June 2006

To Kathy,

I hope this book supports you in your healing work.

Christine Courtois

D0190698

HEALING the
INCEST WOUND

HEALING the INCEST WOUND

ADULT SURVIVORS IN THERAPY

Christine A. Courtois, Ph.D.
PSYCHOLOGIST, PRIVATE PRACTICE
WASHINGTON, D.C.

W. W. NORTON & COMPANY • NEW YORK • LONDON

First published as a Norton paperback 1996

Printed in the United States of America.

Library of Congress Cataloging-in-Publication Data

Courtois, Christine A.
   Healing the incest wound : adult survivors in therapy / Christine
A. Courtois.
      p.   cm.
   "A Norton professional book"—P. facing t.p.
   Bibliography: p.
   Includes index.
   1. Incest victims—Mental health. 2. Psychotherapy. I. Title.
   [DNLM: 1. Incest. 2. Psychotherapy—methods. 3. Stress
Disorders, Post-Traumatic—therapy.   WM 610 C866h]
RC560.I53C68   1988
616.85′83—dc19
DNLM/DLC
For Library of Congress   88-1661
                                                                 CIP

ISBN 0-393-31356-5

W. W. Norton & Company, Inc.
500 Fifth Avenue, New York, N.Y. 10110
www.wwnorton.com

W. W. Norton & Company Ltd.
Castle House, 75/76 Wells Street, London W1T 3QT

        8 9 0

To my parents, Normand and Irene Courtois, who provided me with a strong model of family and marital love, trust, and support.

To the victims and survivors of incest. My intent in writing the book is to communicate that I appreciate your pain, that you are not alone in your experience, and that healing the incest wound is possible.

It is not necessarily emotional deprivation that leads to psychic disturbance but above all narcissistic wounds—including sexual abuse. These wounds occur at the time in life when the child is most helpless and are concealed by subsequent repression. While this repression ensures parents that their secret will be safe, the child's lack of conscious knowledge blocks access to his or her feelings and vitality. Not being able to talk about or even know about these wounds is what later leads to pathological developments.

An unacknowledged trauma is like a wound that never heals over and may start to bleed again at any time. In a supportive environment the wound can become visible and finally heal completely.

—Alice Miller, *Thou Shalt Not Be Aware: Society's Betrayal of the Child*, pp. 124, 182

My father stabbed me repeatedly when I was a child. My mother stood by and watched and did not do anything to stop the stabbing or to get me assistance. She too stabbed me—with her aversion and neglect.

I coped as best I could—I became a model child at school where I was able to relax a bit and get some positive attention. Outside the house and outdoors, I was magical and invincible. I could pretend that I was loved and strong and powerful enough that nobody could get me. But at home and anytime I was near my parents, I was on constant alert for danger. By night I stayed awake and hid in closets or locked myself in the bathroom to escape my father. By day I took care of everyone in the family and pretended everything was normal. I covered my wounds as best I could, hoping that someday I could get out and get the help that I needed. But I kept getting wounded—my father grew more insistent and violent in his sexual demands as I grew older. My mother grew more estranged and hateful. And although members of our extended family knew from my behavior that something was wrong between my parents and me and that I feared my father, no one asked me about anything and no one helped.

I just kept bandaging the wounds and tried to keep them from getting infected. An early marriage got me out of the abuse and gave me enough respite from the incest to start growing scar tissue. But it wasn't enough. My wounds were too infected and were festering, causing difficulties in my day-to-day life. I sought therapy but my first therapist made me feel cheap and dirty—he was only interested in the sexual details of what happened to me and not in my wounds. My current therapy is different. For the first time, I am able to talk about what happened to me and how much the stabbing and the neglect hurt me. And I can talk about what I had to do to cope and how the scars covered the wound but never healed it, how it's been festering. I'm learning about how my scars and bandages distorted my development but got me through. My therapist and I are now in the process of removing the bandages and probing the scars to get at the wound underneath. Our goal is to disinfect the wound so that it will stop festering and, this time, heal properly. Cleansing the wound is very painful, sometimes excruciatingly so. It makes me feel the original pain but I know it's the only way for me to heal. The pain is made bearable by knowing that I am not alone and that I am being attended to. My incest is no longer being denied and the hurt it caused me is no longer being ignored. I have been given hope and am hopeful of recovering and of living a healthier life.

—A therapy client who had been sexually abused by her father from ages 2 to 18

Acknowledgments

THIS BOOK WAS made possible by a number of individuals who, over the years, have offered me personal and professional support as I researched and studied the problem of incestuous abuse and by those women who shared their personal incest histories with me. Each of them made a considerable contribution. The completion of this book gives me the opportunity to acknowledge and thank them.

Of necessity, those individuals who told me their incest stories, either as research subjects or as my clients, must remain anonymous. Participants in my research studies were motivated by a desire to break the silence around incest and to help others. This book is, in part, the result of their efforts. My clients have allowed me access to their inner lives in hopes of alleviating the trauma and healing the incest wound. This book is a reflection of what I have learned from each of them. Both groups of survivors shared what for many were the most painful times of their lives. This book is a testament to their spirit, their endurance, and their recovery from the past.

My professional colleagues have been outstanding in offering both their expertise and their personal support and encouragement. Special thanks go to Drs. Judith Sprei, Deborah Watts, Claire Walsh, and Lynne Hazard for their critical reading of parts of the manuscript and their comments and suggestions. Judi Sprei in particular has had a profound influence on my thinking about incest therapy as co-leader of our four-year incest treatment group, as the co-author of several papers and presentations, and the co-leader of professional workshops on incest therapy. As she noted in the introduction to a manual she wrote on group treatment, our ideas have developed through such close collaboration that it is sometimes hard to remember who thought of what. She further noted that no one should undertake this work without a colleague who can offer support when the work is at its most painful and join in celebration when change and growth are observable. With Judi I have been fortunate to have such a collegial relationship.

I owe a long-term debt of gratitude to staff members of the University of

Maryland and Cleveland State University Counseling Centers. Each group encouraged me and contributed to my professional development. Ruth Anne Koenick has also given her support over the long haul; we have been personally associated and active in the sexual assault field since 1972, when we co-directed the University Women's Crisis Center at the University of Maryland. She was the first to suggest that I write a book on the therapy process.

Other significant professional associates include Joyce Thomas, R.N., M.P.H., and Carl Rogers, Ph.D., of the Center for Child Protection and Family Support in D.C.; David Lloyd, Esq., of the Center for Missing and Exploited Children; Sandra Butler, M.A., pioneer incest researcher and author of *Conspiracy of Silence*; the staffs of the Arlington County, Virginia, Victims of Violence Program and Adult and Child Services, and the Montgomery County, Maryland, Sexual Assault Services; Leslie Jadin, Ph.D., and Cathi Sitzman, Ph.D., with whom I meet weekly for mutual professional support; Barbara Hampton, Ph.D., Edith Herman, M.S.W., A.C.S.W., Maureen Kearney, Ph.D., I. Lisa McCann, Ph.D., Jim O'Neil, Ph.D., Philip Silverman, Ph.D., Michele Sullivan, Ph.D., Trey Sunderland, M.D., and others too numerous to mention individually. All have given me invaluable support.

Equally important are those friends and family members who make up my personal network. At no other time have they been as important to me as during this past year. They have supported the book effort wholeheartedly and coaxed and pushed me back to the computer at those times when I was most discouraged by the magnitude of the task and the stress associated with other professional and personal obligations.

My parents, Normand and Irene Courtois, and my sister, Claire Riley, were always available long-distance and my other sister, Norma Courtois, locally. Banks Chamberlain encouraged my writing for years and provided a computer and technical support to produce the manuscript. Banks and Virginia Chamberlain, Amber Chamberlain, Robbie Brockwehl, Bro. Raymond Dufort, S.C., and Dennis and Gail Sirois provided additional family encouragement.

Joyce Avedisian, Cherie Seidman Brownstein, and Phyllis Van Orden Nathanson indicated their phone availability day or night. Unfortunately for them but fortunately for me there were occasions when they made good on that pledge. Cherie and Jeb Brownstein, John and Waldi Crawford, Lynne and Neil Hazard, Katie and Bill Holmes, and Melissa Nielson and Ed Yawn opened their homes to me and provided me with creature comforts, including many good meals and social contacts, which gave me temporary respite from the effort.

Finally, special thanks go to Susan Barrows, editor of Norton Professional Books, for supporting the publication of this book and for her suggestions and expertise. She has a gentle but effective editorial style and I deeply appreciate her understanding and her patience.

Contents

Introduction

I HAVE BEEN INVOLVED in the sexual assault field since 1972 when I co-founded a campus rape crisis center at the University of Maryland. Although the mission of the center was to provide assistance to women immediately after a rape, it was not long before we started to get calls from women who had been raped in the past and had never told anyone before. Some of these callers confided that they had been assaulted not by strangers on the street but by men they knew and by family members, including fathers, brothers, uncles, grandfathers and cousins. And for some of them, the assaults had never stopped—they were still caught in the situation. Our small crisis center mirrored what was happening across the United States. As rape crisis centers opened to respond to a growing awareness of stranger rape, they too were receiving calls from incest victims desperate for understanding and assistance.

We didn't know how to help these women. Mostly, we applied the techniques that we had learned to use with rape victims: We accepted these women's stories, told them they were not to blame, and urged them to keep trying to disclose the experience and to find someone who would help them escape if their situation were ongoing. We realized that we were dealing with another type of rape, one even more taboo than stranger rape, one that was harder to talk about and harder to recover from. We began to conceptualize incest as a compounded form of rape.

We searched the literature for guidance and found articles highly biased against women—they were blamed or treated as though they were irreparably damaged or their experiences were minimized. Fortunately, the related field of domestic violence was beginning to develop and offered some preliminary ways to conceptualize intrafamilial abuse and to help victims. Then, in 1977, we read Rush's now famous feminist analysis, "The Freudian Cover-up," which charged that Freud's change from the seduction to the oedipal theory had the effect of denying the scope of the problem and the reality of women's experience. Following close upon this, in 1978, four books on incest were published: *Betrayal of Innocence* by Susan Forward and Craig Buck, *Conspiracy of Silence* by Sandra Butler, *Incest* by Karin Meiselman, and *Kiss Daddy Good-night* by Louise Armstrong. Blair and Rita Justice wrote a fifth resource, *The Broken Taboo*, published in 1979.

In 1978, as my dissertation research and at the urging of Lenore Walker, Ph.D., who had just completed a similar study of battered women, I undertook an interview study of women who had been incest victims in childhood and adolescence. My intent was to learn firsthand about the experience of incest and to compare the responses of this group of women with the information in the literature. Many of the characteristics of the incest circumstances were consistent between the two data sources, but missing in the old literature was a description of the women's pain and the terrible toll the incest took on their lives. Also lacking was a description of the creative ways these women had devised as children and adults to cope with their experience and its aftermath. They were survivors in the truest sense of the word.

I came away from my research traumatized by what I had learned about the world of some little girls and the level of dysfunction and incredible selfishness of the men and women who abused and neglected them. But I also felt enormous respect for the resiliency of the human spirit in the face of adversity, and I had learned a great deal about the variability in incest experience and its aftereffects. My subjects described many commonalities of response, but they also offered unique perspectives on their abuse experiences, families, and perpetrators. To the last one, however, they described predominantly negative aftereffects and complained that the incest had robbed them of their childhoods and who they might have been. In 1980, I replicated this research with very similar results.

As a practicing clinician, I speculated about the implications of my research and the new incest literature on treatment. There were no treatment guidelines available. My treatment experience began with my very first client in my first professional position as a counseling psychologist at the Cleveland State University Counseling Center. A young and attractive new freshman entered my office, extended her arm on which she had carved in large block letters "HELP ME," and handed me a letter detailing a history of horrendous multiple incest in her family. She had disclosed and sought outside assistance and her father had been arrested, but he had been allowed to return to the home where he continued his pattern of abuse. Her mother was a debilitated woman who was unable to consistently believe her daughters, much less offer them effective assistance. The family, solidly upper middle-class and appearing to be well-functioning to the outside community, was in reality rife with serious problems and multiple losses. My client was so desperate that she repeatedly went to the police and the courts for assistance, only to be repeatedly frustrated. She moved to Cleveland on a scholarship which allowed her to separate geographically from her family, a separation she was unable to make psychologically.

Needless to say, this young woman was highly traumatized. Our work together over the course of two years was an emotional roller coaster for both of us. Every time it seemed that we had her somewhat stabilized, a new crisis would erupt of either her own making or the family's. I did not know about traumatic reenactment at the time and so was thoroughly perplexed. Also, this client was highly anxious, depressed, strongly hysteric/borderline, self-destructive and self-mutilating, and very dissociative. She fainted regularly during the course of our sessions and when under greater than usual stress. It was necessary to hospitalize her twice when she could not assure her safety and when she was so dissociative that she could not function. And yet, she was thoroughly engaging. Her symptoms needed to be understood in the context of her experience. In retrospect, I see her as a walking manifestation of the post-incest syndrome described in this book.

I struggled with this case, combed the literature for information, and relied heavily on my colleagues for direction. Also, I began to apply what I had learned through my rape crisis work and through my research. I listened, I believed, I offered as much support and understanding as I could, and I worked hard to develop a therapeutic alliance. I took every opportunity to talk to other therapists working with incest cases; in this way we cross-validated our work and supported one another.

Then I began to present my research findings and conduct workshops on incest, including treatment approaches. I found that therapists were hungry for the information. They too were struggling with incest victims, but without the same wealth of information I had gained from my research. These workshops and the positive response to my approach strengthened and refined these early formulations. At this time, I was fortunate to begin to work with Dr. Judith Sprei, a psychologist with perspectives on sexual abuse very similar to mine. We provided mutual support for each other's cases and began to offer an incest therapy group. Together we decided that the most accurate diagnosis for incest response was post-traumatic stress disorder, an idea that seemed heretical at the time (1981) because PTSD was highly associated in the minds of clinicians with the Vietnam veteran. Judi and I began to write and conduct workshops and, once again, found strong validation for our work. Meanwhile a literature was developing that provided some substantiation and guidance.

This book is a direct outgrowth of all of these experiences and the thousands of therapy hours I have spent with incest survivors in both individual and group treatment. I have made every attempt to present the state-of-the-art in terms of treatment, but a strong caveat must be made that our information is preliminary and much remains to be learned. At present, the therapy is grounded in available theory from the fields of feminism, traumatic stress/victimization, self development, and loss. The effectiveness of this therapy has strong clinical support, but is for the most part empirically untested. Its effectiveness for all survivors is certainly not documented.

Nevertheless, this book provides a working model for incest treatment designed to provide healing for the incest wound and to move the victim from the status of victim to that of survivor and even beyond. The underlying philosophy of this book is that in order to heal the survivor must acknowledge the victimization and its reality, must understand it in the context of both the family and the larger culture, and must allow and experience the feelings associated with the trauma. The survivor must psychologically separate from the past in order to develop her unique self, separate from the abuse and its supporting family ethic. The therapy is similar to the cleaning and disinfecting of a wound, although the wounds of the incest survivor are primarily invisible (the clinician will occasionally see survivors bearing visible physical scars as well).

This book is deliberately written about the female survivor because available research indicates that females are incestuously abused far more often than are males; however, in no way do I wish to minimize the fact that males are so abused. The treatment approach described here is applicable to males as well as females, with some modifications. The male incest survivor is described in Chapters 3, 4, and 13.

This book is roughly divided into three sections. The first, comprised of Chapters 1 through 5, is a general introduction to incest by category, type, characteristics, and dynamics. In order to treat incest effectively, the clinician must be knowledgeable about how it develops in a family and its various permutations.

Chapters 6 through 8 make up the second section of the book, which outlines the predominant symptoms and aftereffects associated with incest and their secondary elaborations. These become the presenting concerns when a survivor initiates treatment. Aftereffects are discussed according to four theories — victimization/traumatic stress, feminist, self development, and loss — which in turn focus and direct the philosophy, process and goals of treatment. The issue of diagnosis is also addressed in this section.

The third section is devoted to a discussion of incest therapy. General treatment strategies and techniques are presented as they pertain to both individual and group treatment. Dynamics associated with past abuse are analyzed according to how they affect the therapy process and the relationship, and common transference and countertransference reactions are discussed. Incest experience often results in unique issues in the treatment, such as family disclosure, confrontation, dissociation, intrusive reexperiencing and self-hurtful behaviors. These are discussed in conjunction with strategies for their management, as are special populations of incest survivors who may have unique needs due to their minority status.

My goal is to offer the clinician comprehensive guidelines for working with adult victim/survivors of incest. The more clinicians know about incestuous abuse and its consequences, the more comfortable they will be in offering effective and healing treatment. The need is great. Let us begin.

HEALING the INCEST WOUND

SECTION I

Incest Characteristics and Dynamics

CHAPTER 1

Incest: If You Think the Word Is Ugly . . .

I BEGIN THIS BOOK by defining incest, not in technical terms (that definition is provided in Chapter 2) but graphically and through the eyes of a victim. This portrayal is a composite — incest is very complex and has many different patterns of occurrence. To understand the incest survivor, it is absolutely essential to understand what she experienced and to see it from her perspective. The clinician must know what to expect about the experience and how ugly it can be.

The reality of incest is infants, babies, little girls, preadolescents and adolescents lying in their cribs and beds in fear. They become hyperattuned to footsteps, creaking stairs, breathing, and the light that appears around a bedroom door when it is opened at night. They are aware of being watched, usually quietly, obsessively, and with lustful eyes. Sometimes all that happens is that he stands at the door or just inside the door or sits on the bed and stares. Sometimes he breathes heavily, rapidly, moans a little and then goes away.

At other times, he touches her. He usually begins gently and talks softly as he rubs her body. He does this when he tucks her in at night after wishing her sweet dreams or later when she awakens to find him back in her bedroom, touching . . . feeling . . . and kissing her. He tells her it's their little secret and to not tell anyone for telling will spoil it. She knows it feels good but doesn't understand the not telling anyone part. She begins to wonder. . . .

Then she awakens to find his hands up her nightgown or down her pajamas, rubbing her breasts, her thighs and buttocks, and "down there."

This chapter title is adapted from an article by Myers (n.d.) entitled "Incest: If you think the word is ugly, take a look at its effects."

He tells her not to worry, that she feels so good to him and that he'll make her feel good too. And sometimes he does. She finds herself liking and hating what he's doing. Why won't he stop and why can't she tell anyone and why her? He now tells her that she'll get in trouble if she tells and that it's her fault for being so attractive and leading him on and that besides he needs her. She's confused: What did I do? Why is going to sleep at night leading him on?

His fondling intensifies and he starts doing other things. She awakens to find his hands all over her, probing her, rubbing her. Sometimes it hurts, sometimes not. Then he does even more. One night she awakens to find a penis in her mouth or his head under the covers, licking her down there. Or he probes her more and more with his fingers until he can finally penetrate her with his penis. She can't believe it. She doesn't know what's going on. She wants it to stop. Sometimes it hurts so much. She tells him all these things but he says this is what fathers do for their daughters and that it's for her own good. But he still tells her not to tell because no one will believe her and it's all her fault. She's confused and frightened. And her body hurts and feels funny.

She can't believe that he's back to being normal in the morning when he greets her at breakfast. He's back to acting like her dad. But sometimes during the day, if they're alone, he'll do some of the same things. Then she knows for sure it's not a dream. She tries to tell her mom but can't. What will she think? She'll be so hurt. That's confusing too because sometimes mom tells her to spend time with her dad and take care of him. Is that what she means? It's better not to bother mom about this.

So she takes to hiding, during the day and especially at night. During the day it is easier. She just stays away and finds things to do to distract her. At night, she goes to her bedroom scared. She wears all the nightclothes she can put on and she pulls the covers up as tightly as she can. Sometimes she sleeps under the bed or in the closet behind the clothes hamper or in the bathroom, in the tub, hidden away. She's relieved to find any room with a lock on the door. She tries to booby-trap her bedroom door. Somehow he always manages to find her or to get through her defenses. And he continues to rub and fondle and probe and enter. Other family members have begun to notice some of the "funny" things she does at night but nobody has asked why. He's been caught in her room a couple of times during the night but he always says she was having a bad dream and he was comforting her. He's always believed and nobody asks her what the bad dream was all about.

As the situation goes on, she finds herself watching from afar and being apart from her body. She looks at herself from the ceiling or concentrates intensely on the wallpaper or the curtains so she can make herself be somewhere else. Anywhere but right where she is, in her bed, with these things happening, with this nightmare. He's crushing her . . . it hurts. She can't get away . . . she squeezes her eyes tightly shut so she can't see him or what he's doing. She pinches herself and digs her fingernails into herself for distraction and punishment. She keeps a hand or foot free and reaches it out over the side of the bed so that he can't have all of her. Inside, she tells herself he can't make her feel and that she just has to wait until she's old enough and can get away. What would her mother think? And is all of this a bad dream? Is it really happening?

THE DEVELOPING AWARENESS OF INCEST

During the past decade, all forms of child sexual abuse, including incest, have received unprecedented societal acknowledgment. Women who were sexually abused as children have begun to discuss their abuse experience, breaking the silence with which it has traditionally been surrounded. Disclosure has been spurred by the Women's Movement, with its interest in all aspects of women's lives and its encouragement of "speaking out" about the previously unspeakable, first about rape and then about all forms of family violence, including incest. A simultaneous development has been the discovery of child sexual abuse by researchers studying other types of family violence such as spouse abuse and by those investigating child maltreatment and physical abuse. As a result, sexual abuse has been acknowledged as a reality in the lives of many children. Social and personal denial and suppression of such abuse have begun to give way to acknowledgment and validation.

Since 1978, research efforts to learn more about the characteristics and patterns of child sexual abuse have intensified. These investigations have yielded some startling findings. Among some of the most striking are the following:

- A very substantial percentage of the female population, possibly as high as 20%, has had an experience of incestuous abuse at some time in their lives, 12% before the age of 14, 16% before the age of 18. Possibly 5% of all women have been abused by their fathers (Russell, 1986).
- Boys are also sexually victimized within the family, but in smaller numbers (Finkelhor, 1984).
- The majority of victims are female, the majority of perpetrators male (Russell, 1986).
- The bulk of child sexual abuse is perpetrated either by a family member or by someone known to the child. Females are more likely to be abused within the family and males outside.
- The usual pattern of incestuous abuse is of repeated and progressive sexual activity, beginning when the girl is prepubertal, usually

between the ages of seven and twelve, but not uncommonly occurring in early childhood. Its average duration is four years. In contrast, abuse outside of the family is usually short-term, without the same progression of sexual activity or the same entrapment.

- Most child sexual abuse does not involve violence; however, it does involve some sort of coercion and a misrepresentation of the relationship and the activity. The child is manipulated by the unequal power in the relationship, that is, by the relationship with the perpetrator on whom she is dependent. The child is further coerced by the perpetrator's strong desire to keep the activity a secret, which has the purpose of minimizing intervention and allowing repetition.
- Victimized children, especially those for whom early intervention is not available, are at risk for developing a range of negative aftereffects both immediately and at subsequent life stages. However, reactions vary. Some reactions are mild, others are life-threatening and severely debilitating. Approximately 40% of all victim/survivors suffer aftereffects serious enough to require therapy in adulthood (Browne & Finkelhor, 1986).
- Despite recent publicity and education, most cases of child sexual abuse are not reported outside the family, resulting in no intervention for the exploited child.
- Intervention in cases of child sexual abuse, particularly incest, is complicated and must be handled with sensitivity by individuals with special training.
- Intervention efforts are improving as programs are being developed and expanded but the vast majority of children either have no access to intervention or experience intervention that is ineffective or, worse yet, that retraumatizes them.

Presently, most children who are sexually abused cope as best they can in isolation and without assistance. When abused by a family member, they generally suffer repeated and progressive abuse which results in more severe repercussions than sexual abuse by a stranger (Russell, 1986). In addition, occurrence in the family hampers disclosure and intervention efforts due to the nature of family bonds and divided loyalty. The child's story is open to challenge and disbelief. Most incestuously abused children are forced to develop survival mechanisms to cope with both the abuse and its consequences.

As serious as this situation is for today's children, it was even worse for adults who were incestuously abused as children. For these victim/survivors, the incest occurred at a time when its very reality was largely unacknowledged due to the taboo and denial surrounding it. Incest is strictly forbidden in most cultures and its occurrence is generally met with shocked and horrified reactions and punishment. Despite such strong prohibitions against it, researchers have uncovered evidence of its prevalence going back to Biblical times (Miller, 1984; Rush, 1980; Ward, 1985). Obviously, it is impossible ever to know the full extent of child sexual abuse, but evidence is accumulating to suggest that it has been embedded in and covertly allowed in most cultures, while being overtly and publicly decried and denied. Thus, its victims have been ensnared in a double-bind or paradoxical situation from which there is no escape. They have had no place to go with their stories and no way to achieve outside validation.

The most famous discovery of incest was made by Freud in the late 1800s. His work with hysterical women patients led him to develop his seduction theory (relabeled the trauma theory by Miller, 1984), which postulated that the symptoms exhibited by his patients were caused by sexual contacts with their fathers. His publication of this theory created quite a stir in Victorian Viennese society. This furor, coupled with his profound personal discomfort with the high prevalence of incestuous abuse reported by these women, led him to abandon his theory. Eventually, he replaced it with the oedipal theory, which in effect negated the reality of incest. Freud's oedipal theory profoundly affected the medical/psychiatric profession and with it the response made to any child complaining of an adult's or parent's sexual behavior. It insured that the complaint was treated as a childhood fantasy and not as reality. It had the additional effect of exonerating the involved adult while allowing for both the continuation of the incest and society's denial of it.

Public ignorance and misperception about incest continued from Freud's time until the late 1970s (Armstrong, 1982, has labeled this period the "Age of Denial"). Incest was then rediscovered, albeit reluctantly (see Armstrong, 1982; Summit, 1982). During this Age of Denial, incest was the subject of occasional clinical, psychiatric, or social work studies. Most of these suffered from serious methodological flaws. Researcher bias against the topic and against women, lack of experimental methodology, lack of control or comparison samples, and investigation of clinical samples or only the most serious cases which came to the attention of social agencies were among the more serious flaws. Most studies did little to contradict the prevalent misconceptions about incest, instead substantiating many of them. These misperceptions included that incest: was an extreme rarity; occurred only in lower-class and chaotic families; was largely the fault of a cold, domineering, abandoning, or absent mother and a not-so-innocent daughter; and was relatively devoid of serious consequences. Also, sibling incest was believed to be the most prevalent and least damaging type, almost always involving mutual exploration between peers.

Some of the early research accurately identified characteristics of the experience that were replicated and substantiated by later investigations. These included that incest most often is nonviolent but coerced; that the average age of the child at onset and termination is prepubertal; that sexual activity escalates over time and covers a broad spectrum of sexual behaviors; and that the oldest female child is most at risk in a family. Moreover, certain variables of the experience, such as the degree of relatedness between victim and perpetrator, the degree of force used, the duration of incest, and the type of sexual activity were seen to be related to the severity of psychological consequences.

Research investigating characteristics and effects of incest has greatly improved since the mid-1970s, although methodological refinement is still needed. The earliest "new data" were in the form of retrospective interviews and narratives provided by victim/survivors. These reports generally showed a remarkable degree of consistency between them as well as with the more experimental studies currently being conducted. Much of the new data is reviewed in this book.

Societal acknowledgment of the prevalence of child sexual abuse, based in large measure on this new knowledge base, has resulted in specialized services directed towards the prevention, detection, and intervention into ongoing abuse. This focus on current abuse is certainly needed and understandable; however, it has had an unfortunate and unintentional side effect of continuing the neglect of former victims. Further, the lack of attention to and services for now grown victim/survivors serves to reinforce such common aftereffects of abuse as negative self-esteem, self-contempt, shame, a sense of being unworthy of good attention, and a lack of trust. Many victim/survivors experience a range of emotions in response to the almost daily media attention paid to child sexual abuse. These include relief that the "best kept secret" (Rush, 1980) is no longer and that today's children are being attended to, sadness, anger, and envy (e.g., why couldn't I have had this?), and shame and guilt for some of these feelings.

The child who is incestuously abused most often suffers chronic inescapable trauma without outside support to either buffer the situation or validate her responses to it. Not only does she suffer sexual intrusion, but it is repeated and escalates over time. Repeated traumas with no assistance leave a child to devise methods to cope—behaviorally, emotionally and socially. She usually does so by developing strong defenses which sap much of her psychological energy. Her development may be stunted, with many developmental tasks neglected or unresolved. The secrecy, silence, and taboo keep her from asking for help and prevent her from getting acknowledgment and validation of her experience. The child's very reality is often negated, leaving her to wonder what is real and what is not.

The lack of response or assistance also leads to a "second injury," to use the term Symonds (1980) coined for victims of other types of crime. The second injury occurs when no assistance is forthcoming from agencies or individuals the victim turns to for help and from whom he/she should rightfully expect to receive it. Butler (1978) conceptualized the second injuries experienced in incest as four levels of betrayal: (1) the abuse itself and the betrayal by the relative/perpetrator; (2) nonresponse by the non-offending parent or other relatives or friends; (3) non-response by such professionals as teachers, counselors, social workers, nurses, and doctors; and (4) betrayal of the self, when the child denies her own reality and experience in order to cope. At this fourth level, the child blames herself for having caused the situation, since no other explanation is available to her and blaming the parent(s) is too threatening. The repeated abuse, the self-blame, and the lack of validation and assistance from others lead to the development of a shame-based identity.

Furthermore, at the time of the abuse, victims develop symptomatology associated with acute post-traumatic stress disorder. These original effects usually go untreated. Although some may remit over time, usually under the influence of relationships that are reparative to the victim in that they allow her to trust others and increase her self-esteem, some become chronic or appear in delayed fashion and spawn secondary elaborations. The most common of these include chronic and atypical depression and anxiety disorders, self-destructive and self-defeating behaviors, eating disorders, substance abuse, sexual difficulties, dissociative disorders, somatization disorders, explosive disorders, and revictimization in other relationships, within and outside of a family setting. These secondary elaborations, in turn, create new problems and are usually what cause the adult survivor to seek treatment.

Because incest occurs during the course of the victims' childhood, it inevitably influences maturation and development. For many victim/survivors, the incest experience, along with its aftereffects and coping mechanisms, has influenced and become integrated into their personality. Herman (1987) described the personalities of some survivors as "walking post-traumatic stress reactions." Some develop the symptoms of specific personality disorders, most commonly those associated with hysteric, borderline, narcissistic, avoidant, dependent, or multiple personalities.

The significance of parental abuse in the development of these disorders, specifically borderline and hysteric disorders, has long been downplayed and is only now receiving research scrutiny. Interestingly, the situation is now coming full circle. To quote Herman and Shatzow (1987, p. 11): "In the light of these findings, it would seem warranted to return to the insights offered by Freud's original statement of the etiology of hysteria, and to resume a line of investigation that the mental health professions prematurely abandoned 90 years ago."

Similarly, the relation of trauma to the development of mental health problems and psychopathologial conditions or the "victim to patient process" (Rieker & Carmen, 1986; van der Kolk, 1987a) is under investigation. According to Rieker and Carmen:

Our model of the victim-to-patient process emphasizes the fragmented identity that derives from victims' attempts to accommodate or adjust to the
judgments that others make about the abuse. The common features of the
accommodation are 1) denying the abuse, 2) altering the affective responses
to the abuse, and 3) changing the meaning of the abuse or, as we define it,
the disconfirmation and transformation of abuse. Within this framework, the
original defenses employed by both child and adult victims are viewed as
adaptive survival strategies that later form the core of the survivors' psychopathology. (p. 360)

At present, the relationship between victimization and delayed maladaptive behavior is complex, unclear as to cause and effect, and increasingly
being investigated; nevertheless, our emerging knowledge about psychological trauma in general and trauma-specific syndromes and treatment is
solid enough to suggest that direct treatment of the trauma is necessary for
the resolution of its aftereffects and secondary elaborations.

Incest therapy involves focused treatment of the incest, its aftereffects,
secondary elaborations, and personality manifestations. Incest is understood as potentially traumatic to most victims due to the dynamics of
traumatic sexualization and betrayal within a trusted relationship, and the
helplessness and stigmatization which ensue (Finkelhor & Browne, 1985).
A primary focus is on understanding the experience from the individual's
perspective. The therapist begins by believing and validating the incest and
identifying it as victimization. Then defenses are understood as survivor
skills developed in the context of chronic trauma to cope with negative and
unhealthy events. The victim/survivor must assess her defenses and socialization practices and any family rules which helped maintain them. She
learns to replace maladaptive ones with others which are self-determined
and healthy. The goal is to move beyond victim and survivor status to
healthy separation and self-determination.

CHAPTER 2
Incest Characteristics
and Categories

THE TRUE CHARACTERISTICS and dimensions of incestuous abuse have been masked by the taboo and silence that have surrounded its occurrence. Recent research demonstrates that incest occurs regularly in our society, perpetrated by individuals who, for the most part, would otherwise be regarded as fairly normal. The taboo on incestuous relations is a deterrent to some would-be perpetrators but not to others. The taboo contradicts the reality of incest prevalence, a fact which led Armstrong (1978) to comment that the taboo has been on the open discussion of incest and not on its perpetration.

Here I begin with a general definition of incest and the characteristics most commonly associated with it. Incest is complex, encompassing a wide range of behavior between individuals of varying degrees of relatedness. The behavior can vary from the relatively mild to the torturous, from a one-time occurrence to chronic behavior occurring several times a day over many years, and from involvement of one perpetrator to several, both within and outside of the family. Incest was always thought to be a rather discrete event between two members of the family (most often father and daughter). Recent clinical and research studies have found instead that it commonly involves more than one perpetrator and victim in the nuclear family and has patterns of transmission across generations. Victims and witnesses of incest in one generation may become the victims and witnesses in the next. Additionally, an as yet undetermined number of sexually abused children, particularly boys, go on to perpetrate abuse in adolescence and adulthood.

Within the general conceptualization of incest, different categories have been recorded. In the second section of this chapter, I present currently available information about different categories organized according to whether the incest is abusive or not, occurs between cross-generational relatives or peers, involves members of the nuclear or extended family, involves biological relatives or those related by marriage or family role, involves same-sex or opposite-sex relatives, and involves more than one perpetrator or victim.

CHARACTERISTICS OF INCEST

Defining Incest

The term "incest" encompasses sexual behavior with a multitude of patterns, variations, causes, types, relationships and aftereffects. Incest is illegal in all states in the U.S., but the laws vary by state as to the behavior and degree of relatedness considered incestuous. In general, incest laws forbid marriage, cohabitation and sexual relations (usually defined as sexual intercourse) between individuals who are closely related by blood (consanguineously), marriage and/or adoption (affinally or contractually). Many states have parallel statutory provisions to define other types of proscribed sexual contact. These expand the definition of sexual relations to include contact by degrees, according to the activity engaged in, the ages of victim and perpetrator, and the age difference between them.

Incest between an adult and a related child or adolescent is now recognized as the most prevalent form of child sexual abuse and as one with great potential for damage to the child. Because of this, it is considered a form of child abuse. It should be noted that incest is not always abusive: In those cases of consensual sex between related adults or *mutual* exploratory sex play between peers such as siblings or cousins, it may be considered non-abusive. Incest constitutes abuse " . . . when a child of any age is exploited by an older person for his own satisfaction while disregarding the child's own developmental immaturity and inability to understand the sexual behavior" (Steele, 1986, p. 284). The child is engaged in sexual activity for the gratification of the adult's needs. She is unable to give informed consent due to the authority of the adult, her own dependent and less powerful status, and the age difference between them. Although our focus is predominantly on those forms of incest which constitute child sexual abuse, we pay some attention to non-abusive incest as well. Abusive and non-abusive incest will be discussed in more depth later in this chapter.

For their research, Benward and Densen-Gerber (1975) developed a comprehensive definition of incest, which because of its inclusiveness is quite useful to the clinician:

> . . . [incest] refers to sexual contact with a person who would be considered an ineligible partner because of his blood and/or social ties (i.e., kin) to the

subject and her family. The term encompasses, then, several categories of partners, including father, stepfather, grandfather, uncles, siblings, cousins, in-laws, and what we call "quasi-family." The last category includes parental and family friends (e.g., mother's sexual partner). Our feeling is that the incest taboo applies in a weakened form to all these categories in that the "partner" represents someone from whom the female child should rightfully expect warmth or protection and sexual distance. Sexual behavior recorded as positive incest ranged from intercourse with consent; intercourse by force; attempted intercourse or seduction; molestation, primarily fondling of breasts and genitals, and exposure. We included other sexual behaviors as intercourse, namely, all penetration, anal, oral, and vaginal, both passive and active. Cunnilingus and fellatio were not uncommon activities, nor was sodomy. (p. 326)

As can be seen from this definition, incest involves a wide range of behaviors alone or in combination. The inability of a child to give informed consent to sexual involvement is implicit in this definition even in those cases where the child or adolescent might argue that she consented or appears to have consented.

Such a broad definition, while useful therapeutically, does not meet the legal criteria for incest in most states. In fact, many behaviors can be considered psychologically incestuous and thus of interest in treatment that do not meet the legal requirements for what constitutes incest. Clinicians must keep in mind the difference between the psychological/psychiatric and the legal definitions of incest (Rosenfeld, 1977) and remain informed about statutory provisions.

In an effort to identify and clarify different types and degrees of sexual abuse, investigators have conceptualized abuse continua based upon the type of sexual activity and other variables. Sgroi, Blick, and Porter (1982), for example, outlined a somewhat hierarchical continuum of sexually abusive behaviors. The range was from exhibitionism to intercourse, often progressing through the following behaviors: (1) nudity; (2) disrobing; (3) genital exposure; (4) observation of the child; (5) kissing; (6) fondling; (7) masturbation; (8) fellatio; (9) cunnilingus; (10) digital (finger) penetration of the anus or rectal opening; (11) penile penetration of the anus or rectal opening; (12) digital (finger) penetration of the vagina; (13) penile penetration of the vagina; and (14) "dry intercourse." This hierarchy does not make a determination of which of these behaviors is most disturbing or damaging to the victim. This varies according to the vagaries of each abuse situation. Of note is that some of these behaviors do not involve touching the child. Incestuous abuse can include gestures, comments, and observation as well as actual body contact.

Summit and Kryso (1978) classified parent-child sexual behavior patterns based on cases observed in their clinical work. Their continuum started with incidental sexual contact between parent and child which is controlled and limited, not used to gratify, and therefore not abusive in most cases. This would include the contact required for normal caretaking and hygienic functions. At times, this type of behavior becomes abusive when it is overly intrusive or obsessive and used to meet the involved adult's needs. An example of such abusive contact is the grandmother who scrubbed her granddaughter's genitals so hard during bathing that she caused injury. This grandmother also closely inspected her granddaughter's genitalia and douched her repeatedly to insure cleanliness. At the other extreme of Summit and Kryso's continuum is willful perverse incest which is used to gratify needs of the adult. This adult might involve his child in prostitution while he observed the sexual activity. Between these two polarities lie other behaviors that differ by causative factor, degree, and seriousness of contact.

Rosenfeld (1977) based his spectrum of sexual abuse upon the type of sexual activity engaged in and the manner in which it was carried out. He placed family sexuality on a continuum. A broad range of behaviors involving elements of sexuality, such as affection, caring, and child-rearing functions, are considered normal. These are placed in the middle of the continuum. Incest, rape, and the sexual misuse of the child are at one end, and lack of affection and neglect are at the other. Rosenfeld's model, while useful, does not account for the situation where sexual violation occurs along with physical and affectional neglect.

Glueck (1965) and many other authorities point out that parents have sexual contact with their children as part of normal child-rearing functions. Sexual misuse and abuse occur as boundaries are crossed, as sexual contact is not controlled or limited, but rather is used to satisfy the dependency, sadistic, control, or gratification needs of the parent or involved adult. As these boundaries are crossed, the child is overstimulated and less able to cope with the demands or the activity on both physical and psychological levels.

Incest as rape has been discussed by Brownmiller (1975), who coined the term "father-rape," and by Ward (1985), who used the term "Father-Daughter Rape" (her capitalization). The use of the term "rape" has been controversial. Some authorities believe that defining all incestuous contact as rape is factually incorrect (Finkelhor, 1978; Herman & Hirschman, 1977), ignores the different dynamics involved in intrafamilial contact (Finkelhor, 1978; Rosenfeld, 1979), and contributes to the taboo surrounding the behavior and thus may cause inappropriate interventions in the family and more serious aftereffects for the victim (Renshaw, 1982; Rosenfeld, 1979).

Ward argues just the opposite: that the use of the term "incest" (especially father-daughter incest) and other terms, such as "sexual misuse," "sexual molestation," and "child sexual abuse," as well as the legal distinctions of types and degrees of rape, dilutes and blurs the reality of the behavior. According to Ward, it does so by focusing attention upon *who* is involved rather than upon *what* is happening and by discounting the gravity of the sexual violation. She further argues that incest is widely understood as an anthropological term and carries the pejorative weight of the term "incest taboo," with its implication of the rarity of such behavior and widespread disapproval of it. Ward coined the term "Father-Daughter Rape" as a generic term for all forms of sexual victimization of girl children at the hands of adult men. Using "father" to connote all adult men from whom girl children should be able to expect sexual distance emphasizes the reality that most children are abused by a male known or related to them. The sexspecific "daughter" is used to highlight that:

> the difference between life as a boy-child and as a girl-child is nowhere more clearly demonstrated than in exploring rape. The known statistics indicate that boy-children are victims in five to fifteen percent of cases. It is obvious from the clinical readings that many of these victims are abused/raped by a father, or father-figure, who is taking advantage of the child-status (powerlessness) of whatever children happen to come under his authority, so that it is the fact that the boy is a child that makes him a rape victim. Many boy-child victims are raped by a Father who also rapes girl-children; the statistical information shows an overwhelmingly heterosexual orientation in men who rape children. (1985, p. 80)

It is clear from recent research findings that rape and incest share substantial similarities but have some differences as well. The differences are to be found in three general areas: (1) duration and progression of sexual activity over time; (2) coercion; and (3) consent. Most incest involves multiple acts of sexual violation over time ranging from several months to many years. The usual pattern is for this activity to escalate. Most incestuous relationships begin not as the result of physical force and violence but rather under the guise of affection or education or as something fun or special. Very often, the inducement is the chance to be involved in a special relationship with a known and valued adult. Usually the coercion is subtle, especially at the beginning. It may intensify over the course of the relationship when threats or misrepresentations of fact are used to insure secrecy and continuation of the activity. Although violence is not the typical *modus operandi*, it is used in a substantial minority of cases.

While neither women who are raped nor incest victims willingly give consent, the child experience differs because of the adult's authority and importance in her life. Many children have been gradually conditioned into the sexual activity and may appear to passively submit to the wishes of the involved adult; they may even seek out sexual contact as a means of meeting needs for affection, for favors, or for material goods. It should be strongly emphasized that, like adult victims of rape, children involved sexually with adults may be said to *submit* rather than to *consent* to the activity and, furthermore, to be unable to give informed consent due to their immaturity, dependence, and powerlessness.

The similarities between rape and incest are most obvious when the incest clearly involves those elements which legally constitute rape, that is, sexual penetration through use of force with lack of consent on the part of the victim. The similarities also become quite obvious when a feminist (but generally nonlegal) definition of rape is used. As so defined, rape is viewed primarily as an act of power exercised through sexual use or violation of the individual. It is an assault on the woman's body, but more importantly on her psyche (Brownmiller, 1975). The feminist definition of rape allows for the extension of the legal definition to include any and all forms of sexual intrusion, be it "merely" fondling or actual penetration.

I use the word "incest" to describe intrafamilial sexual violation because it is the most commonly used term; however, rather than stressing the differences between rape and incest, I emphasize their similarities. Incest is a form of rape (as defined from the feminist perspective)—rape within the family, with additional potential for damage to the victim due to the relationship between perpetrator and victim. The relationship increases rather than decreases the traumatic impact of the abuse. The dynamics of incest distinguish it from rape perpetrated by a stranger, the most pertinent having to do with the adult's access to the child by virtue of kinship ties and authority, the secrecy, the betrayal of trust, the child's powerlessness, and the repeated and developmentally inappropriate nature of the violations. Further support for conceptualizing incest as a form of rape comes from the reactions suffered by victims. They can best be described as compounded and intensified rape trauma reactions with some differences due to the special dynamics of incest.

Prevalence of Incest

Until fairly recently, incest was believed to be exceedingly rare. Estimates were that it occurred at the rate of one or two cases per year per million population (Weinberg, 1955). Revised estimates based on a variety of data collection systems and studies conducted in the late 1970s and early 1980s have established that sexual victimization of some sort in childhood is anything but rare. While statistics vary by study because of the populations surveyed, the definitions used and the sensitivity of the questions asked, the prevalence rate for child sexual abuse in the U.S. is believed to be in the range of 10–30% of all girls and 2–9% of all boys (Finkelhor, 1984). These statistics are believed to be conservative. The best statistics currently available about incestuous abuse indicate that approximately 20% of all women have had at least one incestuous experience before the age of 18 (Russell, 1986*; Wyatt, 1985). It is also believed that the rate of sexual abuse of boys is currently underestimated.

*Russell (1986) has conducted the most methodologically rigorous large-scale study of incestuous abuse of girls to date. Her findings are therefore reported in this section as the most accurate so far collected.

According to Russell's analysis, it appears that incestuous abuse has increased, in large measure, due to the following factors: child pornography and the sexualization of children; the sexual revolution; the backlash against sexual equality; untreated child sexual abuse; and the increase in cohabitation, divorce and remarriage, with its resultant increase in blended families.

Duration and Frequency of Incest

Incest can range from a one-time occurrence to literally hundreds of contacts spanning decades. It may involve occasional contact or be compulsive/addictive in nature; in some cases, it occurs once in a while, in others several times a day. The average duration is approximately four years. According to Russell's findings, 48% of the time it occurred from two to twenty times and in another 10% over twenty times (twenty times was the maximum frequency recorded in her study). Clinical reports and survivor descriptions indicate that frequency most often exceeds twenty times over the average four-year duration.

Force, Violence and Coercion

Current indications are that incestuous abuse usually does not involve much physical violence, although, as found with other characteristics, a wide range in the actual use of force and violence is evident. Russell determined that in over 68% of her sample no physical force was involved; 29% involved physical force at a mild level of pushing or pinning down the victim; 2% involved more serious physical force at the level of hitting or slapping; and 1% involved violence at the level of beating or slugging. Analysis according to a violence scale combining the use of verbal threats, weapons, and other physical force or violence by the perpetrator yielded these figures: 65% of the cases were completely nonforceful; 31% involved some force or violence; and 3% involved substantial violence.

Verbal threats and implied threats are often used by the perpetrator to ensure the child's silence and compliance. The child may be threatened with family breakup, dissolution of the special relationship with the perpetrator, shame or blame. Or the perpetrator may threaten to commit suicide or to hurt the victim, other members of the family, family pets, or valued possessions if the incest is disclosed and/or stopped.

Age of Victims

Russell's respondents reported the following concerning their age at onset: 11% were abused for the first time before the age of five; 19% between the ages of six and nine; 41% between the ages of ten and thirteen; and 29% between fourteen and seventeen. These data support the view that incest most commonly begins when the child is of latency age, usually defined as being between the ages of eight to twelve; however, it is likely that these data err in the direction of older age at onset. Emerging data (Herman & Schatzow, 1987; Walsh, 1986a) suggest that younger age at onset is associated with the use of massive repression as the primary ego defense mechanism. Thus, younger victims are more prone to have protectively "forgotten" their early experiences of abuse and so are unable to report them.

Age and Sex of Perpetrator

Most perpetrators are older, usually considerably older, than their victims. Russell found that in 16% of her cases the perpetrators were 40 or more years older; in 39%, 20 to 39 years older; in 30%, 5 to 19 years older; 13% less than five years older; and in 2% the same age or younger. Most currently available data indicate that perpetrators of incestuous abuse are predominantly male, who on average abuse at more serious and traumatic levels than do female perpetrators (Russell, 1983).

Types of Sexual Behavior and Their Progression Over Time

Sgroi et al.'s list (see p. 13) gives us some idea of the progression of sexual behaviors. It is well recognized that in the average incest case the initial sexual contact is rather mild, consisting of mutual observation, kissing, disrobing, and touching; contact progresses to fondling, masturbation, oral sex, and then penetration. The abuse of younger children usually does not involve penetration, while the abuse of adolescents usually does.

Russell and her research team devised a schema of 18 different degrees of sexual abuse, according to whether or not force was used and the degree of sexual violation involved. This typology was collapsed into three categories: (1) least severe sexual abuse; (2) severe sexual abuse; and (3) most severe sexual abuse. Of her sample, 23% of the cases qualified as very severe, 41% as severe, and 36% as least severe. These data offer support for the fact that most incest moves beyond the initial more mild contact to more extensive and intrusive sexual behavior, perpetrated with some degree of force. The following cases illustrate each level of severity:

- *Least Severe*: On several occasions, Susie's grandfather French-kissed her and fondled her breasts and genitals when she would sit on his lap. She was always fully dressed and he never attempted to remove her clothing.
- *Severe*: For a period of several years, Jennie's uncle would babysit for her when her parents went out. At first he would kiss and fondle

her while she was dressed but over time he undressed her and became more demanding. He fondled her breasts and genitals and insisted that she masturbate him.

- *Very Severe*: Audrey's stepfather molested her several times a month for a period of 12 years. Although he began with manual stimulation, he later forced oral sex on her and made her fellate him. At age 13, he forced her to have intercourse and, when she tried to push him away, he threatened her. He attempted anal intercourse but it was so painful to her that he stopped.

Location of the Abuse

As would be expected, most incestuous abuse occurs in the victim and perpetrator's shared home or, if they do not live under the same roof, in either one of their homes. (Russell found that in 68% of all cases where location was mentioned, the incest occurred in the home of either victim, perpetrator, or both.) Incest has also been found to occur at the homes of other relatives and in cars or other unspecified locations.

Social Factors

Incest has commonly been thought to occur more often in families of lower socioeconomic class, in ethnic minorities, and in rural families. These beliefs were not substantiated in Russell's study. In fact, girls in high-income families were more frequently abused than girls in low-income families, the percentage of incest victims was comparable across all ethnic groups studied (with the exception of Asian women, who were at lower risk), and rural background was not a risk factor. Women of Jewish religious upbringing were less likely to be incestuously abused than Catholic and Protestant women, and women raised with stepfathers were much more likely to have been abused than women having grown up with their biological fathers.

CATEGORIES OF INCEST

Each case of incest can be categorized depending on how it occurred and with whom. A category offers general information about the incest dynamics and about possible sources of distress or trauma for the victim, some of which are specific to a particular category. Although considerable variation exists, certain categories have been found to correlate with particular types of aftereffects. Victim/survivors should not be *assumed* to have experienced particular effects because of the type of incest they experienced, yet knowledge of these categories allows the clinician to develop some working hypotheses to explore with the client. As an example, incest between closely related individuals has been found to have more serious aftereffects, on average, than incest between distant relatives. Certainly this correlation does not hold in all cases; nevertheless, the clinician can use it as a valid speculation and modify it according to how well it fits the experience of a particular client.

Abusive vs. Nonabusive Incest

Not all incest is abusive. At times, it is difficult to determine when incest constitutes abuse. Some of the criteria which have been used to make this determination include the age of participants, whether both parties consented to the activity (considering the related question of whether a younger, less powerful participant is able to give fully informed consent), and the aftereffects and participants' subjective reactions to the behavior.

Although some disagreement exists, it is now rather widely accepted that incest should always be defined as abusive when it is cross-generational, because the adult can use his/her power and standing as an adult to coerce the child into the activity. This view holds that a child is unable to consent due to her age and lack of power in the relationship. Even if a child or adolescent seeks out sex with an adult or has positive feelings about it, the activity is still considered abusive because of the power/age/experience discrepancy between the participants and the potential for harm to the less mature (Finkelhor, 1984). The age at which consent is possible has been debated, with age 14 being set as the standard by some researchers, age 16 or 18 by others.

Whether incest is abusive when it occurs between peers is less clear, since the age/power differential is less distinct. It has been widely assumed until recently that peer contact was almost always mutually desired and included nothing more than mild experimentation between participants. It is clear that this is not always the case. In fact, individuals who are technically peers can vary widely in age, size, power and influence. Nevertheless, at present some researchers are using age distinctions as gauges of power differences in determining whether peer incest constitutes abuse. An age difference of five years or more between participants has been used to define abuse in research, but even that distinction has been called into question. For example, Russell (1986) observed that such criteria are rather arbitrary and potentially discount valid cases of abuse perpetrated by close-in-age or even younger peers.

Incest can be considered *nonabusive* when it occurs between brothers, sisters, cousins, or other relatives who are age peers *when it is mutually desired and without coercion.* Also, it is nonabusive when engaged in freely, mutually, and without coercion between adults, whether they are peers or not. Nonetheless, most nonabusive incest is still illegal.

Russell incorporated many of these points in the definition of incestuous *abuse* she developed for her research and which we adopt as a working definition:

> . . . any kind of exploitive sexual contact or attempted contact that occurred between relatives, no matter how distant the relationship, before the victim turned eighteen years old. Experiences involving sexual contact with a relative that were wanted and with a peer were regarded as nonexploitive and hence nonabusive. (p. 41)

The clinician should be aware that the aftereffects of incest do not determine whether it was abusive or not. Incest can be abusive and not be traumatic or result in negative reactions. Positive, neutral, or ambivalent feelings can result from incestuous involvement in childhood or adolescence (whether peer or cross-generational), and should not be taken to mean that the activity was nonabusive. Further, many victims cope with incestuous experiences by downplaying or denying the consequences. Such responses do not indicate that the experience was nonabusive, but rather that these victims have not yet been able to acknowledge its full impact.

On the other hand, incest which is of the nonabusive type is not always benign and can cause later distress. One or both participants in nonabusive, mutual incest may later experience subjective negative reactions from having participated and broken the taboo against sexual contact between relatives and from having engaged in an illegal activity. These reactions do not, however, make the incest abusive retroactively.

Incest between Blood Relatives, Relatives by Marriage and Quasi-Relatives

Consanguinal incest refers to sexual contact between blood relatives. Affinal incest involves individuals who do not have genetic ties but are related due to contract or statute (as in the case of relatives by marriage or adoption). Quasi-relative incest involves individuals who have no blood or contractual ties but are quasi-related by virtue of an individual's involvement in a family and taking on a family role and its associated functions and responsibilities (for example, a live-in lover or a foster parent).

Sexual relations between the most closely related blood relatives, i.e., those within the nuclear family (between parent and child and between siblings), are the most forbidden because they have the most serious potential for harm and disruption. The strength of the taboo decreases when incest occurs outside of the nuclear family in direct proportion to the degree of kinship between individuals. Thus, grandparent-grandchild incest is more taboo than incest between second cousins.

The taboo applies less stringently to individuals who are affinally related and varies according to the roles they occupy with one another. Stepparent-stepchild incest is the most proscribed, followed by stepsibling contact and then contact between other members of the extended family. The societal taboo is even weaker when individuals are unrelated but occupy family roles and perform family functions (quasi-relatives), as in the case of a live-in lover who takes on the roles of husband and father.

State incest laws prohibit sexual intercourse and marriage between individuals who are related by blood but are not uniform concerning the degree of relatedness which is prohibited. Most of these laws also prohibit sexual contact between affinal relatives. Quasi-relatives are not covered by the incest laws because no blood or legal relationship exists between the involved individuals; rather, sexual contact between them is proscribed by state statutes covering rape, sexual assault, child sexual abuse, domestic abuse, or criminal sexual contact. For our purposes, sexual contact between quasi-relatives is considered incest even though it is not so defined legally because this contact has incestuous connotations and aftereffects for the involved child. Calof (1987) has extended the definition even further to encompass what he calls "implied incest," when family members do not adequately respond to abuse perpetrated by someone in a close relationship to the family.

The prevailing legal and professional view has been that incest perpetrated by a blood relative has more serious consequences than incest involving affinal or quasi-relatives. While this may well be the case, some recent research findings suggest another possibility: that consanguineous incest has somewhat less traumatic impact. Russell's (1986) sample reported that incestuous abuse perpetrated by blood relatives was at a somewhat less severe level and was less traumatic than abuse involving affinal relatives. Daughters in this sample were found to be at much greater risk of abuse from stepfathers than from their biological fathers because stepfather abuse was at a more severe level. The perpetrator who is not a blood relative has fewer restraints and may be more sexually violating. This, coupled with the perpetrator's violation of the family role and its boundaries, may contribute to greater trauma. Russell speculated that the incest taboo may, in fact, serve to inhibit the majority of biological fathers from abusing their daughters. For stepfathers and other affinal or quasi-relatives it may not provide enough of a restraint or inhibition. Clearly, these data are preliminary and in need of replication; they should not be used to minimize the seriousness of incest between blood relatives.

Incest in the Nuclear and Extended Family

Incest within the nuclear family refers to sexual contact between a parent (or anyone in a parental role) and a child and between siblings. Extended family encompasses all family members outside of the nuclear grouping. As mentioned above, incest between members of the nuclear family is the most taboo, with the taboo lessening as the degree of relatedness and the potential for harm and conflicted roles decreases. The comparative prevalence of nuclear family versus extended family incest is not clear at this time, making additional investigation necessary. Russell (1986) found that 62% of the incest experiences reported by her sample occurred outside of the nuclear family.

Incest involving members of the nuclear family, on average, seems to have the greatest potential for trauma. Parent-child incest, which in most cases means father/stepfather-daughter, is consistently reported as the most damaging type of incest, followed by sibling incest perpetrated by brothers. Many aspects of the nuclear family are potentially related to the greater traumatic impact: the degree of relatedness and contact between victim and perpetrator and therefore the degree of betrayal involved, along with the greater opportunity for contact and entrapment and its related opportunity for incest of longer duration, greater frequency, and greater severity. Russell (1986) and others also reported that a child caught in nuclear family incest of a severe sort and of long duration is less likely to receive assistance.

Cross-Generational Incest

Cross-generational incest involves sexual contact with a partner of a considerable age difference who is a parent, stepparent, in-law, grandparent, aunt or uncle, or second cousin. It may also involve a quasi-relative who is in a parental or guardian role with the child and from whom the child should be able to expect sexual distance. Incest with an older sibling or cousin can also be cross-generational but for ease of discussion is presented under the category of peer incest. Likewise, aunt/uncle incest is discussed as cross-generational, even though some aunts or uncles are close in age to their nieces and nephews, technically making them peers.

Until recently, cross-generational incest was believed to occur less frequently than peer incest but to hold greater potential for trauma due to the age difference between perpetrator and victim. Father-daughter incest was thought to be the most frequent form of cross-generational incest. New research and clinical findings are challenging some of this thinking. Experts now believe that cross-generational incest is more prevalent than peer incest, a belief which received research support from Russell's investigation. Father/stepfather-daughter incest has consistently been found to account for a large percentage of the cross-generational incest, but in the Russell study was exceeded slightly by uncle-niece abuse. This was a surprising finding, since uncle-niece incest has not been assumed to be very prevalent, nor has it been the object of much investigation.

From the available research and clinical evidence, cross-generational incest tends to have a greater potential for trauma than peer incest because of several factors, including the severity of the sexual violation and its duration (which are likely to be greater in cross-generational incest, depending on the perpetrator), and the age difference and degree of relatedness between victim and perpetrator. Incest between father and daughter is consistently predictive of the most serious aftereffects (Browne & Finkelhor, 1986; Russell, 1986).

Peer Incest

Peer incest involves sexual contact between individuals who are close in age and from the same age cohort. Most sibling (including step and half-sibling) and cousin incest falls within this category, although, as noted earlier, where a large age difference exists between participants cross-generational incest may be the more appropriate category.

Juvenile perpetrators of child sexual abuse have recently received increased research and clinical attention. Russell found that more than one in every four incest offenders reported by her sample was a juvenile. Many juveniles abuse younger children as a traumatic reenactment of their own abuse (whether intrafamilial or extrafamilial) or because they have had inappropriate sexual stimulation or modeling in their own families.

When incest is between close-in-age individuals, it has been assumed to have less potential for damage than when a large age discrepancy exists. Generally, this seems to be the case, but new data indicate that some peer incest, particularly involving older brothers/cousins and younger sisters/cousins, has more serious consequences than has been previously estimated. Russell found that the duration of these incestuous experiences was typically shorter than that of relationships perpetrated by older relatives, but that the severity of the sexual violation was the same for brothers and cousins as for fathers and uncles. She also reported that the severity of the abuse was the variable of the incest most correlated with traumatic response.

Another assumption concerning incest between age peers deserves consideration: that it is always mutually desired, exploratory in nature and therefore nonharmful. Strong enough evidence now exists to debunk this assumption. There is no question that sexual curiosity, observation, and exploration between agemates is normal in humans; however, it moves beyond this point when it is nonmutual and/or forced. Russell's sample reported that brothers and first cousins used more force than any other category of relatives, although most were not reported to be violent.

Opposite-Sex and Same-Sex Incest

Males perpetuate incest in far greater numbers than females, most often abusing female children. As mentioned earlier, abuse by men tends on average to be more traumatic than abuse by women because the abuse itself is of a more severe degree over a longer duration. When females abuse, they tend to abuse boys more often than they do girls. According to Russell and Finkelhor's research review (Russell, 1986): "We concluded that only about 5% of all sexual abuse of girls and about 20% of all sexual abuse of boys is perpetrated by older females" (p. 308). Females sometimes function as co-offenders or accessories to male abusers, as is discussed in Chapter 4.

Same-sex incest, whether involving males or females, has been underreported, leading at least one clinician to conclude that it is a rarity (Raybin, 1969). Recent research suggests that same-sex incest is not rare but only underinvestigated and underreported, because its occurrence involves the breaking of two taboos — incest and homosexuality.

Same-sex incest seems to involve more commonly boys than girls. A review study of male versus female perpetrators of sexual abuse conducted by Finkelhor and Russell (Finkelhor, 1984) concluded that males abuse far more often than do females and that females are more frequently the victims (by a margin of two to three girls to every one boy). When a boy is sexually abused, either within or outside of the family, he is much more likely to be abused by a man than by a woman (Finkelhor, 1984). Sex differences have also been found between how abuse is perpetrated and its aftereffects. Abuse by women is typically at a less severe level and of shorter duration than abuse by men. As a group, victims of female perpetrators report less trauma than victims of males (Russell, 1983).

Groth (1982) advised that same-sex incest should not be assumed always to indicate a homosexual orientation on the part of the perpetrator. The incest may instead represent a traumatic reenactment of the perpetrator's own sexual molestation at a particular age, as well as a symbolic identification with the victim. It is thus seen as a traumatic stress response and a narcissistic choice rather than a homosexual one. It may, nevertheless, be very confusing and traumatizing for the victim and cause a questioning of his or her sexual orientation.

Another perspective was presented in a preliminary study of a community sample of lesbians and gay men (Simari & Baskin, 1982). These researchers found an unexpectedly high rate of incestuous involvement in their sample — 38% for females and 46% for males. All of the incest reported by the males was homosexual; for the females 64% was heterosexual, 36% homosexual (with aunts and female cousins). A significant difference was found between homosexual and heterosexual incest: For females, all the heterosexual incest was reported as being "other" generated; for homosexual incest reported by both the men and women, no differences were found among cases that were "self," "other," or "mutually" initiated. So an unknown percentage of these incestuous experiences could be defined as consensual/voluntary/exploratory rather than coerced/involuntary.

Differences were found in the aftereffects reported by both groups. Only a small percentage of the males reported their homosexual incest as being negative, and those who did had experienced nuclear family cross-generational incest (usually father-son). The females reported all of the heterosexual incest as negative, but none reported their homosexual incest as such. Another finding of note: Only a small percentage of females had thought of themselves as homosexual before the incestuous experience, while almost all of the males so identified prior to the incest. The authors suggest that what may be true for heterosexual incest within heterosexual populations may not be true for homosexual incest within homosexual populations; however, they do not discuss the possibility that negative aftereffects were discounted or minimized by their respondents. Same-sex and opposite-sex incest is futher discussed in Chapters 4, 5, and 13.

Multiple Incest

The term "multiple incest" has been applied to those situations in which a victim is abused by more than one perpetrator either concurrently (as in group incest) or sequentially, as well as to situations in which a perpetrator abuses more than one victim. Increasingly well-documented is the fact that a substantial proportion of incest survivors has experienced multiple incest by members of the nuclear and/or extended family and that many perpetrators abuse more than one child (Courtois, 1982; Russell, 1986; Walsh, 1986a). Some stay strictly within the family, while others involve other children as well (for instance, a child's friend or a neighbor child). Some abusers involve more than one child at a time or approach various children in the family in an opportunistic, pedophiliac way. Others engage children sequentially, usually beginning with the oldest, most vulnerable and/or most favored child (usually the oldest daughter) and then move on to others.

Not infrequently, investigation of a family in which one incestuous dyad has been uncovered reveals additional pairings at both the peer and cross-generational levels. These can be conceptualized as horizontal (peer) or vertical (cross-generational) on a genogram. Once the incest barrier is breached, there is little to disinhibit additional incestuous activity; incest becomes the "normal" way to interact and seems to become unconsciously embedded within the family, even though the abuse is commonly kept secret. In some families, the extent of incestuous involvement across and within generations may be truly amazing. MacFarlane and Korbin (1983) described a family where all 11 adult females in one generation of an extended family had been abused by either a father/uncle or an older cousin/brother. I have worked with a number of cases where all the siblings were incestuously involved with one another in a variety of pairings and one or more were abused by the father and by uncles and grandfathers as well. Multiple incest and incestuous family norms are discussed more fully in Chapter 3.

It stands to reason that the multiply victimized survivor suffers additional aftereffects. She has to contend not only with the original incest but with the additional abuse as well. She often views the subsequent victimization as proof that *something about her* causes others to abuse her. The additional abuse further solidifies her victim identity. In her chapter entitled "Ravaged Lives," Russell (1986) presented three case descriptions of women who had been incestuously abused by several perpetrators and documented their increased vulnerability to continued revictimization later in life. These examples are dramatic portrayals of the victim/survivors' attempts to cope with wave after wave of exploitation by both family members and strangers.

In conclusion, incest has many categories and almost innumerable permutations. In this chapter, we have introduced incest by reviewing its predominant characteristics along with its major categories. This information is useful to the clinician in making preliminary estimates of aftereffects. The next chapter addresses the dynamics of abuse, including characteristics of the family which foster incestuous involvement among its members.

CHAPTER 3

The Dynamics of
Child Sexual Abuse
and the Incestuous Family

C HILD SEXUAL ABUSE and incest have been found to follow a rather pre-
dictable pattern of occurrence, a pattern which must be understood
by the clinician who works with the sexually victimized child or the formerly victimized adult. This pattern is delineated in this chapter, followed by a
discussion of the most common dynamics and characteristics of the incestuous family. Incest has been found to occur in conjunction with other
shame-based family dysfunctions and to have intergenerational patterns of
transmission. These too make up the subject matter of this chapter.

STAGES AND DYNAMICS OF CHILD SEXUAL ABUSE

The pattern of occurrence in child sexual abuse has been most clearly
articulated by Sgroi, Blick, and Porter (1982); much of the following
material on dynamics is drawn from their formulation. According to these
authors, sexual abuse usually consists of five separate phases: (1) the engagement phase; (2) the sexual interaction phase; (3) the secrecy phase; (4)
the disclosure phase; and often (5) a suppression phase following disclosure. Each phase has its own dynamics.

The *engagement phase* encompasses (a) access and opportunity, (b) relationship of participants, and (c) inducements. Child sexual abuse is usually
perpetrated by someone who has ready access and is known to the child,
either through kinship ties or by being placed in a position of caretaking/
authority (e.g., babysitter, neighbor, friend, clergy, troop leader, daycare
worker, teacher). Privacy allows for the opportunity. Although the initial

encounter may not have been planned, later encounters are created or watched for by the perpetrator. According to Sgroi et al.:

> . . . . the dynamics of child sexual abuse most involve often [sic] a known perpetrator who is in a legitimate power position over a child and who exploits accepted societal patterns of dominance and authority to engage the child in sexual activity. It is impossible to overemphasize the significance of the exploitation and misuse of accepted power relationships when assessing the impact of sexual abuse on the child. (p. 13)

The adult's position of authority communicates to the child that the behavior is acceptable. Specific methods of inducement range from very subtle and low-key to overt, forceful, and violent. Most perpetrators do not need to resort to violence or coercion. Instead, they engage the child by suggesting that the activity is a game, something special, a way to gain exclusive attention or particular favors. Special attention is a most effective lure with a child who is neglected or lacking in appropriate adult attention. Sgroi et al. note that the more adept the perpetrator, the less likely it is that he will need to use threats or violence to involve the child. Studies of pedophiles reveal that they seek out children who appear to be vulnerable and in need of attention.

The *sexual interaction phase* typically includes an escalation of some or all of the aforementioned sexual activities, as discussed by Sgroi et al.:

> The typical scenario is a progression from less intimate types of sexual activity such as exposure and self-masturbation to actual body contact (such as fondling), and then to some form of penetration. Oral penetration may be expected to occur early in this progression, which is often followed by digital penetration of the anus or vagina. Ejaculation by a male perpetrator, sometimes against the child's body can occur at any time in this progression. (p. 12)

Although a progression from less to more intrusive activity is the most common sexual pattern in child sexual abuse, it is not the only one. A victim's story should not be discounted if it does not match this escalation. The clinician should expect to hear of such variations as penetration on first contact or penetration first followed by oral sex, mutual masturbation, and fondling, etc.

In the *secrecy phase* concealment is used to eliminate accountability and to allow for the repetition and continuation of the activity. Child sexual abuse has been described as an addiction/compulsion for the perpetrator due to the powerful reinforcement accompanying the behavior, including sexual pleasure and orgasm, enhanced self-esteem due to feeling wanted and cared about, and a sense of power, dominance, and competence in a relationship where few demands are made for mutuality and reciprocity. To continue to engage in this pleasurable activity the perpetrator must pressure or persuade the child to maintain the secret. Here again, the authority and power of the adult actively play into the process. Some perpetrators threaten or use violence to maintain secrecy, but most use coercion of some other sort instead. For example, the perpetrator may threaten anger ("If you tell, daddy (or mommy) will be very angry at you"); separation ("If you tell, daddy will go to jail, or mommy (or daddy) will leave, or you will be kicked out of the family"); blame ("Nobody will believe that it's not your fault. You liked it and wanted it or you would have said something before"). He may threaten to harm himself, the child, or someone or something else ("If you tell, I'll kill myself/you, your sister/brother/friend/pet, etc.") and/or to withdraw his affection or leave altogether.

These different forms of blackmail are usually enough to enforce the child's silence. Additionally, the child remains silent when she is unsure about what is taking place or does not have the language to communicate about it. Or she may have been told and come to believe that she is the member of the family responsible for pleasing the perpetrator and that doing so protects other members of the family and/or keeps the family together. Sgroi et al. also note that some children maintain secrecy not because of direct coercion but rather because of the pleasure and attention gained in the relationship:

> . . . the child may keep the secret because he or she enjoyed the activity and wants the behavior to continue. This premature introduction to sexuality by a known and valued perpetrator, a person who is a "significant other" for the child, may feel good on several levels—pleasurable sexual stimulation, enhancement of self-esteem, feeling important to another person in a special grown-up fashion, and so forth. Although not especially pleasing to contemplate, to deny that the pleasurable aspects of the sexual behavior may be self-reinforcing for the child, is to ignore the obvious and to nelect [sic] to consider one of the most important dynamics. (p. 16)

Many more idiosyncratic reasons and beliefs account for a child's silence. To illustrate: One of the women in my research study did not attempt to stop her grandfather from fondling her because he would provide her with school lunch money afterwards. She and her siblings would have no lunch otherwise. Other survivors describe submitting to abuse in hopes that the perpetrator's mood would improve, that he would stop drinking, not be violent, etc. And some children are abused as infants and babies, at a time when they are preverbal and have no words to associate with their experience. In this case, the abuse is kinesthetically rather than verbally coded. Later retrieval of abuse experiences may come through kinesthetic memory.

Most sexually abused children have kept the secret for months, years or their entire lives. Adult survivors received little if any of the prevention and safety training now given rather routinely to children. What warnings they did receive had to do with "stranger danger" and not with the dangers of sexual exploitation within the home. For the child caught in intrafamilial abuse, secrecy often seemed the only option. Many learned that there was no place to go, no one to tell, no one who would listen, and that disclosure was risky. Yet, we now know that many children were so desperate that they tried to tell, some through direct means and some indirectly.

In the *disclosure phase*, the secret escapes either accidentally or purposefully. External circumstances, such as observation by a third party, physical injury or sexual infection, pregnancy, precocious sexual activity, or spontaneous disclosure made in anger during a family conflict, lead to unplanned divulgence. Since neither of the participants is prepared in advance, unplanned disclosure typically results in crisis reactions and calls for crisis intervention aimed at protecting the child, lessening anxiety, supporting the reality that sexual abuse does occur, validating the report, and supporting all family members.

Purposeful disclosure is characterized by deliberate intent to reveal the abuse, almost always on the part of the child. It is highly unusual, in fact almost unheard of, for the perpetrator to be the one to disclose. Since the child may have various motivations for disclosure, the clinician must assess the reasons for the revelation at the time it occurs (or occurred). Purposeful disclosure allows for more planful intervention, although crisis intervention may also be necessary. Whether the disclosure is accidental or planned, the family typically responds with anxiety and alarm. The perpetrator's role in the family and family loyalty are among the factors that determine how the family reacts. It is an unfortunate reality that "Parents of a child who has been sexually abused by someone other than a parent are likely to react in a more protective fashion toward the victim. The degree of protectiveness toward the child will depend in part on the identity of the perpetrator" (Sgroi, et al., 1982, p. 22).

Divided loyalty and protection of the family unit are major factors when the abuse has occurred within the nuclear family and may be present to a lesser degree in the extended family, especially when a grandparent is involved. Perpetrators usually react to disclosure with denial, defensiveness, and hostility toward the child and anyone either within or outside of the family who supports the child. The family tie allows the perpetrator access, influence, and authority with which to challenge the child. Many mothers of victims respond in a concerned and protective fashion, although it is not uncommon for some to deny the abuse or to attack or blame the child for its occurrence. Some may have known about the abuse all along or may have encouraged or participated in it. These knowledgeable or participant mothers are likely to join the perpetrator in denial, with self-protection as the primary goal.

The mother who does support the child's allegations faces enormous pressure within the family to retract that support. She may be threatened with violence or with loss of family, economic and/or social status, and emotional support. Many mothers are unable to resist the pressure without strong outside assistance. Even with support, many reverse their initial stand, rather than face the conflict, uncertainty, and discomfort entailed in siding with the victim. On the other hand, some mothers are unwavering in their support of their children. At present, several mothers are incarcerated because they refused to obey court orders allowing unsupervised visitation between fathers and daughters following abuse.

Siblings and members of the extended family react in various ways, ranging from denial and attack of the victim, envy if she is perceived as having had a favored status, personal defensiveness and self-protection through withdrawal, and finally, staunch support.

The final phase is *suppression,* which occurs whether disclosure has been accidental or purposeful. Family members attempt to suppress the child's report and to minimize the severity of the abuse or the child's response to it. They want to rid themselves of the aggravation and discomfort of the situation and to avoid adverse publicity as well as intervention by the police or social services. Pressure for suppression is usually most intense when family members have continued access to the child and opportunities to threaten her with a variety of dire consequences if she persists in her allegations or her cooperation with authorities. In addition, family members often attempt to discredit the child to investigating authorities or displace their emotions (particularly anger) about the abuse and its disclosure onto those investigators (Solin, 1986). Many children succumb to the pressure by recanting their allegations or refusing to cooperate with anyone attempting to intervene.

These five phases of child sexual abuse provide an overview of *how* abuse typically occurs. Understanding these phases gives insight into the child's experience. As can be seen, the burden of both the (repeated) sexual assault and of disclosure and proof usually fall on the child, the individual least capable of dealing with them due to physical and emotional immaturity and economic and emotional dependence. In all likelihood, the child who complains of incest faces disbelief, criticism, and hostility rather than concern, compassion, and protection.

Although these phases are characteristic of all types of child sexual abuse, they are usually more pronounced in intrafamilial abuse, *precisely because* the abuse occurs within the family. In our society, family is seen as the protected place, a place of safety and security which nurtures the growth and development of immature children. In contrast, strangers are the source of danger, the people from whom the child needs to be protected. Abuse within the family therefore contradicts everything a family should be. Until fairly recently, the exploitation of a child by an adult relative was so shocking and contrary to the view of family as a sanctuary that its possibility was routinely denied. To this day, in our society, the prerogatives of relatedness and family are strongly encouraged and protected. Family members maintain access and responsibility for children, except in the most serious and irrefutable transgressions.

THE SEXUAL ABUSE ACCOMMODATION SYNDROME

Summit (1983) writes that any understanding of child sexual abuse is incomplete without consideration of the child's perspective. The typical response of the child to sexual abuse flies in the face of adult logic unless understood *in context*, that is, from the child's point of view. If she is misunderstood or blamed, her report of abuse rejected, and her experience invalidated, the most damaging effects of the abuse are reinforced rather than ameliorated. Summit contends: "Acceptance and validation are crucial to the psychological survival of the victim" (p. 179).

Summit has described a syndrome, the *child sexual abuse accommodation syndrome*, bringing together the victim responses seen most frequently in his practice and by other clinicians. The syndrome includes both the common responses to abuse and additional or atypical responses. Summit calls attention to the fact that it is possible to identify a syndrome associated with child sexual abuse but that abuse experience and aftereffects show a high degree of variability as well.

The child sexual abuse accommodation syndrome is composed of five categories, which address both the vulnerability of the child and the reality of sexual assault: (1) secrecy; (2) helplessness; (3) entrapment and accommodation; (4) delayed, unconvincing disclosure; and (5) retraction. The first two categories are preconditions to the occurrence of sexual abuse. The last three are "sequential contingencies which take on increasing variability and complexity. While it can be shown that each category reflects a compelling reality for the victim, each category represents also a contradiction to the most common assumptions of adults" (p. 181). It is crucial for the clinician to have an understanding of the child's reality and also to understand that, in most cases, it confounds and contradicts adult logic concerning abuse.

The *secrecy* category refers to an all-pervasive aspect of sexual abuse. As discussed earlier, the reality of sexual abuse is kept secret even among adults. If adults do not know of its possibility, the child is even less prepared and must rely on the perpetrator for whatever meaning is to be given to the experience. The perpetrator's need and intent are to keep the activity secret. Even when gentle explanations are used and no overt intimidation is present, the pressure for secrecy communicates to the child that something is wrong or that it is dangerous to tell.

The secrecy is both the source of fear and the promise of safety: "Everything will be all right if you just don't tell." The secret takes on magical, monstrous proportions for the child. A child with no knowledge or awareness of sex and even with no pain or embarrassment from the sexual experience itself will still be stigmatized with a sense of badness and danger from the pervasive secrecy. (Summit, 1983, p. 181)

Additionally, if the child does attempt to disclose, she is met with adult disbelief and shock or with minimization or rationalization of the offending adult's behavior. In this process, her perceptions and her complaints are disconfirmed. It is typical for the child to be told that what she has complained about is nothing to be concerned about, something she misunderstood or blew out of proportion, or something that she should simply ignore.

The most common response is for the child not to tell. Most children take the admonitions or threats of the perpetrator very seriously and/or independently conclude that they will be blamed or not supported. So they maintain the secret and in the process isolate themselves with the reality of their experience. The maintenance of secrecy has an additional unfortunate consequence. If the child discloses at a later time (either in adolescence or adulthood), she will be misunderstood and/or blamed for not having told. Typical responses, even to disclosure in adulthood, include: "Why didn't you tell me?" "How could you have allowed it to go on for so long?" "You must have enjoyed it at some level to keep quiet for so long." "You can't expect me to believe that about your father/uncle/grandfather."

The category of *helplessness* refers to the child's dependent and subordinate position in the family, the group of people on whom she relies for protection and security. When a child is incestuously abused, the reality strongly contradicts what she has been taught about the meaning of family. Family members are safe; strangers are dangerous and are to be feared. Summit writes:

The prevailing reality for the most frequent victim of child sexual abuse is not a street or schoolground experience and not some mutual vulnerability to oedipal temptations, but an unprecedented, relentlessly progressive intrusion of sexual acts by an overpowering adult in a one-sided victim-perpetrator relationship. The fact that the perpetrator is in a trusted position of authority with the child relates to the child's helplessness. (1983, p. 183)

Much sexual abuse occurs as the child is preparing for sleep or once the child is asleep. The child's bed, her place of safety, security and "sweet dreams," is repeatedly violated and made nightmarish. In addition to his authority over the child, the perpetrator thus gains the advantage of the child's being in a defenseless state and a state which causes her to question whether what happened was real or was a bad dream. He uses this to his advantage, often relabeling any outcry on the part of the child as a nightmare or bad dream.

The most typical response of the child to both the initiation of the behavior and its continuance is to pretend that it is not taking place. Children pretend to be asleep or somewhere else, anywhere but in their beds being abused. Summit referred to the child's attempts to pretend the abuse was not occurring or to not respond as "playing possum" (p. 183). Many survivors describe a process of dissociation. They separate their minds from their bodies in order not to feel their bodily sensations and not to be present. Their attempts to become part of the wallpaper or woodwork or to blend into the wall serve as protection and as a means of coping with the abuse.

Despite the child's attempts to distance from the activity and the credence the attempts lend to her wish for the activity to stop, the inability to otherwise resist or ask for help reinforces self-condemnation on the part of the child. Instead of learning about her own effectiveness, she learns that she is powerless, that what she wants, says, or does makes no difference. The child perceives that she somehow invited the activity and allowed its continuance by her inability to stop it. Of course, this self-condemnation does not acknowledge a most salient characteristic of the circumstance — her dependent and powerless position as a child.

The next category in Summit's schema is *entrapment and accommodation*. He writes:

> If the child did not seek or did not receive immediate protective intervention, there is no further option to stop the abuse. The only healthy option left for the child is to learn to accept the situation and to survive. There is no way out, no place to run. The healthy, normal, emotionally resilient child will learn to accommodate to the reality of continuing sexual abuse. There is the challenge of accommodating not only to escalating sexual demands but to an increasing consciousness of betrayal and objectification by someone who is ordinarily idealized as a protective, altruistic, loving parental figure. Much of what is eventually labeled as adolescent or adult psychopathology can be traced to the natural reactions of a healthy child to a profoundly unnatural and unhealthy parental environment. (1983, p. 184)

The contradiction between what the parent (or other perpetrator) *is* and what he *is supposed to be* is too great for the child to reconcile. She copes with this contradiction as best she can, usually by reversing it. She sees the perpetrator as good in order to protect herself from the disillusionment that would result if she were to view him as bad. She sees *herself* as the bad one who somehow provoked the behavior. (In some cases, she is told this or some variation on the same theme by the perpetrator.) She attempts to be good, both to deal with her guilt and to earn the acceptance and love she so desperately craves. Her reasoning is along the lines of, "If only I can be good enough, then the behavior will stop. Since it is not stopping, I must be bad and have to keep trying to be good."

In order to survive the situation and its disconfirmation, the child develops other coping mechanisms. Outwardly, she may appear to be very well-adjusted and responsible, but a closer look frequently reveals a depressed, anxious child. Many of these children cope by being model children at home and at school; they are skilled at appearing normal and in pleasing teachers and peers. Furthermore, as part of the family dynamics, they may have responsibility for the functioning of the entire family (e.g., meals, laundry, care of siblings, budgeting, marketing), almost as an extension of the pattern of role reversal inherent in the sexual relationship. The child often utilizes such defense mechanisms as splitting, repression, reaction formation, "sliding" or multiple personalities, and conversion reactions to cope and to maintain her "normal" appearance.

If the child expresses her rage, it is usually during adolescence, when she begins the process of self-determination and separation from her family, often through rebellion. Consistent with her self-blame and powerlessness, the expression of rage is likely to be directed towards herself in self-defeating and self-destructive ways, including suicidal gestures and behavior, self-mutilation, substance abuse, poor choice of friends and intimates, sexual promiscuity and prostitution, and runaway attempts. These serve to reinforce her self-hatred and often result in misunderstanding, criticism, and rejection on the part of the family and others. These, in turn, reinforce her mistrust of others and her expectation that she does not deserve good attention because she is tainted.

Summit's fourth category is *delayed, conflicted, and unconvincing disclosure*. Typically, the abuse is never disclosed, at least not outside the immediate family. However, disclosure can occur accidentally, particularly during the intense family conflicts characteristic of adolescence. Adolescence often provokes a crisis for the perpetrator. As the victim attempts to distance from him, the possibility of outside love interests increases, and as she acts out her rage, he may become increasingly jealous and controlling. Such behavior may intensify the desperation and anger of the adolescent, leading her to act out or impulsively disclose the abuse. This type of angry disclosure, stemming from intense conflict with the parents and attempts by the parents to curb or control acting-out behavior, usually results in disbelief of the adolescent's story. Alternatively, the compliant, outwardly well-adjusted child who seeks to disclose the incest in adolescence faces similar disbelief because she has coped so well. Either way, the burden of proof is on the victim, and neither pattern of accommodation increases her credibility with already skeptical adults. Rather than being seen as real, the child's complaint is viewed as impossible or invalid. This is even more so if the family and perpetrator are of "good stock" and of good standing in the community. Higher family status and professional standing of the parents make reports of abuse even less credible to adults already inclined to doubt that abuse has occurred.

The final step of the sexual abuse accommodation syndrome is *retraction*. Summit summarizes: *"Whatever a child says about sexual abuse, she is likely to reverse it,"* and, *"Unless there is special support for the child and immediate intervention to force responsibility on the father, the girl will follow the 'normal' course and retract her complaint"* (p. 188, author's italics). The aftermath of disclosure is usually so stressful for the child, with many of the threats used to maintain secrecy coming true, that she recants. She admits to lying as she attempts to do what is "good" to preserve the family and to undo the "bad" that threatens to destroy it. Summit summarizes the category of retraction by saying:

> This simple lie [the retraction] carries more credibility than the most explicit claims of incestuous entrapment. It confirms adult expectations that children cannot be trusted. It restores the precarious equilibrium of the family. The children learn not to complain. The adults learn not to listen. And the authorities learn not to believe rebellious children who try to use their sexual power to destroy well-meaning parents. (1983, p. 188)

So it can be seen that the child caught in an abuse situation has few effective options, leaving her to devise coping strategies. Unfortunately, it also seems that the child caught in the most desperate situation is the one who is *least likely* to receive effective assistance and intervention, a fact Russell (1986) documented in her research. She discovered that the more closely related the incest participants and the more severe the level of abuse, the more unlikely that the victim would receive a supportive response. In other words, the victim of repetitive serious abuse perpetrated within the nuclear family is likely to be entrapped with little or no help available. Her only hope to break the pattern of secrecy and denial is strong intervention from the outside, assistance that is only now becoming available. The formerly victimized women who are the subject of this book had even fewer resources than the children of today; the clinician must therefore expect that they employed massive and varied coping mechanisms and that serious, repetitive abuse within the nuclear family called for the strongest psychological defenses and adaptations of all.

DYNAMICS OF THE INCESTUOUS FAMILY

The general dynamics of child sexual abuse and the accommodation syndrome supply a context in which to consider the dynamics and characteristics of the incestuous family. These have been discussed in the literature from several different perspectives: (1) psychodynamic, which focuses on the personality dynamics and backgrounds of the various members in the incestuous family as well as the interactions among family members; (2) sociological or sociocultural, which focuses on social and cultural factors

conducive to the development of incest; (3) family systems, which examines the family as a unit to determine dynamics, interaction patterns, and
family roles; and (4) feminist, which analyzes family roles and patterns in
the context of societal norms and sex-role stereotyping. In the discussion
below, the family systems perspective is emphasized since the other perspectives are discussed elsewhere in this book.*

Before beginning this discussion, several caveats are necessary. The first
is that most of the information about family dynamics has been derived
from the study of father-daughter incest, the type that has received the
most intensive scrutiny to date. The second is that the study of incestuous
behavior, like other forms of family violence, is relatively recent. Moreover,
most of the investigations of incest conducted thus far have suffered from
bias and a lack of scientific rigor. The third is that these characteristics are
not static; rather, they are dynamic and fluid within each family. And the
fourth is that no single factor or single factor theory is sufficient in and of
itself to explain incestuous abuse (Finkelhor, 1986), since incest is multifac-
torial in origin. It occurs under a variety of circumstances for many reasons. Meiselman (1978), in her review of incest and its dynamics, was quite
specific on this point:

> No single personality disturbance or pattern of family dynamics is *the* cause
> of father-daughter incest, but some commonalities have emerged over many
> studies of incest in different research settings and in different societies. Each
> incest situation, like each human being, is absolutely unique in its details and
> yet can be validly seen as representative of types of incest situations that
> have no doubt been recurring almost universally since the inception of the
> taboo. (pp. 140–141)

Finkelhor (1984) has proposed the four preconditions model of sexual
abuse to account for the various factors which relate to sexual abuse. This
model incorporates sociological and psychological explanations of abuse
factored down to the following four preconditions which must be met for
sexual abuse to occur:

(1) Motivation to sexually abuse: The potential offender must be
    motivated.
(2) Internal inhibitions: The potential offender must overcome inter-
    nal inhibitions against acting on the motivation.
(3) External inhibitions: The potential offender must overcome exter-
    nal impediments.

---

*The psychodynamics of the different types of incest are presented in Chapters 4
and 5; sociocultural and feminist issues and perspectives are discussed in Chapters 2 and 7.

(4) Resistance by child: The potential offender or some other factor (e.g., loneliness) undermines or overcomes a child's possible resistance (p. 54).

The Family Process

From the family systems perspective the typical incest family has been found to have rigid boundaries with regard to outsiders, that is, to be socially, psychologically, and physically isolated. Family members are mutually dependent on one another to get their needs met and are said to be enmeshed. Appropriate boundaries are lacking between individual family members and between generations. Children are involved in role reversal with the parents, the most extreme example occurring, of course, when the child becomes sexually involved with the parent. Another common manifestation is the child who becomes the caretaker for one or both parents or for the entire family.

Despite the enmeshment found in these families, emotional and physical deprivation predominates. These are quite often "low touch" families, with affection expressed sexually. Consequently, the children may be starved for affection, with the contact surrounding the abuse their only source of nurturance.

According to Kempe and Kempe (1984), there appear to be two broad family types in which incest occurs most regularly, the chaotic family and the "normal-appearing" family. The chaotic family has been considered the prototypical family in which incest develops because it has been the type most researched until just recently. It is characterized by problems spanning generations, relatively low socioeconomic standing, marginal functioning of individual family members and the family as a whole (e.g., brushes with the law, alcohol abuse, drug abuse, public assistance, instability of intimate relationships and community involvement, limited education and vocational achievement, etc.). In this family, it is not at all unusual for many family members to be sexually involved with one another, for pregnancies to result, and for the resulting children to be raised in the family. The blurring of paternity and generations is just one more blurred boundary in this family.

Children in chaotic families are basically left to raise themselves and, without adult supervision, are vulnerable to all forms of abuse inside and outside the family. Some typically become caretakers, others "lost children," and others rebels. When and if incest and/or other forms of abuse in this family come to the attention of authorities, the perpetrators are more likely to be prosecuted and even jailed than are their more economically and socially stable counterparts. They have neither the community standing nor the financial resources to mount a strong legal defense.

The "normal-appearing" family, as the name implies, is just that. From the outside, the family appears to be solid and well-functioning. The parents are usually established in a long-term marriage, are socially and financially stable, and seem well-integrated in the community. Typically, the family follows the traditional model of the husband as "head of the household" and the wife as subordinate, although in some families this structure is a façade to cover the reality that the wife is the dominant partner and the husband dependent.

The family is not as stable internally as it appears on the outside. The parents often lack the emotional energy to adequately nurture one another, much less their children. Both are affectionally needy as a result of their own emotionally impoverished and/or abusive upbringings. Over time, they become estranged from one another, emotionally and sexually. Not infrequently, they have developed work and social schedules which allow them to avoid interacting with one another on much more than a superficial level. Alcoholism or other shame-based problems are often in evidence and contribute to the barren emotional family climate. Children are left to cope as they can and over time both parents engage them in caretaking functions. The mother turns to her daughter for help in running the household and the father turns to her for emotional and sexual sustenance. Children often turn to one another to meet emotional or other needs and, not infrequently, their relationship becomes sexual. Another sibling variation is the brother who becomes sexually predatory towards his sister in direct modeling of his father's incestuous behavior.

When and if incest in this family comes to light, it is greeted with disbelief and incredulity and treated as no more than a temporary aberration on the part of the father/family. Abusers have the resources to hire a competent (and often aggressive) legal team which attacks the child's credibility while emphasizing the father's community and professional status. These men are rarely found guilty and in almost all cases are free to return home — most often to abuse again.

In Chapter 2, we mentioned that incest can be limited to one perpetrator and one victim as a rather self-contained phenomenon but that multiple incest in one family may be the norm. It appears that in many families, the breakdown of the incest taboo allows for its continuance either within one generation (horizontally) and/or across generations (vertically). This has led to the investigation of the family process in the development of incest, specifically the roles and interactions of family members and mechanisms of transmission.

Incest is now believed to be transmitted from one generation to the next through several such mechanisms. Calof (1987) discusses incest as a symptom of a transgenerational family process with both intrapsychic and interpersonal components. He believes that the intrapsychic process is the "mechanism of incest promulgation." As such, it is the mechanism in need of intervention to stop the abuse cycle. Denial and dissociation are primary aspects of this intrapsychic process. These are explained in more detail below.

Cooper and Cormier (1982) documented several patterns of intergenerational transmission of incest. In incestuous families, it is not unusual for both parents to have been emotionally deprived and/or sexually or physically abused during their childhoods. The mother with an unresolved history of incest with her own father (and possibly with a brother as well) may be unable to prevent an incestuous relationship between her husband and daughter. The research of Goodwin and DiVasto (1979) substantiated this pattern. They found that such an incest history impedes some women from adequately functioning as a mother at all. These women are so needy that a role reversal is established with their children from a very early age. In another pattern, the father witnessed sexual abuse of sisters or was himself sexually abused by his father or another family member or nonrelative. Pelto (1981) found evidence of this pattern in his study of incestuous fathers.

According to Rist (1979), children in these families are involved in destructive triangulation—they meet the needs of their parents while their needs go unheeded and their development unattended. Triangulation occurs because child protection and caretaking functions in a particular family are weak and the children are used both to shore up the parents' self-esteem and to compensate for their marital estrangement. Krugman (1987) discussed the concept of triangulation across generations as the basic pattern in the organization and transmission of family violence. He noted:

> In effect, it means that adults take it out on children when they cannot manage tension and conflict among themselves. . . . In one pattern, the classic scapegoating sequence, parents maintain their alliance and stabilize the family system by blaming and punishing the child. In another pattern commonly associated with sexual abuse, the child is elevated into the parental hierarchy and the system stabilized through role reversal. The child may thus be either covertly allied with one parent against the other, or parentified and obliged to care for a parent suffering from alcoholism, depression, or another disability. The child may also be assigned the role of surrogate parent for other children or, in the case of father-daughter incest, the role of surrogate wife. (p. 139)

In a similar vein, Fossum and Mason (1986) have noted intergenerational patterns of shame in families suffering from single or multiple dysfunctions such as addictions or compulsions in addition to physical, sexual, or emotional abuse. They concluded that shame was the organizing intrapsychic principle in these families' dynamics, "masked by a myriad of well-developed, sophisticated defense systems" (p. xi). Like Calof (1987) and other researchers, they noted that denial was a primary defense mechanism, further supported by intense family reliance and loyalty, in turn fostered by the insecure family atmosphere. Denial leads to forced silence and causes a selective restructuring of reality. Children in these circumstances must contend with the obvious manifestation of the family dysfunction, be it alcoholism or abuse or a combination, yet are not free to identify it as such because it carries such shame and to do so would be considered disloyal. Instead, the child is forced to distort reality to something it is not and then to distort her own feelings in reaction.

The dysfunction and its associated denial contribute to an unstable atmosphere supported by inconsistencies of response on the part of the parents. What brings praise and affection one day results in abuse and rejection on another. Children cope with this inconsistency by learning to be mistrustful and wary and by responding in ways that help them avoid further conflict, criticism or punishment. In extreme cases and when children have high dissociative potential, they begin to split off these different experiences of reality, a process which ultimately develops a fragmented rather than integrated sense of self. Children from abusive homes often complain of not feeling whole and of having holes in their sense of themselves. Thus, they very adequately convey the consequences of having grown up in an environment which fosters fragmentation rather than intactness.

A child's splitting off of reality corresponds to and reinforces the adult's own denial of reality in much the same way as the co-dependent family member's support of the alcoholic enables his continued denying and distorting. Without outside intervention to break the cycle, it becomes self-perpetuating. It contorts and distorts the individual personality of family members and the relational patterns among them.

Traits and Characteristics of Incestuous Families

We see that these families are characterized by a shifting reality used to maintain family integrity and to avoid dissolution. Calof (1987) has provided a summary of the traits most often used by incestuous families to maintain the integrity and homeostasis of the family unit:

(1) Collective denial and shared secrets about a multitude of problems, not just the incest. These include problems such as alcoholism and other addictions, major illnesses, family illegitimacies, previous marriages, etc.
(2) Duplicity and deceit between family members. The family goes to great lengths to protect itself and develops protective myths as defense mechanisms.
(3) Social isolation, which is generally enforced by the parents.

(4) Parents who are expert at manipulating the context of a situation and shifting reality. As an example, abuse, alcoholism, or other family problems are denied while their reality is, in fact, obvious.

(5) Role confusion and boundary diffusion both within and outside of the family.

(6) A child who is triangulated into the parents' marriage, which is often characterized by a failed sexual relationship. The child is used to defuse the situation and to keep the family intact.

(7) Poor tolerance for differences from the family norm and for anger and conflict.

(8) Overly moralistic. In some families, religious beliefs are quite rigid and intolerant and are used to cover transgressions. For example, the child is often faced with strong moral injunctions about sex outside of marriage and the evils of sexual temptation even while she is being sexually used and stimulated.

(9) No touch except for bad touch. Being abused comes to be equated with love.

(10) Inadequate parenting. Children grow up too quickly by having to attend to their parents' needs. Their own needs are unmet and their development compromised.

(11) Low humor and high sarcasm. Emotional abuse may characterize the interactions in these families. Children may be consistently criticized and belittled, with little or no encouragement. Praise or reward is lacking. These families are said to be "character and initiative-assassinating."

(12) Dead, missing or part-time parent(s). The job of parenting may be abandoned in favor of other activities (work, drinking, etc.).

(13) Children may be unwanted and treated that way. Herman (1981) documented enforced pregnancies among mothers of incest survivors. It stands to reason that children conceived under such circumstances will be emotionally neglected or worse.

(14) Unpredictability and intermittent reinforcement. Like physically abusive families, many incestuous families are inconsistent towards children, who may be loved one day and abused the next for the same behavior. The child learns to "expect the unexpected" and thus is deprived of basic security. These families may also be inconstant in other ways. Family life may be chaotic and characterized by interchangeable family members (sequential live-in lovers and their families, stepsiblings, or members of the extended family who move in and out), and frequent geographic moves (as in military families or evicted families).

(15) Violence and the threat of violence. The threat of violence may be always present even if violence is not exercised. In some fami-

lies, actual violence is the norm and in the most extreme cases reaches the level of being torturous.

(16) No time for recovery and no one to turn to. The child may be so isolated and the abuse so pervasive that she has no opportunity to process it. Consequently, she contains it and copes as best she can. The most extreme form of such non-integration is multiple personality disorder, where experiences are split off into various personalities.

Family Rules and Injunctions

The family process is maintained by a system of family rules and injunctions. These intrapsychic components must be identified during therapy in order for the survivor to become consciously aware of them and to be able to develop apart from them. A number of authorities on child abuse and incest have identified that double binds are most characteristic of these families. Wooley and Vigilanti (1984) provided an account of the double bind in incestuous families, a description quoted here at length because of its completeness:

> The double bind in incestuous families is defined as a no-win situation in which the person who is sexually abused received conflictual messages from the system (i.e., the family) in a manner that does not allow escape. The most salient feature of the double-bind process is a failure to achieve separation/individuation. Separation/individuation is . . . a process by which the individual forms a sense of self, differentiated from that of the parents, by separating one's own identity from that of the parents and thus beginning the development of one's own individuality. . . .
>
> The double-bind process may be conceptualized as follows:
>
> *The Participants.* The double bind is a recurrent process which includes two or more persons. In this case, the participants are: the perpetrator of sexual advances (generally, but not always, a father figure); the recipient of sexual advances; and other involved family members (oftentimes the mother figure).
>
> *The Primary Negative Injunction.* The recipient of sexual advances is repeatedly exposed to a primary negative injunction which comes from the abuser and can take the form of "If you do not submit to my sexual advances, I will punish, ignore, or reject you." The mother figure may also play a part by communicating helplessness, or an inability to recognize or change the situation. . . .
>
> *The Secondary Negative Injunction.* A secondary negative injunction is imposed on the recipient by the abuser to the effect of "Do not see me as making sexual advances, because this is not really sex," or "This is really good for you and I am not abusing you," or, "This is your fault for turning me on." Again, the mother figure, or others, may collude in the paradox by implying that "Good girls don't do such things."
>
> *The Tertiary Negative Injunction.* A tertiary negative injunction is involved which prevents the victim from leaving the situation emotionally, often even

after she has left home and has a family of her own. If the incest begins early in childhood, escape is, of course, impossible. However, later, the tertiary injunction may involve promises of love, material goods, etc. Often, the abuser is the only person in the family to whom the recipient feels close. There is commonly a clear love bond between the victim and the abuser. The victim may consciously choose to continue or encourage the relationship if she feels her emotional survival is threatened, or if she learns other family members escaped punishment as long as they were sexually compliant. Others acquired special goods that were denied other family members.

The Failure of Separation/Individuation. The end result of the double-bind pattern is that the recipient is unable to undergo the normal process of separation/individuation and continues in a no-win cycle of love/hate and fear/dependency, both in the family of origin as well as other significant relationships. After a period of time, symptoms, including low self-esteem, poor interpersonal relationships, dissociative states, depression, and phobias, which result from a paradoxical situation, can be triggered by only one component of the system and not the entire process (p. 348).

Speigel (1986) discussed one other important aspect of the double bind — an enforced rule that the paradox not be openly discussed. In this way, the victim is placed in a position of forced silence, which intensifies traumatic reaction (Lister, 1982). Furthermore, according to Speigel, not only is dissociation the defense against the trauma of the impossible situation but

> . . . it may also represent a dramatic symbolic expression of the patient's response to the parent's demand that the patient be two contradictory people at the same time. That is indeed what the patients become. . . . their response to the double bind imposed on them by their parents is to become the paradox, to become two or more discontinuous and conflicting people, and thus become all good, all bad, all cooperation, all defiance at the same time. (p. 69)

The family develops a series of messages or rules for members to follow to protect the family. Many of these overlap with messages found in the alcoholic family. The most predominant of these messages are:

- Don't feel. Keep your feelings in check. Do not show your feelings, especially anger.
- Be in control at all times. Do not show weakness. Do not ask for help.
- Deny what is really happening. Disbelieve your own senses/perceptions. Lie to yourself and to others.
- Don't trust yourself or anyone else. No one is trustworthy.
- Keep the secret. If you tell you will not be believed and it will not get help.
- Be ashamed of yourself. You are to blame for everything.

Families also develop their own, more idiosyncratic rules which the therapist should seek to discover with the survivor.

To recapitulate, incest is a manifestation of family dysfunction which is supported by intergenerational family process. The family functions in such a way that its reality is distorted, the distortion treated as the reality. Although incest occurs, it is largely denied and unacknowledged by all family members. This disconfirmation allows for its continuance while communicating to the victim that it is something that is not to be discussed. Victims are placed in a double bind made all the more intolerable because it cannot be escaped and cannot be discussed. In order to contend with the paradox inherent in the bind, they transform their reality and ultimately themselves to suit the family rules and injunctions.

CHAPTER 4
Parent-Child Incest

I N THIS CHAPTER, we examine incest between parent and child. Father/ stepfather and daughter incest is by far the most frequently occurring of this type. It has been the most extensively investigated and is therefore the type of incest about which the most is known. In contrast, other forms of parental incest are less prevalent and less studied to date. The discrepancy between the different types is reflected in the information presented below.

Parent-child incest has the greatest potential for harm because it involves the betrayal of the parent's role as nurturer and protector of the immature child. The child's development is compromised in a number of significant ways when a parent meets his/her own needs through sexual contact with the child. Furthermore, the child's accessibility and dependency allow parent-child incest to continue over long periods of time and contribute to the child's entrapment and powerlessness.

FATHER-CHILD INCEST

A substantial minority of fathers sexually abuse their children, abusing daughters in far greater numbers than sons. This disparity was found by Finkelhor (1984) in his analysis of the American Humane Association (AHA) National Reporting Study of Child Abuse and Neglect of 1978 (1981). Boys were sexually abused within the family much less often than girls, but like girls they were more likely to have been abused by the father when a parent was the perpetrator. Those boys abused within the home were more often subject to physical as well as sexual abuse than their sisters. Additionally, if the boys were not sexually abused themselves, they often witnessed abuse of sisters.

Incest between fathers and daughters seems to be the most prevalent of any type (although a surprising finding of Russell's study was that father-daughter incest was slightly exceeded in prevalence by uncle-niece incest; this finding is in need of replication). Russell (1986) also found that stepfathers abused daughters in much higher percentages than did biological fathers and in disproportionate prevalence to their actual numbers.

Researchers have found incestuous fathers to be quite diverse. Characteristics which appear repeatedly in descriptions of these fathers include: poor impulse control, overdependency and desertion anxiety, low self-esteem, insensitivity to the needs of others, an endogamous family orientation, and a history of having witnessed abuse or having been physically and/or sexually abused as well as emotionally deprived and rejected in their families. A bipolar personality pattern has been observed: at one extreme, fathers who are passive, meek, and rather ineffectual; at the other, fathers who are dominant, tyrannical, and controlling. Some of these fathers have stable employment histories yet others are chronically unemployed. Some are professional men — "pillars of the community" — who lead private lives far different from their public personae. Others have public and private lives that are less at odds — they may be known for explosive tempers and aggressive behavior. Gross psychopathology has been found in only a small percentage of these fathers. By and large, since they do not seem to differ significantly from the profile of the average man who is generally in good psychological health, their pathology has been termed "restricted" (Wells, 1981). However, as is the case in incest research in general, the research on abusers is seriously flawed both conceptually and methodologically (Finkelhor, 1986), making this information preliminary.

Father/Stepfather-Daughter Incest

Incest between father and daughter has been the most documented type because of its prevalence, its violation of the taboo against sex between parent and child, and its potential for wreaking havoc in the nuclear family. The father's traditional family role of provider and protector is grossly betrayed when he perpetrates incest. Instead of protecting, he violates. Instead of nurturing, he uses. Family roles are violated and generational boundaries are blurred. The parents' relationship is triangulated, resulting in conflicted roles. The mother loses her status and authority in the family and becomes a rival of her daughter. The daughter is removed from her role as a child as she is made her father's lover.

Let us begin this discussion of father-daughter incest by looking at the members of the family triangle.

The Father. The available data on incestuous fathers have been derived mostly from clinical studies. Despite this limitation, they provide quite detailed and largely consistent information about these men. They have been found to be a rather heterogeneous group, and for this reason researchers have found it useful to organize them by type. The comprehensive typology of Justice and Justice (1979) is representative of several different typologies. These authors described four types of men who engage in father-daughter incest: (1) symbiotic, (2) psychopathic-sociopathic, (3) pedophiliac, and (4) "other." The symbiotic category is the largest, accounting for 80–85% of all perpetrators.

(1) The *symbiotic father* came from a nonnurturing family and so was emotionally deprived as a child. He has strong unmet needs for closeness and affection, which he has learned to satisfy in sexual ways since he does not know how to establish a close relationship in a nonphysical or nonsexual way. Symbiotic incestuous fathers have been organized into four subtypes according to the ways they use to achieve closeness through sex: introverted, rationalizing, tyrannical, and alcoholic.

The *symbiotic introvert* is the prototype of the isolated, distant incestuous father. Even if he appears outgoing, this man is unable to reach out to others and to be genuinely close. He may appear strong, competent, and capable of intimacy, but beneath this façade he is starved for affection and craves someone to nurture and comfort him. From the outside, this father appears to be the "good husband and father." He typically spends his nonworking hours with his family (endogamous family orientation) and has few, if any, outside social or professional contacts or sources of support. He may feel highly stressed by his work and family responsibilities and cope by withdrawing and expecting solace and safety from his family. In part, his withdrawal, isolation, mistrust of anyone outside of the family, and inability to ask for or seek help are explained by depression. However, his coping strategies only exacerbate his dysphoria. Although his wife may initially provide for him and serve as his link to the world, over time she may tire, withdraw, and seek outside activities. Sexual estrangement, which is usually part of this withdrawal, leaves the father without his main method of achieving closeness. In this context, he turns to his daughter, whom he may view as "belonging" to him, substituting her for his wife.

The *symbiotic rationalizer* finds ways to justify his incestuous behavior with his daughter. Most often he rationalizes it both to himself and to the child as a special love game; as special sex education preparing her for the future; as protection from other men who are characterized as corrupt and lascivious; as protection of the purity of the family bloodline (unlike most other incestuous fathers, this one would like the incest to result in pregnancy, enabling him to have a dynasty); as his right, since he views his child as his exclusive property to do with as he pleases; and finally, as harmless and healthy sexual liberation and recreation.

The *symbiotic tyrant* dominates his family, issuing orders and demanding total loyalty and obedience. He tolerates no opposition and uses force, including physical abuse if necessary, to get his way. Family members fear him and avoid upsetting him. This father may also play the part of the proud patriarch who views his family as his property subject to his wishes. He goes to great lengths to give the impression that everything is under control at home, when in reality he and his wife are estranged and he has turned to his daughter for sex and affection.

Approximately 20% of symbiotic fathers are tyrants. They are often macho in their attitudes towards sex. Sex is an expression not of closeness but of manliness, of "being a real man." Women are "made to be laid." The tyrant's daughter is appealing in her weakness and vulnerability because he can dominate her and show affection without appearing weak. He communicates his sexual attitudes to his sons, with whom he does not have a close relationship; rather, he is authoritarian and exacting and may get them to comply with his wishes by physically abusing them. His brutish exterior may camouflage tender feelings for his daughter, which she welcomes because she is starved for affection and attention. His daughter's adolescence usually is a time of crisis for the tyrant. He can be quite jealous, paranoid, judgmental, and even violent when his daughter begins to date. Her dating and other attempts at independence feel like a betrayal and reinforce his feeling that no one can be trusted.

At least 10–50% of men who commit incest are *alcoholic* or psychologically dependent on alcohol. These symbiotic fathers use alcohol to "loosen up" their anxiety about getting close to other people and to deal with their guilt about the incest. Alcohol serves mainly to disinhibit incestuous behavior. After the fact, it provides an excuse and a rationalization. Many unrecovered alcoholics have high unmet dependency needs and fear abandonment. They use alcohol to hide these from themselves and those close to them, thereby contributing to the alcoholic cycle. The alcoholic family has been found to have seriously dysfunctional interactions, characterized by denial and enabling of the alcoholic. Over time, as alcoholism escalates, a common pattern is for the wife to tire of providing care and to rely on her oldest daughter to take her place. The daughter comes to believe that if she provides sufficient care and comfort her father's drinking will stop. The father, in his drunken state, may begin to see his daughter as a substitute wife and be disinhibited enough to act on his sexual urges. If no intervention takes place, a pattern develops which may continue for years — drinking, acting out, feeling guilty, and then drinking more to diminish the guilt (Crigler, 1984).

Carnes (1983) has written about multi-addictive patterns, that is, compulsive gambling or sexual behavior, for example, along with alcohol or drug addiction. Among the most serious sex addicts are those individuals who compulsively perpetrate incest. Very often, their alcoholism serves to mask and excuse their sexual addiction. According to Carnes, treatment of the alcoholism alone is not sufficient to treat the sexual addiction; each needs separate, focused treatment.

(2) The *psychopathic-sociopathic* personality type is quite different from the symbiotic type. Fortunately, psychopaths make up only a small percentage of incestuous fathers. Instead of using sex with the daughter as a way to get closeness and nurturing, these fathers use it for stimulation and novelty and as a channel for excitement and hostility. They quite often use violence to achieve their ends and show little capacity for guilt, remorse, and empathy with others, although at times they may be charming and rationalize their behavior in such a way that they resemble the symbiotic rationalizer. Although a minority of these men are also psychotic, the chaotic and disorganized quality of their families and relationships is due largely to their inability to form stable or lasting attachments and their constant seeking of thrills and sexual gratification. These men were so deprived and/or abused in their childhoods that they are driven as adults by hostility and a need for excitement and stimulation. They are unable to love or develop emotional attachments and trust no one. Sex is used as an expression of intimacy but strictly as physical stimulation—the psychopath is indiscriminate in whether he is sexual with men, women, and children, including his own, although not all psychopaths are incestuous.

(3) *Pedophiliac* incest offenders are attracted to their daughters when they are young and nonthreatening and when they have not yet developed secondary sex characteristics. They may lose interest as a daughter ages and turn to her younger sisters for their gratification. These men are themselves immature and inadequate in their ability to maintain an adult relationship. When rejected by their wives or otherwise under stress, they turn to their children for comfort. Often they do not engage in intercourse, confining the sexual activity to kissing, genital fondling, and observation. Only rarely does the pedophile also have psychopathic and psychotic characteristics, a combination which is extremely dangerous for the child victim.

(4) Among "other" types, Justice and Justice (1979) included *psychotic* and *culture-permissive* incestuous fathers. Three percent of all incestuous fathers are believed to be psychotic, that is, hallucinatory and delusional. Another 3% are pedophiles with psychopathic or psychotic tendencies. These men, along with the psychopaths, most often use force in the perpetration of incest.

The *culture-permissive* incestuous father comes from a cultural group or family background which allows sexualized contact with children. Meiselman (1978) noted that the father from a rural or isolated cultural group constitutes a type of endogamous father whose orientation is characteristic of the culture rather than of his personality type. The modern sexually liberalized family, where children are encouraged to explore their sexuality with other family members or to observe family members in sexual activities, is a contemporary version of the culture-permissive family.

While Justice and Justice's four groups — symbiotic, psychopathic, pe-dophilic, and other — are quite distinct, overlap exists and fathers in one group may show characteristics of another. Meiselman (1978) included two other types not mentioned by Justice and Justice — mental defectives and situational abusers. Mental defectives, as the name implies, are those men whose low intelligence has contributed to reduced ego controls concerning incestuous impulses and behavior. Situational incest occurs when life stresses, life events, and circumstantial opportunities break down the de-fenses, inhibitions, or resistances in a man who otherwise would not be incestuous. Incest of this type occurs only once or is of short duration.

Two recent investigations of incestuous fathers shed additional light on their characteristics. Pelto (1981) found that incest offenders suffered more trauma in their childhoods regarding sexual experiences and exposure to incest than did non-offenders. Over half of his sample were incestuously victimized; in many cases, they were subjected to more than one type of sexual activity and were victimized by both male and female perpetrators. Half of the incestuous sex offenders in his sample had witnessed incest between their fathers and sisters in their families of origin. Significantly more incest offenders than non-offenders had been sexually victimized in childhood through bribes, pressure, and assault. This research suggests that incest exposure or modeling and the sexual abuse of boys (whether incestuous or not) constitute risk factors for sexual abuse in the next gener-ation and possibly that more boys have been abused than has yet come to light.

Parker and Parker (1986) documented additional antecedents of father-daughter incest. They found that inadequate bonding of the father with his own parents and lack of early physical contact and involvement with his child were the two best predictors of incest. These authors were careful to note that these predictors do not in themselves constitute a sufficient cause of incest and that family relationships, personality characteristics, and even subcultural differences in the strength of the incest taboo are also relevant. Nevertheless, both biological and stepfathers who were deeply involved with their infant daughters were unlikely to abuse them, while those who were physically and emotionally distant were more likely to become incestuous. The authors recommended that fathers become more involved in caring for and nurturing their young children to strengthen later incest avoidance. Herman (1981) made a similar recommendation after analyzing the characteristics of the typical incestuous family and the roles engaged in by all family members.

The Stepfather. Russell (1986) found that stepfathers abuse their daugh-ters at much higher rates than do biological fathers and that they abuse at a more severe level. It is now clear that some men seek to marry women who are mothers in order to gain sexual access to the children. These men are possibly pedophiliac in orientation, but choose a family setting and thus behave as incestuous pedophiles. It is not uncommon to find that they abuse children inside and outside of the family and that they have been involved in serial relationships/marriages with women having children of their preferred age range.

Applying Parker and Parker's findings to stepfathers, it is plausible that many of these men would be disinhibited from abusing their stepdaughters because their bonding with them is weaker or because they were not involved in nurturing them in their formative years. Further, the incest taboo is weaker and thus less restraining in stepfamilies (Finkelhor, 1979).

The dynamics and characteristics of stepfamilies increase the risk of stepfather-daughter incest in many ways. Children who have been the products of a failed marriage or of serial live-in relationships may be quite needy and therefore vulnerable to the advances and attention of their stepfather. They may also feel displaced by him and rivalrous with him for their mother's attention. They may behave seductively or seek their stepfather's attention due to their neediness or as a gesture of revenge or hostility against their mother. (This does not mean that the child/adolescent is responsible for any incestuous contact which occurs; it is clearly the stepfather's responsibility to discourage and prevent any sexual activity with his stepdaughter.) Stepfathers may also marry into a family when the adolescent children are sexually developed. If the age difference between stepfather and daughter is less than that between biological father and daughter, blurred generational boundaries and role slippage may facilitate the development of a sexual relationship between stepfather and daughter.

The Mother. The mother's upbringing provides background information about her dependence and relative powerlessness within the family. Her family history has been found to be similar to the father's, characterized by domestic instability and emotional deprivation. In all likelihood, her family followed the traditional patriarchal structure, so that as a female she was taught that her role was subservient and involved taking care of other members of the family, without attention given to her needs. She may have been placed in a position of responsibility for the family from an early age, in a role reversal with her mother or as a mother substitute. Not infrequently, she herself was incestuously abused. Her negative family experiences have left a residue of low self-esteem, unsatisfied dependency needs, and strong separation anxiety, making it likely that she would use an early marriage as a means of escaping her family of origin and as an attempt to gain the nurturance and care she previously lacked. As an adult she is vulnerable to rejection and abandonment by her husband and children. Unfortunately, she is also likely to choose a marriage partner from a similar background and whose personality style she complements. Justice and Justice (1979) identified three types of mothers—*dependent, caretaking,* and *submissive* — who complemented the various subtypes of symbiotic fathers and whose marriages were distinguished by the power imbalances and communication and sexual difficulties described earlier.

Recent research findings offer evidence that a link exists between the past incestuous victimization of mothers and the subsequent abuse of their children. In a study of the backgrounds of abusive mothers, Goodwin, McCarthy, and DiVasto (1981) found that a high percentage were incestuously abused. These women had inhibitions and fears about tenderness traceable to unresolved issues from the childhood incest. These issues impede adequate parenting and are risk factors in the development of either physical or sexual abuse in the family. Studies of family violence have documented that a disproportionate number of abused women are incest survivors and that battering husbands often sexually abuse both their wives and their children (Walker, 1984). Other investigators have discovered that many incest mothers suffer from sexual dysfunction and chronic depression, which may be aftereffects of their own incest. It is possible that these findings — previous abuse and resultant depression, parenting difficulties, learned powerlessness, and sexual difficulties — are related and contribute to the development of incest in the next generation.

Daughters also run a high risk of sexual victimization if their mothers are absent from the family or suffer from some sort of disability. Mothers are sometimes permanently absent due to death, desertion, or divorce and loss of custody. It has been noted that even temporary absences during times of family transitions or stress (such as childbirth or a mother's attending to elderly, sick, or dying family members) or due to her work schedule can render a daughter vulnerable. Studies of mothers in incest families have found that some have serious, incapacitating physical illnesses and disabilities. Some also suffer debilitating psychiatric illnesses, including major depressive disorders, personality disorders, psychotic disturbances, and alcoholism (Herman & Hirschman, 1981).

Estrangement between mother and daughter leaves the daughter emotionally vulnerable and without adequate support and protection. It is a sad but unfortunately true commentary that, as Herman stated, "It appears that only a strong alliance with a healthy mother offers a girl a modicum of protection from sexual abuse" (1981, p. 48).

Herman summarized her description of the mother in the incestuous family:

> In short, even by patriarchal standards, the mother in the incestuous family is unusually oppressed. More than the average wife and mother, she is extremely dependent upon and subservient to her husband. She may have a physical or emotional disability which makes the prospect of independent survival quite impractical. Rather than provoke her husband's anger or risk his desertion, she will capitulate. If the price of maintaining the marriage includes the sexual sacrifice of her daughter, she will raise no effective

objections. Her first loyalty is to her husband, regardless of his behavior. She sees no other choice. Maternal collusion in incest, when it occurs, is a measure of maternal powerlessness.

As for the question of the mother's responsibility, maternal absence, literal or psychological, does seem to be a reality in many families where incest develops. The lack of a strong, competent, and protective mother does seem to render girls more vulnerable to sexual abuse. Maternal disability of any sort represents a significant family stress and is perceived by all family members as a deprivation.

But no degree of maternal absence or neglect constitutes an excuse for paternal incest, unless one accepts the idea that fathers are entitled to female services within their families, no matter what the circumstances. (1981, p. 49)

It must be recognized that the majority of mothers do not collude in incest, nor are they offenders or even participants in its occurrence. And many mothers, who as a group go largely unacknowledged, are outraged by their daughters' victimization and attempt to provide them with protection. Russell (1986) found that mothers may not even know about severe abuse because their daughters go to great lengths to keep them from knowing. Nevertheless, it is clear that some mothers are not entirely ignorant of the incest when it occurs and even knowingly tolerate or participate in it. And some deny or discount signs or signals that indicate that a sexual relationship between father and daughter is about to or has developed. Russell also found that, when incest occurs with the biological father and is of the long-term endogamous type, the mother may be less able to offer her daughter any protection. Specifically, Herman (1981) and others have argued that the powerless position that many women hold in these families accounts for their inability to effectively deter incest or support their daughters when they disclose its occurrence. These mothers are often so emotionally and/or economically bound to their relationships that believing their daughters and taking effective action would mean giving up their own base of security, no matter how unhealthy.

The Daughter. Daughters are a heterogeneous group in terms of personality style. Although certain personality traits and physical characteristics may make them more susceptible to incest, these are not its cause. Daughters become vulnerable due to the dynamics at play in the family which distort their development, undermine their security, and condition them into roles of passivity and/or pseudo-maturity. Since emotional support is lacking in many of these families, children feel abandoned and insecure from a young age, not uncommonly predating the incest.

The oldest daughter in the family is the most likely to be incestuously victimized, but younger sisters may follow as the father "progresses" through the family. When the daughter is abused as a preschooler, it is due almost exclusively to her accessibility and dependence on the father.

Abuse of the preschooler usually involves kissing, fondling, masturbation, and oral sex; less often it progresses to intercourse and other types of penetration. The child failing to understand the nature of the activity, may feel little shame or guilt. Instead she may be eroticized by the incest and conditioned to the special relationship and special games. Another scenario involves the young child who is traumatized or who learns that the activity is wrong. She is apt to utilize strong defenses such as repression to cope. Although not all of these youngsters are "parentified" in the family, some of them clearly are. Children as young as four and five have been known to function as caretakers of their parents and their siblings in severely dysfunctional families.

When the unabused but parentified daughter reaches latency age or older, she may be vulnerable to incestuous abuse not only due to her accessibility but also due to her functioning as an adult in the household. She may have had to assume family responsibilities, such as household chores, family budgeting, and childcare, well beyond the responsibilities associated with her chronological age, caring for both her parents and her siblings. Her family role may substitute a sense of importance and power for the nurturance that she is lacking. Physically or sexually comforting the father may initially be perceived as part of this caretaking role. But since the daughter herself is emotionally needy, the contact may be gratifying, at least at first. It may later put her in a totally untenable position with each parent.

The continuation and intensification of the incest fuel these difficulties. The daughter becomes burdened with the necessity of keeping the activity a secret. The family's intense dependency and insecurity, her father's warnings about the dire consequences of disclosure, and her own perceptions about the consequences all function to keep her silent. She may also be quite protective of both parents and keep the secret in an attempt to guard them and to keep the family together. The entrapment and "forced silence" often cause an incorporation of feelings of anxiety, guilt, shame, helplessness, and responsibility for the incest. Although victims have been found to employ a variety of resistance strategies, many develop a stance of passive and fearful compliance, either until their adolescence or until they are able to leave home, usually by running away or marrying prematurely.

The Siblings. The siblings in the incestuous family have been largely ignored by researchers and clinicians, although there can be little doubt that either they are profoundly affected consciously or unconsciously. Incest is often perpetrated on more than one of the sibling group, especially the daughters; brothers may witness incest, resulting in their sexually victimizing others, often their sisters and later their own daughters (Pelto, 1981). The rescue of a younger sibling from suspected or threatened abuse is a common reason for disclosure. Victims may be unable to break the silence to stop their own abuse but may do so when they learn of the abuse of their siblings.

Cohen (1983) had the following to say about the siblings:

> There is no clear information as to the siblings' level of knowledge and awareness about the incest itself, but one wonders about their coping with the emotional and structural family pattern which allowed the incest to take place. The siblings, younger or older, might develop rivalry and intense resentment toward their sister, because she is perceived to be father's favorite offspring, sometimes to their total exclusion. Also, given the low level of the mother's functioning and the many times strict authoritarian attitude of the father, it would be safe to assume that siblings, especially males, would feel rejected by both parents. In addition, in many families, the incestuous daughter is the only one who assumes parental responsibility toward the siblings, thus no appropriate limits are set for them. One can speculate therefore that given this family constellation, the potential is strong for the siblings to develop behavior difficulties. . . .
>
> It seems that siblings within the incestuous family are the "undetected victims" and deserve more attention from a theoretical dynamic point of view as well as in relation to therapeutic intervention. (p. 157–158)

Berry (1975) described another sibling variation, which she labeled "incest envy." She reported that serious psychological disturbances might be experienced by the "unchosen" daughter, who was aware and envious of the special relationship between her father and sister. Of course, brothers could be similarly affected. DeYoung (1981b) further described this phenomenon:

> An overwhelming feeling of rejection often overcomes the siblings. Although they certainly may not crave the sexual victimization, they do desire the attention and physical contact that often accompany it. That they were not 'chosen' by the incestuous father creates a strong feeling of worthlessness, which may be so pervasive and persistent that it can produce emotional problems. (p. 566)

Dynamics. In Chapter 3, I described the dynamics and progression of behaviors known as the child sexual abuse accommodation syndrome (Summit, 1983) and the family dynamics characteristic of "classic father-daughter incest." The discussion below offers more specifics concerning the development of father-daughter incest. Keep in mind, however, that there are many variations. The clinician must be open to each survivor's unique story.

Father-daughter incest is usually a symptom of family dysfunction; however, one characteristic of the endogamous incestuous family is that it appears normal and well-adjusted. A closer look reveals that the family's inner reality does not match its external appearance. A great deal of stress, strain, and turmoil underlies the façade. Furthermore, the family alternates between overly rigid or overly loose rules and relationships within and outside of the family.

A troubled marital relationship is almost always in evidence in families where father-daughter incest develops. Sexual dysfunction and power imbalances are characteristic of these marriages (Waterman, 1986), and the mother is often described as being absent, incapacitated, or unavailable physically, psychologically or both. In the typical case, the couple is sexually estranged—the most commonly reported pattern is for the wife to be sexually disinterested, unresponsive, unavailable, and/or rejecting, and the husband consequently to be sexually frustrated. Cases have been reported where the husband suffers from some sort of sexual dysfunction, such as hypersexuality, which causes the couple sexual distress. In other cases, the couple has a seemingly active and satisfying sex life.

Various causes may underlie the sexual problems in these marriages. The following have been noted most frequently: The couple may have been sexually incompatible right from the start of the relationship, or the husband may be overly demanding, selfish, or otherwise sexually unattractive. Further, the wife may avoid sex because of fear of pregnancy. Herman (1981) noted that enforced childbearing is the norm in some patriarchal incest families. The wife may be unavailable due to illness, depression, exhaustion, or disability, or she may suffer a disorder of sexual desire or response due to her own unresolved sexual abuse experience.

An imbalance of power between the partners is also common. One pattern involves a tyrannical, authoritarian father who dominates his family, who has little or no regard for others' feelings, and who maintains control through violence or other types of coercion. His controlling behavior masks profound feelings of inadequacy. The wife is usually passive and acquiescent, with strong emotional and financial dependence on her husband. She may also be "beaten down" or "worn out" by the demands placed on her by her family of origin, her husband, and her children. To relieve her the daughter takes over many aspects of the mother's role.

A second pattern involves a father who is shy, introverted, and rather inept both socially and occupationally, who marries a controlling or caretaking woman on whom he relies emotionally and often financially. Like the tyrannical father, he may feel a sense of inadequacy in his male role and harbor a great deal of anger towards women; instead of bullying his family, he is demanding, needy, and passive-aggressive. Over time, excessive caretaking needs, as well as the needs of other family members, overwhelm his wife to such a degree that she withdraws emotionally, sexually, and physically. This woman may have initially functioned rather adequately as a parent, but with increased demands she turns to her daughter as a helpmate. The daughter provides her with much-needed emotional support and assistance with the housework, other family responsibilities, and caring for father. The mother may directly or indirectly encourage her daughter to take care of the father, even to the extent of meeting his sexual needs.

Whatever the case, when the mother withdraws or is otherwise absent, a vacuum is left within which father-daughter incest can develop, other conditions being conducive to it. The father, who feels abandoned, frustrated, emasculated and angry, turns to the daughter and sexualizes the relationship, in effect making the daughter both mother and wife in the family. Most frequently, the daughter continues in her conditioned role as family caretaker, her father's sexual well-being becoming one more thing for which she is responsible. Since her caretaking role has required that she forego nurturance in the family, she may be starved for attention and affection. She may welcome the attention she receives, even if she does not like the sexual contact itself. Later she may be confused by her mixed emotions and take her need for attention to mean that she wanted the sexual contact.

There seem to be three developmental patterns in father-daughter incest, one involving incest with a preschooler, the second involving the latency or preadolescent child, and the third involving the postpubertal adolescent. The daughter's average age at the onset of incest has long been found to be age eight, but the range is from infancy to adulthood.

According to Waterman (1986), the social factors conducive to incest seem similar for families with preschool children and those with older children; these include the presence of stress in the family, social isolation, opportunity for sexual contact, and a sexualized climate in the home. Similarly, the two major characteristics of the marital relationship—little communication and intimacy and an imbalance of power—are often in evidence in families of abused preschoolers. The dominant mother/dependent father variant may be more common in the development of incest with the preschool child than in the development of incest with the preadolescent or adolescent.

At least three major differences between the preschool, the latency-aged and the adolescent victim have been noted (MacFarlane et al., 1986). First, the preschooler bears less resemblance to an appropriate adult sexual object than the preadolescent or adolescent. Second, the preschooler generally has little knowledge about sexual functioning and is usually unaware of the stigma and taboo associated with incest. She may, therefore, feel less shame and guilt than the older child; however, because of her stage of cognitive development she may suffer more trauma if told she is bad or that bad things will happen if she tells anyone. The third difference concerns the developmental tasks and levels of the different age groups. Preschool children going through the oedipal phase are often curious about the anatomic differences between the sexes. This normal development curiosity may be misinterpreted by the needy father and lead to his sexual abuse of his child.

Finally, differential parental dynamics have been observed.

Those who abuse preschoolers may be relatively more concerned about the issues of nurturance, abandonment, and separation, while the prime concerns of those who abuse older children may center more frequently on power and dominance. Additionally, those who abuse very young children may be more likely to view children as their primary sexual objects than those who abuse older children who more closely resemble adult sexual objects. There are certain characteristics of the fathers that seem common to a majority of incestuous families regardless of the age of the children; these include poor impulse control (at least in certain situations), sexual concerns, and alcohol or drug use.

There also may be significant differences between the mothers. Two major possible differences are these: (1) Mothers of preschoolers may tend to be less threatened at a deep self-esteem level by the incestuous behavior than mothers of older children; and (2) mothers of preschoolers may tend to be less dependent in their marital relationships than those with older children. (Waterman, 1986, p. 216)

Mothers of preschoolers may be more willing to separate or divorce when incest is disclosed than mothers of older children, largely because they are less emotionally dependent on the father and less locked in to the marriage, even though they may be financially dependent. Additionally, these women may be less likely to be personally threatened or to see the child as a rival. They will be more outraged and driven to action when the victim is a toddler or young child.

Suzi's stepfather began molesting her when she was two and still sleeping in a crib. He would masturbate her and digitally penetrate her, abuse he continued until she was five and he was caught in the act by Suzi's mother.

If the incest goes undiscovered or attempts at intervention are ineffective, the incest begun in the child's toddler years may well continue into adolescence. Similarly, incest begun during *latency* usually continues to the teen years. The preadolescent girl may be approached because of her availability and innocence. She may be conditioned in a fashion similar to the younger child but she may feel more guilt, shame, and conflict because she is more aware of prohibitions and the reasons for the injunction to secrecy.

When Julie was about four, her father began to abuse her while bathing her or tucking her in for the night. At first he rubbed and massaged her to help her go to sleep. Then he began to lie next to her and kiss and fondle her. Over a period of years, his behavior progressed to the point where he would masturbate her and perform oral sex on her. At times he would enter her room at night, come close to the bed, masturbate and ejaculate.

In a third developmental pattern, incest begins at about the time of *puberty*, when the girl is developing secondary sexual characteristics. From the available research evidence sexual activity commonly progresses to intercourse when the incest begins at or continues into adolescence. The father is no longer inhibited by the child's physical immaturity and is often quite infatuated with his daughter's sexual development. He may be much less gradual and more forceful and threatening in his introduction of intercourse with his postpubescent daughter, since she is more likely to resist his attempts than her prepubescent counterpart. The older daughter is less likely to be as conditioned or entrapped, but she may feel more embarrassment and shame than the younger child, and thus may also have difficulty disclosing its occurrence.

Lila's father began to abuse her when she was eight. He planned times when they could be alone to play special games. These began in a nonsexual way but gradually became sexual. When Lila protested, her father first sought to bribe her; when that failed he coerced her by telling her no one would believe her and saying that she must have liked it because she never told before. Lila later realized that her inability to disclose emboldened her father. As his alcoholism worsened so did the abuse and the level of force and threat. He forced intercourse on her when she was 12 and continued this abuse several times a week until at age 14 she finally confided the abuse to a school counselor.

As the daughter gets older, her striving for independence and peer involvement is usually enough to terminate the incest, despite her father's attempts to continue it. As her social life develops, and particularly as she begins to date, the father may play the part of jealous suitor and behave in a paranoid and persecutory way in an attempt to restrict her activities. The daughter often rebels at his increased pressure and becomes more willing to break away from the relationship. In fact, it is not unusual for an unprepared disclosure of the incest to take place during an argument with parents concerning more independence or privileges. Unfortunately, a disclosure only sometimes precipitates effective action to end the incest. Most often, even when the daughter is initially believed, her revelation does not result in intervention strong enough to effect a cessation of the incest (See Chapter 3).

Teenage girls who are still entrapped in the incest must often resort to extreme measures to put a stop to it. Most frequently, they marry at an early age (sometimes due to a deliberate pregnancy) or they run away from home. Substance abuse, promiscuity, self-destructiveness, rebellion, and defiance of authority figures are also used by many adolescents to dull or escape from the pain of the incest. Occasionally, the incest will terminate when the daughter emphatically and assertively refuses to submit to it any longer. Or she may become so desperate as the sexual demands intensify that she reports it to her mother, to another adult, or to authorities. Unfortunately, as Summit (1983) has noted, the teenage girl is less likely than a younger girl to be believed or to receive appropriate intervention, especially if she is angry, rebellious, defiant, or promiscuous, on one hand, or a model child, on the other. Instead, she is likely to be blamed for being unmanageable or seductive and her report thus discounted. Her report will also be discounted if she has been too "good" and has never shown symptoms or aftereffects.

Walsh (1986a) identified another aspect of the early versus late development of father-daughter incest that has gone largely unrecognized—the younger the age at onset, the more likely that the child will be multiply molested either within or outside of the family. Girls who were multiply molested reported that their experiences of incest occurred more frequently, lasted longer, included the most sexually deviant acts, and were traumatic.

Controversy has long existed about the age of onset of incest and whether it is a factor predictive of more severe aftereffects. Some authorities have maintained that younger age at onset is related to less serious consequences. Their line of reasoning is that less serious sexual behavior is likely to be involved and that the child's physical and emotional immaturity shield her from fully experiencing its impact. As an extension of this reasoning, the latency-aged child is thought to suffer more because the sexual behavior is usually more intrusive and she has more awareness of its inappropriateness. Other authorities take just the opposite view—that younger age at onset is more predictive of trauma. They point to the child's increased developmental vulnerability and use of repression as a coping mechanism. Walsh's findings offer a different perspective, since they suggest that even if the child did not fully react to her early sexual experience, such an early experience somehow put her at greater risk for revictimization in childhood or adolescence.

Father-daughter incest has been found to be highly traumatic due to the betrayal of the father's role, the convoluted relationships which develop between parents and daughter, and the entrapment inherent in the nuclear family. As we will see in Chapter 5, this type of incest profoundly affects the daughter's ego development and sense of self-worth, as well as her sexual and interpersonal functioning, including her capacity to adequately parent and protect her own children.

Father/Stepfather-Son Incest

Father/stepfather-son incest is less clearly documented than incest between fathers and daughters because of the small number of case reports in the literature. In their 1978 article on father-son incest, Dixon, Arnold, and Calestro speculated about the lack of discussion of this type of same-sex parent-child incest: "It is unclear whether this conspicuous dearth of information reflects a very low incidence of homosexual incest; . . . a tendency to label this behavior pattern as simply homosexual rather than incestuous; . . . clinicians' failure to recognize the problem; or a combination of all three factors" (p. 835). It is likely that all three factors have played a part and that the prevalence of father-son incest, like that of other forms, has been underestimated and underreported, resulting in its being underinvestigated. The 1978 American Humane Association National Reporting Study of Child Abuse and Neglect contained 199 cases of father-son incest, the largest cohort reported to date. Of the father-son cases reported in the AHA study, the median age of the sons (at reporting) was 9.36 years, 49% were oldest children, and 14% were only children (Finkelhor, 1984). Stepfather-stepson incest is even less well documented and awaits research attention.

The available case descriptions suggest that father-son incest may result from intrapsychic conflict or a psychological breakdown of some sort in the father, family difficulties, or some combination of the two. The father's conflicts about latent homosexuality, feelings of inadequacy, anger or revenge, a distant, powerless, or sexualized relationship with his own mother, alcoholism, unresolved past sexual abuse, sociopathy and violence towards family members all are mentioned as causes, as are marital strain and distress. Mrazek (1981) offers perhaps the most comprehensive description of the father to date:

> The father frequently has had severe problems with his own mother, being rejected and deprived during his formative years. His problems with women continued with inhibited relationships with girls during his teens and severe marital problems, sometimes including sexual estrangement, with his wife. Latent or conscious struggles with homosexual impulses usually have been a major determinant for some of the father's long-term behavior and character style. Frequently, there have been other homosexual incestuous experiences with brothers, uncles, cousins or even fathers during childhood and adulthood. Homosexual relationships outside the family are less common. The homosexual incest is a living out of the father's own adolescent conflicts. The father often is intelligent, successfully employed, and without a history of severe psychological disorder. Often he is under the influence of alcohol during the incestuous episodes. Half of the cases in the literature report simultaneous physical and sexual abuse of the child. The father may also foster other incestuous relationships, such as between siblings, or a son and an uncle, or engage in additional sexual activities himself with his other children, both male and female. (p. 102)

Mrazek's description is consistent with the data from the American Humane Association study. In other studies, the role of past sexual abuse as a precursor to father-son incest, whether inside or outside of the family and most frequently same-sex, is receiving more emphasis.

The mother's role in father-son incest has been less clearly articulated than her role in father-daughter. As in other forms of incest, mothers may be aware of the abuse but unable to directly acknowledge it and/or protect the child. Disclosure of same-sex incest between father and son or multiple incest with children of both sexes may have two quite opposite consequences. It could be more outrageous to the mother, making it more difficult to deny and easier to report, or its very outrageousness may lead her to disbelieve and/or repress what she has seen or heard.

Besides the general effects associated with incest, some are mentioned as specific to father-son abuse. Intense anger and homicidal feelings towards the father have been noted. The popular press has recently carried stories of sons who (like some daughters) have killed or attempted to kill their fathers to prevent them from further physically or sexually assaulting their mothers, siblings, and themselves. Negative feelings can alternately be directed towards the self in suicidal, self-mutilating, and other self-destructive behavior. A devalued sense of self may be displayed through self-degradation and self-punishment, such as prostitution. Several authors mention psychosis as an outcome in a number of father-son cases, especially when the boy reaches adolescence and his conflict and anxiety intensify.

Sexual identity problems may result from being homosexually assaulted. The boy may question whether he is homosexual and be confused about his role in the abuse and about any sexual arousal he experienced. He may have suffered an acute threat to his masculinity due to the stress of finding himself in a role reversal of the expected male role—helpless rather than in control. As a consequence, he may feel extremely shamed and uncertain about his masculinity and be ineffective in his attempted relationships. Even when sexual identity is not in question, father-son incest is harmful. Simari and Baskins (1982) found that among the homosexual men they studied who had had incestuous experiences, incest with the father was reported as negative and as causing significant problems.

For some victims, the effects may not be discernible until they turn to children (their own or others) in an attempt to meet their needs or to master or reenact their victimization experience. Prior to this, there may have been simultaneous or subsequent incestuous experiences with brothers, male cousins, uncles, or peers.

John, diagnosed as emotionally disturbed, was placed in a state hospital from ages 8 to 13. He began to have sex with other boys his age in his dormitory; generally they performed fellatio on him. From his description it is unclear whether he was molested or participated voluntarily. Whatever the case, he subsequently came to identify himself as gay.

When he returned home he told his parents about his sexual orientation. From age 13 until he left home at 18, his father abused him about once a month. His father would complain about being hot and hard for John, usually after he had been drinking and had primed himself with pornographic pictures. He and John would engage in mutual fellatio and anal sex. John felt that he had no choice but to engage in the sex because he felt his father used "psychological warfare" on him; moreover, his father was physically violent when displeased.

MOTHER-CHILD INCEST

Until recently reports of mother-child incest have been quite rare, leading to the widespread belief that its occurrence is similarly rare; however, new research and clinical evidence indicates that mothers, in larger numbers than previously estimated, may be accomplices or co-offenders in father-child incest or may be sole perpetrators with children of either sex (McCarty, 1986). Finkelhor and Russell (as reported in Russell, 1986) have concluded that adult females who abuse do so in much smaller percentages than do males; approximately 5% of all sexual abuse of girls and 20% of all sexual abuse of boys involve women. The relative percentage of mothers who abuse their own children is unknown at this time.

In his analysis of the AHA study for 1978, Finkelhor (1984) found significant differences between mothers and fathers who abuse and the sexual abuse they perpetrate. Mothers who abused were more likely to be poor, black, and single and to combine physical and sexual abuse. They tended to abuse children younger than those abused by fathers, yet like fathers they usually chose the oldest child. These findings are tentative and in need of replication. The characteristics of these mothers may be accurate or may be artifacts of reporting and detection, since poor families make use of social service agencies in greater numbers than do more well-to-do families.

The literature on mother-child incest has almost universally ascribed the incestuous behavior to gross pathology on the part of the mother. The routine assumption has been that severe psychological disturbance or psychosis is necessary for a mother to violate the societal proscriptions against incest with her child. Meiselman (1978), Ward (1985), and other feminist authors have commented upon the fact that no such routine assumptions or predictions are made when the perpetrator is the father. Ward's term, the "asymmetrical incest taboo," was coined to call attention to the double standard that incest by a male/father is more "normal" and acceptable than similar behavior perpetrated by female/mother. Groth (1982) described mothers who incestuously abuse their children from a less pathological orientation:

> Typically such women are described as retarded or psychotic, but in fact our clinical research would suggest that incest offenses by mothers may be more frequent than one would be led to believe from a review of the few cases documented in the literature. The socially accepted physical intimacy be-

tween a mother and her child may serve to mask incidents of sexual exploitation and abuse on the part of a mother. It may be that only sexually abusive
mothers who are handicapped by serious mental illness or intellectual defi-
ciency are detected since, by reason of their psychological impairment, they
lack the skills to conceal successfully this behavior.

In the limited contact we have had with cases of mother-child incest, the
same dynamics and motivations found in regard to the incestuous father are
evident in regard to the incestuous mother. Where she is a co-offender or
accomplice, her dependency on her spouse is a major contributing factor,
and where she is an independent offender (especially if she is the only
parent) her need for nurturance and control appear prominent. Some factors
which may contribute to the evolution of mother-child incest may be the
absence of this parent during the child's early years, relatively little discrepancy between the ages of the parent and child, sexual (especially incestuous)
victimization of the mother as a young girl, the loss of spouse and the
assuming of adult responsibilities (such as helping to support the family) on
the part of the child, a history of indiscriminate or compulsive sexual activity
on the part of the mother, and a history of alcohol or drug abuse. (p. 231)

In their report on maternal-neonatal incest, Chasnoff, Burns, Schnoll,
Burns, Chisum and Kyle-Spore (1986) found similar characteristics in
mothers they studied. They were estranged from their sexual partners,
were quite isolated in their living arrangement, had no ongoing sexual
relationships, and thus could be said to be motivated in part by loneliness.
They demonstrated some confusion regarding sexual identity and had
problems with chemical dependency.

Finally, in an important recent study, McCarty (1986) examined case
records of incestuous mothers. She organized them into three categories
described by Groth: (1) independent offender, (2) co-offender, and (3) accomplice. Her summary of each category is as follows:

. . . the typical independent offender had a troubled childhood (92%) during
which she was sexually abused (78%), usually by a brother. She is of average
intelligence (100%) and is able to maintain steady employment (67%). She
married as a teenager (83%) and that was her only marriage (75%). She is
now living independently (67%). She may abuse drugs (46%) and may be
seriously emotionally disturbed (50%). Her victim is most often a daughter
(60%), whom she views as an extension of herself (67%). The average age of
the female victims is 6 and the male victims 10.

The typical co-offender had a troubled childhood (100%), during which
she was sexually abused (100%), usually by an adult caretaker. She is borderline in intelligence (56%) and does not work outside the home (78%). She
married as a teenager (100%) and is now in her second (44%) or third (44%)
marriage. She has a history of sexual indiscretion (56%). She has a strong
need to be taken care of and that need takes precedence over the needs of
her children (100%). Her victim was as often her son (average age 9) as her
daughter (average age 7), and she was a neglectful parent (66%).

The typical accomplice is of average intelligence (80%) and is employed outside the home (100%). She married as a teenager (60%), and had a strong need to be taken care of; that need took precedence over the needs of her children (100%). The victim was most often a daughter (75%) whose average age was 13. (pp. 456–457)

McCarty's findings and Groth's description offer preliminary information on the incestuous mother. Further information is available according to the sex of the maternally abused child.

Mother-Daughter Incest

Forward and Buck (1978) believe mother-daughter incest to be the least frequent and least reported of all types, although data from the AHA study show far more reports of mother-daughter than mother-son incest. While these AHA findings must be regarded as tentative, they are consistent with McCarty's findings cited above. Regardless of the true prevalence, the clinician must be aware that such types of abuse do occur and may be difficult for the client to reveal because of their relative rarity. Reports in the literature describe the mother in two ways which can overlap: as very needy and emotionally dependent and/or as disturbed and possibly psychotic or sociopathic. The daughter often plays a caretaker role in relation to the needy or disturbed mother; however, with the more sociopathic mother she may serve as the object of her mother's intrusive, exploratory, and sometimes sadistic sexual contact. In all reports of mother-daughter incest the mother has been the initiator.

The needy mother often views her daughter as an extension of herself. The sexual activity is best described as highly intrusive, narcissistic, and almost masturbatory in nature. The contact may begin as an extension of the mother's normal nurturing and caretaking functions or as a gradual progression in physical contact and closeness. The daughter may enjoy this level of contact because caring, tenderness, and dependency are demonstrated. In time and usually with more insistent or intrusive contact, she may begin to feel smothered but may not define the behavior as incestuous or abusive (Goodwin & DiVasto, 1979). She does, however, stay in the relationship due to her mother's obvious neediness and dependency and/or physical or mental illness. In situations of the latter type, fathers are usually physically or emotionally absent and may have even abandoned mother and daughter, with the expectation that the daughter care for her ill mother.

Goodwin and DiVasto reported that sexual behaviors in mother-daughter incest vary greatly, ranging from voyeurism through kissing, fondling and mutual masturbation to digital exploration and penetration with objects. The more intrusive behaviors characterize mothers with a more controlling, hostile, or sadistic bent. These mothers abuse their daughters as a reenactment of their own abuse or as an expression of hostility or projected self-hatred. Mothers of this type are receiving increased attention, especially in the literature on multiple personalities. An account of one such mother was provided in the book *Sybil*, another in the stage play and movie *Agnes of God*. Some of these mothers have been found to offend alone, some in conjunction with an abusive male or female as a co-offender, and some as accomplices who do not directly engage in the sexual activity.

Incest between mother and daughter has been reported to cause aftereffects similar to those resulting from other forms of incest. In addition, Goodwin and DiVasto's study highlighted an aftereffect that is of particular interest to the clinician. In two of their cases, the presenting concern for treatment was sexual abuse by the father when, in reality, the abuse had been perpetrated by the mother. Careful therapeutic investigation was needed before the victim could disclose that the incest had occurred with her mother. The therapist must be aware that victims feel additional shame and stigma when their incest experience is "out of the ordinary." As a result, they are even more scared and reluctant to disclose the incest than victims of other, more commonly discussed types.

Gail is an only child whose mother has been diagnosed as schizophrenic. Her father left home when Gail was 14, complaining that "he couldn't take it anymore." He has since cut off all contact with Gail and her mother. Gail is her mother's sole support and caretaker, except when her mother gets so bad that she has to be hospitalized—only then do members of the extended family become involved. Otherwise, they want nothing to do with the "crazy lady."

Gail's mother has been overprotective of her and overdependent on her since Gail was a little girl. Gail feels as though her mother was always touching her and that she couldn't get away from her. She would confide in Gail when she and Gail's father would have a fight and would regularly sleep with her at those times and when father was away on business. When her father left permanently, Gail's mother insisted that they sleep together because she was afraid to be alone. Her touching became more intimate and intrusive over time, as she tried to make Gail a substitute for her absent husband. Gail sometimes liked being close to her mother and being held by her. She did not like the sexual contact but did not say anything for fear of precipitating another breakdown.

Gail attends a commuter college and continues to sleep with her mother. She sought counseling for feelings of derealization and depression. It took months of testing her therapist before she could disclose what her therapist had come to suspect, the sexual abuse by her mother.

Mother-Son Incest

Meiselman (1978) and Ward (1985) reviewed the various case reports of mother-son incest in the literature. They found it necessary to categorize cases according to whether they were son-initiated or mother-initiated to account for the differential dynamics and effects of each.

Mother-Initiated. Early investigations of mother-initiated incest with a son almost universally reported gross pathology on the part of the mother. It now appears that the severely disturbed or psychotic mother is but one type. Alcoholism and other types of character problems have also been identified, as have loneliness, neediness, and role reversal. The son has infrequently been identified as disturbed at the time of mother-initiated incest, although any later disturbance he exhibits has typically been attributed to its occurrence. Mrazek (1981), from her review of the literature, suggests that some sons may have been subject to early maternal rejection or to rejection alternating with overprotection and/or overdependence. She believes that these sons have a variety of problems resulting from the maternal rejection prior to the actual incest.

In contrast to the intact family pattern usually associated with father-daughter incest, mother-initiated incest with a son ordinarily involves an absent partner, the father. Two family variations have been documented: an intact family where the father is absent or unavailable due to work commitments or other reasons, and the single-parent family with no father/husband. In either case, the son may be expected and even directed to be the "man of the house" and to take care of his mother. The mother seeks from her son what she would normally expect from her husband, with the incest developing from this role reversal, which becomes eroticized and sexualized over time.

Similar to what has been documented for father-daughter incest, mother-son incest may be situational, characterological, or both, and involve a progression and variety of sexual behaviors. Crigler (1984) discussed a situational form of mother-son incest arising in military families where a son becomes a substitute for the absent father. The mother and son become emotionally dependent on each other in their loneliness and neediness. This emotional attachment may at some point become sexual.

Mother-initiated incest which is of a more characterological sort can involve a needy, dependent, or smothering mother who usually has no partner and/or one who is promiscuous with a series of partners. The single mother may have been abandoned or rejected by her partner; instead of seeking other adult male companionship she turns to her son as a substitute. He is usually her only child. She may be jealous, demanding, dependent, overpossessive, and smothering of him, placing him in the roles of her protector/confidant/companion from an early age. These roles make him feel powerful and needed.

This type of mother is usually gradual and tender in approaching her son, pledging him to the secrecy of their special love and her special attention. As in the analogous form of mother-daughter contact, the incest develops as an inappropriate and sexualized extension of normal maternal caretaking. The latter provides her with a convenient rationalization and cover for her behavior, but it is usually a source of confusion for the son. As an example of this circumstance, the mother may continue to bathe her son beyond the age at which it is appropriate for her to do so and sexualize the activity by bathing with him or insisting that she must carefully wash or inspect his genitals. This mother may also insist that her son sleep with her, ostensibly for protection or to keep her company. While outright sexual contact may not occur, the son's sexual arousal and development are compromised, since they become associated with his mother.

The promiscuous mother goes through a succession of lovers and/or husbands. She lacks appropriate sexual controls and boundaries and is overtly seductive or sexual in front of her son. It is not unusual for her to deny that her indiscretion or influence have had any harmful effects on him.

Forward and Buck (1978) described three variations in sexual contact involved in this type of mother-son incest: (1) no overt sexual contact but closeness and a sexual seductiveness on the part of the mother that make her the object of her son's sexual fantasies while frustrating these same fantasies; (2) no intercourse but sexual contact that is more overt, possibly including stimulation to ejaculation; (3) regular intercourse. The latter is believed to be the most rare form, but not necessarily the most traumatic. In each variation, there exists strong potential for the sexually inexperienced boy's sexuality to become associated with his mother, causing him to have difficulty becoming sexually aroused by anyone else. He may later become impotent.

Whether intercourse occurs or not, a son seduced by his mother may be overcome by conflicted emotions, especially guilt, desire, confusion, anger, love and hate. He may exhibit low self-esteem and poor social skills and be mistrustful, insecure, isolated, and uncomfortable with peers and particularly with women. Justice and Justice (1979) noted that the son may be psychosocially inept and cope by never growing up and leaving his mother. In some cases, discomfort may turn to resentment. Nasjleti (1980) discussed one possible consequence of this resentment: ". . . the seduction of a boy by his mother, mother surrogate or significant adult female in his life is detrimental to a boy's psychosocial development. The negative effects of such sexual experiences are numerous, and most endanger the well-being of women and children who become victims of men who, as boys, were sexually abused by women" (p. 271). If this resentment is self-directed, the son may become self-destructive.

The son may seek therapy for some of these and other symptoms commonly associated with incest without making an association between them and the behavior with his mother. The memory of the incest may be repressed, or he may be so shamed, both by being with his mother and being abused by a woman, that he feels he cannot disclose it. Additionally, the son may be unaware that what happened was abusive, both because mother-son incest is popularly treated as benign and even as very exciting, and because the activity is frequently, although not always, embedded in tenderness and caring.

Son-Initiated. Meiselman (1978) found that in the majority of son-initiated cases the son was psychologically disturbed and that the psychopathology observed in the sons after the incest was a continuation of the disturbance that fostered the occurrence of the activity in the first place. The mothers in these cases were not found to be grossly disturbed, although some were blatantly promiscuous in a way that antagonized and sexually tempted the son. The father was not present in the home in any of the cases on which Meiselman based her summation (pp. 301–302), although he was in the case described by Shengold (1980). Most of the son initiators described in the literature are adolescents or adults at the time they are sexual with their mothers. Arroyo, Eth, and Pynoos (1984) presented an exception in the case of sexual assault of a mother by her preadolescent son (age eight). This boy had access to pornographic materials, came from a highly disorganized family, and likely was sexually assaulted or incestuously abused himself.

Ward (1985) suggested son-initiated mother incest may occur when a son has been conditioned to be incestuous within the family where father-daughter or father-son incest has occurred and where he models his behavior on his father's. Weiner (1964) even reported a case where a father forced his two teenaged sons to have intercourse with their mother while he watched. Ward wrote:

> In a family where the Father is raping the Daughter(s), the Son has the ultimate patriarchal model. Some attempt resistance; some repress the knowledge; some, however, follow suit. Just as the Daughters in these families are receiving the most thorough conditioning into rape-passivity, so too are the Sons learning the right of males to rape. . . . (p. 182, author's capitalization)

Ward reanalyzed reported cases of son-initiated incest and relabeled those involving late adolescents or adults as "sons raping their mothers." In the professional commentaries on these cases, the mothers themselves had been accused of having caused the incest by being seductive, despite strong evidence to the contrary in the case reports. This type of allegation parallels those found in other forms of rape—that it is the woman's fault and that she must have done something to cause it or deserve it. Ward reported that son-mother rape is increasingly being reported and raised the possibility that this type of intrafamilial sexual abuse may be substantially underreported because of the difficulty that women have in admitting to its occurrence.

Thus far, little mention has been made in the literature of the effects of son-initiated incest on either the mother or son. The case descriptions of Margolis (1984) and Shengold (1980) offer the most extensive information about the sons. Both clients were diagnosed as neurotic, as opposed to borderline or psychotic, and suffered from pervasive feelings of shame, guilt, and a need for punishment for the incestuous behavior; neither was able to complete his treatment. Shengold's patient had completely re-pressed the incest, which returned to consciousness during treatment. Margolis commented, "My clinical impression is that acts of incest are unsuccessful attempts to deal with internal conflicts that may lead to retraumatization and even more untoward pathological results" (p. 383). No descriptions of sons who would be labeled mother-rapists are available as yet.

Ward reported that, as would be expected, mothers raped by their sons suffer severe aftereffects. One such mother committed suicide after leav-ing a message for the local rape crisis center explaining that she no longer wanted to live since she had come to recognize the hatred that many men have for women (Ward, 1985, p. 185).

Stepmother-Stepson Incest

Stepmothers and stepsons become sexually involved in some yet un-known numbers. This type of incest is either mother- or son-initiated. Like stepfather/daughter incest, it may be due to the weaker taboo on sexual activities in stepfamilies, a lack of bonding when the child is young, a needy, vulnerable or hostile child who feels displaced, or blurred genera-tional boundaries between close-in-age stepparent and child. It too may result in negative aftereffects.

In conclusion: The child who is sexually abused by a parent is likely to suffer grave consequences. Such abuse violates the child's safety and matu-ration by triangulating the child into the parents' relationship and by pre-maturely sexualizing the child. Stepfather-daughter incest is the most com-mon form of parent-child incest, followed by father-daughter. Father-son and mother-child are much less common.

CHAPTER 5

Incest Between Other Relatives

PARENT-CHILD INCEST is but one type. Incest occurs between other relatives as well, both within and outside of the nuclear family. In this chapter, other types of incest involving kin of various degrees of relatedness are discussed in terms of dynamics and aftereffects. Sibling incest, which is presented first, rounds out our presentation of nuclear family dyads. Different types of incest involving members of the extended family are then discussed.

SIBLING INCEST

Sibling incest refers to sexual behavior between brother and sister, brother and brother, or sister and sister of a more intimate nature than is usually included in normal child sexual development and experimentation. Although father-daughter incest is believed to be the most commonly *reported* type, incest between an older brother and a younger sister has been thought to be the most commonly *occurring* type (Finkelhor, 1979; Weeks, 1976), but may be exceeded by uncle-niece incest (Russell, 1986). Cole (1982) writes that little is known about sibling incest because: (1) Reported cases are rare, since most parents who discover incest are unlikely to "turn in" a son or daughter, and (2) sibling incest is largely believed to be nondamaging. The predominant view of sibling incest has been of mutual sexual exploration among children within the same age range; this is seen as a normal occurrence in a child's psychosexual development. Furthermore, sibling incest has been seen as far less potent and damaging to the family than father-daughter incest and as less likely to result in serious repercussions for the participants.

Russell's (1986) research findings caused her to decry the "myth of mutuality" as obscuring the serious aftereffects that can result from sibling incest. Finkelhor's investigation (1979) offers support for a range of possible sibling incest pairings and outcomes: 13% of his respondents reported sibling sexual experience — 74% heterosexual and 26% homosexual. Of the same-sex experiences, 16% were between brothers and 10% between sisters. The sample was divided equally about effects, with roughly one-third reporting positive effects, one-third negative, and one-third so-so effects. The more negative effects correlated with greater coerciveness and greater age difference between the siblings. Russell discussed the necessity of distinguishing between abusive and non-abusive sibling incest and of appreciating that the aftereffects may be discounted. In her research sample, 48% of the sisters reported being very or extremely upset by their brother's sexual abuse of them, 24% were somewhat upset, and 28% reported no long-term effects.

Forward and Buck (1978) discussed the circumstances usually associated with positive effects:

> Under certain very specific circumstances sibling incest may not be a traumatic, or even unpleasant, experience. If the children are young and approximately the same age, if there is no betrayal of trust between them, if the sexual play is the result of their natural curiosity and exploration, and if the children are not traumatized by disapproving adults who stumble upon them during sex play, sibling sexual contact can be just another part of growing up. In most such cases both partners are sexually naive. The game of show-me-yours-and-I'll-show-you-mine is older than civilization, and between young siblings of approximately the same age is usually harmless. (p. 85)

Loredo's (1982) observations about the possible reasons for sibling incest are quite inclusive:

> Sibling incest occurs for numerous and multiple reasons. It may be a result of sexual curiosity and experimentation among siblings and may evolve out of sex play that has "gone too far." Sibling incest may exist due to situational pressures, personality disorders and dysfunctions within a family system, or assumptions of inappropriate roles within the family system. Sometimes, the sexual interaction(s) may be encouraged or forced by a third party, perhaps the parents.
>
> Sibling incest may not always be a situation involving one victim and one aggressor. Both may willingly engage in the behavior as an attempt to cope with unmet needs. Such needs may include a desire for affiliation and affection; a combating of loneliness, depression, and a sense of isolation; and a discharging of anxiety and tension due to stress. Other more violent forms of sibling incest occur involving a clear aggressor who acts out sexually with a weaker sibling to gratify needs for retaliation, retribution, power, or control. (p. 178)

Loredo also delineated a number of issues that can assist the clinician in differentiating sexual behavior that is generally harmless and developmental in nature from that which is potentially harmful and an expression of underlying individual or family pathology. These include: determining whether the sexual behavior has involved victimization or whether, in the case of two or more willing participants, some form of psychopathology is evident; the type and duration of sexual activity and whether it was consistent with the developmental level of the involved children; how the participants became involved, whether through mutual agreement or deception, enticement, intimidation, coercion, or force; the intent of the participants, including their motivations, such as exploration, retribution, power-control needs, and sadism, and whether the behavior became a preoccupation to the exclusion of other activities; the age of the siblings, particularly a large age discrepancy between them; the personality predisposition of the siblings; contributory family dynamics, especially the possibility of other types of incestuous activity within the family and factors which would dispose a family to support the perpetrator and abandon the victim (as when the perpetrator is the more valued child, usually a boy, who will be believed rather than the less favored or girl child); and disclosure of the activity and actions taken or not taken by other family members, particularly the parents.

Mrazek (1981) noted that the parents may not provide adequate supervision of their children and may communicate conflicted messages about sexuality. One of the parents, usually the mother, may be excessively rigid and puritanical about sexual matters. This repression might stimulate the children's interest in the "forbidden." Alternatively, some parents create a highly charged sexual atmosphere in the home through nudity, pornographic books and films, excessive discussion of sex, and even the acceptance of the observation of parental intercourse and outright encouragement of sexual contact between the children. I have worked with two survivors of sibling incest whose families contained a very confusing blend of both positions: one parent was excessively rigid and restrictive (the father in one family, the mother in another), and the other excessively exhibitionistic, voyeuristic, and provocative. Multiple incest occurred between all siblings in both families.

As in other types of incest, variations by age and sex of partner in sibling incest have unique dynamics which must be understood by the clinician. These are discussed below. This discussion is also meant to apply to step- and half-siblings, with the caveat that these types are less taboo and involve additional family dynamics.

Older Brother-Younger Sister Incest

This type of incest may have similar dynamics to father-daughter incest, but it is not as potentially explosive to the family since it lacks the rivalry of the parent-child triangle; however, as discussed in Chapter 4, a son may model his behavior after his incestuous father's following father-daughter or father-son incest. Or a victimized brother/son may become an incest perpetrator in an attempt to master his own sexual abuse experience.

Several researchers, notably Finkelhor (1979), Meiselman (1978), and Russell (1986), have found that girls who were sexually abused by their brothers were likely to come from large families without adequate attention or parental supervision (particularly around sex play). Furthermore, some parents may have provided faulty sex models, and/or the personality characteristics of the brother and sister may have caused them to seek contact with one another. In my clinical practice, I have repeatedly observed this pattern when older brother-younger sister incest is reported.

Older brother-younger sister incest has three main variations: (1) when the pubertal brother uses his younger and more naive sister for sexual experimentation and learning; (2) when a socially inept or parentally neglected brother substitutes a sister for unavailable female peers or for lacking affection or nurturance; (3) when the brother who may be quite a bit older than his sister and may himself have been physically and/or sexually abused forces her into sexual activity through violence and coercion. Overlap may exist between these in any particular case. It should also be noted that the younger sister is infrequently the initiator, although this situation has been rarely reported.

In the first variation, the incest activity may be compulsive while ongoing but relatively short-lived. The incest typically stops when the brother gets involved with his peers outside the family. In the second variation, the brother turns to his sister for contact and affection because she is seen as safe and accessible and he lacks social skills, experience, and confidence. As the sexual behavior becomes compulsive, he may find it difficult to stop even when he wants to. It usually ends when the sister refuses further contact, leaving the brother feeling bereft but possibly relieved as well. This brother may feel a great deal of guilt and anxiety about having taken advantage of his sister, but may also feel acutely her loss when the activity stops.

In the third variation, the brother resembles the incestuous father and may have an abusing father on whom he models his sexually predatory behavior. He himself may have witnessed incest or been emotionally, physically, or sexually abused within or outside of the family. The sibling incest may become a means of coping with his own victimization or with other conflicts and problems within the family. It may also be a manifestation of the brother's psychopathology. This brother may abuse more than one sister and engage in many different sexual activities. Increasingly, the literature is documenting that older brother-younger sister activity is often coerced, with the sister being bribed, compromised, or threatened to keep the activity a secret. Violence and rape are not uncommon, nor are instances of brothers' sharing their sister(s) with friends, cousins, or other brothers. Brother-in-law incest is also being documented more regularly.

This type may involve severe levels of sexual coercion and behavior and result in significant conflict for the victim who hesitates to report the abuse out of loyalty to her sister. Through this form of incest, she is made her sister's rival and fears that disclosure will terminate her sister's marriage and alter the sisters' relationship with each other.

Meiselman (1978) found that brothers who have been studied had no outstanding neurotic or psychotic symptoms and were not alcoholic or mentally defective. Rather, this brother is often the oldest brother in a large family with weak or absent parents, a situation which allows him a measure of intrafamilial power. In the minority of cases, the brother is found to be psychopathic or sociopathic, with a propensity to use other family members as objects for his gratification. In such a case, the parents may be either unwilling or unable to control his activities, including the incest.

One other aspect of this type of incest deserves mention: Brothers may persist in their incestuous behavior throughout their lives and in time become incestuous with their own daughters or nieces. This pattern is suggested by survivors who are fearful for the safety of their brothers' children and equally fearful for their own. I have found that it is not unusual to hear about this type of intergenerational pattern in clinical practice. I make it a policy to take worries of this type seriously and to suggest that a reason exists for a sister to be fearful about her brother's behavior. Protective measures should be taken when children are around these men.

Cole (1982) contends "that older brother-younger sister incest is not benign, even when the age difference is small and even when one or both of the participants report the experience as 'positive'" and that "neither the seriousness of sibling incest nor its complexity have been adequately appreciated" (p. 80). More research on this type of incest is clearly needed. In general, studied aftereffects are similar to those experienced by daughters of father incest, including disillusionment, guilt, self-blame, fear of being disbelieved, lack of trust, fear of intimacy, poor self-concept, anger, and, for some, gratification at the attention. The effects of sibling incest reflect the importance of siblings to one another.

Russell (1986) found serious consequences associated with brother-sister incest: Victims may be less likely to marry than victims of other incest perpetrators; may be more likely to be physically abused in their marriages if they marry; and are more likely to report unwanted sexual advances by an authority figure or other forms of sexual harassment. As children they were more fearful about sexual assault, and as adults they continue to be fearful.

Meiselman noted some interesting differences in presenting problems between incestuously abused sisters and daughters in her research population. Her findings indicate that aftereffects may be very similar but differ in severity, especially when the brother is of the same approximate age, is not violent, and is not in an authority/father position in relation to his sister. In Meiselman's study, sisters, compared with daughters, were: not so obese; more likely to be married with a more stable marital history, even though their marriages seemed very unsatisfactory and had a masochistic quality; less likely to have problems with the family of origin; not as often alienated from brother (father) although they were distrustful of him; as likely to have difficulty relating to their own sons due to displacement of feelings from the brother (father); more inclined to be experimental and promiscuous than to withdraw from sex; more likely to have been raped; and more likely to express an aversion to sex.

I have observed that guilt and feelings of complicity may be more diffi-cult issues for sisters to resolve than for daughters, particularly when the participants are close in age, when the sexual activity was mutually desired or became compulsive, and/or when the brother is valued. Many sisters feel as though their inability to stop their brother amounts to their being the initiator or "asking for it." Another pattern shows up in those families where the boys are clearly more valued than the girls and the children are taught that the girls' responsibility is to serve everyone else in the family. Some sisters engaged in or enjoyed sexual contact with brothers precisely because association with the brother gave them status or made up for some of the devaluation they experienced. In these families, additional shame, guilt, and confusion may have resulted for the girl if the incest was discov-ered and was either ignored or seen as entirely her fault. Unfortunately, this is not an unusual response.

Adrienne was sexually abused by her older brother from the ages of 8 to 13. This brother, the oldest child, was aggressive and unmanageable from a young age. The parents made little attempt to control him since their attitude was "boys will be boys." Adrienne's brother forced oral sex on her when she was six and forcefully initiated vaginal and anal intercourse when she was seven. Adrienne never told anyone about the abuse directly be-cause she knew she would be blamed for not stopping it and she didn't want her parents to know such an awful thing about their son. Her silence has continued into adulthood.

Older Sister/Younger Brother Incest

Older sister/younger brother incest may be similar to mother-son incest with two variations — sister-initiated or brother-initiated. In sister-initiated, seductiveness and tenderness may be demonstrated toward the brother by the older sister. She is likely to be insecure with peers or within the family and to use her brother for affection, security, and reassurance. Or she may be quite aggressive, possessive, and demanding of him sexually and other-wise. In this case, the brother usually suffers the more severe aftereffects. As in mother-son incest he may feel guilt, shame, and remorse, as well as great ambivalence towards his sister. His guilt and anxiety may later impede his ability to perform sexually with women in his peer group.

In some cases, younger brothers behave much like older brothers and are the initiators/aggressors in the sexual contact. Even though younger than their sisters, they may be larger and stronger, as well as more valued or less controlled by the family. In this circumstance, effects would be more serious for the sister, resembling those found when an older brother is the initiator.

Same-Sex Sibling Incest

Few reports of same-sex sibling incest appear in the literature, making its dynamics relatively obscure. In young children, same-sex contact does not imply homosexuality; however, same-sex activity between older siblings may be indicative of a homosexual orientation. The homosexual preference of the initiator generally precedes the incest, rather than being its outcome, although such incest may lead to confusion on the part of the victim about his/her sexual identity. As in other types of incest, the greater the age difference between participants, the greater the potential for non-mutuality, coercion, and violence, and thus for trauma.

Same-sex sibling incest may have a variety of outcomes. At best, when it is mutually initiated and when both partners identify as having been homosexual prior to the incest, the effects may be benign as suggested by the research of Simari and Baskin (1982). However, these researchers also found that when incest involves members of the nuclear family effects are more likely to be in the negative direction. Same-sex sibling incest may be deeply troubling and have very serious consequences, as demonstrated by two cases presented by Kaslow, Haupt, Arce, and Werblowsky (1981). A dual suicide was the result of one case of brother-brother incest, while the victim in a case of sister-sister incest presented for treatment with fears of hurting her husband and children, guilt over refusing her husband and boyfriend sex and their subsequent raping of other women, depression, past suicide attempts, and polydrug abuse. Other documented aftereffects include depression, guilt, anxiety, low-self esteem, self-hatred, and confusion. Victims may attempt to master their experience by setting themselves up for revictimization, as in prostitution, or by victimizing others.

INCEST IN THE EXTENDED FAMILY

Grandfather-Granddaughter/Grandson Incest

Estimates of the prevalence of grandfather-granddaughter incest range from 6% (Russell, 1986) to approximately 10% of all reported cases (Courtois & Hinckley, 1981; Goodwin, Cormier, & Owen, 1983), yet this type has not received much attention or discussion. Grandfather-grandson incest is rarely mentioned, although it occurs with some unestablished prevalence. Grandfather incest is yet another type that has been considered benign and rather inconsequential, in part due to the stereotyped perception of grandfathers as nonsexual and kindly towards grandchildren and a related conclusion that any sexual abuse would be due to senility.

Goodwin et al. (1983) found that eight of the ten grandfathers they studied had a total of 33 known victims and that eight of the 18 grandchildren were victimized by multiple perpetrators. They suggested the grandfathers were pedophiles and that this form of incest should be further investigated because of the potential for intergenerational abuse. A majority of these men had molested their daughters and later turned to their granddaughters. This pattern of multiple abuse and multiple perpetrators within one family across several generations is being recognized as more common than formerly believed. Russell's findings led her to conclude that "some grandfathers may play an initiating role in what became a history of revictimization for their victims" (p. 320). They may further be patriarchs of a family system of sexual abuse. Russell also found that stepgrandfathers, like stepfathers, pose a risk for children. Due to the fact that they have no biological bond, they may be more prone than natural grandfathers to molest their granddaughters.

Reported cases involve both maternal and paternal grandfathers, none of whom was found to be senile or otherwise mentally defective. Forward and Buck (1978) reported two types of grandfather perpetrators—relatively young men in their forties and fifties where the incest pattern followed that generally found in the father-daughter type, and older men who may have begun to feel the effects of their age. These older grandfathers appeared to be motivated by the social effects of their age rather than by senility, namely by loneliness and loss, low self-esteem and depression, physical helplessness and deterioration, need for affection and for reassurance about their sexual potency and desirability. Anger about getting old and about being stereotyped or given stereotyped roles such as babysitter may precipitate incest. Alcoholism is implicated in a minority of the cases. The grandfathers are usually gentle in their approaches to their granddaughters and, as found in father-daughter incest, may engage in a progression of activities over the duration of the incest. But they usually have limited access to their granddaughters and as a consequence abuse less frequently than do fathers. Children may have difficulty disclosing this type of abuse due to divided loyalty: They would be reporting a perpetrator who is the parent of one of their parents. Such conflicted loyalty surely makes it easier for some grandfathers to abuse over a long duration.

Some of the grandfathers in the Russell sample conformed to the "dirty old man" stereotype. Forty-four percent of them were known to have sexually abused at least one other relative, and some appeared to be predatory old men who were attracted to prepubescent or adolescent girls. Grandfathers in the Russell study were more likely than other incest perpetrators to abuse their victims at the least severe level, yet they tended to use force and to have a relatively high frequency of contact over a long duration.

Goodwin et al. (1983) found a pattern to the incestuous activities. In more stable families, no intercourse was involved. In chaotic, disorganized families where parenting difficulties, including an inability to adequately supervise children, were evident, intercourse was attempted or consummated. Additionally, eight out of the ten incestuous grandfathers studied had sexually abused their own daughters.

Grandfather-grandson incest is assumed to occur only rarely. As with other forms of incest, this should not be taken to mean that it does not occur. Clearly the potential exists for fathers who abuse their own sons to abuse grandsons as well and for intergenerational contact and transmission to occur in this way.

A wide variety of aftereffects and severity has been reported for grandfather-granddaughter incest; most of these can be presumed to also apply to grandfather-grandson incest. Goodwin et al. found that victim aftereffects differed by group. Those victims from chaotic families showed educational and behavioral symptoms and those from more stable families exhibited fears and phobias. Meiselman (1978) and Courtois and Hinckley (1981) found that the effects experienced by adult survivors resembled those associated with other types of incest. They supported Forward and Buck's observation of compounded guilt reactions for those victims whose grandfather died during the course of the incest or shortly thereafter. Many of these victims may have wished the grandfather dead as a means to stop the activity. When the wish became a reality, the grandchild was left with additional guilt, confusion, and remorse to work through.

Ellen's grandfather used to French-kiss her and masturbate against her when she was a young child. The abuse would occur whenever he was alone with her, in either of their homes or in his car. Ellen hated his sexual demands but never said anything to keep her grandmother and mother from knowing—she didn't want to hurt them. Ellen later found out her grandfather had done the same thing to her mother and to all his female grandchildren.

Grandmother-Granddaughter/Grandson

Incest involving grandmothers and their granddaughters or grandsons is also underreported in the clinical literature. An account of sadistic, misogynistic grandmother-granddaughter abuse is included in Bass and Thornton (1983). More research and case reports are needed to understand dynamics and effects, although we can speculate that both are consistent with those reported for mother-daughter/mother-son and grandfather-grandchild incest.

Uncle-Niece/Nephew

Incest perpetrated by uncles is mentioned throughout the incest literature, yet to date this type of incest has not been adequately investigated in its own right, nor has it been treated as serious. New research and clinical evidence concerning the frequency of such abuse and its possible dynamics, particularly those concerning intergenerational patterns, indicate that this is a significant omission in the incest literature. Russell's research substantiated the findings of the Kinsey (Kinsey, Pomeroy, Martin & Gebhard, 1953) study that uncle-niece incest was the most common form of intergenerational incest, occurring slightly more often than the father-daughter type.

Russell (1986) remarked, "The fact that uncle-niece incestuous abuse occurs outside the nuclear family makes it particularly important theoretically" (p. 323). This is so because uncle-niece incest occurs apart from the interplay of family problems which is theorized as being partially causative of father-daughter incest. In some cases, however, incestuous fathers are also known to be incestuous uncles. Patterns of incestuous abuse are evident throughout some extended families, with brothers of one generation abusing the daughters and nieces of the next and following a model established by the father/grandfather.

I found a pattern of multiple victimizations in all five uncle-niece cases in my research sample where the uncle was reported as the principal perpetrator and in eight additional cases where he was reported as secondary (Courtois, 1982). Victims identified loneliness, alcoholism or drunkenness, poor relationships with women, and an incest norm in the family as possible causes of the incest.

As in other forms of incest, incest perpetrated by uncles includes a variety of sexual behaviors with either prepubertal or postpubertal nieces. Russell (1986) found that the average case of uncle-niece incest involves sexual abuse of a less severe level, perhaps because the majority of uncles, like grandfathers, have limited access to their nieces. Nevertheless, cases at the very severe level were also found in her research and in mine as well.

Uncle-nephew incest is discussed sporadically in the literature. It is likely that dynamics resemble those found in father-son incest, but without the nuclear family issues. Uncles who abuse their nephews may themselves have been abused and may be seeking mastery through repetition, and/or they may more simply be seeking to satisfy their needs through their sexual involvement.

Victims of this type of incest sometimes find it difficult to report because of conflicted family loyalties. Victims may be reluctant to tell a parent that they are being sexually abused by an uncle, the parent's brother; they may want to save the parent from hurt or may fear being either disbelieved or blamed.

The effects of uncle-niece/nephew incest may range from mild to severe and resemble those found in other forms of intergenerational incest. Meiselman wrote that sexual contacts with uncles were likely to be more damaging when the uncle functioned in a father role to the niece (and by implication to the nephew) and when coercion was involved. This formulation does not always hold and ignores other potential sources of trauma, as noted by Russell. I also found that other sources of trauma could be at play: Even when the uncle was not an active member of the nuclear family and was not particularly coercive or violent, strong negative reactions in all categories of aftereffects were reported by a substantial proportion of my subjects (all female) (Courtois, 1979). In uncle-nephew incest, the same-sex dimension of the sexual contact may cause additional aftereffects, particularly regarding gender identity.

Olivia's uncle used every opportunity to be alone with her. He began fondling and kissing her when she was 8 and raped her when she was 12. Since then, she has worked hard to avoid him. She is now 15 and is convinced that he will rape her again given the opportunity. Olivia also believes he has been incestuous with his own daughters. She never disclosed what happened because of her shame — her uncle told her that he only did what he did because she was a "fox who led him on."

Aunt-Niece/Nephew

Like other female perpetrators, aunts have been found to be sexually predatory towards nieces and nephews, but much less often than uncles. Until further information is gathered about this type of incest, it can be assumed that both the dynamics and the effects parallel those for incest perpetrated by mothers; however, the nuclear family dimension is lacking, except when an aunt lives with the family and/or functions as a caretaker to the children. Aunt-niece/nephew incest is more likely to be circumstantial and to occur with a lower frequency over a shorter duration than incest within the nuclear family.

Cousin Incest

Cousin incest receives only occasional mention in the professional literature and is probably considered the least serious form of incest between blood relatives. In fact, first-cousin sexual contact is legal in some states.

Cousin incest, which may be peer or cross-generational, certainly occurs with more regularity than has been previously recorded.

Russell found that incest perpetrated by first cousins was similar to incest perpetrated by brothers in terms of the degree of physical force used, the severity of the abuse in terms of the sex acts involved, and the age disparity between cousins and their victims. It was different in that cousins tended to abuse less frequently over a shorter duration and that incest with brothers was rated as somewhat more severe. Incest with cousins was, however, only slightly less upsetting. Over one-third of the victims of first cousins reported some or severe long-term effects, so it is inaccurate to consider this type of incest as non-harmful. Even in mild cases with no reported serious aftereffects, it may be damaging by virtue of being disillusioning for the victim who holds such sexual contact between cousins to be taboo.

Step-, Half-, In-Law and Quasi-Relative Incest

Several other variations exist involving affinally related individuals, further extending the complexity of incest. It may occur between step-relatives, half-relatives, in-laws, and quasi-relatives such as foster parents and children. The incest taboo applies in a weakened form to all of these liaisons because the relational bond is affinal and contractual rather than due to blood ties. Many researchers of the contemporary family have expressed concern that the high divorce rate in the U.S. and the resultant high level of reconstituted and blended families, as well as loosened sexual mores and standards which enable couples to live together without benefit of a marriage contract, put children at risk for higher rates of this type of incest. The lack of clear relationship bond and a strong taboo may lessen inhibitions associated with incest.

Despite the fact that no blood tie exists, the aftereffects of this type of incest can be serious because the relational role has been violated and because an adult in an authority position has transgressed. Due to its high prevalence, stepfather-daughter incest (discussed in Chapter 4) has received the most research attention thus far. Russell (1986) found some of her sample to be highly distraught about sexual abuse perpetrated by brothers-in-law, a situation also evident for some of my research subjects (Courtois, 1979). These women reported feeling very uncomfortable about being compared to or made rivals of their sisters (usually older sisters). They were reluctant to disclose their brother-in-law's approach for fear of hurting their sisters, causing a marital split, or being blamed.

Finally, although few hard data are available to support the fact, it is nevertheless widely recognized that a foster placement may put a girl at risk for sexual abuse at the hands of a foster father or brother. Although uncomfortable to contemplate, some foster parents take children in to molest them and not to shelter them. Some abusive foster fathers abuse their charges serially. By the same token, girls with repeat foster home placements may go from one abusive relationship to another. Compounding this tragedy is the fact that foster placement is often the only option for an abused child. Most foster families receive little if any training on the special needs of these children. Foster families with inadequate boundaries may be ill-equipped to handle abused children, particularly those who are sexually precocious, provocative, and/or promiscuous. An incestuous/pedophilic foster parent has a ready source of victims.

Messer (1969) used the term *Phaedra Complex* to describe situations of incestuous attraction between stepparents and stepchildren and suggested ways for blended families to heighten the parental role of the stepparent to guard against the development of a romantic role. This strategy should be extended to other family-type relationships to help guard against the sexual misuse of children entrusted to the care of these adults. Foster parents, in particular, need careful screening as to any abuse history or potential. Once selected, they should be carefully trained and monitored concerning sexual abuse and handling the special challenges of the incestuously or otherwise abused foster child.

It is obvious from this and the previous chapter that incest can take many forms and that particular aftereffects are associated with how the incest occurred and with whom. The clinician should be aware of these different incest manifestations and the dynamics unique to each in assisting survivors who are reluctant to divulge experience with less common forms of incest. In addition, such specialized knowledge will enable the clinician to better plan and focus the treatment.

SECTION II
Symptoms, Aftereffects, and Diagnosis

CHAPTER 6

Incest Symptoms, Aftereffects, and Secondary Elaborations

I NCEST, A FORM OF chronic traumatic stress, can lead to a host of initial and long-term aftereffects. Like child sexual abuse in general, it poses a serious mental health risk for a substantial number of victims. According to Browne and Finkelhor (1986), who reviewed the empirical studies of aftereffects of child sexual abuse, at least one-fifth to two-fifths of all sexually abused children manifest pathological disturbance in the immediate aftermath of abuse. In adulthood, victims as a group show impairment of some sort when compared with nonvictims; 20% of these victims show serious psychopathology.

In all likelihood these findings underestimate aftereffects, since research instruments are only now being developed which specifically address the effects of child sexual abuse and are sensitive enough to tap its less obvious effects. Furthermore, it is likely that these findings underestimate the effects suffered by incest survivors as a distinct subpopulation of the sexually abused. A number of researchers have noted that incest survivors tend to minimize their distress due to their shame at having been involved in a taboo activity and their desire to protect or excuse the abuser or other family members. Abuse within the family has particular characteristics which have been associated with the most severe reactions: longer duration and frequency, a closer relationship and a greater age difference between perpetrator and victim, the use of force, multiple abuse, and the greater intrusiveness of sexual activity (Russell, 1986). Moreover, the chronic nature of the abuse, the nature of the family, including its dynamics and defenses, the child's dependence on and entrapment in the family, and her loyalty necessitate her use of strong defenses to cope. Denial and dissociation allow her to discount, minimize, or otherwise suppress her abuse memories and reactions. These defenses frequently persist into adulthood.

As a result, victim/survivors may appear asymptomatic and as not suffering long-term aftereffects, when in reality they are constricted emotionally due to the trauma.

As evident from preceding chapters, the majority of former victims had little chance either in childhood or later to get effective assistance to end the abuse or to treat its effects. These untreated effects (whether immediate or long-term) become chronic or delayed and spawn secondary elaborations. These secondary elaborations, in turn, create new problems which are usually what cause the adult survivor to seek treatment (Gelinas, 1983). The most common of these include chronic and atypical depression, eating disorders, substance abuse, anxiety, dissociative disorders, somatization disorders, and explosive disorders. Survivors might also present as victims of domestic abuse or other types of sexual violence.

Incest occurs during the course of the victim's childhood and inevitably has an influence on her maturation and development. For many victim/survivors, the incest experience, along with its aftereffects and coping mechanisms, has influenced and become integrated into the personality. Some develop the symptoms of specific personality disorders, most commonly those associated with hysteric, borderline, narcissistic, avoidant, or dependent personalities.

The etiological significance of parental abuse in the development of these disorders, specifically those of the borderline and hysteric type, has long been downplayed and is only now receiving research scrutiny. Similarly, the relation of trauma to the development of mental health problems and psychopathological conditions or the "victim-to-patient process" (Rieker & Carmen, 1986; van der Kolk, 1987a) is under investigation. At present, the relationship between victimization and delayed maladaptive behavior is complex, unclear as to cause and effect, and in pressing need of additional research. Our emerging knowledge about psychological trauma in general and trauma-specific syndromes and intervention suggests that direct treatment of the trauma is necessary for the resolution of its aftereffects and secondary elaborations.

In the following pages I detail the aftereffects and secondary elaborations most common to the incest experience, as well as the defenses victims use as they attempt to cope. The information is drawn from three sources: (1) retrospective reports of survivors; (2) clinical descriptions and studies; and (3) empirical studies. My intent is to present an inclusive compilation of the aftereffects that have been recorded thus far, but this inclusive approach must be qualified. First, the bulk of the evidence suggests that incest is a negative life event for the majority of victims. As discussed above, it has devastating consequences for a sizable minority of victims. Since this book is directed towards clinical intervention, the most negative aftereffects and their secondary elaborations are emphasized. Yet, as demonstrated in Chapters 4 and 5, incest experiences are tremendously variable, occurring for numerous reasons under a wide variety of circumstances. Aftereffects are similarly variable in their development, range, and severity. While typical responses and patterns have been documented and are presented here as the most common aftereffects, heterogeneous and idiosyncratic responses have also been noted. In my research, I found that my interviewees carefully discriminated between categories of aftereffects and their severity when asked to describe and rate them. They took care to point out that some effects developed or remitted over time and some were much worse or better than others. On average, subjects rated their incest experience as predominantly negative, yet individual differences among aftereffects and their rated severity were notable (Courtois, 1979, 1982).

A second qualification: The clinician must be cautious about predetermining both the aftereffects and their severity and must make every effort to individually assess and diagnose each case. The clinician should take a balanced perspective and recognize that some survivors will report horrendous experiences, aftereffects, and secondary problems, while others will report experiences which are neutral, mildly discomforting, or positive. Reactions at either extreme of the continuum may be difficult for the clinician to accept or acknowledge. It is important for the client to be able to discuss and explore all aspects of the experience and its aftermath and to expect an accepting and empathic response.

SOURCES OF INFORMATION ABOUT AFTEREFFECTS

Until recently, most of the information available on the aftereffects of incest was speculative at best, derived from seriously flawed empirical and clinical studies and case descriptions. Their generalizability was limited because samples were small, were not representative of the population of incest victims, and had no control groups for comparison. Specifically, many of these studies investigated cases that had been reported to the authorities and were in mandated treatment. These tended to be the most desperate cases from the most disturbed families, largely from lower socioeconomic groups. Less serious cases or those that occurred within more intact families with the resources to avoid the detection of social service and law enforcement agencies and/or to afford private treatment were thus excluded. As a result, the information gleaned from these studies was biased and incomplete.

Despite the problems with these studies and reports, many showed consistency in their descriptions of family dynamics, characteristics of incest occurrence, and aftereffects. A range of predominantly negative intrapsychic and interpersonal consequences, both immediate and long-term, was found to be associated with incestuous abuse. A few reports found no obvious damage, and some discussed positive benefits.

At present, the findings of these studies and clinical reports are being replicated and extended by two previously unavailable sources of data: self-reports of victim/survivors and methodologically sound empirical studies. Since the late 1970s, a number of victim/survivors have written about their incest experiences. These have been published either in short story or book form or as contributions to anthologies. Women have met in consciousness-raising and self-help groups and shared their stories. Several extensive case descriptions have been provided by clinicians. Retrospective studies of clinical and nonclinical samples have been conducted by professionals using both structured and unstructured interview formats, some of which included batteries of standardized psychological instruments. For these studies, researchers solicited volunteers in mental health populations or in the public at large who were willing to discuss their incest experience.

These personal accounts have provided in-depth subjective descriptions of both the experience and its aftereffects. Victims have described what it was like to be involved in an incestuous relationship and discussed their perceptions of family functioning and causes of the incest. They have also addressed whether from their perspective its effects were positive, negative, neutral, or mixed. Overall, these first-person accounts document mostly negative effects, many of which have been previously cited in the clinical literature. These self-reports have particular value because they provide a subjective perspective on what has been objectively observed and recorded. Further, they help respondents to break away from the secrecy and silence and to talk about that which has been considered unspeakable. Despite the value of personal reports, they too are subject to charges of bias. Their most serious limitation lies in their nonrepresentativeness and in the possibility that only individuals with the most serious experiences and aftereffects would volunteer to talk about them.

Carefully constructed empirical investigations have been undertaken in the last decade. Several studies have compared clinical with nonclinical groups and both with matched controls. Broad-based community surveys of randomly selected subjects have been conducted to compare victims to nonvictims and to assess the prevalence of child sexual abuse in the population at large. In general, these studies have found significant differences between victims and nonvictims: Victims as a group have more psychological difficulty on both objective and subjective measures of adjustment. These results support previous findings that negative sequelae result from incest and child sexual abuse and are not simply an artifact of samples drawn from a clinic population; however, they document a range of response possibilities as well. Effects can vary quite substantially, and some victims suffer much more serious aftereffects than others.

Browne and Finkelhor (1986) conducted a thorough review of available research on the impact of child sexual abuse. They concluded the following:

Summarizing, then, from studies of clinical and nonclinical populations, the findings concerning the trauma of child sexual abuse appear as follows: In the immediate aftermath of sexual abuse from one-fifth to two-fifths of abused children seen by clinicians manifest pathological disturbance (Tufts, 1984). When studied as adults, victims as a group demonstrate impairment when compared with their nonvictimized counterparts, but under one-fifth evidence serious psychopathology. These findings give reassurance to victims that extreme long-term effects are not inevitable. Nonetheless, they also suggest that the risk of initial and long-term mental health impairment for victims of child sexual abuse should be taken very seriously. (1986, p. 72)

In summarizing their findings about the long-term effects of sexual abuse, they stated:

Empirical studies with adults confirm many of the long-term effects of sexual abuse mentioned in the clinical literature. Adult women victimized as children are more likely to manifest depression, self-destructive behavior, anxiety, feelings of isolation and stigma, poor self-esteem, a tendency toward revictimization, and substance abuse. Difficulty in trusting others and sexual maladjustment in such areas as sexual dysphoria, sexual dysfunction, impaired sexual self-esteem, and avoidance of or abstention from sexual activity have also been reported by empirical researchers, although agreement between studies is less consistent for the variables on sexual functioning. (p. 72)

Browne and Finkelhor's review addressed the impact of all forms of child sexual abuse. Several of the studies included in their review offer data suggesting that the impact of incest is more serious than the impact of other forms of child sexual abuse and that overt incestuous contact has more serious ramifications than covert, seductive behavior between family members. Two studies in particular, those conducted by Herman (1981) and Sedney and Brooks (1984), are illustrative. Sedney and Brooks surveyed a nonclinical population of college women concerning their history of childhood sexual experience, current symptoms and demographic background. They found that adults who had been victims of abuse as children reported significantly greater symptoms, generally indicative of depression, anxiety, and self-abusive behavior. Women whose experience occurred within the family were at greater risk for disturbance than women whose experience was outside the family. They commented:

The pattern that evolved was of a greater likelihood of symptoms in the early sexual experience group than the control group, with the negative effects more apparent in the incest group than the nonfamilial sexual experience group. In other words, early sexual experience with a family member seemed to have negative consequences over and above those resulting from just the early sexual experience itself. (p. 217)

Herman compared victims of serious and overt incest to victims of mild or covert incest (with seductive fathers) and documented similar symptomatology between the two groups. She found that:

In general, having grown up with a covert or mild form of incest, the daughters of seductive fathers exhibited a mild form of the incest-victim syndrome in adult life. Like the incest victims, they tended to feel contempt for women and to hold men in excessive regard. Like the incest victims, they had many difficulties in establishing rewarding personal or sexual relationships, difficulties that were ultimately related to their own lack of self-respect. Unlike the incest victims, however, they did not develop a confirmed negative identity as the guardian of a malignant secret. They did not think of themselves as irredeemably evil and did not feel doomed to exclusion from normal society. (p. 124)

Russell's 1986 study of incest victims, the most methodologically sound conducted to date, offers valuable information on the variability of reaction to incest and the most damaging aspects of the incest experience. Her data help to explain Sedney and Brooks' and Herman's findings. The incest victims in her randomly selected community sample reported a considerable range in their degree of subjective trauma. Approximately one-quarter reported a great effect, one-quarter some effect, another quarter little effect, and 22% no lasting effect. Certain characteristics of the experience were found to be associated with more serious aftereffects, characteristics which are more typical of incestuous abuse than of other forms of child sexual abuse. They derive from the fact that the child is in a dependent relationship and is in essence captive within the family where she is being abused. These characteristics include abuse of longer duration and frequency, abuse involving closer relatives (particularly fathers and father figures) as compared to all other types of perpetrators, a large age difference between victim and perpetrator, abuse perpetrated by males, sexual behavior which is more serious and involves penetration, greater use of force and coercion, and multiple abuse experiences.

Russell reported that many of the incest victims in her sample seemed to minimize or downplay the effects of the incest and that in reality effects were more serious than acknowledged. These observations are in line with those of other clinicians and researchers and with survivor reports as well. They are consistent with the data emerging about traumatic stress response, particularly in relation to chronic trauma and traumatic experiences in childhood (see Chapter 7). In order to survive their experiences of repeated and progressive abuse and to cope with the double binds found in many incestuous families, incest victims deny, dissociate, and repress the abuse and their reactions to it. This disconnection or blunting is a survival strategy which often persists into adulthood. It may be quite functional in allowing the victim to cope, but it also masks reactions to the trauma and prevents resolution. Additionally, it causes incest survivors to appear asymptomatic or less injured when in reality they are emotionally deadened as part of the trauma response.

The clinician should be aware that the aftereffects of incest do not manifest solely because of the sexual nature of the abuse, nor are they discrete from other personality factors, family characteristics, and life events; rather, they are entangled with them in such a way that causation is often impossible to determine. Numerous factors before, during, and after the incest serve to influence aftereffects and their severity. Premorbid factors, such as the child's personality and health and the family's functioning, may contribute to the child's vulnerability to abuse or to the intensification of her traumatic response. For example, a shy vulnerable child or one who is sickly and demanding may be more at risk for abuse than her outgoing and assertive sibling. Early bonding disturbances between the child and her parents may increase her vulnerability to abuse and aggravate her reactions to the incest. She may have learned to be mistrustful about the reliability and trustworthiness of others long before the incest occurred. Similarly, her self-esteem and cognitive abilities may determine how she interprets the incest.

As discussed earlier, specific characteristics of the abuse, such as age at onset and termination, the chronicity of the abuse, the use of force or coercion and the relationship of participants, interact and influence outcome. Family factors, such as the child's relationship to the perpetrator and non-offending family members and whether the child is otherwise physically and emotionally nurtured, neglected, or abused, are significant. The presence or absence of overall family pathology and dysfunction, the family dynamics, specific family problems or crises (physical abuse, alcoholism, serious illness, divorce or death), family support systems, and personality characteristics of family members have an impact. Attempts at disclosure and the response of family members and of others have a weighting, as does the development of a supportive relationship outside the family circle or later in life. Sources of trauma may be compounded in multiproblem, chaotic families and for those survivors who experience multiple traumatic experiences and victimizations. Comprehensive assessment to determine aftereffects and diagnostic considerations and formulations are addressed in Chapter 8.

THE SYMPTOMS OF INCEST

A number of *behavioral, physical,* and *familial symptoms* in childhood, adolescence, or adulthood offer clues to the occurrence of incest and serve as indicators of aftereffects. In ongoing cases, these symptoms often provide signals indicative of abuse strong enough to validate the child's experience in the face of the family's or child's denial. Such symptoms are similarly useful in retrospective validation. In cases where the incest is not consciously available to the adult in treatment due to strong denial, repression, or dissociation, these symptoms provide the clinician with reason to suspect or evidence to substantiate the incest. Some survivors are able to link symptoms directly to the abuse and its aftereffects. For others, the links are not be obvious and must be made by the clinician.

Symptoms in Childhood and Early Adolescence

Behavioral symptoms of incest manifest according to the developmental stage of the child and her level of physical and psychosexual maturity. Lewis and Sarrel (1969) discussed age-and phase-specific symptomatology, which only becomes trauma-specific as the child matures. The infant and very young child show signs of acute anxiety as a result of being overstimulated/assaulted. These symptoms are nonspecific to the sexual trauma and include failure to thrive, withdrawal, fretfulness, whining and crying, clinging behavior, movement impairment, feeding disturbances, and later, speech disturbance.

In early childhood, a wide variety of neurotic symptomatology, again phase-specific and not trauma-specific, can develop, including thumb-sucking, scratching and picking behavior, self-injurious behavior, tics, enuresis, speech problems, conduct disturbances, and sleep difficulties. Trauma-specific symptoms may begin at this time including compulsive and inappropriate sex play, and sexual activities, and sexually aggressive behavior with peers, adults, and objects. The child may be sexually precocious and show an understanding of different types of sexual activity inappropriate to her age. She may be quite seductive with males (and less so with females) when the perpetrator is a male. On the other hand, she may exhibit fear when around males and make obvious efforts to avoid the perpetrator as well as other males.

In middle childhood, these same phase-and trauma-specific symptoms may occur on a transient basis or be relatively persistent. Besides the sexual symptoms, other symptoms include those associated with depression (nightmares, sleep disturbances, concentration problems, suicidal feelings); fears and phobias; eating disorders; delinquent behavior; pseudo-mature behavior; and possible borderline and psychotic states. School and social functioning may be impaired or, just the opposite, appear normal.

Sgroi (1978) commented on the possible range of behaviors exhibited by a child:

> Children can exhibit the entire gamut of behaviors in response to a sexual assault, ranging from the negative to the positive. Unsophisticated observers may note calm and unconcerned behavior or outright denial of the situation or positive response by the child to the suspected perpetrator . . . and mistakenly conclude that no sexual assault could have occurred because of the child's reaction. It is essential that helping professionals who come in contact

with these children be knowledgeable about the wide range of possible reactions that may be exhibited. (Sgroi, 1978, p. 135)

In adolescence, acute anxiety and rage may be acted out in angry, rebellious, delinquent behavior, including sexual promiscuity and substance abuse, or may result in a depressive state characterized by social withdrawal or overly compliant "good girl" behavior. Psychosomatic complaints may continue and be transient or relatively stable. Attempts to develop a peer group identification may be impeded as strong feelings of shame, worthlessness, embarrassment, and being different from others and "out of synch" emerge. An early pregnancy or series of pregnancies or abortions, early marriage and/or runaway behavior may also be indicative of an abuse history.

Physical symptoms serve as indicators of abuse in some cases. While most children do not sustain physical injury, trauma to the mouth, genital, urethral, or rectal areas signals the possibility of sexual abuse. Trauma may include lacerations, tears and bruises, abnormal swelling or dilation, or the insertion of objects into these body cavities. In some cases, the injuries are very serious and damage is significant. The child may experience difficulty with urination or defecation and may have blood stains or semen on underwear or bedclothes. Some children will have serious physical discomfort and pain, resulting in difficulty performing such normal physical activities as sitting, walking, or playing sports. Violent or forceful abuse can also result in soft tissue bruises, cuts, and abrasions to the breasts, buttocks, lower abdomen and thighs. Sexually transmitted diseases and pregnancy are also consequences of abuse.

Other physical symptoms include gastrointestinal disturbances and pain, including gagging, nausea, eating disorders, ulcers, and stomach cramps; sleep disturbances, including insomnia, nightmares, night terrors; and such symptoms of anxiety, depression, and trauma as migraine headaches, startle responses, dissociation, fear of being trapped or attacked, lethargy, passivity, frozen watchfulness, self-soothing behavior, inability to concentrate, and signs of self-injury.

Children sometimes hide their injuries or deny their origins in order to maintain the incest secret, especially if they have been threatened or feel they must protect the family or perpetrator. Unfortunately, such a disclaimer is all too often believed and some other explanation found for the symptoms, even the most obvious ones. In her pioneer article on the medical treatment of child sexual abuse, Sgroi (1977) challenged medical professionals to stop denying that child sexual abuse was the cause of such symptomatology as sexually transmitted diseases and genital trauma. Many survivors report that they were medically examined and treated for their various symptoms, but for the most part the symptoms were never attributed to abuse even when the evidence was obvious. Instead, symptoms were most frequently described as psychosomatic or without basis or another diagnosis was given.

Certain *family symptoms* are associated with incest and provide cause for speculation about its occurrence. These have been covered in Chapters 3 and 4.

Symptoms in Adolescence and Adulthood

According to Gelinas (1983), many *behavioral symptoms* in adulthood are actually secondary elaborations of the untreated negative effects of incest. The client seeking therapy usually presents with a "characterological depression with complications and atypical impulsive and dissociative elements" (p. 326). The results of a study by Briere and Runtz (1985) confirm these observations, in that sexual abuse victims scored higher than nonvictims on indices of somatization, anxiety, depression, and dissociation.

Behavioral cues are associated with each of these scales. The survivor may manifest clear symptoms of depression intermittently or constantly throughout childhood and adolescence and into adulthood. These include low self-esteem, feelings of worthlessness and hopelessness, passivity, lethargy, eating disturbances resulting in weight loss or gain, helplessness and lack of personal efficacy, inability to concentrate, withdrawal and isolation, anhedonia, and self-injurious behavior, including self-mutilation and suicidal ideation and gestures. Depression may result in a disregard for personal hygiene and a drab and unkempt personal appearance. An unattractive appearance, including layered clothing and deliberate weight gain, has been used by some survivors to pad themselves and make themselves as unattractive and sexually unappealing as possible. Anorexia may provide an alternative way to not be sexual or sexually attractive by reversing secondary sexual characteristics.

Impulsive behavior includes a history of running away (which, in many cases, was appropriate behavior geared to escaping the intolerable home situation and therefore should not be considered solely as a sign of delinquency); uncontrolled and impulsive spending, sexual activity, and substance abuse involving alcohol, drugs, and food; impulsive flight from relationships, particularly those that hold promise of positive regard and nurturance for the survivor; impulsive development of relationships with inappropriate, untrustworthy, or unsavory people; and behaviors such as self-mutilation, "accidents," and suicide gestures and attempts.

Dissociative symptoms are manifest by recurrent nightmares and night terrors, amnesia especially for small or large segments of childhood, trance states, perceptual distortions, feelings of depersonalization or of seeing the self from afar, feelings of derealization, fainting spells, migraine headaches, epileptic-like seizures, and "sliding" or multiple personalities. Addictive patterns of food, alcohol, and drug intake can provide a means of chemical dissociation. Additional anxiety symptoms include feeling trapped and afraid of or phobic about particular people and places, panic attacks, hyperventilation, and flashbacks.

Physical symptoms may be seen in illness or somatic symptoms which defy medical diagnosis. Many of these are symptoms of anxiety and tension, often involving a disturbance of gastrointestinal functioning. Nausea, "nervous stomach," stomach pain, and ulcers may be freestanding symptoms or related to substance abuse problems and either anorexia nervosa or bulimia. Some of these symptoms relate to the locus of the abuse, e.g., gagging and vomiting resulting from forced oral sex.

All forms of sexual problems and aversions have been identified as consequences of sexual abuse. Some survivors are sexually abstinent and phobic, while others are compulsively and indiscriminately sexual. Other sexual problems include pain, discomfort, and numbness or stimulation in sexual areas of the body. Memory fragments or flashbacks of forced sex, pregnancy, and abortion may offer clues to past abuse. Early and/or repeated pregnancies may characterize some survivors. Sexually transmitted diseases may occur at the time of the abuse and then lie dormant for months or even years, only to flare up in adolescence or adulthood.

A tendency to react to body touch with flinching, withdrawal, violence, tearfulness, or paralysis may suggest past abuse experiences. Other physical effects include physical injury to different parts of the body, sometimes resulting in disabilities, and scars of injuries inflicted during the course of the abuse by the perpetrator or scars resulting from self-inflicted injury used to anesthesize, distract, or heighten the abuse experience at the time or later.

The *family symptoms* and roles observed in childhood may continue in similar fashion in adulthood if there has been no change or intervention to alter the patterns. Several of the most common patterns are as follows. In father-daughter incest, the triangulation may persist. The father may continue to exhibit obsessive and possessive behavior, including attempts to be sexual towards his favored daughter, even after she leaves home. On her visits home, the daughter may feel very pressured as she attempts to fend off her father's attentions and to receive positive attention from her mother. Instead, she may find that her mother blames and rejects her for her father's behavior.

Another pattern demonstrated by some incest fathers is to ignore or reject the older daughter(s) as she becomes an adolescent. His rejection may be triggered by his fears of pregnancy or by her seeking more autonomy or rejecting his advances. He may then become more obvious in his attentions to any younger sisters. The older daughter may feel especially betrayed if her involvement with her father was contingent upon his promise not to abuse other siblings. She may become hostile to him and may seek every opportunity to hurt him or to challenge his authority. The deterioration of a formerly favored, exclusive relationship to the point of extreme hostility between father and daughter may be symptomatic of past or current abuse. Other related behavior, such as running away from home, promiscuity, and substance abuse may be indicative as well.

The role reversal between parent and child is another pattern which may continue into adulthood, even if the daughter no longer lives at home and/or has established her own family. Not infrequently, she has her own children when she is quite young. Nevertheless, she may continue to function as the caretaker to her family of origin, performing many of the traditional wife/mother/housekeeper roles with no reciprocal caretaking of her needs. Her inability to set limits on the demands of her family, often complicated by her guilt about the incest with her father and her conditioning to behave in a compliant manner, sooner or later result in her becoming exhausted and depleted. She then copes by withdrawing and becoming emotionally unavailable to her partner and children and by parentifying one of her own children. In this way, dynamics conducive to incest develop in the second generation. A variant of this pattern is the daughter who is excessive in her gift-giving to her family, even when she receives no gifts or even thanks in return. She may go so far as to put herself into debt to show others how much she cares and how good she is. For example, one of my clients wanted to buy her mother a house to expiate her guilt about the past incest.

One further family pattern is indicative of possible incest. In those families where wives are battered, it is not uncommon for them to suffer marital rape as well and for the children to be incestuously assaulted. According to Russell's (1986) and Walker's (1984) research studies, a high percentage of battered women were themselves incestuously abused as children. Incest history puts women at greater risk for revictimization experiences, both within and outside of the family. Family violence should be considered a risk factor for incest occurrence.

Other family behavior patterns may lead one to suspect incest. Some incest survivors "divorce" themselves from their family and refuse to have any contact as a means of protecting themselves from further abuse and harmful family interactions. The divorces are so complete in some cases that the survivors maintain their privacy by moving away from their family of origin, by not listing their addresses and phone numbers, by changing their surnames and/or by denying that they have a family. They often seek out substitute families, either through marriage or with friends, or give up on families altogether. Some survivors don't go to the extreme of stopping all contact but are selective about which family members they see or set stringent limitations or conditions on family interactions.

Fear or avoidance of a particular member of the family or refusal to have any contact with him or her is often associated with abuse experience. So too is the refusal to allow children to interact with that family member or a tendency to allow contact only with close supervision. A contradictory response, leaving a child totally unsupervised and/or neglected, may make the child especially vulnerable to sexual involvement with another family member.

Finally, since multiple incest is so common, disclosure of incest by one family member may well offer evidence that incest has occurred between other family members.

THE AFTEREFFECTS OF INCEST

Incest has been found to impact the victim intrapsychically and interpersonally. For ease of presentation, the intrapsychic and interpersonal effects will be categorized into the following six groupings: (1) emotional reactions; (2) self-perceptions; (3) physical/somatic effects; (4) sexual effects; (5) interpersonal relating and functioning; and (6) social functioning.

The Initial Effects

Initial incest aftereffects and their symptoms develop at the time of the abuse or shortly thereafter (within two years of termination of abuse, using the criteria developed by Browne and Finkelhor, 1986). They may be transient and remit over time either spontaneously or with assistance of some sort. Alternatively, as the child develops they may persist and become long-term or may develop in delayed fashion.

Emotional Reactions. Anxiety, fear, confusion, guilt, anger, and depression along with loss and grief reactions are common emotional effects associated with ongoing incest or its immediate aftermath. These feelings may be absent at the beginning of the activity, particularly when the sexual behavior is presented slowly and gently and when the child has been misled about the activity. In those cases where the abuse is forcefully committed with no tenderness and no attention to the relationship, the child is likely to experience the immediate fear and anxiety found in other types of sexual assault. In either case, she will probably show symptoms of depression, including sadness, lethargy, and concentration and memory impairment, along with related feelings of guilt and confusion.

The anxiety and fear may show up in compulsive or ritualized behavior and phobias; sleep disturbances such as nightmares, night terrors, and fear of sleeping alone; perceptual distortions; dissociative reactions; mood swings; hypervigilance and hyperactivity. The fear may be related to a number of different aspects of the abuse — fear of being blamed, of not being believed, of being rejected, of causing the family to break up, of causing mother (or other family members) distress, or of physical injury or other retaliation by the perpetrator.

According to Green (1983), children caught in situations of chronic abuse with unpredictable and inconsistent caretaking develop a traumatic neurosis which greatly affects their emotional development. This neurosis includes ego disorganization and regression, narcissistic injury, and a painful affective state. These, in turn, activate primitive ego defense mechanisms and compulsions to repeat the trauma in an attempt to master it. Abused children often show signs of emotional and physical constriction such as frozen watchfulness as they attempt to deal with their painful emotions and to protect themselves from further abuse. Emotional shutdown, sometimes referred to as "emotional anesthesia" or an "arrest in the development of affect," characterizes the most severely traumatized children. In the worst case, the child may become psychologically dead and psychically closed off.

Self-Perceptions. An insidious effect of incest for many children is the erosion of a positive sense of self and the concomitant development of a negative identity. The secrecy, entrapment, and betrayal by a trusted family member, coupled with feelings of guilt and complicity, cause shame and stigma reactions. Some children compensate for and defend against these feelings by always trying to be good, in the belief that being good will make the abuse stop. This shame and stigma become compounded if the incest is disclosed and the child is blamed or disbelieved; these reactions cause the child additional feelings of isolation, worthlessness, or hopelessness. Further, as the child comes to realize that others her age have not had the same sexual experiences with family members, she may feel she is marked, disgusting, freakish, and unworthy of good attention from others. Powerful self schemata develop around these self-perceptions.

Some survivors have also described feeling powerful but in a malignant way. Their special relationship and favored status with the perpetrator and their parentified role in the family often give them influence beyond their years and can result in grandiose feelings. Taken together, the shame and grandiosity explain the development of a sense of negative power. These children learn that they can make or break the family with their terrible secret.

Emotional and social withdrawal, self-carelessness and risk-taking behavior, and self-defeating and self-injurious behavior may be the most obvious immediate manifestations of negative self-esteem.

Physical/Somatic Effects. These physical and somatic symptoms have been associated with sexual abuse: regressive behavior (e.g., bedwetting in a child who is already toilet trained); the sudden onset of diffuse aches and pains such as headaches, gastrointestinal, and genitourinary discomfort or pain; dissociation, fainting, and epileptic-like seizures; eating disorders, including loss or gain of appetite and weight; signs of depression and anxiety, such as lethargy, inability to concentrate, rashes, and phobias; signs of physical and genital trauma and infection; pregnancy; perceptual disturbances; fear and terror reactions, such as gaze aversion, frozen watchfulness, speech and movement inhibition, and the repetition of the trauma (either as victim or aggressor) in dreams, fantasies, play and with others; and sudden behavioral or personality change.

Sexual Effects. As previously discussed, the sexual effects of abuse may be exhibited in age-inappropriate awareness of or excessive curiosity about sexual activities, compulsive behavior such as masturbation and exhibitionism, repeated attempts to engage peers or adults in sex play, and sexually abusive behavior towards other (usually younger) children. Through these behaviors, the child may be attempting to resolve feelings (particularly anxiety) about the sexual abuse, exhibiting and discharging the overstimulation she has experienced or demonstrating an identification with the perpetrator. Yates (1982) has discussed how some children involved in intense, "stable state" long-term incest become eroticized by the experience. She notes that these children are easily aroused and find sexual activity pleasurable, which differentiates them from other children who engage in compulsive sex play to discharge their anxiety. This abnormal sexual responsiveness is in itself a problem because it affects psychosexual development and interpersonal relationships.

Some children react in just the opposite way and avoid any type of physical contact with others. Touch may be perceived as threatening and negative. These children may also have developed feelings of disgust about themselves and their bodies. They may feel that something about their bodies, their sexuality, or their sexual response caused the abuse and may be particularly confused about any feelings of sexual stimulation they experienced. Some survivors have described this as a feeling of self-betrayal and as a secondary secret associated with the incest. Often children react by blunting or dissociating from their bodily sensations or by engaging in self-injurious behavior to hurt themselves or call attention to their plight.

Interpersonal Relating. Many victims suffer a marked impairment in their ability to relate to and trust others within and outside of their families as a result of the betrayal inherent in the incest. In families where the child has been emotionally neglected as well as sexually abused, she is likely to show signs of withdrawal but be very needy and dependent. Her very isolation and neediness may make her an easy target for revictimization, further eroding her trust in others and her experience with non-exploitive relationships.

The eroticized child may have another set of difficulties. She is prone to relate to others sexually due to the conditioning she received in the incest. Her interpersonal relationships may be marked by others' keeping their distance from her due to discomfort or, alternatively, becoming involved with her sexually. This latter response frequently results in being revictimized.

The neediness of many victims is masked by parentified or compliant behavior. On the surface, such a child appears to be mature beyond her years. She is often charged with taking care of everyone else in the family while receiving little nurturance or attention for herself. While she may take on such a role because it is expected of her, it also provides her with some power, with a means of compensating for her badness, and of getting others to like her.

Some children act out their distrust by withdrawing from interpersonal and social contact or by becoming hostile, aggressive, and unmanageable. These feelings may be directed towards the perpetrator or towards others inside or outside of the family. This withdrawal can be extreme and is to be expected in those children who have suffered the most extreme forms of abuse with little or no adult support or soothing.

Social Functioning. The psychological overload inherent in situations of chronic abuse may potentially distort cognitive development and compromise a child's ability to learn. Some children develop memory and learning difficulties, concentration problems, and a shortened attention span. They may have associated behavior problems in school and problems socializing with other children. They may also show language and movement deficits.

Some survivors describe the opposite pattern of excelling at school and in relations with peers and teachers. For them, school represented a place where they could escape from and temporarily forget the incest. It was also a place to compensate for the incest by being good and by getting good attention from teachers and peers for exemplary behavior and performance.

Long-term Effects

Long-term aftereffects and their symptoms are defined as those which develop two years or more post-abuse (Browne & Finkelhor, 1986). They may be chronic manifestations of acute aftereffects or develop in a delayed fashion. Some appear and remit sporadically and rather spontaneously.

Emotional Reactions. The emotions associated initially with incest often persist over time but may fluctuate in continuity and intensity. Generalized anxiety and fear continue for many survivors, who report apprehen-

sion, anxiety attacks, sleep disturbance and nightmares, and various phobias including fears of other people, fear of enclosed places, fear of the
dark, etc. Anxiety and apprehension may become especially pronounced
around issues of sexuality and sexual functioning as the survivor moves
through adolescence and repressed or latent fears and anxieties come to
the fore.

Depression, an aftereffect that frequently becomes chronic, is seen in
self-damaging behavior and suicidal ideation and attempts. Some recent
empirical investigations have shown that rates of depression for abuse
victims are not significantly different from those found in the general
population; however, significant differences have been found repeatedly
between the two groups in terms of suicide attempts and behavior and self-
destructive wishes. Abuse victims are much more likely to consider or
attempt suicide and to engage in self-mutilating or other types of self-
harmful behavior (Briere & Runtz, 1986).

In adulthood, the abuse survivor may continue to feel helpless and
powerless, the powerlessness alternating at times with feelings of being
powerful but malignant. She may further report self-estrangement and
emotional deadness. Her detachment may be the extension of the defensive repression and suppression of feelings that she learned in childhood.
Additionally, it may be due to her fear that, if she does allow herself to feel,
the feelings (especially anger) will be so intense that she will victimize
others, go crazy, or cause others to abandon and reject her. Feelings of
emptiness may also be associated with loss and grief.

Self-Perceptions. A fairly consistent finding is that survivors' perceptions
of themselves are predominantly negative. Many have incorporated a
marked sense of badness and shame, a sense that something is wrong with
them, making them inherently unlovable. They feel stigmatized and different from others, marked by their incest experience. Related to this are
strong feelings of confusion. While many survivors blame themselves and
their very existence for having somehow provoked the incest, they also
have existential questions. They wonder, "Why me? Why did it happen to
me? How could someone who is supposed to love me do this to me?" In the
absence of information to the contrary, they answer this question in their
own disfavor: They assume that they did something to cause the abuse or
that something about them signaled to the perpetrator a willingness to
engage in a sexual relationship. Past lack of effective assistance and intervention unfortunately provides some substantiation for this position, for
someone would have helped them if they had not been so reprehensible
and responsible. The perpetrator's insinuations that the child liked/want-
ed/was to blame/would be blamed for the behavior are often taken as
additional substantiation.

Physical/Somatic Effects. Many physical and somatic effects are related to negative feelings about the self which are contained in or projected onto the body. Not infrequently, it will appear that the body is fighting itself. In keeping with the feelings of self-blame and self-hatred discussed above, many survivors feel betrayed and disgusted by their bodies; they both extend their self-hatred somatically and use their bodies to manifest these feelings. They may continue the injunctions they learned during the abuse to disregard their body state and their own needs. At the most extreme, some survivors are so alienated from their bodies that they do not experience impulses to eat, rest, or sleep and so deprive and abuse their bodies unmercifully.

Physical effects may be related to the type and locus of the abuse and be manifested directly or in conversion symptoms. The more trauma-specific effects are related to the breasts, thighs, buttocks, genitals, or genitourinary organs. These include discomfort, chronic pain, infection, unpredictable and unexplained feelings of stimulation, and fears and phobias about genitourinary organs and functioning. Some survivors were so sexually shamed and humiliated that it is very difficult for them to touch themselves or to undergo any type of medical procedure, particularly one of a surgical or gynecological nature. (This problem is discussed in more detail in Chapter 14.)

Some gastrointestinal and respiratory effects also relate specifically to the locus of the assault. Nausea, gagging, vomiting, and choking reactions may be due to being choked, to forced oral sex and the swallowing of semen. One of my clients described chronic feelings of nausea when brushing her teeth and an aversion to chewing gum with liquid in the center. The toothpaste foam and the liquid center were uncomfortable reminders of semen. Over the course of treatment, this particular aversion lessened.

Rectal discomfort, pain, hemorrhoids, constipation and diarrhea are associated with anal intercourse, enemas, or analingus. Less localized though nevertheless trauma-specific physical reactions include dissociative and conversion reactions occurring in an automatic fashion when specific stimuli or anxiety are experienced. One survivor complained of a sore index finger while working in therapy on the recovery of memories of her incest experience. As the memories emerged, so did the explanation for the sore finger: As part of the abuse, this woman was forced to digitally penetrate her father's anus. Her finger stopped hurting once the association was made.

More generalized physical effects are quite varied in nature. Anxiety and fear-related symptoms are among the most pronounced and include gastrointestinal disturbance and problems, respiratory distress, muscular tension, and stress problems such as migraine headaches, tempero-mandibular jaw (TMJ), high blood pressure, frozen joints (e.g., frozen pelvis or clenched fists), ringing in the ears, hyperalertness, and hypervigilance. Substance abuse of any sort usually provides a means of blunting or, conversely, of intensifying the pain while punishing oneself. Obesity and anorexia are additional signs of distress.

Effects on Sexual Functioning. The evidence suggests that incest strongly affects the later sexual behavior and experiences of many survivors; a high proportion seem to have developed sexual difficulties of one sort or another, although some have escaped essentially undamaged. This latter group has been described as sexually counterphobic by one sex therapist (O'Connor, 1986).

Many aspects of the incest experience can be sexually damaging, from the actual sexual behavior itself to its influence on the various components of intrapsychic and interpersonal development. According to Maltz and Holman (1987), the sexual repercussions of incest are evident in three major areas: (1) sexual emergence in early adulthood; (2) sexual orientation and preference; and (3) sexual arousal, response, and satisfaction. These authors note that other factors can affect sexuality:

> It is important to keep in mind that each woman's sexuality is affected by a variety of influences, such as biological drive, religious training, educational awareness, and social group. These influences can exert themselves powerfully on her sexual development. While a history of sexual abuse *can* constitute the most dramatic influence, conclusions about its strength must be tempered by these other factors. (p. 69)

In terms of *sexual emergence*, childhood sexual abuse creates a disruption in normal developmental tasks, including dating patterns and the development of intimate relationships. Survivors often describe being sexually "out of synch" and always in jeopardy of being more informed or of behaving in a sexually inappropriate fashion with their peers. During adolescence and beyond, whether the abuse has stopped or not, two predominant sexual styles emerge: Survivors tend to become socially and sexually withdrawn or indiscriminately sexually active. Some survivors find that they alternate between the two. Both styles can be seen as a way for the victim to achieve some control over her body and her sexuality. In either style, she may turn to drug and alcohol use to cope with her anxieties about sexuality.

The withdrawal response usually reflects negative emotions and self-concept, as well as fears about relationships, sexual feelings, and sexual activity. Social withdrawal and celibacy may be seen as a way to compensate for past "badness" and to avoid any sexual feelings.

The alternative style of unusually frequent sexual activity has many possible motivations. It may allow the survivor to own herself, to continue to feel special power over men and to use them sexually, or to get back at the abuser. On the other hand, sexually indiscriminate behavior may be intentionally self-destructive and self-degrading. It may result in a negative reputation, revictimization, unwanted pregnancies and abortions, and sexually transmitted diseases.

Several studies have documented that quite a high proportion of prostitutes were sexually abused as children. Prostitution may provide a means of acting out negative self-esteem and gaining some control. Myers (n.d.) described her experience in this way:

> I felt marked. I knew that, wherever I went, men would find me and abuse me. So, my attitude towards prostitution was, "Why not?" If I have to have sex . . . why not get something for it? I felt I deserved the money: other men were going to have to pay for every time my father had me. . . .
> Since I thought the only thing men wanted was sex, the only way I could see to get power in a relationship was by making them pay for it. . . . Prostitution was another way of expressing my rage, of getting back at all of them for what had been done to me. I thought I was ripping them off rather than the other way around. (p. 13)

In another variation of sexual development, survivors describe how their dating patterns and sexual activities were relatively trouble free until they became involved in a committed intimate relationship. At that point, they felt trapped in the relationship and into meeting sexual demands. When the young woman marries, the sexual activity is once again taking place with a relative, a fact which may cause sexual anxiety and the cessation of sexual feelings.

Whether childhood sexual abuse causes a change in a survivor's *sexual orientation and preference* is unclear, although surely it influences sexual development in many ways. Some survivors report that they believe their sexual abuse affected their sexual orientation while others do not. Maltz and Holman (1987) speculate that these women represent two different groups: women who are lesbian and who happen to be incest survivors, and women who are basically heterosexual or bisexual and who have experimented with female partners as part of their trauma reactions or healing process. Another group would seem to be survivors who are either bisexual or indiscriminate in choosing the sex of the partner, just as they are in choosing partners in general.

Lesbian incest survivors may find that the incest did not alter their preference for women; rather, it supported it. For some lesbians, however, the incest may have obscured their preference for female partners by conditioning them to sex with men. Some may have developed aversions to other women due to their rage at a mother who failed to protect them or due to mistrust and contempt projected onto all women for their perceived weakness.

Survivors who are basically heterosexual may choose to have women as their sexual partners because of their fear of men and their belief that they can only be safe from sexual abuse when with a woman. They may view all men as potential abusers and therefore as unsafe. Sex with another woman may further be a defense against fears and phobias about anything male, including secondary sex characteristics, body size, body hair, deep voice, penis and semen, all of which serve as painful reminders of the abuse and cause avoidance reponses. Incest treatment should help resolve sexual fears and allow the survivor a sexual preference based on choice rather than fear and avoidance.

In comparison studies, incest victims have been found to suffer more *sexual problems* than nonvictims. Sexual problems may have developed at the time of the abuse or relatively soon afterward or may surface later in life. Schover, Friedman, Weiler, Heiman and LoPiccolo (1980, 1982) have outlined six categories of sexual difficulties and dysfunctions* which a colleague and I (Sprei & Courtois, 1988) found useful in discussing the sexual problems experienced by survivors: (1) desire disorders; (2) arousal disorders; (3) orgasmic disorders; (4) coital pain; (5) frequency and satisfaction difficulties; and (6) qualifying information.

Desire disorders are divided into two areas, both of which are common for incest survivors: (1) low sexual desire where desire is inhibited and results in a low frequency of sexual activity, and (2) aversion to sex characterized by such negative emotions as helplessness, fear, shame, and disgust. Some survivors avoid sex due to the negative conditioning and residual fear of the past abuse. They have fears associated with being coerced or terrorized, of being out of control of their bodily reactions, of being in physical pain, or of doing things that were once repulsive to them. Sexual activity has the potential to stimulate memories that are highly negative or those which are pleasurable yet filled with shame and guilt. Certain smells, positions, activities, and words may be aversive, with oral sex most frequently cited as problematic. As Maltz and Holman noted: " . . . negative conditioning is very strong in survivors because the sexual abuse usually constituted their first experience with overt sexual stimulation, and their negative feelings were reinforced through the repetition of the sexual abuse" (1987, p. 76).

Arousal disorders involve the ability to become sexually aroused and to perform sexually. Lubrication difficulties, including partial or complete failure to attain or maintain lubrication-swelling response throughout the sex act and a lack of sensation or feeling in the vaginal or pelvic area, are

---

*The terms disorder and dysfunction are used here with the understanding that they developed in response to traumatic sexualization and therefore should be understood either as effects associated with trauma or as survivor skills that were functional for the victim.

disorders which may inhibit sexual functioning for incest survivors. Feelings of arousal may be threatening because they remind the survivor of her negative experiences and so cause feelings of conflict and disgust.

Orgasmic disorders are common. They constitute a response to the fear of being out of control or a manifestation of or defense against guilt and anxiety associated with sexual pleasure. Primary or secondary anorgasmia or orgasm achieved only with masturbation is typical. Masturbation is "safe" because it does not involve trusting another person or relinquishing control. Even so, self-stimulation may be too threatening for the survivor who is unable to touch herself or to perceive her own sexuality as anything but dirty and shameful.

Coital pain includes: dyspareunia, defined as pain located in the genital area that occurs during the sexual act; vaginismus, the conditioned involuntary phobic response which causes muscle spasms which interfere with coitus; and other pain, such as lower back pain which is exacerbated by sexual activity. These problems have been linked to feelings of shame, self-hatred, and guilt, and to trauma associated with intercourse, making incest survivors likely candidates for such difficulties. Pain may also be due to actual physical injuries suffered during the abuse.

Frequency and satisfaction difficulties are prevalent, showing widely divergent and alternating patterns. As discussed above, some survivors are totally celibate, while others are hypersexual. Some alternate between periods of abstinence on the one hand and compulsive and/or promiscuous sexual activity on the other. Whatever their sexual patterns, many survivors report not being able to feel any sexual satisfaction or only feeling it sporadically.

Qualifying information refers to a number of other factors which may have an impact on sexual functioning. For survivors, post-traumatic stress reactions and any other negative conditioning associated with the abuse can impair the ability to function sexually. Intrusive/reexperiencing symptoms such as flashbacks or memories can be triggered by sexual behaviors, positions, feelings, sounds, and smells. These triggers and the anxiety they generate usually result in a cessation of sexual arousal or pleasure and involuntary responses. For instance, one of my clients described spontaneously and involuntarily throwing her husband out of bed the first time they attempted intercourse, which triggered an intense and terrifying flashback to her childhood abuse. Her abuse experience had been totally repressed prior to this event.

Denial/numbing symptoms such as depersonalization, derealization, and dissociation may allow the survivor to be sexual but not be present. She may find that she is unable to allow herself to experience feelings of stimulation and intimacy. This behavior has been described as "spectatoring" in the sex therapy literature. The survivor may also be so conditioned to attend to her partner's sexual arousal and pleasure that she does not focus on her own and has no knowledge of her own sexual responsiveness.

Other cognitive or automatic symptoms, such as hyperalertness, the inability to relax, insomnia, phobic avoidance of situations that arouse memories of the trauma, or exacerbation of symptoms on exposure to situations that resemble the traumatic event, also impede sexual functioning. Several other factors have been found to have a bearing on sexual functioning: confused sexual orientation and preference; sexually deviant behavior such as promiscuity and prostitution; increased vulnerability towards sexual and/or physical revictimization; the tendency towards reenacting the trauma by victimizing or abusing others; instability, mistrust and abuse in intimate relationships; and substance abuse.

Sexual difficulties are certainly related to difficulties in the next category, interpersonal relating.

Interpersonal Relating. Concerns pertaining to relationships have four variations: general relationship difficulties with both men and women; problems in intimate and/or committed relationships; problems with parents and other family members and with authority figures; and problems in parenting. Some of the more common relationship patterns were described in the previous two chapters so they will be presented in somewhat abbreviated fashion here. (Relationship difficulties are often in evidence in the therapy process and relationship. See Chapter 11 for a discussion of the therapy relationship.)

Difficulty trusting others due to the past betrayal by one or more family members is at the core of problems in interpersonal relating. The attitude that many survivors hold is: "If I couldn't trust my family, who can I trust? No one is trustworthy." Unfortunately, this conclusion becomes self-fulfilling if the survivor does not come into contact with others are are honorable or if she is revictimized. Survivors also may not have had the opportunity to develop relationship skills in their families and may relate according to the role they played in family interactions.

Many survivors characterize their relationships as one-way, empty, superficial, guarded, idealized, conflictual, or sexualized. They bring their feelings about others, including fear, disillusionment, mistrust, overvaluation, devaluation, and hostility, to bear in any interaction. Some feelings are gender-specific and are often directed at authority figures. For instance, the incest survivor who had a hostile or estranged relationship with her mother may project her feelings onto all women. Similarly, the survivor whose hostility is primarily directed towards a male perpetrator may project similar feelings onto other men. Feelings about others interact with feelings the survivor has about herself and her abuse experience to influence both her ability to relate and the quality of her relationships.

Incest survivors seem to have special difficulties in intimate and/or committed relationships. These relationships require trust and openness that are experienced as threatening rather than gratifying. Not infrequently, survivors describe feeling trapped within intimate relationships and unable to allow closeness to develop beyond a certain point. These feelings are exemplified by several of my clients who are unable to wear their wedding bands, which to them symbolize being trapped and out of control rather than being committed. Several studies have found that heterosexual survivors remain unmarried in disproportionate numbers to a non-abused comparison group. Possibly this is due to difficulties developing and maintaining intimate relationships along with mistrust of men.

Abuse dynamics may be reflected in choice of partner and in the subsequent interactions. Although men may be feared, they are often idealized and overvalued. The survivor may seek out a dominant and/or older man who can take care of her and provide her with protection. Or she may continue in her caretaking patterns and find an immature partner who requires her attention but can give her little in return. Paradoxically, yet somewhat predictably, a number of incest survivors end up in abusive relationships with others who, like themselves, were abused or neglected as children. Their partners, whether male or female, are often abusive to or neglectful of them and so recapitulate their early family experience while reinforcing a negative sense of self-worth and a mistrust of others.

Conflicted relationships with parents and siblings most often continue into adulthood, particularly when the incest was of the classic nuclear family type. Hostility and rage may characterize the relationship with father, mother, or both, and may extend to all members of the family. The survivor may continue in familiar roles and relational patterns with the family or try to establish some distance. In some cases, family interactions continue to be noxious and to include abuse (of the survivor, her children, or other family members), so that she finds that she has no option but to distance herself or refuse any further contact.

Difficulties with parents can also extend to in-laws and authority figures. Survivors may project their feelings about their own parents onto in-laws and other relatives and onto anyone in a position of authority or perceived as an authority figure. Family relationship patterns and unresolved difficulties are continued with new players.

Relationship difficulties due to past abuse frequently affect the survivor's ability to adequately parent her children. The individual who experienced a poor relationship with her parents often repeats the familiar mode of relating with her offspring. She may have little understanding of or skill in parenting and her own unresolved abuse experience may prevent her from developing emotional and physical closeness with her children. This distance may set the stage for further abuse. An additional issue relating to poor parenting has to do with early and/or repeated pregnancies. Young mothers often do not have the knowledge, skills, patience, or support to contend with the demands of children, especially when they themselves are immature and were emotionally deprived. On the other hand, some survivors are good and even exceptional parents, driven by their determination not to do to their children what was done to them.

Parenting issues may be gender-related: Survivor/mothers may harbor *fears about* their sons, especially as sons mature and develop secondary sex characteristics. These women may *fear for* their daughters or feel rivalrous towards them. They may cope with these feelings by being overly distant from their children or overly protective of them. In some cases, these emotions lead to child abuse and, in the worst case, murderous impulses towards the child. Green (1982) described a case where a decompensated survivor developed filicidal impulses towards her daughter when she reached the age at which the mother had been abused. The filicidal impulse seemed at once the urge to protect the child from abuse and a traumatic reenactment in which the mother identified with the aggressor.

Social Effects. Social functioning of survivors shows wide variability, ranging from isolation, rebellion and antisocial behavior to overfunctioning and compulsive social interaction. The personal disillusionment and interpersonal disturbance that accompany human-induced victimization may cause an alienation that pervades all aspects of the survivor's life. According to van der Kolk (1987a), many people who were traumatized as children suffer from a later "disorder of hope." Victimization has also been described as a "break in the human lifeline" which may lead to the experiencing of one's social world as dead or constricted (Krystal, 1984). A minority of survivors experience this deadness and maintain a life of total mistrust and withdrawal. These women might be labeled as paranoid, hostile, antisocial, and/or eccentric in their communities. This emotional deadness might be present even in someone who outwardly appears to be functioning fairly well. One of my clients describes herself as flat and with no color while the world around her is vibrant and colorful. She has been quite self-abusive in her survival mechanisms and described self-abuse as a way to get some color. Her specified therapy goal was to learn to have color in her life in more positive ways.

Some survivors are less extreme in orientation but mistrust and rebel against any authority or organization they perceive to be oppressive. These women might vent the rage they feel about their abuse in social causes and social movements. A less pervasive disillusionment is at play for many others. Russell (1986) found a significant relationship between incest victimization and religious defection in adulthood, a finding which pertained to my research sample as well. Survivors who defected described a lack of faith in a just and loving deity and an unwillingness to accept a male god and/or a religion oriented towards and dominated by males.

An impaired ability to function well either occupationally or socially characterizes some survivors. The disruption of developmental tasks, chronic anxiety and depression with or without impulsive and hostile characteristics, low self-esteem, substance abuse, mistrust of others, social withdrawal and post-traumatic stress responses affect the survivor's functioning on the job and in the community at large. Tomarchio (n.d.) has hypothesized that vocational development is one of the developmental tasks interrupted or distorted by child sexual abuse. The effects of incest on career development and occupational and social functioning have not yet been adequately investigated.

In contrast to survivors with impaired functioning, some women function quite well. They extend the childhood pattern of successful school functioning to their social, occupational, and familial functioning as adults. Often, they are outstanding in the community, as workers and as parents. Their success is frequently enhanced by survivor skills learned in childhood: scouting behavior or perceptiveness about the needs and behavior of those around them, pleasing behavior towards others especially those in authority, caretaking of the needs of others, and the ability to handle multiple stressors and responsibilities successfully. Summit (1986) has noted that many practitioners in the helping professions were formerly victimized children. A similar observation has been made by researchers studying survivors of other types of family abuse, notably adult children of alcoholics (Wood, 1987).

Even though these women are successful when assessed on a number of criteria, many describe themselves as feeling disconnected from their skills and accomplishments and as impostors waiting to be found out. These "superwomen" types are susceptible to burnout and other stress-related maladies due to the self-neglect that usually accompanies their overfunctioning. Herman and Schatzow (1987) observed a similar pattern in the survivors they studied:

> A striking characteristic of many . . . was the contrast between the relatively high levels of competence and achievement evident in their working lives and the painfully constricted, isolated, or chaotic and self-destructive character of their intimate relationships. Moreover, though many functioned effectively in a caretaking role on the job or as parents, deficiencies in self-care were often remarkable. (p. 3)

Studies of women involved in antisocial and deviant behavior (e.g., prostitution, drug abuse, delinquent and criminal behavior, involvement with criminals) and studies of inpatient, outpatient deinstitutionalized, and chronically victimized populations are remarkably consistent in the finding that a high percentage have experienced childhood sexual abuse. Incest can definitely be a factor in the development of antisocial behavior and of self-destructive and revictimizing behavior. Additional research is needed on these populations. Hopefully, acknowledgment of the significance of abuse experience and treatment of emotional reactions will allow these survivors to live a less marginal and impeded life.

Some survivors function moderately well and do not fit into either of the patterns described above. Still others alternate between periods of functioning competently or times of falling apart, and others find their lives disrupted by delayed aftereffects. Reexposure to events which resemble the trauma may cause an upsurge of disabling symptoms. The following case description is a rather dramatic example of this type of impairment.

I interviewed a survivor who had had complete amnesia for her violent incest experience at the hands of her father. Her social and occupational development had been exemplary—she had been well-regarded in her community for her civic involvement and she had held a high-level administrative position in social services in her state.

When I met her, she was unemployed, virtually homeless, and desperate. An attempted rape had stimulated total recall of her incest experience, along with the emergence of multiple personality disorder and a host of debilitating and terrifying intrusive symptoms. She had had a personality switch after the assault and was amnesic for several weeks when she "awakened" to find herself in Washington. In our meeting, she was stunned and disoriented about what had happened to her.

A final *social effect* is what has come to be known as revictimization. From the available data, it seems that victims of incest/child sexual abuse are much more likely than nonvictims to suffer sexual revictimization both inside and outside of the family (Runtz, 1987; Russell, 1986; Walker, 1984). Runtz suggests that factors specific to child sexual abuse, particularly the traumatic sexualization, combined with overvaluation and overidealization of men, impaired ability to identify others who are trustworthy, and learned helplessness, render abuse victims vulnerable to repeat episodes of sexual exploitation.

SEVERITY OF EFFECTS BY TYPE OF ABUSE

The characteristics of incest most associated with serious afteraffects have been the subject of speculation since the earliest clinical writing on this topic. The characteristics of primary interest are:

- *Duration and frequency*: Incest which occurs more frequently and is of longer duration is believed to be more harmful than short-term, less frequent abuse.
- *Type of sexual activity*: Sexual abuse involving penetration of any

sort is considered to be more harmful than that involving other forms of sexual behavior.

- *Use of force and aggression*: The more force or violence used, the more serious the consequences.
- *Age at onset*: The influence of the child's age at onset has been debated. Some researchers predict that younger age of onset causes more damage; others that younger age provides some measure of insulation for the child and that the older child will be more damaged.
- *Age, gender, and relationship of the perpetrator*: The more closely related the victim and perpetrator and the wider age difference between them, the greater the damage. Also, abuse perpetrated by a male is believed to be more damaging than that by a woman.
- *Passive submission or willing participation on the part of the child*: The child who goes along with the wishes of the perpetrator and submits without struggle or who willingly participates is theorized to suffer more negative effects in the long run.
- *Overt or disclosed incest with lack of assistance*: The lack of assistance when the incest is known or disclosed is believed to be more damaging than incest which remains hidden.
- *Parental reaction*: Negative parental reactions upon discovery or reporting of incest are believed to cause further trauma for the child.
- *Institutional response*: Negative, stigmatizing response or ineffective assistance on the part of social service and law enforcement agencies contributes to trauma.

Browne and Finkelhor (1986) reviewed the available empirical studies on effects by type of abuse and concluded:

> From this review . . . it would appear that there is no contributing factor that all studies agree on as being consistently associated with a worse prognosis. However, there are trends in the findings. The preponderance of studies indicate that abuse by fathers or stepfathers has a more negative impact than abuse by other perpetrators. Experiences involving genital contact seem to be more serious. Presence of force seems to result in more trauma for the victim. In addition, when the perpetrators are men rather than women, and adults rather than teenagers, the effects of sexual abuse appear to be more disturbing. . . . When families are unsupportive of the victims, and/or victims are removed from their homes, the prognosis has also been shown to be worse. . . .
>
> Concerning the age of onset, the more sophisticated studies found no significant relation, especially when controlling for other factors; however, the relation between age and trauma is especially complex and has not yet been carefully studied. In regard to the impact of revealing the abuse, as opposed to the child keeping it a secret, current studies also suggest no

simple relation. Of all these areas, there is the least consensus on the effect of duration of abuse on impact. (p. 75)

These findings are largely consistent with those reported by Russell (1986). In addition to the types reported above, Russell found that abuse of longer duration and multiple abuse correlated with greater trauma in her sample. Two recent studies on clinical populations suggest an interrelation between age at onset, duration, violence, and multiple abuse on the one hand, and the type of ego defense used and severity of symptoms, on the other. Herman and Schatzow (1987) found that earlier age of onset and/or violent abuse correlated with the use of repression as a defense mechanism and resulted in severe symptomatology in adulthood. Walsh (1986a) found that earlier age of onset was correlated with multiple abuse and that repression was the major defensive operation used by these victims. Although these findings are preliminary, they suggest that younger children may seem asymptomatic because of their use of more primitive defenses. These studies propose directions for future research on these factors.

To summarize: Child sexual abuse has been found to affect the victim's personality development and every major life sphere, either at the time of the incest and/or later in life. The severity of aftereffects is not uniform and varies by individual circumstance. In a clinical sample, the aftereffects are by definition more serious than in the population in general and have become symptoms associated with an array of mental health disturbances. Therapeutically, these disturbances need to be recognized as consequences of the untreated original effects of the abuse. Treatment must therefore be directed towards addressing the original trauma as well as its initial and chronic aftereffects.

CHAPTER 7

Theories Pertaining to Aftereffects and Treatment

W HAT THEORIES GUIDE our treatment of incest survivors? Here we examine incest and its aftermath from four different theoretical models: feminist, traumatic stress or victimization, self developmental, and loss theory. The treatment approach described in the following chapters is derived from these four theories. Although each provides a distinct perspective on the understanding and treatment of the victim/survivor, the theories also complement one another.

FEMINIST THEORY

Feminism has brought family violence and violence against women to public awareness. Were it not for the feminist movement, these abuses would continue to remain hidden, their victims enshrouded in the pain of their isolation. Rape was the first form of violence against women to be addressed. The predominant myths about rape were identified and challenged: Rape was clearly labeled as sexual victimization perpetrated on a woman for which she was not to blame. Power and degradation were identified as the predominant motivations of rape, the sexual violation providing the *modus operandi* (Brownmiller, 1975). As rape issues were publicized and more women sought help, they divulged other forms of sexual violence, some of it outside the family (e.g., sexual harassment), but the majority perpetrated within the family by male relatives. It began to appear that the family was the breeding ground for women's sexual exploitation in the larger society, a radical formulation when it was first made, but one that is holding up as more is learned about incest and other forms of domestic violence.

The feminist perspective extends beyond the family unit to examine the societal perspective and its influence on the development of incest. The recent documentation that child sexual abuse/incest (particularly of female children by adult males) has been accepted yet unspoken in many cultures (Rush, 1980) and findings regarding its high prevalence (Russell, 1986) have led feminists to conclude that it is an endemic societal manifestation of the power imbalance between the sexes (Herman, 1987; Russell, 1986). From this perspective, men are conditioned into roles of power and domination with regard to females, who are conditioned to be passive and dependent. Incest is seen as the tragic and most extreme manifestation of this power imbalance and a within-the-family conditioning of women to their roles in society.

Instead of receiving nurturance geared towards their full development as individuals, girls are subjugated and abused based on their gender. They learn from an early age that to be female means to be less valued, less important, and sexually used. As Brickman (1984) so forcefully stated:

> The immediate effects of incest as described by . . . victims is that they are driven out of their bodies. . . . In this manner their bodies become the property of men, and females are deeply and seriously alienated from the one piece of territory every human being possesses, her own body. . . . Incest victims learn at an early age that sex is for male pleasure, for the benefit of men. For her, sexuality is connected to pain and humiliation; it is something to endure. (p. 66)

Feminists challenged a main tenet of the psychoanalytic tradition, the oedipal theory, as a misconstruction. They argued that Freud's original theory (his seduction theory, which has since been relabeled the trauma theory by Miller, 1984) was accurate and that its replacement was nothing short of a coverup which denied the reality of the abuse while excusing the perpetrators (Rush, 1977). They argued against the sexism of psychoanalysis, best exemplified by the position of blaming the child and the colluding mother for the development of incest while exonerating the abusing father. And they held that the oedipal theory had the effect of perpetuating incest and its negative effects rather than ameliorating them by reinforcing dynamics of denial, disbelief, and blame of the victim.

Incest was reconceptualized as victimization with high traumatic potential for the exploited child. As a form of rape it was and is viewed as the ultimate violation of the self short of homicide. Its occurrence within the family by a supposedly trustworthy individual was seen as compounding its traumatic impact and its potential to seriously injure the developing child.

Feminism has as its focus *women's reality*. It stresses the subjective knowledge of the individual and seeks to validate women's experience in a world where the experience of men has been held as the standard. In terms of incest, this means that a victim's experience is central and must be accepted and validated (Brickman, 1984). Feminism also offers a conceptualization of symptom formation as a creative adaptation to highly negative circumstances rather than as pathology. Symptoms are viewed as survival skills that allowed the victim to cope with the incest and its aftermath. Subsequently, these same coping mechanisms may have become maladaptive, spawning secondary elaborations and associated life difficulties. The work of therapy is to validate the reality of the original injury, to identify survival skills, and to dismantle them so that the injury can be healed and the arrested process of development completed. The survivor is seen as the authority on her own experience, which she is assisted to explore. Because her control was negated so definitively through the incest, treatment is geared to helping her reestablish a sense of personal power.

TRAUMATIC STRESS OR VICTIMIZATION THEORY

The aftereffects of incest have been shown to resemble those of other traumatic life events and to have physiological as well as psychological manifestations. Figley (1985) offered concrete definitions of trauma and traumatic reactions. "Trauma" represents "an emotional state of discomfort and stress resulting from memories of an extraordinary, catastrophic experience which shattered the survivor's sense of invulnerability to harm" (p. xviii). Traumatic stress reactions are the first indications of the presence of a trauma and are natural behaviors and emotions which occur during the catastrophe. "Post-traumatic stress reactions" are defined as "*a set of conscious and unconscious behaviors and emotions associated with dealing with the memories of the stressors of the catastrophe and immediately afterwards. . . . A post-traumatic stress disorder* is the clinical manifestation of problems associated with trauma induced during the catastrophe and represented by the post-traumatic stress reactions" (p. xix, author's italics).

That incest is potentially an experience of catastrophic proportions which shatters a victim's sense of invulnerability to harm is now well-documented. Unfortunately, as we noted above, it is not an experience that is out of the ordinary in terms of its prevalence; however, it *is* extraordinary to the victim who cannot escape it. Finkelhor and Browne (1985) analyzed the dynamics of child sexual abuse/incest to determine which factors are most related to its traumatic impact. They postulated four trauma-causing factors or "traumagenic dynamics": traumatic sexualization, betrayal, powerlessness, and stigmatization. They wrote:

> These traumagenic dynamics are generalized dynamics not necessarily unique to sexual abuse; they occur in other kinds of trauma. But the conjunction of these four dynamics in one set of circumstances is what makes the trauma of sexual abuse unique, different from such childhood traumas as the divorce of a child's parents or even being the victim of physical child abuse.

> These dynamics alter children's cognitive and emotional orientation to the world, and create trauma by distorting children's self-concept, world view, and affective capacities. (pp. 530–531)

Traumatic sexualization refers to a "process in which a child's sexuality (including both sexual feelings and sexual attitudes) is shaped in a developmentally inappropriate and interpersonally dysfunctional fashion as a result of the sexual abuse" (p. 531). *Betrayal* refers to "the dynamic by which children discover that someone on whom they were vitally dependent has caused them harm" (p. 531). Children experience betrayal not only when they are sexually violated, but also when the non-offending parent remains silent or joins with other family members, as well as any others, who disbelieve the child or fail to offer assistance.

Powerlessness refers to "the dynamic of rendering the victim powerless . . . the process in which the child's will, desires, and sense of efficacy are continually contravened" (p. 532). *Stigmatization* refers to "the negative connotations — e.g., badness, shame, and guilt — that are communicated to the child around the experience and that then become incorporated into the child's self-image" (p. 532).

Finkelhor and Browne are careful to point out that the dynamics are not narrowly defined; in fact, each can be seen as a clustering of harmful influences with a common theme. Further, reactions to abuse are multiply determined and only rarely reliant upon one factor or dynamic. In determining the effects of the abuse, the contributions of pre- and post-abuse situations must be analyzed along with the four traumagenic dynamics.

In Chapter 6, the aftereffects of incest were described as they manifest at the time of the incest and then later in life. These effects meet the *Diagnostic and Statistical Manual-III-R* (American Psychiatric Association, 1987) criteria for the diagnostic categories of post-traumatic stress disorder, acute, and PTSD, chronic and delayed (see Chapter 9). Victims experience a host of highly variable effects which differ by intensity and degree and which frequently alternate between symptoms that are emotionally numbing and constricting and those of the intrusive/reexperiencing sort. Children have been found to cope somewhat differently with traumatic events than do adults because of their immaturity. Incest victims, as children, show symptomatology in age- and stage-specific ways. Immediate efforts at remediation help, but, as Terr (1983) has demonstrated, aftereffects can be long-lasting even then.

Symptoms have been found to most closely resemble those found acutely in the rape trauma syndrome, including fear, guilt, sleep and eating disturbances, genitourinary difficulties, anxiety and depression (Courtois & Watts, 1982; Goodwin, 1985). The parallel symptoms are understandable in that incest, like rape, is human-induced, premeditated, involves sexual violation and ultimately a violation of the victim's selfhood. But the hallmark of incest is that it is rape perpetrated repeatedly by the same related individual(s) which intensifies over time. Goodwin (1985, p. 159) commented: Incest victims . . . "have not been exposed to a single, discrete, overwhelming incident but to hundreds of assaults, spanning years and developmental phases, and to the concealment, lack of empathy or protection, and hypocrisy that fill the interstices between assaults." Because of this, incest aftereffects also resemble those found in situations of chronic trauma involving conditions of captivity and terror. Herman (1987) and others have likened it to concentration camp internment, where the victim is not only victimized but reduced to absolute emotional and physical dependency on the captors. The captor's ultimate end is to achieve total control over the victim and her responses and for the victim to become a willing participant and to enjoy the abuse. To achieve this end, many incest offenders take great pains to sexually stimulate their victims to arousal and orgasm to establish "proof" that they "really wanted it." Victims are thus often brainwashed into believing that they are to blame.

Incest has yet another hallmark—its perpetration not by a stranger but by a parent or other relative who is a member of the victim's primary affiliative group, the family. It is a form of child abuse perpetrated within the family setting on an immature child, adding to the potential for distress. All of the characteristics of the family process described in Chapter 3 entrap the child in the situation while disconfirming both the reality of the abuse and her reaction to it.

Speigel (1986), who discussed the double bind inherent in much intrafamilial abuse, had this to say:

> Severe trauma inflicted by parents, as opposed to that inflicted by strangers, has elements of a macabre double bind. A beating or rape by a stranger, traumatic as it is, is in some ways easier to assimilate psychologically. It is a tragic event imposed from outside, seemingly for no reason. But rape by a father or physical abuse imposed by a mother has the bizarre quality of combining intense and longed-for attention from the parent with pain and humiliation. Furthermore, frequently the parents rationalize the behavior by telling children that it is "for your own good," will "whip you into shape," will "teach you what you need to know about life," and so on. Thus, these patients are left with intense and irreconcilable feelings, pain, fear, and humiliation on one hand and on the other the desire for something positive from their parents and the half-belief that the mistreatment is indeed for their own good. Furthermore, when such events happen in childhood, the victims have little ability to understand independent causation. They think in concrete terms and necessarily interpret what is done to them in light of their own conduct and role in eliciting it. They are made helpless to control both their own body and their own internal state. . . . Such patients become structurally or spatially fragmented, unable to incorporate their history of trauma and conflicting parental messages into an acceptable unified sense of self. The defense against trauma becomes itself a source of distress. (pp. 69–70)

Like the feminist model, traumatic stress theory posits that traumatic symptoms are not in and of themselves pathological; rather, they develop as natural and healthy responses to out-of-the-ordinary catastrophic events. In some instances they remit fairly quickly or over a short time; in others they persist and become chronic; in still others they develop in delayed fashion. Typically, these symptoms alternate between those which are numbing and emotionally constricting and which serve to contain and blunt reactions, on the one hand, and those which are intrusive and reexperiencing and which cause a vivid return of the trauma and its associated painful emotions, on the other. Over time, these symptoms (whether of the numbing/constricting or intrusive/reexperiencing sort) give rise to other problems, which have come to be known as secondary problems or secondary elaborations. According to Krugman (1986, p. 128): "Secondary elaboration is a characterological adaptation to traumatization that includes depression, avoidance of intimacy, and 'relational distortions.' These features are most evident when the trauma has been neither acknowledged nor treated as such." The chronic nature of most incest allows the child little time for recovery or integration. The child's energy is spent staving off further assault and contending with aftereffects and their elaborations. A post-traumatic decline—"... an impoverishment of activity and role function secondary to psychological constriction and phobic avoidance" (Krugman, p. 128)—is evident in many of these children.

The original effects, their secondary elaborations, and associated difficulties are brought to treatment. According to traumatic stress/victimization theory, the trauma must be treated directly in conjunction with its symptoms and secondary problems. Although short-term treatment models are available for traumatic stress (Horowitz, 1986), the chronic nature of intrafamilial abuse, its impact on the victim's personality development, and the severity and intensity of symptomatology typically require treatment of longer duration. Furthermore, because incest is human-induced, it disturbs the individual's ability to trust others and to develop a positive self-concept. Treatment must insure a safe and consistent atmosphere and therapeutic relationship from which to explore the trauma and its impact. The goal of treatment is the abreaction of the trauma and the improvement of associated problems, including the development of positive affiliative bonds and the resumption of development arrested by the abuse.

SELF DEVELOPMENTAL THEORY

Incest may well be the most destructive form of child abuse. Anna Freud (1981, p. 34) wrote, "Where the chances of harming a child's normal developmental growth are concerned, it ranks higher than abandonment, neglect, physical maltreatment or other forms of abuse." It is interesting to note that while the impact of child sexual abuse on development is regularly mentioned in the abuse literature, abuse is hardly mentioned in the developmental literature. Russell (1985) has commented that the deleterious impact of incest on human development in general and the psychology of women in particular has yet to be fully acknowledged.

Authorities on child abuse of all sorts agree that abuse by family members, when chronic, inevitably alters the full development of the child. It involves the sacrifice of the self to the satisfaction or care of the family. It results in serious damage to the child's sense of self, often causing a fragmented identity to develop. Moreover, such chronic intrafamilial trauma causes a compounding and exacerbation of post-traumatic stress reactions. The sense of a "normal self" is lost as defenses and symptoms become integrated into the child's developing personality.

In general, child abuse involves a disregard for the child by the caregiver and gross inconsistencies of care and interaction. Care often alternates in an unpredictable pattern with hostility and abuse (Steele, 1986). Typically, caretakers themselves were abused and use their children to shore up their fragile sense of selves. These parents can be conceptualized as suffering from post-traumatic adaptation (van der Kolk, 1984). They are characterized as being easily aroused to anger and anxiety and lacking in the ability to empathize with their offspring and to offer them secure attachment and soothing. This lack of empathy in the context of abuse is itself traumagenic and contributes to abuse across generations. According to van der Kolk:

> The earliest and possibly most damaging psychological trauma is the loss of a secure base. When caregivers who are supposed to be sources of protection and nurturance become simultaneously the main sources of danger, a child must maneuver psychologically to reestablish some sense of safety, often becoming fearfully and hungrily attached, unwillingly or anxiously obedient, and apprehensive lest the caregiver be unavailable when needed. (1987b, p. 32)

The child most often is left in an acute anxiety state and exhibits clinging behavior, hypervigilance, and constricted affect. The child does not develop a healthy sense of herself because her needs and her feelings are not encouraged or attended to; in a sense they fall by the wayside.

To survive, the child must resort to such primitive ego defenses as denial, projection, introjection, splitting, avoidance, and distancing. Since these same defenses are employed by the parents, their use is modeled and reinforced. They are most evident in terms of the child's object relations. The child's object world is distorted, with love, violence, sexuality and aggression fused (Krugman, 1986). The child splits the parent into the "good" and "bad" and introjects the parent as good despite his bad behavior. The split-off bad parent is attached to the self. The child identifies herself as bad and as deserving the parent's treatment, thereby maintaining the image of the good parent. Although this maneuver allows the child to maintain an illusion of safety and of being in control, it negatively affects self-esteem. Wood (1987) described this circumstance as applied to the adult child of the alcoholic; her description pertains to the adult incest survivor as well. She wrote:

> Instead of providing their children with support, encouragement, and unconditional regard, alcoholic and enabling spouses are likely to abuse, exploit, and neglect them. When children are hurt by their selfobjects instead of nurtured by them, the result is a severe disturbance of the internal object relationships that form the foundation of the self and extensive fragmentation (splitting) of the psyche that also weakens the self.
>
> First the "true," or nuclear self—when it feels itself threatened by the parents—retreats to a place of hiding in the unconscious. That is, it is "split off" from the central, conscious ego. Though the true self may make its existence known through acts of impulse or subjectively experienced longing, it is never allowed direct expression and remains alienated from, and misunderstood by, the conscious self. A "false self" arises to carry on conscious transactions with the external world and to provide the true self with the camouflage it feels it needs. Though the false self may contain many socially valued elements, and may realize a certain degree of success in academic and vocational pursuits, it is inherently unstable, and never feels entirely "real" to the adult child. Moreover, feelings of frustration, futility, and loneliness emanate from the true self, isolated as it is, and deprived of meaningful intrapsychic and interpersonal intercourse. These feelings periodically build up, overwhelm the adult child's capacity to split and repress, and become outright, conscious psychic pain. The erection of a false self also interferes with the struggle to separate and individuate, since it masks and weakens the parts of the self that are truly distinctive and that form the "lost heart of the self" necessary for the full realization of one's individuality. (pp. 67–68)

Incest and other forms of chronic child abuse interfere with the completion of the developmental tasks associated with each life stage (Erikson, 1980), beginning with the most basic task, trust versus mistrust. When abused by parents, children learn to mistrust in their most significant relationships. This is best exemplified by the survivor question, "If I couldn't trust my parents, who can I trust?" At subsequent stages, children are prone to develop a shamed sense of self, low self-esteem, identity diffusion, and difficulties in intimate relationships and productivity.

The clinician must be aware that while the trauma of chronic child abuse has high potential for a host of negative sequelae, individual variability is also very much in evidence. Some children fare far better than others due to their strength of character, their natural resiliency, the availability of other nurturing individuals in their lives, and interventions. A hopeful note is that, while the original abuse never can be undone, its effects are subject to modification and healing. Treatment involves the search for the "true self" and the gradual dismantling and dissolution of the "false self" that developed as protection. In Chapter 10 this is conceptualized as working with "the child within" or "finding the little girl." The survivor is urged to remember the trauma of the incest and to feel the emotions which were split off in order to survive the abuse ordeal. With the therapist she examines family rules and messages which served to reinforce the incest and to disconfirm her experience. She is assisted in extricating herself from the family pattern and her traumatic reenactments and encouraged to develop a more integrated, stable sense of self. According to Rieker and Carmen (1986), the abuse is recontextualized, allowing the survivor to restore accurate meanings and emotions to her past experience. The therapeutic environment is warm, responsive and open; it is deliberately made reliable and consistent to counter the inconsistency of the past. A safe environment is a necessity when one undertakes the work of self-development with traumatized individuals.

LOSS THEORY

Victimization of any sort involves loss — of control, of life assumptions, of a sense of safety in the world, and very often of the self as it was before the victimization. Victimized individuals often describe themselves as altered by the trauma — they conceptualize themselves as pre- and post-victimization selves (Bard & Sangrey, 1986). Benedek (1985), in discussing children and psychic trauma, took note of the fact that losses in human-induced violence may be overlooked because they are personal rather than property losses. The loss of self-esteem, sense of personal worth, and body integrity is often much less outwardly dramatic than the loss of home and property. And yet, it is so much more significant and profound.

The incest survivor loses a sense of possibilities. Many of the survivors I interviewed for my research told me that they felt the incest irreparably changed them and that they did not develop *as they might have been*. I was struck by the remarkable consistency with which 50 women described this loss to me. Survivors described themselves as feeling as though they have holes in themselves and in their development, as though they don't know where other people leave off and where they begin, and as so burdened with the demands of others that their own needs remain undefined.

A survivor might not recognize this lack of definition and development as loss because of the tendency for these areas to be overlooked in general and particularly in her family of origin. Yet she might be engaged in a compulsive pattern of seeking out lost objects and lost opportunities in a futile search for what was denied her in childhood. Repetition compulsions or traumatic reenactments put survivors at risk for continued bad relationships and for a life of searching for what was and continues to be unavailable. In order to heal, the survivor must accept her losses, stop trying to heal her family and stop the self-sacrifice entailed in the effort. Swink and Leveille (1986) offered this description of loss acceptance:

> As the former victim realizes that she usually cannot transform her family members(s) into the people she wants and needs, she must make a decision to stop trying to change them. This necessitates giving up the hope that she will someday get the mother/father/sister/brother that she has always needed. Giving up the hope is experienced as a huge loss even though the only losses are a fantasy, the old burden of responsibility for the family, and the frustration of trying to change something out of her control. She must grieve this loss. Then she must break old patterns with the family so that she refuses to be the scapegoat any more, refuses to be the martyr, or to be used and manipulated in other ways. She learns to say no to them. Often the pressure to return to them is so great, that for her own self-protection she must break all ties with the family—no longer attending family functions/ rituals, no longer having contact with the family. She will usually feel very guilty about this and the family will certainly promote her guilt; but she must take care of herself, not them any longer. Then she will feel free of the degradations, manipulations and abusiveness. (p. 136)

Accepting the loss means admitting the inability to control the circumstance. Paradoxically, attempts to control only contribute to more loss. As losses are accepted and the lack of control acknowledged, the pain associated with grief is experienced. The survivor grieves for the loss of her original self as well as for her lost family dreams. Survivors describe grieving for the little girl, lost good parents, lost childhood, lost security, etc. In a similar vein, it is necessary for her to mourn all of the losses brought on by the traumatic responses, their secondary elaborations, and any traumatic decline.

Grieving is a natural and painful process that leads to healing. During the process, the survivor must adjust to the loss, a process which can be quite discomforting. The structure of the familiar, no matter how dysfunctional, has changed and a new structure remains to be built to take its place. During this phase, the survivor is encouraged to look forward and not back and to see separation as allowing individuation and the development of a healthier, much less encumbered life. Emotional energy is withdrawn from past relationships and reinvested in the self and in the development of new relationships. This does not mean that the survivor no longer cares about her family but that she is separating from them to reclaim herself and her development.

Grieving is very much part of incest therapy and usually proceeds simultaneously with the experiencing of anger and outrage over past abuse and neglect. The survivor is encouraged to understand the pain as a natural consequence of the numerous losses inherent in incest and as a necessary but uncomfortable part of the healing process. The support of the therapist and empathic others is invaluable during this stage of the process.

In conclusion, four theoretical perspectives help us understand the incest response and direct our treatment. Incest is viewed as "having a gender" (Butler, 1985) and as being related to women's conditioning to the victim role in the family and the larger culture. To decrease their sense of stigmatization and isolation survivors are encouraged to view their experience from a sociocultural rather than an individual perspective. Incest is conceptualized as a unique form of victimization which almost inevitably influences the course of the child's development and alters her sense of herself. In order to heal, the survivor must grieve for the losses which accompanied her abuse experience and separate from her family. Although she cannot undo her experience, she can be helped to disengage from it in order to proceed with her own self development.

CHAPTER 8

Presenting Concerns and Diagnosis

M ORE WOMEN THAN EVER before are seeking professional help to cope with past incest. This previously forbidden topic is being discussed more than at any time in history. The pervasive publicity and discussion of child sexual abuse are problematic for some survivors, however. In particular, those who have repressed or "forgotten" their incest experience or who have dissociated to remain only marginally aware may without warning be flooded with feelings and memories. Many of these women, thrown into panic and crisis, seek therapy for acute symptoms and crisis reactions.

Despite recent publicity, most survivors do not divulge their incest experience during intake or early in treatment. The complicated dynamics of incest support continuing secrecy and silence rather than disclosure, especially if the client is middle-aged or older. Often indirect clues are what signal a history of incest. The therapist must be sensitive to these clues and prepared to raise and explore the possibility of incest. If the therapist misses the clues or dismisses abuse as unimportant when it is disclosed, the survivor frequently retreats to a position of silence and secrecy. Like the abused child, she may even retract her story. As a consequence, incest aftereffects are further compounded rather than alleviated.

This chapter discusses the various ways survivors present for therapy, assessment issues, and diagnostic considerations. Special attention is given to incest clues embedded within the client's presentation in therapy.

PRESENTATION IN THERAPY

Among all therapy patients, incest survivors are well represented. Studies of outpatients place prevalence rates at 25% to 44% (Briere, 1984; Rosenfeld, 1979; Spencer, 1978; Westermeyer, 1978)—and these percentages reflect only those cases where the incest is disclosed to the therapist.

Studies of inpatients have reported similar percentages. In their study of hospitalized children, Emslie and Rosenfeld (1983) found that 37.5% of nonpsychotic female subjects, 10% of the psychotic girls, and about 8% of all the boys had been incestuously abused. Carmen, Rieker, and Mills (1984) found that 43% of the adult inpatients they studied had a history of physical and/or sexual abuse. When Goodwin, Attias, McCarty, Chandler and Romanik (in press) questioned a group of inpatients specifically about childhood sexual abuse, 50% responded affirmatively and 35% described incest experiences. These researchers noted that few inpatients volunteer this information, especially as they become more chronic.

The Disguised Presentation

Many incest victims who have attempted disclosure either in childhood or adolescence have encountered disbelief in their families, in the larger community, and within professional circles (Butler, 1978; Summit, 1983). The pressure to keep quiet or to accept blame for this unmentionable abomination has reinforced the trauma itself. For many adult survivors, disclosure is blocked by feelings of alienation, guilt, badness, inadequacy, "craziness," and helplessness. This pattern of silence often persists into adulthood, as well as into therapy. Approximately half of all survivors who seek treatment do not disclose their incest history during intake and assessment; rather, they make a disguised presentation for a number of reasons. The most common are the following:

Lack of Awareness About Having Been Abused. A number of women who have been incestuously abused enter therapy without an awareness of having been abused. This non-awareness is due to the use of various ego defenses and denial/numbing mechanisms used to contain the trauma, most notably repression, amnesia, and dissociation. The delayed onset of symptoms when defenses weaken or crumble often precludes association of current distress with the abuse experience.

Massive repression seems to be the main defensive operation available to very young children and/or the violently abused. According to Herman and Schatzow (1987), severe memory deficits may characterize those survivors who resemble Freud's classic hysterics. They state:

> In Freud's time, these women would undoubtedly have been diagnosed as suffering from hysteria. They would readily have recognized their own afflictions in the anxiety attacks, the bodily disgust, the "mental sensitiveness" and hyperreactivity, the crying spells, the suicide attempts and the "outbursts of despair" . . . (p. 3)

Many life circumstances, including therapy, can cause the defenses to abruptly crumble and trigger memory recall and symptom development. For instance, media reports may evoke memories.

Pat read a first-person account of incestuous abuse in her local newspaper. In it the victim described herself lying in bed in a state of hypervigilance and frozen watchfulness, acutely attuned to footsteps on the stairs and a light appearing around the bedroom door as it was opened. Suddenly Pat was flooded with previously repressed memories of her own abuse and feelings of terror. In particular, she remembered lying in her bed as a child dreading for the light to appear around her door as her father entered her room to abuse her.

Naivete or Ignorance about Abuse. The victim may be ignorant of the abusiveness of her experience, especially when the abuse was embedded within patterns of "normal" family behavior and interaction, when it clearly served a positive purpose for her, or when it was presented positively by a favorite adult who did not use pressure or coercion.

Joanne's father used to observe her while she was dressing, bathing, or using the bathroom. Occasionally, he would ask her to take off her clothes so he could see what a developing girl looked like. Because this behavior continued throughout childhood and adolescence, did not involve touching, and often occurred in her mother's presence, Joanne had not considered it to be abusive, although she was aware that it made her feel uncomfortable.

Age and Chronicity of Symptoms. As Goodwin et al.'s study (in press) documented, the age of the survivor and the chronicity of her symptoms and/or treatment, particularly treatment during which the incest remained hidden, serve to inhibit disclosure. *Older survivors* were abused before incest was publicly discussed and before women's groups, victimization studies, and survivors themselves began to identify current problems as dysfunctional extensions of attempts to cope with past trauma. Many older survivors have experienced severe and chronic mental health problems for which they underwent years of treatment; unfortunately, their problems were treated without awareness of or attention to sexual abuse. In other words, the symptoms were treated but not the cause. Consequently, many of these women "never got better." It was not unusual for them to have received multiple diagnoses and to be labeled as chronic with little or no hope for improvement. Those women who did attempt to disclose their incest histories all too often found their reports discounted, dismissed, or treated as evidence of mental illness. Or, as van der Kolk (1987a) noted, "When a history of such a psychological trauma is obtained, it usually is recorded as a fact with little relevance to current psychiatric problems" (p. 19).

An unfortunate and unintended consequence of the focus on psychopathology has been the reinforcement of the patient's sense that *something is wrong with her*, not that something is wrong with the system or that she has developed symptoms as a reaction to prolonged trauma. Treatment may have taught her the same lesson as the incest—that she is helpless, crazy, and powerless. Having experienced this societal and psychiatric climate, older survivors often feel that the conditioned pattern of silence and fear is too strong to break. For them to divulge or discuss the abuse would be to "air dirty laundry" and would serve no purpose.

The *adolescent survivor* may also make a masked or disguised presentation. Appropriately focused on establishing her own identity and separating from her family of origin, she may avoid or resist discussing anything about family relationships. Asked, "How do you get along with your parents?" she may respond with silence. If the perpetrator is still making advances or actively coercing or blackmailing her (as is sometimes the case in extended father-daughter contact) or if she is being pressured by other family members or fears for their safety, she may remain silent or recant any disclosure. She may continue to protect and rescue her family by being complacent and good.

Very often, the adolescent will engage in post-traumatic acting-out behavior as a means of distracting herself from painful events and memories and their associated anxiety and/or as a way of expiating her guilt. Substance abuse, delinquent or self-destructive behavior, and provocative, indiscriminate sexual activity are often successful in alienating others and deterring inquiries into the past. The victim may find herself blamed once again, while her parents receive sympathy for having to contend with such an unmanageable teenager.

The adolescent survivor may be particularly uncooperative, suspicious, and guarded during intake and later in therapy. Her distrust of authority figures may surface in the clinical situation, fostering resistance to forming a relationship or learning about the abuse. Her projections onto the therapist may prevent her from disclosing much, if anything, about the incest or the rest of her life. She may be more comfortable talking with a group of her contemporaries, although she is also afraid of peer rejection should her secret become known.

Means Used to Silence the Survivor. The type and degree of intimidation used to silence the victim are closely linked with her ability to disclose either at the time of the incest or years later. Numerous survivors continue to fear reprisal if they violate the injunction to "keep our secret." Coercion has been found to take many forms, including a range of threats, from severe physical punishment (death, mutilation, or battering) to psychological penalties (rejection, blaming, and abandonment). Some perpetrators threaten to commit suicide, to harm other members of the family or family pets, to destroy prized possessions, or to withdraw privileges. In some cases, threats have been carried out, particularly through the torture or killing of animals and even cherished pets, to underscore the abuser's seriousness.

Family rules and patterns, such as intense family loyalty, shame, denial of problems, enmeshment, mistrust of others, and closing of ranks to outsiders, also serve to reinforce silence. Reported threats concerning disclosure should always be taken seriously by the therapist, since they can take on a life of their own for the survivor.

Amy attempted suicide after disclosing that her father sexually molested her for years. Her father had silenced her by saying he would kill her if she ever told anyone. Her suicide attempt was due to her fear that his threat would be carried out and her decision that she did not want to give him the satisfaction. She would deny him by killing herself.

Previous Negative Experiences with Disclosure. Some victims have disclosed despite the admonishments and threats, only to find that help is not forthcoming or available or that disclosure worsens rather than relieves the situation. Many have been pressured to retract their allegations and to continue to protect the perpetrator and the family. They may have also learned the hard way that the perpetrator told the truth—they were the ones to be castigated, rejected, or disbelieved. In some cases, the abuse escalated after unsuccessful disclosure, due to the perpetrator's increased rage and/or his realization that little or nothing would be done to stop him. Little wonder that previous negative experiences with disclosure limit the ability to disclose in therapy.

Feelings of Stigma. Having been involved in a taboo activity results in feelings of shame, guilt, low self-esteem, and stigma. A number of survivors do not disclose incest because of their feelings of self-contempt, self-hatred, and badness. Their fearful belief is that no one could possibly view them as anything but contemptible and responsible. These feelings prevent them from disclosing, even though they may desperately wish for attention and support. Closely related to this is a fear of losing control. Many victims have survived by utilizing intense self-control. Disclosure may trigger fears of going crazy, exploding with homicidal or suicidal rage, being sent back to the family, being unable to stop crying, or becoming totally engulfed by the past. Additionally, the victim who had the role of scapegoat or "identified patient" in her family may feel that her family's view of her as crazy will come true if she discloses.

Silence As Protection. Silence often serves as a way to keep the family intact (e.g., "If I don't tell, daddy won't go to jail or have to leave") or to protect certain family members from the pain of knowing about the incest. The daughter involved in a role reversal learns to take care of the needs of others at her expense and is rewarded in the family for doing so. A related pattern is for the oldest daughter (usually the first to be abused) to enter into a pact with the perpetrator (usually the father). She agrees not to tell if he promises not to "bother" her sister(s). It is not uncommon for disclosure to occur when she discovers the molestation of sisters despite her sacrifice. Disclosure may also occur only when the perpetrator or non-abusing parent dies and so no longer needs protection. Apart from these special circumstances, a survivor's disclosure in therapy may represent a betrayal of all she has worked hard to protect. She may feel that any divulgence on her part will bring immediate shame to the family and that it is *she* who is betraying them.

Mistrust of Others. Finally, survivors may resist disclosing their past due to mistrust of nonsurvivors and authority figures, whom they perceive as belonging to the "establishment." They may believe that only another survivor could accept or understand them. They may be quite suspicious about the clinician's motives and project their self-contempt by implying that the clinician working with survivors is seeking out freaks or vicarious thrills. For instance, during intake, one survivor asked me in a hostile tone, "Why are you interested in working with lepers like me?"

Characteristics of the Disguised Presentation

Gelinas (1983) described the common characteristics and manifestations of the disguised presentation. She labeled the symptoms elaborations of the untreated negative effects of the incest and found that the most commonly presented constellation of symptoms consisted of "a characterological depression with complications and atypical compulsive and dissociative elements" (p. 326). It is of note that this constellation resembles Freud's description of hysteria, with its components of anxiety, depression, somatization, and dissociation (Herman & Schatzow, 1987).

Gelinas called particular attention to the "parentified" survivor who presents for treatment as competent, responsible, confident, and mature. Probing by the therapist reveals that her social and professional achievements are genuine but mask other difficulties and concerns. The "parentified" child resembles the "responsible child" found in many alcoholic families. She excels at taking care of others but has been emotionally neglected; she has parented herself and others but has not received adequate attention and nurturing. As a result, she is emotionally needy, with hidden feelings of low self-esteem and shame. Her achievements and caretaking behavior, besides being conditioned, additionally serve constantly to demonstrate her lovability to others and to compensate for her low self-worth. Her efforts to please and take care of others are frequently of heroic proportions. It is typical for survivors who fit this pattern to be emotionally and physically exhausted. In this group in particular, many previously hidden and/or unrecognized symptoms are likely to emerge during treatment.

Ellenson (1986) outlined a predictive syndrome to assist in identifying masked incest histories. Survivors are likely to have the following: thought content disturbances, including recurring nightmares which reflect the childhood trauma experience; persistent phobias, which occur most often in the bedroom and next in the bathroom; recurring and unsettling intrusive obsessions associated with increased risk of being abusive or abused; and recurring dissociation, often accompanied by unusually large gaps in childhood memory. Perceptual disturbances include: recurring illusions when alone, again usually in the bedroom; recurring auditory hallucinations, which somewhat resemble flashbacks; recurring visual and tactile hallucinations of shadowy figures who touch and push, the former being the most powerful single indicator and the latter less common but powerfully predictive of an incest history.

While Ellenson's symptoms are often not severe enough to warrant a diagnosis of schizophrenia, Beck and van der Kolk (submitted) found that chronically hospitalized patients with an incest history (nearly half the cases) had a variety of psychiatric diagnoses, schizophrenia being the most common. They also found that incest victims had a higher incidence of affective symptoms and substance abuse. Based on previous studies that have shown that affective stimulation associated with post-traumatic stress disorder may cause a disorganization of thought processes, they hypothesized that psychotic decompensations in these patients were caused by a response to affective stimulation that was appropriate to earlier childhood trauma. In effect, in their "psychotic" states they may have been partially reliving earlier traumatic events. The authors recommended that the content of incest victims' psychotic thoughts be examined to determine to what degree their "delusions" might be related to actual events.

Lees (1981) has listed additional cues to identifying women with incest histories. She has observed common bipolar patterns of affect, behavior, and cognition. Some survivors rigidly maintain one extreme, others the polar opposite, and some alternate between the two. Fossum and Mason's (1986) cycle of control/release in shame-bound families and individuals (described in Chapters 3 and 4) resembles the bipolar pattern described by Lees. Because of differential sex-role socialization, some of these patterns are more typically exhibited by women and some by men. The polarities are summarized in Table 1.

When the clinician suspects past incest, s/he must begin by "sifting the evidence" and looking for confirming clues. One overwhelming symptom may certainly be cause for suspicion; however, a pattern of symptoms should be determined before drawing conclusions. In addition, the therapist needs to be aware that some of the symptoms associated with child sexual abuse overlap with symptoms of other types of familial abuse, neglect, and dysfunction (e.g., physical abuse, parental alcoholism) or with reactions to other traumatic events. Further, many of these symptoms are

TABLE 1
Polarities Observed in Incest Victims

Feeling bad or no good, "lower than the lowest"	Feeling superior to, better than anyone else
Feeling totally mistrustful of others	Feeling totally (naively) trusting of others with no ability to discriminate
Feeling powerless and victimized in life with difficulty saying "no"; helpless and out of control	Feeling powerful with special or magical powers or behaving rigidly and in an overbearing and controlling way towards others
Behaving in an overly nice and pleasant fashion, presenting a pleasing, ingratiating exterior	Behaving overly unpleasant and "un-nice" (M)
Selflessly taking care of others and not getting own needs met; people-pleasing behavior, attention other-directed and other-determined	Selfishly not taking care of others; attention totally self-directed; expect to be taken care of (M)
Behaving in an over responsible manner; taking the blame and responsibility even when it belongs to someone else	Irresponsible; blaming of others
Feelings of total despair and desperation (no one can or will understand; no one cares; no one notices; nothing will ever change)	Denial of negative feelings "Pollyanna-ish" optimism and naivete (everything is fine, nice, just right)
Extreme isolation and withdrawal	Hypersocial, inability to tolerate being alone
Abhorrence of physical touch or sexual activity; likely to be celibate or abstinent; may be overweight, have poor personal hygiene, and dress in a way that is unappealing and designed to hide the body	Compulsive sexuality and promiscuous sexual activity; physically intrusive and demonstrative; may dress in extremely seductive and revealing clothing
Feeling different from others, inhuman, regretting that she was born	Feeling and living in an overnormal, overconforming way
Compulsive/addictive behaviors	Excessive inhibition

(M)=trait more commonly exhibited by men.

Adapted with permission from Lees, 1981.

seen in certain personality disorders, such as borderline, multiple, and histrionic personality, which are themselves commonly the result of an abuse history.

Presenting Concerns

Symptoms and aftereffects of incest correlate directly with the concerns for which survivors seek treatment. Typical presenting problems (whether the incest is disclosed or not) cluster in the categories assigned to the aftereffects in Chapter 6:

- *Emotional reactions* including fear, anxiety, depression, and self-destructive thoughts and behaviors.
- *Self-perceptions*, which are predominantly negative and indicative of low self-esteem, shame, and stigma.
- *Physical and somatic effects*—direct physical expressions of the abuse or physical manifestations of emotional reactions.
- *Sexual effects*, including the full range of disorders usually associated with anxiety and physical or psychological trauma.
- *Interpersonal relating* characterized by mistrust and conflictual, non-nurturing, or superficial relationships with friends, coworkers, partners, parents, and children.
- *Social effects*, ranging from underfunctioning to overfunctioning, from people-pleasing and extroverted behavior to hostile schizoid behavior and patterns of victimizing others or revictimization.

The Crisis Presentation

A crisis will most likely develop due to delayed aftereffects of the original trauma, reexperiencing of the trauma, or exposure/reexposure to events that symbolize the traumatic event and which trigger symptoms. All of these situations fit the *DSM-III-R* diagnostic criteria for post-traumatic stress disorder. The reemergence of the trauma, along with intrusive symptoms, is distressing to just about anyone; however, it is most distressing to those victims with no conscious memory of having been abused. For incest survivors, various life events or behaviors can trigger intense, intrusive symptoms or numbing of responsiveness. These, in turn, can precipitate acute symptoms of anxiety or depression, including decompensation and psychosis, or explosive, impulsive or vegetative behavior. Immediate crisis intervention is called for with such intensely disabling symptoms.

Many life crises and transitions, whether happy and incremental, such as an intimate relationship, marriage, pregnancy, and the birth of a child, or sad and decremental, such as illness, death, separation and divorce, have been associated with the onset of symptoms. Some survivors have been unable to allow themselves to feel anything or to break through the amnesia barrier until the death of the perpetrator and/or the death of the silent or non-offending parent. The loss or death of any other significant person can similarly disrupt dormant affect and memories or alternatively create a numbing of response. Incremental transitions can cause crisis reactions in two ways: They may signify enough safety and security to allow for a lessening of defenses and the emergence of memories, or they may precipitate negative affect such as anxiety and guilt.

Following the death of her mother, Liz found herself obsessively ruminating about her abuse experiences. She had kept these hidden in order to protect her mother, who, she was convinced, did not know. She had recurring nightmares and became increasingly agitated and phobic. She sought treatment because she felt as though she were going crazy.

Exposure to events which symbolize or resemble the original trauma may be particularly difficult for the survivor and may provoke a reaction which matches the abuse in intensity. Episodes of revictimization including other experiences of sexual molestation and sexual assault (both within and outside of intimate relationships) violence and physical abuse, episodes of criminal victimization, such as a rape or a physical assault, and recurrent or delayed sexually transmitted disease recreate the trauma directly and may cause a sudden flood of intrusive emotions and symptoms.

Some perpetrators continue the abuse throughout the victim's adolescence and into adulthood. Usually in adolescence, intercourse is initiated, with or without contraception. A crisis may therefore be precipitated by pregnancy and resultant panic on the part of the victim, the perpetrator, and other family members. Venereal or sexually transmitted disease or other gynecological injury or problem may also cause severe enough distress to break silence and cause a crisis. Further, in those cases where the victim has been coerced through violent means or where violence has been used or escalated due to an adolescent's attempts to escape or otherwise put a stop to the activity, a crisis may result from being in extreme physical danger, from actual injury, or from escalating threats. In such circumstances the victim is in immediate need of safety and shelter, much like a battered woman attempting to leave her mate.

Victims who have been able to leave home but who return on a periodic basis (such as college students who return home for holidays or vacations) may have intense reactions to being reconnected with or "recontaminated" by the family environment. Some families have been known to make financial support contingent on the daughter's "taking care of daddy" and "not making waves" when she returns home. These daughters are highly stressed by the discrepancies between their "normal" college environment and their "abnormal" family environment. Walsh (1986b), who runs a university sexual assault recovery service, has seen enough instances of this pattern to have labeled it "parental prostitution." It is not unusual for a daughter caught in such a bind to return to campus in a highly agitated, dissociated, or suicidal state. I have seen several cases where hospitalization was considered because the reactions were so disabling.

Discovery of other incest in the family, committed, say, by her partner/ spouse, by the same perpetrator (e.g., in the case of siblings, cousins, or one's own child), or by other family members, is particularly distressing. "Anniversary dates" of past traumatic events may precipitate some symptoms, which may or may not be consciously linked with the trauma. Events that resemble or symbolize the trauma in less direct ways may continue to be overpowering. Certain locations, activities, textures, smells, tastes, and body positions (whether sexual or not) may be aversive and evoke strong emotional response. Medical examinations, particularly gynecological and breast examinations, or surgery, may stimulate strong memories and reactions (see Chapter 14 for a discussion of medical concerns and their management). Other body treatments, such as acupuncture, massage, psychodrama, and movement therapy, can bring up kinesthetic memories of abuse, especially abuse that occurred when the child was at a preverbal level of development.

Similarly, the pervasive media coverage extended to child sexual abuse in recent years is highly disruptive for some survivors. While most of them applaud the fact that incest is finally being acknowledged, the same acknowledgment can lift the protection of repression and dissociation. A flooding of memories, emotions, and symptoms can ensue. Additionally, the way sexual abuse stories are publicized causes intense reactions. Media reports are quite regularly either sensationalized or trivialized. Stories of adult survivors always seem to stress how abuse causes long-term emotional devastation and that past abuse experience causes survivors to later abuse their own children. Survivors who hear these stories and who have no access to other information can become panicked over their implications. Finally, some media stories on false allegations and inadequate response by child protective services evoke reactions of rage and helplessness and reinforce feelings of guilt and the survivor's questioning of the reality of her own experience and that of other children.

Crisis presentation calls for immediate response, reassurance, stabilization, assurances of safety, and a nonjudgmental response. As in other crisis situations, sedation and hospitalization may be needed to stabilize intense depressive, anxious, explosive, or self-destructive reactions.

ASSESSMENT AND DIAGNOSIS FOR
TREATMENT PLANNING

Encouraging Disclosure

Whatever the mode of presentation, the therapist should ask about childhood sexual experiences with related or unrelated adults as part of routine intake, psychosocial, and history-taking procedures. Asking gives the client permission to discuss such experiences and indicates the therapist's willingness to hear about abuse. The recommended approach is to ask, either verbally or in writing, in a straightforward, matter-of-fact manner about any sexual experiences with adults which occurred either in childhood or adolescence. Or the therapist can ask, "What was it like to grow up in your family?" or "How were things in your family when you were growing up?" "Sexual abuse," "incest," "victim," or words with similar connotations should not be used initially, unless the woman herself uses them. Many women do not see themselves as victims or what they experienced as incest or victimization. Others may be quite fearful about admitting to behavior which is so labeled.

Should the woman deny knowledge of abuse despite indications to the contrary, the therapist can gently probe, suggesting that the symptoms she has described are sometimes related to a history of sexual abuse. The therapist might also describe what constitutes incest. At times, therapist and client will conclude that incest occurred even without conscious validation or memory on the part of the client. As mentioned above, some memories return gradually over time, some recur quite intrusively as flashbacks, and some occur somatically or kinesthetically. The remembering process may be very difficult. The inability to remember either childhood in general or specific details can be very frustrating, especially when a strong effort is made to recapture lost time and events. Usually, the most conflictual and traumatic memories are those most solidly repressed. Nevertheless, when some of these memories do emerge, they may be so distressing that they cause the woman to doubt her sanity or to regret she ever remembered.

Obviously, the recollection or reexperiencing of the event(s) is stressful and anxiety-provoking for many survivors. For some, it may create a secondary crisis, since it symbolizes losing control and losing that which allowed her to function. Loosened control can feel life-threatening and lead to self-destructive or self-mutilating gestures. Remembering may symbolize disloyalty and betrayal of the family, leading to a need for self-punishment. All current relationships, especially those with family members, may be called into question when abuse memories surface. The survivor may have to confront perviously denied realities, such as neglect or non-assistance on the part of significant others both within and outside of the family. At times, neglect and abandonment predated incest and contributed to its occurrence and impact.

The disclosure of incest is not uncomfortable or stressful for all survivors and should not be assumed to be so by the therapist. At whatever point a client discloses a history of incest and however she discloses, the therapist should proceed with caution and sensitivity. As Renshaw (1982) noted, noncondemnatory listening is called for; the comfort of the client relates directly to the comfort of the professional in addressing the topic. A "blank screen," authoritarian, or abstinent interview approach is to be avoided. Instead, the therapist should present as approachable, understanding, and responsive to the survivor.

Josephson and Fong-Beyette (1987) have conducted the first empirical investigation of personal and background factors of the client, attributes of the counselor, and aspects of the counseling relationship as they relate to self-disclosure of incest experiences during counseling. They have found that client readiness for disclosure is assisted by public information and education about incest and by counselors' direct and indirect questioning. Counselors who are calm and receptive and do not become outraged by descriptions of offenders and non-offending parents assist clients in making fuller disclosures, as opposed to those who communicate discomfort, minimize the effects and importance of the incest, show excessive interest in sexual details, push clients, ignore the disclosure, and become angry with the client or the offender. Moreover, participants in this study emphasized that incest victims need reassurance, encouragement, and validation at the beginning of the treatment process. Helpful counselors were described as patient, calm, caring, warm, nonjudgmental, empathic, honest in their responses, and interested in clients as people. Many participants sought out counselors experienced with incest survivors. Table 2 presents Josephson and Fong-Beyette's guidelines for assisting disclosure of incest.

Even when the survivor talks openly about incest, she may have difficulty discussing specifics. In order to anticipate possible adverse reactions, the therapist should attempt first to discern the meaning of the disclosure and childhood messages and beliefs about giving up the secret. Then the therapist should carefully monitor how the client is reacting to discussing the experience. Most importantly, the therapist must make explicit that the survivor's story is believed, that she is safe, that she is and will be supported, and that she will not be rushed. In cases of selective amnesia or conflicting details and memories, the therapist should indicate a willingness to work with the client to explore the material and its significance. The victim/survivor needs the assurance that her experiences, whatever they are, will receive validation and not be subject to further suppression.

It must also be made explicit that disclosure does not mean resolution but rather signifies the beginning of the working-through process. Scur-

TABLE 2
Guidelines for Assisting Disclosure of Incest

Responding to Client Needs During Counseling

1. Counselor reassurances that:
    Clients are believed and not blamed.
    Responsibility for incest belongs to the offender.
    Clients did the best they could have done to survive the circumstances.
    As children, clients were not in control of the situation.
    Details of the counseling will remain confidential.
    Clients are "survivors" and can recover from their victimization.
    Clients can get over their feelings of shame.
    Counselors' feelings toward the clients will not change as a result of hearing about the incest.

2. Counselor encouragement and validation that:
    Clients may temporarily feel worse about disclosure before they start to feel better.
    Clients have the right to feel anger and grief.
    Clients have the right to have positive feelings toward the offender.
    Clients did not deserve the abuse.
    Clients are making gains despite how small the gains seem to the clients.
    Clients are important and intelligent people.
    Clients' coping mechanisms are seen as "survivor skills" and adaptive.

Addressing Incest During Counseling

1. Counselors could elicit disclosure by:
    Asking directly if sexual abuse occurred during childhood.
    Using a structured questionnaire such as an intake form to receive a complete early sexual history.
    Mentioning that the symptoms clients are describing have been related to histories of sexual abuse in other clients.
    Defining incest to clients.
    Asking about best and worst experiences during childhood.
    Being persistent in probing sexual abuse histories.

2. Once disclosure takes place, counselors should:
    Identify incest as primary cause of clients' difficulties.
    Acknowledge and validate significance of incest.
    Relate specific difficulties in adult life to coping skills developed to survive incest.
    Not minimize incest even if it occurred infrequently.
    Encourage clients to "dwell" on incest.
    Be fully aware of their own reactions to hearing about incest.

From Josephson and Fong-Beyette, 1987.

field's (1985) observation about trauma survivors is particularly applicable to the incest survivor:

> A trauma survivor may not yet be ready to acknowledge the possible impact of the trauma, let alone be able or willing to discuss it in any detail. Thus, one must be alert to vacuums in history, areas that perhaps can only be adequately explored following engagement in a therapeutic trust relationship. . . . The axiom "diagnosis follows treatment," may be more characteristic of PTSD than any other clinical diagnosis. (p. 238)

Assessment

A comprehensive assessment inclusive of more than the incest trauma is needed for initial diagnosis and for treatment planning. Such an assessment is time-consuming and does not occur only during intake; rather, it unfolds during the treatment process. A number of elements should be included: identifying data, chief complaint and symptoms; history, including family constellation, family history, and pre-trauma developmental and psychosocial history; the traumatic event(s) and immediate coping attempts; developmental and psychosocial history; any revictimizations or other significant crises; and adult adjustment, including post-trauma psychosocial context and reactions.

The Identifying Data and Chief Complaint and Symptoms. These should be recorded in as much detail as possible at the time of the assessment. Symptoms which arise during the course of treatment should also be noted since they contribute to a more comprehensive diagnostic picture over time.

Family History and Pre-trauma Functioning. A thorough assessment of the family history and pre-trauma functioning (if remembered or available) includes: demographic and relational data on the family of origin going back at least two generations and including data on addictions and physical and sexual abuse; family-of-origin functioning; relationships and family rules; religious history; parent-child, sibling, peer, and authority figure relationships; and behavior patterns and functioning in family, school, work, and social life. Data should be gathered about both positive and negative pre-incest factors and relationships, since they may be associated with the degree of trauma experienced. For example, a positive relationship with a significant authority figure or success in school or sports may mitigate some of the negative impact of the abuse or abandonment experiences with parents pre-incest may reinforce it.

The Traumatic Incestuous Events and Any Additional Trauma. These should be carefully assessed, with a focus on the individual's subjective interpretation of the experience. Incorporating Scurfield's (1985) categorizations for the assessment of traumatic events, the following should be included:

- *Objective factors*: The frequency, intensity, duration, sexual behaviors engaged in and progression of behaviors, age at onset and at termination, location, identity of perpetrator(s), the means of involving the child, and the roles of other family members.
- *Active/passive role*: Whether the survivor was actively involved in any way in the initiation or maintenance of the behavior. Some children are conditioned or eroticized into seeking involvement. Others may be motivated by their need for affection or by motives of anger or revenge. Others do all they can to get out of the situation or submit or experience total paralysis. Information about activity level is very useful in determining the meaning and impact of the abuse and in working on the conflicts associated with responsibility and blame.
- *Idiosyncratic meaning of the incest*: The individual's perspective on her abuse or her overall life experience. Some survivor's feel that the abuse irreparably and irrevocably changed and damaged their lives. Others feel that they learned from the experience, learning which allowed or forced them to develop in ways they would not have otherwise. Making some sense of the experience is an important component of self-understanding and recovery (Courtois, 1979; Russell, 1986; Silver, Boon, & Stones, 1983).
- *Immediate post-incest reactions*: While a range of reactions is possible during and following abuse, it should not be assumed that numbness or lack of stress reactions immediately after the trauma indicates no traumatic aftereffects or lack of relationship between the symptoms and the event. A latency period of months or years is typical of delayed or chronic post-traumatic stress disorder.
- *Attempts at disclosure*: Whether the client ever disclosed her experience and the results of doing so. This would include disclosure both at the time of the incest and later, either within or outside of the family. Multiple attempts at disclosure should be assessed, as should reactions to the aftermath of each disclosure. Often, repeated disclosures are necessary before any response is forthcoming.
- *Involvement of any social agencies and personnel*: Whether disclosure led to the involvement of any social agencies and personnel and the results of intervention. Reactions to the interventions should be assessed.
- *The psychosocial context and developmental adjustment post-abuse*: Such an assessment is necessary to understand the individual's adjustment process and any factors which have contributed to the

delaying, prolonging, exacerbating, or ameliorating symptoms. Factors to be assessed include social class and economic standing, sex and sexual orientation, ethnic group, family support and relationships, social networks and friendships, occupational functioning, financial history, relational and sexual history, medical history, and recreational and cultural activities. In addition, symptoms and reactions must be assessed. According to Scurfield:

> Post-trauma symptoms and reactions can include one or more of a common set of symptoms. The particular configuration of symptoms is at least partly a function of the nature of the unique elements about the person. The major emotional states, or themes, that occur include various combinations of symptoms, behaviors and cognitions, any or all of which one should be alert to in assessing and treating. . . . (p. 232)

The following case example of two incestuously abused sisters illustrates different post-trauma functioning and outcomes:

Claire and her sister Marsha were both abused by their father for many years. Claire was abused by their brother as well. Both women entered early marriages to escape their family, but their lives differed remarkably from that point on.

Once married, Marsha refused further contact with her family and built a successful career as a corporate executive, despite having only a high school education. The early years of her marriage were satisfactory, but as she developed occupationally her capabilities and independence threatened her husband. Her marital difficulties which culminated in divorce, in addition to the death of two significant friends, triggered a delayed onset of serious depressive and dissociative symptoms, which caused her to seek treatment. Although her recovery process was difficult, she has been able to maintain her career and economic status and to function well socially.

Claire's first marriage was unsuccessful and she proceeded to marry four more times, each time to an abusive and/or inadequate man. Between marriages she returned to her parents and depended upon them for financial support. They would at times withhold support so that she was forced to go on welfare and/or resort to prostitution to support herself. Claire, an alcoholic with a violent temper and occasional severe mood swings, is the identified patient of the family. Her social adjustment is poor—she has no friends other than the man she is involved with at any point in time.

In assessing the severity of reactions across all of the major categories or life spheres, the therapist must differentiate between "dysfunctional" and "normal stress" responses. According to Horowitz's (1986) theory, the therapist can make this determination by assessing the individual's degree of control over and/or preoccupation with any intrusive/repetitive thoughts

and the severity of impact of post-trauma symptoms on spheres of functioning. For example, have flashbacks made it impossible for the individual
to engage in sexual relations, or have depression and constricted affect or
anxiety symptoms made it impossible for her to function socially and
occupationally?

Several other areas of investigation are recommended. A *developmental
and psychosocial history* should be taken to determine whether the survivor
met major developmental milestones and whether she had any deficits
developmentally and in her psychosocial experience and adjustment. Developmental and psychosocial problems pre-incest may have made her
more vulnerable to abuse. Post-abuse, these same problems may have compounded the aftereffects. The therapist should ask about *the onset and
recurrence of symptoms* and whether the client is aware of life events conducive to symptom development. *Any additional traumatic event(s)*, either
prior to or after the abuse, should also be assessed. Unfortunately, many
victims have suffered multiple trauma in childhood and later. The clinician
should be aware that sometimes revictimization can be so constant and
chronic across a victim's life as to seem incredible. I'm reminded of a case
on which my consultation was sought:

*Jennie was a 15-year-old whose mother arranged for her to be married to
"get her off the street." She had dropped out of school, which she could
legally do at 15 because of her married status. Over the years, she had come
to the attention of the teachers and school counseling staff because she
often appeared battered, had learning difficulties, and had a brother who
obsessively hounded her at school.*

*Forced and violent sibling incest was suspected and confirmed in con-
versations with Jennie. Jennie calmly (she almost always appeared calm but
in a numb sort of way although substance abuse was not suspected) recounted to the counselor that she had been abused since early childhood
by a number of men who had been her mother's lovers. Her brother had
physically abused her and was compulsive in his sexual demands. At the
age of 12, her victimization outside of the home began and she was used to
"service" men in their cars. Through all of this, her mother offered her little
assistance and protection. The only exception to this (and this was certainly questionable in terms of protection) was the forced marriage to a Viet-
namese man with a known history of violence. Compounding the tragedy
and victimization, Jennie's case had been repeatedly reported to Child
Protective Services, which investigated, made recommendations, and
closed the case each time.*

*Jennie sought treatment at a family counseling service when she be-
came pregnant. She was near panic at the time of intake. She was terrified
of delivering the baby because she was uncertain of its paternity. Her
marriage had not deterred her brother from abusing her and she feared*

*that the baby would be caucasian rather than oriental and that her hus-
band would learn of her terrible secret and harm her or her baby.*

Russell (1986), in particular, has discussed the credibility problems associated with multiple revictimization and the tendency to disbelieve or
blame the victim who reports such a history. She has challenged mental
health practitioners to use the information from her study to expect and
understand these multiple occurrences. In numerous instances, the dynamics of child sexual abuse contribute to multiple revictimization of
victims, some of whom do not live to tell their stories (for example, in the
case described above, a domestic homicide would not be an unlikely outcome — both the brother and husband were violent men) and most of
whom never have the opportunity or courage to tell it. The clinician must
specifically inquire about multiple abuse experiences and should expect
them to be revealed only gradually as the survivor develops trust in the
therapy relationship.

Assessment Instruments

While information about incest can be gathered using a standard intake
protocol, several assessment instruments have been designed by researchers specifically to assist in the identification of incest history and to gather
information. The reader is referred to Donaldson (1983; 1987), Ellenson
(1986), Gelinas (1983), Mayer (1983) and Renshaw (1982) for various types
of instruments. I have found my research questionnaire, a detailed structured interview (Courtois, 1979), useful in therapy. It covers most of the
areas Scurfield (1985) recommended and discussed above. The questionnaire has been revised for clinical use and is found in Appendix A along
with suggestions for its use. An incest questionnaire can be reassuring to
the survivor since it communicates that incest is sufficiently common to
warrant its own assessment instrument.

Many of my research subjects (all volunteers) expressed relief at having
discussed their incest in a structured interview format. They indicated that
the interview was on target and "asked the right questions," demonstrating
to them that someone understood their experience in its various dimensions and complexities. I have had similar responses when I have used the
instrument in clinical information-gathering. As with assessment in general, the therapist should be careful to move at the client's pace when making
direct inquiries about incest experience.

Any of the instruments can be self-administered to save time or alleviate
discomfort. As with verbal inquiry, the therapist should monitor how the
client is reacting to the written questions and encourage her to pace herself. The material may be overwhelming for some and apparently not at all
distressing for others. Goodwin et al. (in press), in their investigation of the

effect of routine questioning of inpatients about childhood sexual abuse, found that of 40 they surveyed eight (five of whom were victims) reported negative reactions. They found the questions disturbing and upsetting. Others were highly positive, and some were ambivalent. Although discomforting to some patients, the inquiry was not found to result in prolonged hospital stays or increased hospitalizations. The benefits of asking (i.e., increased information about the patient and the relevance of an abuse history to diagnosis and treatment) seem to far outweigh the discomfort although, as previously mentioned, the level of discomfort must be continuously monitored.

As part of either the assessment and/or the treatment process, the therapist may want to encourage the survivor to keep written or audio records of dreams, fantasies, and flashbacks, and to write an autobiography, leaving blank spaces for any periods of time for which she is amnesic. Keeping records impedes the defensive process of "reforgetting," which is fairly common.

Diagnosis

Post-incest syndrome or disorder is not available as a diagnosis in *DSM-I, -II, -III* or *-III-R*, nor are other similarly descriptive diagnoses, such as child sexual abuse disorder (Corwin, 1986), post sexual abuse syndrome (Briere, 1984), or sexual abuse accommodation syndrome (Summit, 1983). It is hoped that at some time in the future such subclassifications will be available, most likely under the generic category of post-traumatic stress disorder (PTSD).*

In the absence of the direct diagnosis of aftereffects of incest/child sexual abuse, we must choose among the other *DSM-III-R* categories. A *DSM-III* multiaxial diagnosis appended with Renshaw's incest diagnosis (presented below) is the most comprehensive.

Accurate diagnosis is further complicated by the number of aftereffects and by presenting concerns that span more than one diagnostic category.

---

*A diagnosis of PTSD is rejected by some survivors as too stigmatizing and too descriptive of their history and thus as an invasion of privacy, especially when included on an insurance form. More specific diagnoses such as post sexual abuse syndrome or post incest trauma syndrome would likely elicit similar reactions. Furthermore, critics have suggested that "disorder" in PTSD and the proposed diagnosis, child sexual abuse disorder, is a misnomer and should instead be "reactions." Clearly, diagnoses having to do with traumatic stress will continue to develop as these syndromes are further researched. In the interim, the clinician might deal with these concerns and for insurance purposes by using a more "neutral" diagnosis having to do specifically with the client's presenting concerns and keeping a more detailed and descriptive diagnosis strictly for treatment purposes.

Moreover, a lack of clarity and rigor in some of the *DSM* diagnostic formulations contributes to the difficulty, as does significant overlap and similarity between symptoms of some of the major diagnoses. For example, post-traumatic stress disorder resembles multiple personality disorder (MPD) in many proposed antecedents and in such symptoms as amnesia; in MPD, the splitting off of the trauma is more complete than is found in PTSD. In addition, traumatic stress responses may resemble and mimic those of major mental disturbances. Unstable, delayed, or even absent symptom presentation is characteristic of PTSD, increasing the likelihood that the symptoms will not be correlated with their cause by either the client or the diagnostician.

As specifically suggested in *DSM-III-R*, multiple diagnoses can and should be given when necessary to describe the current condition. Multiple diagnoses within an axis are listed in descending order of priority. Of note is the fact that some syndromes which developed after the incest may need direct treatment before the underlying trauma can be addressed (see Chapter 14).

Renshaw's Incest Classification. To assist the clinician in specifying the nature of the incestuous contact, Renshaw (1982) has devised a three-stage classification system describing the different types of incest. Her justification for a separate incest diagnosis is, the more comprehensive the description, the more useful it is clinically. A clear understanding of the type(s) of incest the survivor experienced allows the clinician to hypothesize about some of the aftereffects and their severity.

The incest diagnosis can be used in conjunction with all other diagnoses, as indicated in the third category. Renshaw proposes the following:

1. Incest diagnosis: More than one may apply and be listed:
    a. Consanguineous (blood relative) or affinity (related by marriage) incest
    b. Consensual, coercive, or forceful
    c. Coital or noncoital incest
    d. Heterosexual or homosexual incest
    e. Adult-adult, child-child, adult-child, or group incest
    f. Rape incest
    g. Pedophilic incest
    h. Exhibitionist incest
    i. Multiple deviant incest (e.g., exploitation, prostitution, transvestism, child pornography, sadomasochism)
    j. Fantasy or dream incest
    k. Incest craving or envy
    l. Incest-accepting family, culture or religion
2. Physical diagnosis (primarily for the physician who is performing a physical examination of the child to validate incest; however, may

also be useful retrospectively when the victim was physically injured or scarred and shows physical symptoms in adulthood)
3. Other psychiatric diagnoses: In addition to incest, is a psychiatric
disorder present or absent? Diagnoses in this category might include no psychiatric diagnosis, alcohol abuse, drug abuse, mental
retardation, infanticide, depressive disorder, conversion disorder,
parricide, avoidant disorder, dissociative disorder, anxiety disorder,
somatization disorder, or adjustment disorder, etc. (pp. 21–22)

Axis I Diagnoses. DSM-III-R axis I encompasses the symptoms and presenting concerns brought to treatment. The majority of disorders listed in
DSM fit into this broad category. Many incest survivors meet the criteria
for clinical depression, usually of an atypical sort. Besides affective disorders, the most common axis I diagnoses applied to outpatient incest survivors seem to be substance abuse disorders, anxiety disorders, somatoform
disorders, dissociative disorders, and impulse control disorders. For inpatients, Beck and van der Kolk (submitted) found a variety of diagnoses, with
schizophrenia the most prevalent. Another research team (Bryer, Miller,
Nelson, & Krol, n.d.) found that inpatient survivors, compared to outpatient survivors, were likely to be characterized by more severe symptoms
and more atypical, psychotic, and major depressive diagnoses on axis I.
Here we review the criteria for the diagnosis of *post-traumatic stress disorder*
and *dissociative disorders* because of their special pertinence to incest survivors.*

In those cases where the required number of criteria for the diagnosis
post-traumatic stress disorder is met, PTSD is suggested either as the principal axis I diagnosis or as a diagnosis listed in order of priority with other
clinical syndromes. The diagnosis of PTSD is broad enough to encompass
a variety of symptoms found to be associated with incest history. In addition, the PTSD diagnosis in and of itself can be quite therapeutic in
reconceptualizing the incest and its effects. This diagnosis directly communicates to the client that her symptoms do not mean that she is crazy;
rather, they result from traumatic circumstances in her life and efforts to
cope with them. In a similar way, the PTSD diagnosis helps the therapist
conceptualize and depathologize the responses to incest and offers concrete directions for treatment planning.

PTSD has been underutilized as a diagnostic category in general and
with regard to incest in particular. This has been partly due to its recent
association with Vietnam veterans and to professionals' reliance on more
familiar diagnoses and concepts. Professionals have been reluctant to asso-

---

*Reprinted with permission from the *Diagnostic and Statistical Manual of Mental
Disorders* (3rd edition, revised). Copyright 1987, American Psychiatric Association.

ciate symptoms of distress (especially long-term ones) with past victimization or external trauma, or they have been uninformed about the possible associations. In particular, PTSD may not be recognized by the diagnostician when the client is in the numbing/constriction phase because it may closely resemble normal functioning.

As victimization has received more publicity, the PTSD diagnosis has been increasingly used and recommended. Strong anecdotal support for the appropriateness and utility of the PTSD diagnosis exists among professionals who specialize in working with incest survivors. In separate clinical studies of incest survivors, Armsworth (1986), Donaldson and Gardner (1985), Frederick (1985) and Lindberg and Distad (1985a) found that the vast majority of these clients meet the criteria for PTSD.

In addressing the multiple causes and the individual character in the development of PTSD in general, Andreason (1985) offered the following analogy, which is useful in understanding the personal dimensions of the response to incest trauma:

> The causes of post-traumatic stress disorder are probably many. By definition, the disorder is caused by a stressor so severe that it is likely to produce psychological trauma in most normal persons. The role of the stressor in post-traumatic stress disorder may be compared to the role of force in producing a broken leg. It is normal for a leg to break if enough force is applied, . . . Individual legs vary, however, in the amount of force required to produce a break, the amount of time required for healing, and the degree of residual pathology that may remain. In most persons experiencing post-traumatic stress disorder, the stressor is a necessary but not sufficient cause, because even the most severe stressors do not produce a post-traumatic stress disorder in all persons experiencing that stressor. A variety of psychological, physical, genetic, and social factors may also contribute to the disorder. (p. 17)

The first criterion for a post-traumatic stress disorder is that "The person has experienced an event that is outside the range of usual human experience and that would be markedly distressing to almost everyone . . . " (*DSM-III-R*, p. 250). Obviously, incest is an experience with the potential to evoke great distress.

Andreason had the following to say about the nature of the stressor:

> Stressors of various types contribute variable amounts to the development of post-traumatic stress disorder. . . . Although the trauma often involves a physical factor, as in the case of rape or accidents involving physical injury, *it always involves a psychological component that produces significant emotional trauma. The psychological component involves feelings of intense fear, helplessness, loss of control, and threat of annihilation.* . . . When the stressor involves intentional cruelty or inhumanity . . . the impact of the traumatic event may also be greater than normal. The impact may also be more severe than normal if the victim feels trapped or cornered and has no opportunity to fight back or escape. (p. 17, italics added)

The same author further discussed the nature of the victim as concerns severity of reaction:

> A variety of personal factors determine a particular person's predisposition to develop psychiatric symptoms in response to trauma. These factors include age at the time of injury, underlying personality traits, previous psychiatric disability, genetic predisposition, and availability of social support. In general, the very young and the very old have more difficulty in coping with traumatic events.... The availability of social support may also influence the development, severity, and duration of post-traumatic stress disorder. In general, patients who have a good network of social supports are less likely to develop the disorder or to experience it in its most severe forms. (pp. 17–18)

These comments further substantiate our view of incest as a traumatic event with the potential to evoke severe aftereffects at the time of its occurrence, which later continue as traumatic stress reactions or develop into a full-blown post-traumatic stress disorder.

The second criterion of this diagnosis is:

> The traumatic event is persistently reexperienced in at least one of the following ways: (1) recurrent and intrusive distressing recollections of the event; (2) recurrent distressing dreams of the event; (3) sudden acting or feeling as if the traumatic event were recurring (includes a sense of reliving the experience, illusions, hallucinations, and dissociative [flashback] episodes even those that occur upon awakening or when intoxicated); (4) intense psychological distress at exposure to events that symbolize or represent an aspect of the traumatic event, including anniversaries of the trauma. (*DSM-III-R*, p. 250)

Numerous incest survivors experience at least one of these symptoms and many experience all of them.

The third criterion is:

> Persistent avoidance of stimuli associated with the trauma or numbing of general responsiveness (not present before the trauma), as indicated by at least three of the following: (1) efforts to avoid thoughts or feelings associated with the trauma; (2) efforts to avoid activities or situations that arouse recollections of the trauma; (3) inability to recall an important aspect of the trauma (psychogenic amnesia); (4) markedly diminished interest in significant activities (in young children, loss of recently acquired developmental skills such as toilet training or language skills); (5) feeling of detachment or estrangement from others; (6) restricted sense of affect (e.g., unable to have loving feelings); (7) sense of a foreshortened future, e.g., does not expect to have a career, marriage, or children, or a long life. (*DSM-III-R*, p. 250)

Criterion four includes:

Persistent symptoms of increased arousal (not present before the trauma), as indicated by at least two of the following: (1) difficulty falling or staying asleep; (2) irritability or outbursts of anger; (3) difficulty concentrating; (4) hypervigilance; (5) exaggerated startle response; (6) physiologic reactivity upon exposure to events that symbolize or resemble an aspect of the traumatic event (e.g., a woman who was raped in an elevator breaks out in a sweat when entering any elevator). (*DSM-III-R*, pp. 250–251)

Duration of the symptoms of these three criteria is of at least one month. Delayed onset is specified if onset of the symptoms was at least six months after the trauma.

The delay in symptom onset is one of the unanswered questions about incest trauma, as with other types of trauma. Lindberg and Distad (1985a, p. 332) suggest that the survivor theory applied to Vietnam veterans is applicable to incest survivors as well: "Following a severe trauma, a pattern of repression, denial and emotional avoidance emerges. This denial-numbing phase, also called a latency period, can last days or decades, then is followed by an intrusive-repetitive phase, in which disquieting symptoms such as nightmares or guilt reoccur." Clinicians must take delayed symptom development into account in their history-taking.

As conceptualized in *DSM-III-R*, PTSD also includes associated features important in both diagnosis and treatment.

Symptoms of depression and anxiety are common, and in some instances may be sufficiently severe to be diagnosed as an Anxiety or Depressive Disorder. Impulsive behavior can occur, such as suddenly changing place of residence, unexplained absences, or other changes in life-style. There may be symptoms of an Organic Mental Disorder, such as failing memory, difficulty in concentrating, emotional lability, headache and vertigo. In the case of a life-threatening trauma shared with others, survivors often describe painful guilt feelings about surviving when others did not, or about the things they had to do in order to survive. (*DSM-III-R*, p. 249)

PTSD may itself lead to a variety of further complications or secondary elaborations. Psychic numbing may interfere with interpersonal or occupational functioning. Phobic avoidance of behaviors or activities which resemble or symbolize the original trauma may cause serious lifestyle restriction. Physiological or psychological dependency on drugs may result from attempts to anesthetize the self to the painful memories and emotions or to heighten their impact as a means of self-definition or self-punishment. Depressive symptoms, such as guilt and hopelessness, may lead to self-defeating behavior, suicide attempts, and completed suicide.

Dissociative disorders including *multiple personality disorder* are underutilized diagnoses particularly applicable to incest survivors. Dissociative reactions are complex psychological mechanisms characterized by an alteration of normal integrated awareness and self-identity. Certain faculties, functions, feelings, and memories are split off from immediate awareness or consciousness and compartmentalized in the mind, where they become separate entities. This process can be conceptualized as a form of autohypnosis resulting in the splitting off of dimensions of the personality into partial or whole alter personalities, each with a different degree of consciousness or lack of consciousness. Dissociation has been found to be on a continuum (Price, 1987), with a range from healthy to unhealthy, from positive to negative, from less to more severe, with weaker to stronger discrete boundaries between dissociated parts.

According to Beahrs (1982), dissociation is necessary for healthy functioning and includes such operations as dreams and fantasies, roles and specific skills, defense functions, projection of positive and negative aspects of the self onto others, and selective amnesia for certain stimuli. Beahrs describes dissociative disorders as arising when the full experience of the continuity of selfhood is lacking, that is, when the self is segmented and the information flow from one to the other is impaired sufficiently to disturb the person's sense of selfhood. Dissociative *disorder* denotes

> personality splitting that is dysfunctional, not useful or maladaptive, limiting instead of enhancing the organism's power for action, or leading to behavior dangerous to self and others. It refers not only to multiple personality, but also to a broad scope of psychiatric problems where a similar dynamic applies, but with less discrete or rigid boundaries between the part-selves. These include neurotic, borderline, and even episodically psychotic disorders which can actually be more disturbed than true multiples, as well as less. (Beahrs, p. 81)

DSM-III-R lists the essential feature of dissociative disorders (or hysterical neuroses, dissociative type) as a disturbance or alteration in the normally integrative functions of identity, memory, or consciousness. When the alteration occurs in consciousness, important personal events cannot be remembered. "If it occurs primarily in identity, the person's customary identity is temporarily forgotten and a new identity may be assumed or imposed (as in multiple personality disorder), or the customary feeling of one's own reality is lost and replaced by a feeling of unreality (as in depersonalization disorder). If the disturbance occurs primarily in memory, important personal events cannot be recalled (as in psychogenic amnesia or psychogenic fugue)" (*DSM-III-R*, p. 269). The dissociation mechanism may account for hysterical conversion reactions and thus be related to histrionic personality disorder.

Four forms of dissociative disorder are listed in *DSM-III-R*. *Psychogenic amnesia* includes a sudden inability to recall important personal behavior or events (not due to an organic mental disorder) which is too extensive to be explained by ordinary forgetfulness. *Psychogenic fugue* involves sudden unexpected travel away from home or customary place of work, with inability to recall one's previous identity and the assumption of either a partially or completely new identity. This diagnosis is not made in the presence of an organic mental disorder. *Depersonalization disorder* is characterized by one or more episodes of depersonalization sufficiently severe to cause marked distress. This diagnosis is not made when depersonalization is secondary to any other disorder, such as panic disorder. *Multiple personality disorder* involves the existence of two or more distinct personalities or personality states, which recurrently take full control of the person's behavior. *Dissociative disorder, not otherwise specified* is diagnosed in those situations where a dissociative symptom (i.e., a disturbance is in the function of identity, memory or consciousness) is present but the total symptom picture does not meet the criteria set forth for the four listed above. These include trancelike states, derealization unaccompanied by depersonalization, and more prolonged dissociated states which occur in persons subjected to intense and prolonged coercion. *Sleepwalk disorder (somnambulism)* involves the essential feature of a dissociative disorder but is classified in *DSM-III-R* as a sleep disorder.

Although many etiological factors have been associated with major dissociative disorders, there is increasing evidence that children who have suffered severe, repeated, and often bizarre physical, sexual, or emotional abuse, most often administered by parents and unpredictably interspersed with affection, are at high risk for their development. Not all victims of sexual abuse dissociate, but most dissociators have been victims and have high dissociative potential. Dissociation as a common response in incest survivors is now well recognized by clinicians. For example, Summit (1983), quoting Shengold (1979), discussed vertical splitting as a coping mechanism, and Brickman (1984) wrote of a range of dissociative responses which she termed "sliding personality." Briere (1984) and Briere and Runtz (1985) found a significant association between sexual abuse and dissociative reactions.

Dissociating serves many purposes. It provides a way out of the intolerable and psychologically incongruous situation (double-bind), it erects memory barriers (amnesia) to keep painful events and memories out of awareness, it functions as an analgesic to prevent feeling pain, it allows escape from experiencing the event and from responsibility/guilt, and it may serve as a hypnotic negation of the sense of self. The child may begin by using the dissociative mechanism spontaneously and sporadically. With repeated victimization and double-bind injunctions, it becomes chronic. It may further become an autonomous process as the individual ages. Dissociation is therefore another type of survival mechanism used by the child. Over time, it commonly changes from being functional (a survival skill) to being dys-functional and getting in the individual's way (a symptom) (see Chapter 14 for further discussion of dissociative reactions).

The most severe form of dissociation, *multiple personality disorder* (MPD), often develops in childhood but is usually not recognized until adolescence or adulthood. According to *DSM-III-R*, multiple personality is "the existence within the person of two or more distinct personalities or personality states (each with its own relatively enduring pattern of perceiv-ing, relating to, and thinking about the environment and self). At least two of these personalities or personality states recurrently take full control of the person's behavior" (p. 272).

MPD is more chronic than other types of dissociative disorders and its degree of impairment is generally more severe as well. While amnesia is not among the *DSM-III-R* criteria for the MPD diagnosis, some experts believe that it is diagnostically essential (Coons, 1980; Putnam, 1984). The individ-ual with MPD splits into two or more personalities; the average number seems to be 8 to 13 but up to 92 have been documented. "Super multiples" (Braun, 1980) are those individuals with 20 or more personalities. In large numbers, the personalities are usually more short-lived, less clearly de-fined, and more incompletely formed. The earlier the chronological age at which major personality splitting occurs, the greater the number of alter personalities that are likely to emerge.

The personalities, whatever their total number, have varying degrees of distinctness and complexity, many with very different habits, values, and ways of expressing themselves. The individual may change dress, speech, mannerisms, body posture, and movement according to the identity of the dominant personality at the time. In fact, the individual personalities may be discrepant to the point of being completely incompatible with one another. Some profess to be of different age, race, class, family of origin, and sex. Personalities have even been found to respond differently to mea-sures of psychological and physiological functioning (Putnam, 1984).

The functions of the secondary personalities vary. They usually devel-oped after the occurrence of trauma as protection against emotional pain. Later they enable the individual to act on aggressive and sexual impulses unacceptable to the original personality. Common alternates include a fearful, dependent, child-like personality; a reckless, promiscuous personal-ity who acts out forbidden aggressive and sexual impulses; and a calming, rational, soothing protector or advisor. At least one personality, usually that of a child, contains the memory of the abuse and the terrifying experi-ences. Other personalities may be avengers or persecutors and may serve to deliberately humiliate or cause distress for other personalities. A trace personality or internal self-helper (ISH) (Allison, 1974) serves as a repository of information about all of the personalities. It is usually neutral in the internal struggle but knows the details about every other personality and about the host personality's life.

The original or host personality is usually a shy, introverted, bland personality unable to deal with strong emotions and passions and unaware of or amnesic for the other personalities, at least initially. Alternate personalities may have partial or complete amnesia for one another. Multiple personalities are often identified by memory gaps and time distortions. They may complain of lost hours, days, weekends, or longer. Switching from one personality to another is commonly preceded by a headache. Multiples have been found to have a high hypnotic susceptibility and to easily learn autohypnosis. As a group, they show high levels of intelligence, creativity, sensitivity, and talent.

The personality that seeks treatment in adulthood commonly presents as depressed, anxious, and suffering from psychosomatic symptoms. Presenting problems include substance abuse, homicidal, suicidal or self-mutilating behavior, auditory hallucinations (usually from within rather than outside of the self), psychotic episodes, amnesia, criminal behavior, hysterical conversion symptoms, phobias, and sexual problems. Some multiples use the term "we" instead of "I" in their conversation and may self-diagnose. Others may be referred for treatment by family members or friends who have witnessed "switching" or conversational indications of multiplicity.

Additionally, the diagnosis of multiple personality should be considered with a client who reports a history of blackouts, time distortions, time or memory lapses, fugue states or other experiences related to amnesia. Other strong indicators are severe headaches, depersonalization, derealization, hypnagogic visions, auditory hallucinations from within the client's head, and histrionic convulsive-like fits and trance-like states.

Multiple personality disorder usually begins in childhood. The clinician should be alerted to the possibility of a diagnosis of a major dissociative reaction, including multiple personality disorder, when the adult client (and/or a family member) describes the presence of several signs and symptoms of dissociative reactions in childhood. The adult may continue to experience and exhibit many of these same symptoms in adulthood. Table 3 is a list of symptoms children exhibit which may be indicative of MPD. The word "children" can be replaced with "adults" in many of the symptoms on this list.

The clinician may use the General Amnesia Profile (Caul & Wilbur, n.d.) to assist in diagnosis. In line with our recommendations about proceeding with caution during assessment and diagnosis, the MPD diagnosis should be carefully presented to the client. Although some multiple personalities self-diagnose and they can be expected to do so with more frequency as the disorder receives more acknowledgment, and while some

TABLE 3
Signs and Symptoms of Dissociative Reactions in Childhood

1. Children who do not remember the actual abuse.
2. Children who seem to go into a "daze" or trance-like state at times.
3. Children who show marked changes in personality, e.g., going from shy and timid to hostile and belligerent, from passive and dependent to autonomous and aggressive, from feminine mannerisms to masculine behavior. One may also note changes in voice.
4. Children who seem unusually forgetful or who seem confused about very basic things, such as the names of teachers and friends, important events, possessions, etc.
5. Children who show marked day-to-day or hour-to-hour variations in skills, knowledge, food preferences, athletic abilities, etc., which would be expected to be stable, e.g., handwriting, knowledge of arithmetic or spelling, use of tools, or artistic abilities.
6. Children who demonstrate rapid regressions in behavior or show marked variations in age-appropriate behavior, e.g., a ten-year-old playing like a four-year-old at times.
7. Children who appear to lie or deny their behavior when the evidence is obvious and immediate.
8. Children who have many rapidly fluctuating physical complaints, especially headaches, and/or hysterical symptoms, such as epileptic-like seizures, paralysis, loss of sensation, blindness, etc., where no medical cause can be found.
9. Children who refer to themselves in the third person or insist on being called by a different name at times.
10. Children who self-mutilate, who engage in dangerous or self-destructive behaviors, or who are suicidal.
11. Children who are abnormally sexually precocious and who initiate sexual behavior with other children or adults.
12. Children who report auditory hallucinations.
13. Children who report conversations with an imaginary playmate beyond age six or seven.

Reprinted with permission. *Justice for Children*, P.O. Box 42266, Washington, DC 20015.

accept the diagnosis with relief, others find the diagnosis threatening. And some are so frightened that they may resist diagnosis by withholding information or lying. When the diagnosis is made, it ought to be presented gradually and explained in detail. Since the therapist wants to gain the cooperation of all personalities, s/he should be careful to present information neutrally, to assume the presence of other personalities, and to invite each to engage in the therapeutic process.

Considering the range, intensity, and instability of symptoms, we can see how the diagnosis is difficult and often missed. Putnam, Post and Guroff (1983) found an average time in the mental health system of 6.8 years from entry to proper diagnosis. Multiple personality should be differentiated from other dissociative states, hysterical personality, hypnotic states, affective disorder (especially manic-depressive illness), sociopathy, organic conditions, alcoholism and other substance abuse where blackouts occur, simulation and malingering, anxiety, somatoform and borderline personality disorders, and schizophrenia. Psychotic states present a puzzle, since multiple personalities may become psychotic and dissociation can occur in psychotic states, particularly schizophrenia (Coons, 1980, p. 332). Diagnosis of MPD is made further difficult by the fact that some individuals remain in one personality for long periods of time without switching and some actively hide from the clinician to deliberately impede accurate diagnosis.

Axis II Diagnosis. Axis II of a *DSM* diagnosis is distinguished from axis I in that its categories are long-standing, developmental, and apply to personality disturbances. Since incest occurs over the course of the child's development, it may significantly affect personality. The narcissistic, borderline, histrionic, avoidant/dependent, atypical, and mixed personality disorders have been the diagnoses most frequently applied to incest survivors, both inpatient and outpatient.

Most commonly, incest victims may be diagnosed as having a *borderline personality disorder (BPD)*. According to *DSM-III-R*, BPD involves "a pervasive pattern of instability of mood, interpersonal relationships, and self-image, beginning by early adulthood and present in a variety of concepts, as indicated by at least *five* of the following:

(1) A pattern of unstable and intense interpersonal relationships characterized by alternating between extremes of overidealization and devaluation.
(2) Impulsiveness in at least two areas that are potentially self-damaging, e.g., spending, sex, substance abuse, shoplifting, reckless driving, binge eating (Do not include suicidal or self-mutilating behavior covered in [5]).
(3) Affective instability; marked shifts from baseline mood to depression, irritability, or anxiety, usually lasting a few hours and only rarely more than a few days.
(4) Inappropriate, intense anger or lack of control of anger, e.g., frequent displays of temper, constant anger, recurrent physical fights.
(5) Recurrent suicidal threats, gestures, or behavior or self-mutilating behavior.
(6) Marked and persistent identity disturbance manifested by uncertainty about at least two of the following: self-image, sexual orientation, long-term goals or career choice, type of friends desired, preferred values.
(7) Chronic feelings of emptiness or boredom.

(8) Frantic efforts to avoid real or imagined abandonment (Do not
    include suicidal or self-mutilating behavior covered in [5]) (p. 347).

In addition to these criteria, it is highly likely that individuals with BPD
develop at least one episode of major depression. The syndrome can be
considered an atypical variant of affective disorder (Herman & van der
Kolk, 1987), an association currently being investigated.

There has been extensive speculation and debate, as well as some research, about the etiology of the borderline disorder. Although the role of
severe physical and sexual abuse perpetrated by parents has been noted, it
has never been given much credence as a factor causing the development
of the personality disturbance (Herman & van der Kolk, 1987). Moreover,
the role of incest has not been systematically investigated, even though a
clear logic now connects adult characteristics to damage of self, abuse of or
lack of boundaries exhibited by the abuser or the family in general, confusion about safety and rules of relationships, parentification, etc. Such investigations are only now underway. Two small studies have documented a
startlingly high percentage of incest in hospitalized patients who carry a
borderline diagnosis: Stone (1981) found a 75% rate of incest and Nelson
found 86% (unpublished study cited in Herman & van der Kolk, 1987). A
study by Wheeler and Walton (1987) showed a clinical sample of incest
victims to have an elevated score for borderline personality when compared with a non-incest sample.

The role of incest in the development of borderline symptoms has been
noted by clinicians working with survivors and by sexual abuse researchers.
Clinically, it is apparent that chronic post-incest reactions of many abuse
survivors fit the criteria for BPD. Briere (1984) substantiated this clinical
hypothesis in a study of women who had been sexually abused in childhood. In his research, he compared abused and nonabused samples and
found significant differences between the two in symptoms indicative of
anxiety, depressive, impulsive, and dissociative disorders. He noted the
congruence between the symptom constellation of the abuse sample,
which he termed the post sexual abuse syndrome, and the criteria listed for
borderline personality disorder in *DSM-III*. The striking similarities between the two led him to suggest that BPD is not an accurate diagnosis and
to propose a post sexual abuse syndrome as a diagnosis that clarifies etiology and assists the clinician in offering effective treatment. Although incest
is beginning to be recognized as related to and causative of borderline-type
symptoms, treatment approaches have not followed suit. Briere wrote:

> To the extent that a significant proportion of "borderline" diagnoses involve
> symptomatology arising from sexual abuse, an absence of training and inter-
> est in sexual abuse trauma among mental health professionals becomes a
> major concern. This is somewhat exacerbated by the fact that current treat-

ment approaches to borderline personality disorder stress theoretical formulations which are relatively devoid of reference to sexual victimization (e.g., Object Relations theory). The absence of traditional treatment approaches to chronic sexual abuse trauma (whether designated "PSAS" or "Borderline") which address childhood victimization may partially explain the traditional wisdom that such cases "rarely get better." Although the outcome data is [sic] incomplete in this area, it is quite probable that treatment approaches which directly deal with the abuse, somewhat in the way that Rape Trauma Syndrome is treated by "working through" the assault (Burgess & Holmstrom, 1979), will be more successful with such clients (Herman, 1981). (p. 14)

The recognition of the underlying trauma and of the borderline symptoms as essentially manifestations of post-traumatic stress disorder focuses on the need for the recovery and integration of the trauma. Many of the difficulties associated with treating borderlines might be alleviated by providing therapy which focuses on the trauma.

A substantial amount of overlap exists among the symptoms of post-traumatic stress disorder, multiple personality disorder, and borderline personality disorder. Each often involves a chronic affective disorder. According to Braun (1986), PTSD can be considered a dissociative disorder that operates through both intrusive symptoms (intrusive thoughts and nightmares) and denial (amnesia, psychic numbing). He further notes that MPD can be considered a special form of chronic PTSD. Putnam (1984) states that the dissociation of MPD may be followed by such residual symptoms as nightmares, flashbacks, difficulty concentrating, excessive irritability, anxiety, and depression which may continue for many years. Speigel (1986) has proposed another way that MPD can be conceptualized as a form of post-traumatic stress disorder. He believes that MPD arises in response to repeated double binding of the child. The child dissociates in order to contend with an intolerable situation; however, the splitting off of the trauma is more complete in MPD than it is in PTSD.

MPD, like borderline personality disorder, is a disorder of the self. Both are characterized by an unstable sense of self, unstable and intense interpersonal relationships, mood instability, impulsive behavior, chronic boredom, inability to tolerate solitude, ego splitting, uncontrolled anger and rage, and manipulative suicide attempts. A number of researchers conceptualize MPD as a type of borderline personality disorder due to the instability of mood and symptoms, the propensity to develop transient psychotic episodes, and the use of such primitive ego defenses as splitting, projective identification, repression, and denial. Beahrs (1982) has written that he agrees that MPD falls under the rubric of the narcissistic and borderline disorders, as opposed to the hysterical, a position also supported by the work of Clary, Burstin, and Carpenter (1984). He further suggests that a combination diagnosis of borderline personality disorder *with* multiple personality is perhaps the most accurate. He believes that a substantial proportion of borderline personalities are actually multiples and raises the possibility that the most severely disturbed chaotic borderlines, whose splitting is possibly too chaotic to form stable alter personalities, are in reality "super-multiples" as delineated by Braun (1980). In support of Beahrs' dual diagnosis idea, Horevitz and Braun (1984) found that 70% of patients with the diagnosis of MPD also qualified for the diagnosis of borderline, and Schultz, Braun, and Kluft (1987) in a preliminary report found a figure of 67%.

Speigel observed an important point of difference between the two diagnoses: Clients with dissociative disorders, notably MPD, split internally and are usually ruminative, depressed, and guilty about their early life experience; in contrast, borderline personalities split external objects into good and bad and tend to be hostile, paranoid, and unable to tolerate dysphoria. Clary, Burstin, and Carpenter (1984) made a similar observation:

> It is our position that the multiple personality represents a "special instance" of borderline personality disorder, that the introjects are indeed composed of a representation of the self, a representation of the object and an affective bond. However, the representation of the object in these cases is the patient's central ego, and in this sense there is a distinct difference from the classical borderline pattern. This probably represents a further development of structuralization and accounts for the finding that patients with multiple personality use both mechanisms of splitting and repression in their defense repertoire. (p. 98)

Finally, as Briere's (1984) study showed, borderline personality disorder can be conceptualized as a post-traumatic stress disorder. Herman and van der Kolk offered this explanation:

> Clinical descriptions of borderline personality disorder, however, are remarkably congruent with descriptions of chronic post-traumatic stress disorder . . . and especially with the form of the disorder described in patients who have been subjected to repeated trauma over a considerable period of time. In both syndromes, major disturbances are found in the areas of affect regulation, impulse control, reality testing, interpersonal relationships, and self-integration. (p. 115)

In summary, diagnosis is complicated by the many symptoms and aftereffects exhibited by incest survivors, their often disguised presentation, and by the many points of overlap between diagnostic categories. From the above review of PTSD, MPD and BPD diagnoses, it is obvious that progress is being made in acknowledging traumatic events as contributing to the emergence of serious degrees of personality disturbance and debilitating symptoms. It is noteworthy that incest history is being independently associated with each of these diagnoses. The application of traumatic stress treatment models to incest offers a way to integrate the trauma and to prevent further symptom formation and recurrence.

SECTION III
Incest Therapy

CHAPTER 9

Philosophy, Process, and Goals of Incest Therapy

RETROSPECTIVE INCEST THERAPY is based on the new information available on incest and other traumatic life events and derived from the theories presented in Chapter 7: feminist theory; traumatic stress or victimization theory; self developmental theory; and loss theory. The basic organizing principle is that incest is a real childhood experience, not a fantasy occurrence or a wish. It has high traumatic potential due the premature sexualization of the child, the abuse of power and betrayal of trust inherent in its occurrence within the family, and the taboo and forced silence which have historically surrounded it. Incest therapy is directed towards the development of a therapeutic relationship from which the survivor can rework the trauma and integrate the self.

THE PHILOSOPHY OF TREATMENT

The philosophical principles of retrospective incest therapy are: (1) to treat the incest directly along with its original and compounded effects; (2) to use traumatic stress, feminist, and family systems models to understand the incest, its effects, and its symptoms, and to plan and implement treatment; (3) to individualize the treatment within the more general process and structure; and (4) to foster the development of a therapeutic alliance and a safe environment within which to conduct the treatment.

Before elaborating on these principles, let us consider how they might contradict or complement a given practitioner's therapeutic orientation. The philosophy of incest therapy is consistent with the basic tenets of some personality theories and schools of therapy but at odds with others. The therapist should consider how his or her preferred orientation might work against or support the perspective presented here. In some cases, a slight philosophical modification is needed; in others, wholesale reversal or abandonment of a central tenet is called for.

The most significant discrepancy is found with any theory or orientation which holds that the sexual abuse of children is impossible or untrue or which blames the child for the abuse. The classic psychoanalytic tradition centered around drive theory and the Oedipus complex is the most obvious and influential in this regard. From this perspective, the reality of abuse has been largely negated in favor of an emphasis on the child's fantasies, desires, and projections.

A problem also arises with theories which acknowledge the reality of sexual interactions between adults and children but view them as natural and beneficial. The child's immaturity is seen as protection against the development of negative effects. This position, espoused by some schools of sex therapy and humanistic therapy, totally ignores the child's experience, the power differential between adults and children, and the potential for exploitation.

Other theoretical departures are less dramatic but nonetheless affect the direction and course of treatment. Some theories accept the reality of incest but due to rigid sex-role stereotyping ignore or minimize the prevalence of the problem, its predominant perpetration by males, and its sanctioning by the sex-role stereotyping found in patriarchal society, as well as its risk for injurious consequences (Brickman, 1984; Butler, 1985; Finkelhor, 1984). Brickman has been most articulate in discussing the drawbacks of traditional and even "nonsexist" therapies when they are applied to the treatment of incest. She writes:

> In the most traditional theories, incest as fact disappears. In its worst and most insidious forms, reports of incest are viewed as fantasies and insisting on their reality considered a sign of serious mental instability. In the few instances where it is acknowledged to have occurred, the therapeutic issues will typically revolve around the girl's desire for her father, her initiation of the act, her seduction of him and others, her pleasure, gratification and gain. It will not necessarily be seen as harmful to her. (p. 55)

Nonsexist therapies are an improvement over the more traditional models in that they attend to sex differences and role inequalities. At the same time they generally fail to address the power imbalances within the family and continue to place exaggerated emphasis on the wife's role as collusive and the daughter's as seductive, with too little emphasis on the role and responsibility of the father (or other perpetrator). Or all family members are held to be victims and equally responsible for the perpetration. The traditional, patriarchal family structure is not viewed as contributing to the development of incest. The result is therapy aimed at reconstituting the family into its traditional roles without attention to power distinctions, the individual responsibility of the perpetrator, or the safety of the children. A number of family therapies, some of which are religiously oriented, have as their goal the maintenance of the family unit above all else. The family is seen as so important and sacrosanct that its maintenance is primary.

Feminist theory, on the other hand, emphasizes the subjective experience of the abused child, the more powerful role ascribed to males in our society and the less powerful to females, and the sexualization of these power differentials. The patriarchal family provides the model for inequality and sex-role conditioning. To quote Herman (1981, p. 206) on the topic: "As long as fathers rule but do not nurture, as long as mothers nurture but do not rule, the conditions favoring the development of father-daughter incest will prevail. Only a basic change in the power relations of mothers and fathers can prevent the sexual exploitation of children."

The four philosophical bases of incest therapy are discussed below.

To Treat the Incest Directly Along with Its Original and Compounded Effects

The reality of incest and child sexual abuse is at the core of this therapy. While this point is self-evident and redundant, it must be continuously reemphasized due to the societal tendency to deny, discount, or dismiss such intrafamilial abuse, as well as the denial inherent in some theories of personality and on the part of some practitioners. In incest therapy, the abuse not only is given credence but becomes the main, although not the sole, focus of the treatment. The client is believed and is actively encouraged to remember what happened and to experience the emotions associated with the incest, with the aim of reworking the trauma and extinguishing the need for dysfunctional defenses and symptoms. Rieker and Carmen (1986) describe treatment for the aftereffects of abuse in this way:

> The core of treatment must be to help the victim, in a safe and controlled way, to recall the abuse and its original affects and to restore the accurate meanings attached to the abuse: that is, to recontextualize the trauma. . . . the turning point for the patient occurs when her or his rage is experienced not as meaningless, but as a response to cruelty. The patient needs to understand that nothing will erase the past. The work of therapy is, rather, to reclaim that traumatic past as a part of one's history and identity. With this kind of understanding, the abused patient will be able to grieve and to let go of both the trauma and the distortions in memory and affects that once were necessary for survival. (p. 369)

To Use Traumatic Stress, Feminist, and Family Systems Models

The medical model of psychopathology is replaced with the traumatic stress and feminist models supplemented by the family systems approach to conceptualize the abuse and its aftereffects. Incest and its context are viewed as potentially and almost inevitably traumatic for the child. If the traumatic impact is untreated and unresolved, attempts at mastery will be seen in intrusive and numbing symptomatology and in compulsive repetitions and unconscious reenactments during childhood and later. The symptoms and defenses are conceptualized as the secondary elaborations of the untreated original effects of the incest.

As part of this treatment, symptoms and defenses must be understood in context and not pathologized. Working through the incest means dismantling the defenses to work with underlying material. This in turn results in symptom remission over the course of the therapy. Some survivors spontaneously give up symptoms when they are no longer needed, while others change them gradually as new skills are learned and substituted. Miller (1984) describes the process in this way:

> The healing process begins when the once absent, repressed reactions to traumatization (such as anxiety, rage, anger, despair, dismay, pain, grief) can be articulated . . . ; then the symptoms, whose function it had been to express the unconscious trauma in a disguised, alienated language incomprehensible both to the patient and to those around him, disappear. (p. 53)

While the individual and her experience occupy center stage, incest is conceptualized within its broad sociohistorical context, a perspective fostered by feminism. Recognizing the social forces which support or produce victims and offenders, such as the hidden acceptance of abuse behind the taboo (Rush, 1980), the economic and power differentials between men and women, the powerlessness of children, and rigid sex-role and family stereotyping, is a step toward seeing the abuse as more than an individual or one-family aberration. The taboo surrounding talking about child sexual abuse has been instrumental in allowing it to flourish while adding to the victim's trauma through forced silence (Lister, 1982) and disconfirmation of her experience (Rieker & Carmen, 1986). Dealing with the effects of not being able to talk about the abuse and of having her reality repeatedly invalidated is a goal of treatment.

Additionally, the fact that the abuse was at the hands of a relative and not a stranger is viewed "as intensifying rather than mitigating the betrayal and the trauma" (Brickman, 1984, p. 64). A feminist perspective on the family is maintained. Family maintenance or reconstitution is not the goal; rather, the safety of children within the family is considered paramount.

Family systems theory reveals the family's interaction patterns. Concepts such as boundaries, role reversal, enmeshment, triangulation, family subsystems, and intergenerational process and transmission assist the clinician in understanding and working with the dysfunctional family. Nevertheless, traditional family therapy is not sufficient in and of itself to treat incest because it is directed more towards modifying family relationships than toward uncovering the family's intrapsychic process. Since intergenerational family process has been found to contribute to the development of incest and other serious family dysfunction, the process and its intrapsychic components must be treated (Calof, 1987). Used in conjunction with feminist and traumatic stress theory, family systems theory broadens our multimodal approach to the complex problem of incest.

To Individualize Treatment

Within the general treatment framework, the therapist strives to understand each survivor and her unique experience and to tailor the therapy to her individual needs. Symptoms are understood as symbolic ways by which each individual communicates about herself and her experience while defenses are viewed as skills devised to survive the trauma. The therapist should expect to hear of highly idiosyncratic experiences. Interventions need to be carefully applied, taking into account the survivor's specific circumstances and needs. Treatment planning includes attention to the following factors:

(1) The abuse experience itself, as well as other traumatic or problematic life events.
(2) The individual's personality structure and her personalized defensive operations and adaptations.
(3) The idiosyncratic meaning of the incest experience.

To Foster the Development of a Therapeutic Alliance and a Safe Environment

It is important for the therapist to maintain a stance of openness to and acceptance of the client. Although the therapist might studiously maintain the neutrality associated with some therapeutic orientations, it is advisable that s/he be active and open in engaging the client. The nonresponsive, abstinent therapist is often perceived as judgmental and unavailable. Such a position recreates dynamics from the past, making it almost impossible for the client to disclose and to engage in self-exploration. The survivor learns through the therapy that she has, possibly for the first time in her life, an advocate, someone who is interested in understanding what happened to her in childhood (Miller, 1984). A warm, caring, but not overindulgent therapist provides the interpersonal environment conducive to disclosure and examination.

The therapist must further avoid being parental or authoritarian with the client or creating an environment where she is without power or where her efficacy is contravened. She is the expert on her own experience; the therapist is available as a supportive person who helps her to explore that experience, to express that which was impossible to express in childhood and is impossible to express alone now (Miller, 1984). Whenever possible, the therapist avoids techniques and interventions which are controlling, authoritarian, or power-laden, so as not to recreate abuse dynamics. Furthermore, the therapist assists the survivor in identifying and reclaiming her personal power, as well as those parts of herself which went undeveloped or were distorted by the trauma.

Rosenfeld (1986) likened the role of therapist to that of midwife/facilitator, someone who assists in the dual processes of remembering and working-through. As such, the basic therapy stance is open, exploratory and noncondemnatory. It is likewise helpful for the therapist to share affectively with the client. Because the survivor has been betrayed in the context of an intimate relationship, other relationships are suspect. The therapist is well-advised to stress the reality of the relationship and to work in the here and now with the survivor so that she develops her perceptive capacities. This occurs in addition to analyzing transference and countertransference reactions. An example serves to illustrate this point.

Early in her treatment, Holly continually asked her therapist "Do you hate me?" after having disclosed something about her past or after having received the therapist's positive regard during the session. Clearly, she projected her feelings of being undeserving and unlovable onto all around her. Rather than exploring or interpreting Holly's question, the therapist chose initially to reassure her that she did not hate her and further to ask Holly to focus on the relationship as she was experiencing it. Over time, Holly became more comfortable within the therapy and was able to receive positive attention without the accompanying feeling that she was hated.

CONCEPTUALIZATIONS OF THE THERAPY PROCESS

Retrospective incest therapy can be conceptualized in a number of ways. It is often labeled a healing or recovery process or an abreaction of the trauma, which generally involves breaking the secret, catharsis, and reevaluation of the incest, its circumstances, and its effects. Butler (1985) has suggested that at its most basic incest therapy is the encouragement of expression at the expense of repression and suppression. Wise (1985) has described it as a remembering process, with the central therapeutic issues being family rules, self-destructive behaviors as survival mechanisms, and internalized shame and guilt. She has also labeled the process the "victim/ survivor paradox," since victims survived childhood abuse through their own efforts and resourcefulness but continue to perceive themselves as victims — without power and at the mercy of those around them. Therapy is geared to illuminating this paradox and facilitating the change from victim to survivor and beyond. Similarly, Wooley and Vigilanti (1984) conceptualized childhood incest as a double-bind situation which the child survived at great personal expense. Its traumatic potential was heightened because the child was forbidden to discuss it and so was allowed no expression or validation (Speigel, 1986). Encouraging ventilation, teaching ways to break the double bind, and fostering separation and individuation from the family and its patterns are critical tasks.

The therapy process can also be conceptualized as a developmental process involving reparenting in the sense that the survivor reexperiences and reworks the tasks of maturation that were either missed or experienced prematurely (Courtois & Sprei, 1988). It is important to stress that the therapist does not become the parent, nor can s/he ever change or make up for the client's past. Rather, therapy provides an opportunity to address the past with a supportive ally and to grieve and make up for the losses of childhood.

The process involves finding meaning in the experience as well as mourning. Silver, Boon, and Stones (1983) discuss the therapeutic benefit of finding meaning in the incest experience, including an understanding of its causes, circumstances, and aftereffects. They caution, however, that some situations have no explanation or meaning, making resolution more difficult. Grieving is poignant enough when the survivor can identify reasons for the abuse and give some meaning to the experience. When no such explanation or meaning is available, she must do the best she can to make sense of the circumstance and to mourn how it affected her.

Conceptualizing the aftereffects of incest within a traumatic stress framework offers a model for understanding the complex symptom picture that survivors often present and a concrete orientation for treatment understandable to both client and therapist. Horowitz (1986) discussed the general principles of this treatment:

> Modifying excessive controls, altering pathological defensive stances, and supporting weak regulatory capacities all are part of the treatment of stress response syndromes. These coping and defensive conditions are set in motion by the impact of the stressor events; yet they are also a product of longstanding personality styles. The patient's character also includes enduring schemata of self, others, and relationships, as well as persistent life agendas encompassing unconscious scenarios of how the person hopes life will turn out. The treatment invariably involves work with coping and defensive strategies, as well as with the repertoires mentioned above, whether or not these levels of immediate reaction or personality are interpreted. Thus the treatment is both specific and general. (p. 112)

Incest survivors, by virtue of having been children at the time of the abuse, have had their development affected and modified. It is likely that trauma reactions are embedded within their personality. A traumatic stress approach involving different levels of interpretation can address both trauma and developmental issues. As the therapy progresses by stages to the discussion of the abuse, the survivor begins to explore warded-off unconscious material about her childhood, material that she had to repress to survive. This exploration allows access to the constructs she developed about herself, her ability to direct and control her life, and her relations with others.

Five treatment principles have been formulated for intervention for delayed or chronic PTSD, according to Scurfield (1985, p. 241): (1) establishment of a therapeutic trust relationship; (2) education regarding the stress recovery process; (3) stress management/reduction; (4) regression back to or a reexperiencing of the trauma; and (5) integration of the trauma experience. These are remarkably similar to the stages of incest treatment outlined by Harris (1986): (1) intake and diagnosis; (2) building the adult relationship; (3) working with the "child within"; (4) integrating the helpless child with the nurturing adult; and (5) disclosure to and confrontation of the family and any involved others. What follows is a description of the process of incest treatment, using the Harris headings and integrating the traumatic stress approach developed by Scurfield.

Intake and Diagnosis

This stage involves the preliminaries in developing the therapeutic relationship. The therapist learns as much as possible about presenting concerns and their severity and assesses the individual's personality style and level of functioning. Once incest is identified, the therapist seeks to learn about its occurrence and its impact, including its secondary elaborations and symptoms. Preliminary diagnostic formulations are made at this stage. (Guidelines for conducting the intake interview and for making the diagnosis are presented in Chapter 8.)

Early in treatment and repeatedly throughout its course, the therapist should offer information about incest/child sexual abuse and stress response and recovery, particularly the bipolar nature of intrusive and numbing symptomatology. Repeated exposure to this information is necessary because it contradicts what the survivor learned and believes about herself and may not be immediately comprehensible or applicable. As is frequently the case in chronic and/or preverbal victimization, these individuals have had their reactions/reality contradicted so many times in childhood and have had such intense emotional reactions that they feel they are going crazy or losing their minds. New material contradicting the old, although initially incomprehensible, is nevertheless very relieving since it validates and depathologizes emotions. Some clients explain that their rational/intellectual self understands and accepts the new conceptualization even though it "does not compute" on an emotional level. Over time and with repetition, the information becomes more emotionally congruent and is assimilated and used.

The therapist should also outline the normal course of treatment, including the fact that symptoms usually get worse before they get better. The therapist can, at this stage and throughout the treatment, offer a supportive alliance to get through the traumatic aftermath. The therapist imparts hope about recovery and offers the assurance that PTSD is responsive to treatment; however, it is essential that the therapist communicate the reality that some symptoms may never completely abate although they will lessen and that treatment does not "make it all go away." Rather, treatment is directed towards helping the survivor better understand her experiences and reactions and reduce or extinguish the need for symptoms and their secondary consequences. She will leave therapy with less need for defensive self-control and with more positive controls in place for herself and her life. The therapy will also help her to examine both the positive and negative meaning and impact of the experience in her life.

Building the Adult Relationship

This stage involves many different tasks: the establishment and deepening of a therapeutic alliance with the therapist and involved others (such as therapy group members); the utilization of the therapist and group members as alter egos who offer support during the experiencing of warded-off feelings; continued education about incest, its effects, and the recovery process; breaking silence and isolation by learning that she is not alone; working with presenting problems and symptoms; learning about family interactions and taking an "adult look" at family dynamics and rules; and acknowledging the "child within."

As discussed in Chapter 9, the survivor may enter treatment with multiple and compounded presenting concerns and symptoms. Early intervention involves deciding what has priority. Two rules of thumb apply. First, the incest material should not be explored in any great detail if the survivor is otherwise in crisis because doing so is likely to precipitate a new crisis, worsen the situation, or promote regression and decompensation. In this situation, crisis intervention aimed at stabilization is necessary. Secondly, problems more severe or life-threatening than the incest take treatment precedence and must be managed before or simultaneously with exploratory work.

Establishing priorities is at times tricky because some problems are not responsive to treatment until their functions and secondary gains are uncovered. For example, acute anorexia or bulimia, self-destructive behaviors, and addictions and compulsions may all be resistant to treatment until such underlying dynamics as self-hatred, the need for self-punishment, and identification with the aggressor are uncovered and lessened. The therapist needs to work towards stabilization of these problems while working on the trauma. These problems and special treatment considerations are discussed in Chapter 14.

The survivor's coping strategies should be assessed with the aim of identifying those which have been effective in the past under certain circumstances. The survivor is encouraged to continue to use these strategies and to develop a repertoire of others. The ability to exert some self-control frees the survivor for more in-depth work on trauma-related symptoms and issues.

Working With the "Child Within"

The focus of the therapy is the recollection, exploration and abreacting of the traumatic material from the adult context. In this stage, the abused child is experientially brought into the treatment. In the context of the supportive relationship and environment, the survivor reconnects with the abused child and reexperiences the trauma and the feelings of childhood, in particular responsibility, guilt, confusion, ambivalence, shame, anger, sadness, and loss. Regression, including a return of intrusive symptoms and body sensations associated with the past, destabilization, and sometimes decompensation, characterize this stage. The survivor may have to get worse before she can recover. Since this work is often the most intensive of the therapy involving affective and autonomic arousal, the therapist must closely monitor the process and help the survivor "dose" and contain her reactions. She should be assisted in managing both her denial and her intrusive symptoms to make them as tolerable as possible. The support of the therapist and of others, such as therapy group members and available family members and friends, assists the survivor to resurface and face cut-off memories and emotions. She thus discovers validation for her experience within her new adult context and grieves for what was lost.

Integrating the Helpless Child
with the Nurturing Adult

This phase of therapy involves integrating the various aspects of the trauma experience, whether positive, negative or ambivalent, into the self and separating from family rules and patterns. A radical redefinition of the self can result. As the survivor increasingly understands the societal and familial patterns and dynamics which contributed to her abuse, she is able to develop a different perspective from which to assess her reactions and adaptations. Doing so enables her to empathize with her difficult childhood position and view herself with compassion rather than self-loathing.

In this way she is able to lessen her sense of badness and to forgive herself. Grieving past losses sets the stage for personal development and empowerment. Old maladaptive mechanisms, patterns, and symptoms are analyzed and replaced with ones that are healthier and more appropriate. A positive self-concept replaces the shame and self-hatred of old.

Survivors who have used dissociation extensively, some to the point of developing multiple personalities, present the most extreme forms of splitting and the greatest challenge in the integration process. When full personalities have developed, they are quite often fearful of any movement towards assimilation because it means annihilation. The treatment must give each part or personality legitimacy and acknowledgment for the function it serves. Treatment involves generating communication between the personalities so that each can learn to appreciate the other(s). They can then work cooperatively as a whole and in this way integrate rather than destroy one another.

Disclosure to and Confrontation of the Family and Any Involved Others

Whether symbolically within the therapy setting or directly with the family or others, disclosure and confrontation allow further integration of the trauma experience. The survivor breaks the silence to become the "reactivated child" who reclaims her selfhood, her experience, and her voice (Harris, 1986). Much preparation and practice are required for this step (see Chapter 15 for discussion of these issues).

Incest therapy, like other forms of therapy, varies greatly in terms of intensity and duration, based on the needs of the client. At its least intense, reassurance, information, the opportunity for ventilation, support, and short-term counseling suffice. For those survivors suffering the most serious effects, long-term exploratory and reparative treatment is needed. Of course there are many points on the continuum between these short-term and long-term models.

In some cases the therapy proceeds in stages. A number of survivors can tolerate only limited amounts of interpersonal contact or exploration before they resort to familiar and comfortable defenses or reinstitute numbing or flight mechanisms. The individual must be ready and motivated to engage in the hard work of therapy. She may have to wait until she feels ready or until she is forced to consider change by crisis circumstances or unbearable symptomatology. Many survivors can nonetheless benefit from an abbreviated therapeutic contact based on the treatment philosophy outlined in the previous section. Breaking silence within an empathic and supportive relationship may provide the only therapy needed or prepare the survivor for a return to therapy when she is motivated once again. Herman (1987) has observed that incest therapy is completed in "episodic" fashion by a number of survivors.

GOALS OF TREATMENT

Treatment goals to alleviate the negative effects of incest generally conform to those for treating a stress response syndrome, which according to Horowitz (1986, p. 123) include "completing integration of an event's meanings and developing adaptational responses." More specific and individualized goals must be established for each survivor. Some clients enter therapy to work on particular problems, e.g., sexual aversions, marital distress, or substance abuse; others complain of symptoms that have become bothersome and disruptive, most frequently intrusive symptoms (e.g., nightmares, flashbacks, startle responses, crying spells). These cause greater distress than numbing symptoms, which are generally more easily overlooked; however, some clients do enter therapy complaining of numbing symptoms (e.g., inability to concentrate, amnesia, derealization and a sense of detachment). Other clients wish to address more general and less specific issues, e.g., to feel better or less depressed, or to deal with the incest. At times, it is necessary to explain to the survivor that specific problem areas will probably not improve if underlying trauma issues are not discussed. For example, Nadelson (1982) and Sprei and Courtois (1988) found that for some women behavioral sex therapy alone is unsuccessful in treating sexual dysfunctions arising from sexual abuse. In-depth treatment addressing salient incest issues is needed for symptom relief to occur.

Concerning the goals of incest therapy, Brickman (1984, p. 63) wrote, "These are long-term goals, rarely accomplished in anything less than two or three years, and certainly not assumed by the mere cessation of abuse. In severe cases, it is a question as to what extent they can be accomplished at all." My experience leads me to agree with Brickman. Long-term treatment is often required due to the chronicity of the abuse, its impact on the developmental process and the character of the victim, and the time required to work with strong defenses and establish a therapeutic alliance. With those survivors who have suffered the most serious repercussions and who present the most serious symptomatology, including multiple personality, other dissociative states, substance dependencies and addictions of any type, and suicidal and self-destructive behavior, the therapist can assume that the therapy is going to take years. Optimally, the therapist-survivor relationship develops slowly, with interventions and interpretations paced according to both the survivor's ability to work with them and the degree of affect and defense they generate.

The survivor herself is likely to be discouraged or enraged by the need for such lengthy treatment, its slow pace, and the disequilibrium inherent in recovering from the incest aftereffects. Quite understandably, some women see therapy as extending the amount of "life time" that the sexual abuse has taken. For obvious reasons, it is important for the therapist to support the outrage, resentment, and discouragement. Explanations of the course of therapy and the reasons for its likely duration can put the process in perspective and offer support and reassurance. Early in the therapy, it is not uncommon for the survivor to believe that therapy will be lengthy because she is so crazy and to use this as a reason to be angry with and blame herself. The therapist must counter such self-perceptions repeatedly and reframe the situation so the client understands that she suffered extensive damage and developed maladaptive symptomatology that can only be undone over time. Moreover, the therapist must counter the survivor's despair with hope that she can recover and with assurance that the syndrome and its symptoms are amenable to treatment.

The general goals of incest therapy are:

Development of a Commitment to Treatment and the Establishment of a Therapeutic Alliance

The survivor may initially contract for short-term work in order to "test the waters" before making a longer-term commitment. She needs to be confident of the therapist's acceptance and understanding before proceeding. Even so assured, commitment for long-term work may be difficult for other reasons. The survivor might shy away when it becomes obvious to her that she will have to face what she has previously avoided and that treatment will involve a considerable amount of pain. She might be so threatened by a redefinition of her abuse experience (discussed below) that she chooses not to continue treatment. Forward and Buck (1978) have cautioned therapists about the tendency of some survivors to flee treatment prematurely in avoidance and/or in a "flight into health." Survivors in this latter circumstance are so relieved at revealing their secret, venting feelings, and receiving affirmation that they leave thinking they are "cured." Another type of avoidance is evident in the survivor who acknowledges the occurrence of the incest but enters therapy with the expressed intent of "making it all go away." Therapists can attempt to head off these possible reactions by addressing them explicitly early in the treatment and by communicating an understanding of the difficulty involved in working with incest. It is good strategy for therapy to begin with an understanding that the client has the right to leave therapy at any time but that she agrees not to do so without first discussing her reasons with the therapist.

The therapeutic alliance, an essential element in any therapy, holds special potential in healing the effects of incest. It is the necessary base which allows the exploratory work to take place. It offers the survivor personal validation along with the consistency and support needed to undo the repression and to face often terrifying memories and emotions. In so doing, it directly counters the survivor's feelings of being alone, worthless, and undeserving. Additionally, it serves as a model of a healthy, non-exploitive, and growth-promoting relationship.

Acknowledgment and Acceptance of The Occurrence of The Incest

Acknowledgment involves breaking old patterns of secrecy and silence, challenging family injunctions and modes of functioning, and countering denial and other coping mechanisms. Acceptance involves believing the experience and memories. The defenses involved in the maintenance of silence need to be dismantled, so the survivor can directly acknowledge what happened and work through the emotional repercussions. Rieker and Carmen (1986) write that the abuse needs to be recontextualized during the treatment process to counter the disconfirmation and transformation processes which occurred at the time of the abuse and afterwards. Acknowledgment, acceptance, and recontextualization are usually very threatening and thus require time. They may alternate with periods of denial and suppression before they are allowed unequivocally. Swink and Leveille (1986) discussed this process:

> To fully accept the reality that this person who was supposed to love, guide, and protect her actually chose to abuse, use, and hurt her requires the breakdown of the fantasy of the perfect family. The loss of this hope is very painful and threatening. Since the victim has [often] grown up being the scapegoat and identified as "crazy" in the family, it is easy to doubt herself. When she dares to share these flashbacks, any feedback which might hint at disbelief or questioning feeds the self-doubt and regresses the process. If, however, she is listened to, believed, supported and accepted, she can begin to trust herself and begin [the] therapeutic process of recovery. (p. 133)

Recounting The Incest

This goal involves the actual disclosure of the incest in the therapy. The recounting process is highly variable. It is done easily in a rather offhanded and matter-of-fact way by some survivors, and with great suspicion, hesitancy, shame, and excruciating pain by others. Some survivors have only the most vague and cursory memories, despite their best efforts to remember. Usually, repression lifts during the course of therapy and memories return, although some survivors have to base their belief that incest occurred on physical cues or outside sources of validation, rather than on concrete memories. Whatever the style and degree of disclosure, the therapist should watch for delayed reactions or backlash emotional responses which may lead the survivor to flee therapy or punish herself.

The incest story may have to be recounted in pieces, taking into account the gradual giving way of repression to memories and insuring that the emotional impact is both tolerable and manageable. The therapist needs to closely monitor this process with the client. A recitation in great and exhaustive detail is necessary for some survivors, but not for all. For some, a general recitation to establish facts suffices. As a general rule, the therapist should seek to learn about the pertinent details of the abuse, its duration and frequency, the child's age at onset and termination, the identity of the perpetrator(s), whether the incest was overt or covert, whether the survivor ever sought out the contact, whether force was used, any disclosure and intervention, and other incestuous abuses and problems in the family (Courtois & Watts, 1982). These issues are discussed in more detail in Chapter 8.

Breakdown of Feelings of Isolation and Stigma

Some of the more persistent effects of incest, such as the sense of being different from "normal people" or of being malignantly powerful, the need to maintain secrecy, the lack of trust, and the fear of intimacy, result in withdrawal and isolation. In cyclical fashion, isolation fosters these same effects while contributing to lowered self-esteem and stigma. The therapy relationship may be the first step in breaking both the isolation and stigmatized self-concept. Group therapy is the treatment of choice to counter these effects, but self-help networks and bibliotherapy are useful as well.

The Recognition, Labeling and Expression of Feelings

The denial, repression, and minimization which allow the survivor to tolerate the abuse later make her feelings unavailable to her except when they break through in flashbacks, nightmares and other intrusive symptoms. Quite commonly, survivors have sealed off their emotions and trained themselves to operate strictly on a rational basis. The therapy challenges this split. With consistent encouragement and support for the exploration of both conscious and unconscious material, the survivor learns to recognize and label her feelings. During the course of therapy, she becomes better able to articulate her emotions and to use them for increased self-understanding and self-determination. To quote Swink and Leveille (1986):

> As the client accepts the reality of what has been done to her, and that she is not at fault for this abuse, she then experiences a range of emotions: pain, sorrow, betrayal, anger, rage. She must accept that she has these emotions and that she has a right to feel them. She has been well-trained to suppress her feelings so she must now unlearn that suppression and relearn ways to

express her feelings. She is afraid that she will lose control of herself if she begins expressing her emotions; yet [if] she dares to open up and let them out in healthy ways she can begin to trust herself, trust her feelings, and find comfortable appropriate means of expression. (p. 135)

Resolution of Responsibility and Survival Issues

A major focus of therapy is the resolution of the issue of responsibility for the incest and the survivor's subsequent coping behaviors. The survivor must analyze her childhood situation and her family makeup and dynamics in order to transfer responsibility from herself to the perpetrator and other nonprotective family members. Once she has done this she can see her coping and survival efforts from a different perspective. The shift in accountability helps her to understand her powerlessness in a compromised situation and offers the potential for heightened self-empathy and self-esteem. This shift can be very threatening for the survivor and so is sometimes actively resisted. It counters everything she was previously taught. Again, quoting from Swink and Leveille, who are most articulate about the difficulties in achieving this goal:

Because of the muddled boundaries, crossed lines of responsibility and role-reversals, the victims have shouldered the blame for the incest. As they begin to look at what was done to them, they realize how they were used by the abusers so that now they can appropriately place the blame/responsibility on the perpetrator rather than on themselves. As long as they are protecting their abusers, they tend to avoid the label "victim" because they don't believe in their own innocence. They will go through a period of blaming others (such as the non-protecting parent) who are less threatening and easier to blame than the abuser. . . .

Frequently at this stage they are afraid of a catastrophe if they place the responsibility on the abuser, even without a confrontation. Does this mean that the abuser will strike back at them somehow? (Abusers are often seen as having super-human knowledge of the victims' thoughts, feelings, and whereabouts.) Does this mean that they have to hate their abusers? (They usually have a mixture of love and hate, but feel guilty for the hate.) Since this is so foreign to their family dynamics, will somebody die or go crazy? When the victim realizes that she is not to blame for the incest, she can give up her martyr role. She can begin to take control of herself, rather than everyone else. She can begin to understand appropriate lines of responsibility in relationships.

As a martyr, she has built her self-concept around her guilt and worthlessness. Without the guilt, her self-concept is shattered. The result is a combination of relief and insecurity/uncertainty. This may precipitate an existential crisis: Who am I? Where do I fit in? What is my role in life if I'm not the martyr? What are people really like? Will I ever be "normal"? The old self-concept which was based on negativity is destroyed so that a new, positive, healthier one can be built in its place. This is so threatening that many incest victims do not choose to even remember their abuse much less confront the issues. (pp. 134–135)

Grieving

The recognition and expression of long-suppressed memories and emotions along with the reconceptualization of the abuse result in grief and require mourning. Feelings of sadness and loss are usually preceded by anger and indignation. The survivor mourns the loss of her pre-incest identity (who she was then), her self-development (who she might have been, what she lost and what price she paid), and her family relationships (how distorted and unhealthy they were for her). Feelings of being cheated, deprived, or stripped of dignity and self-worth are common. Unfortunately, the losses often continue in the present and may even be required as part of the healing process. For instance, the survivor may have to suffer the actual loss of her family or an intimate relationship to recover. These too must be mourned.

It is the therapist's function to encourage grieving and then to foster the conditions which allow it. Grieving is likely to be one of the most painful parts of the therapy and requires support and compassion from the therapist. In order to get better, the survivor must give up attempts to control that which she cannot and accept the losses involved in incest. As the survivor processes her multiple losses, she comes to realize that she cannot change what happened to her but that she can affect and control her future.

Cognitive Restructuring of Distorted Beliefs and Stress Responses

As a result of the stress of an incestuous childhood, many survivors internalize negative and distorted beliefs about themselves. During therapy, as self-esteem and self-confidence increase, the survivor learns to identify family myths and injunctions which supported the incest and affected beliefs about herself. She is then better able to separate beliefs from facts and to critically examine beliefs about herself in light of her new perspective. She comes to restructure her beliefs about herself more positively and to reconceptualize her stress responses in more favorable ways. This change allows behavior change, which in cyclical fashion reinforces the changed cognitions.

Self-Determination and Behavioral Change

Gradually, the survivor determines who she is apart from her family and her incest experience and makes changes in her behavior consistent with this determination. She breaks away from patterns of behavior conditioned by fear, anxiety, and guilt to those determined by what she wants and feels. As she is less encumbered by the past, she is more free to reclaim those lost or undeveloped parts of herself: She works to resolve conditioned fears and phobias, challenges her learned helplessness, learns new roles and new ways of relating, and develops an acceptance of her body and sexuality. These changes take time and effort together with rehearsal, repeated encouragement, and patience. They become self-reinforcing as they enhance her self-control, self-esteem, and self-efficacy. As noted above, they also reinforce changed cognitions.

Wooley and Vigilanti (1984) describe separation and individuation as a final therapeutic task, not completed during treatment but continuing afterwards. They write:

> This process includes the ability to practice new ways of relating and behaving, including being able to experiment with adult behaviors rather than relying on parent/child interactions, dependency and manipulation. In essence, it is gaining and unfolding a differentiated personality.... The woman who is undergoing separation/individuation is in the process of resolving the anger/love/fear conflict and sees herself as better able to cope with ambivalence in relationships, including marital relationships, as well as more readily expressing appropriate emotions without the threat of the loss of the relationship. In other words, she is able to behave more as an adult with the opportunity for continued individuation and independence. (p. 351)

Education and Skill-building

Children from incestuous families, like children from other types of dysfunctional families, grow up with misinformation or a lack of information in various life tasks and skills. They have missed the normal learning experiences of healthy family life. The therapist may need to function as both parent surrogate and educator in teaching such basic life skills and information as communication, decision-making, conflict-resolution, friendships, intimacy, sexuality, parenting, and boundary-setting. In particular, education about incest and any other major family problem, such as alcoholism, should be included in the therapy process. Skill-building courses and/or exercises and bibliotherapy are often necessary adjuncts to therapy. These are discussed in Chapter 10, along with other treatment strategies and techniques used to implement the goals of incest therapy.

In this chapter, we have reviewed the philosophy, process, and goals of incest therapy. The therapist must individualize treatment for each survivor although the therapy will likely follow the process of re-experiencing and integrating the incest trauma as outlined in this chapter.

CHAPTER 10

General Treatment Strategies and Techniques

V ARIOUS STRATEGIES and techniques from many different theoretical schools are useful in achieving the goals of incest therapy. Since systematic study of incest/child sexual abuse is relatively new, it follows that treatment techniques and strategies are still being developed, applied, and evaluated. The most commonly used therapy approaches and modalities are discussed in this chapter. Most are standard techniques drawn from the major schools of therapy, others are adaptations of commonly used techniques, while some have been developed specifically to treat incest survivors.

Contemporary development of treatment for adult victim/survivors began in the mid to late 1970s with the seminal work and publications of Armstrong (1978), Butler (1978), Giarretto (1976), Forward and Buck (1978), Herman and Hirschman (1977), and Meiselman (1978), in conjunction with work on such related topics as family violence and rape. Although much has been published on incest since 1975, the treatment literature has tended to focus on therapy of children and families involved in ongoing abuse. Treatment of the adult victim/survivor has received less emphasis, and only in the last several years have articles appeared specifically addressing treatment needs and guidelines.*

*Since 1979, four national conferences on the sexual abuse of children have been held in the United States sponsored by the Division of Child Protection, Children's Hospital National Medical Center. Although treatment needs of adult survivors have been addressed at these conferences, the major focus has been intervention into and treatment of ongoing abuse. The only national professional conference to specifically address adults (Counseling the Sexual Abuse Survivor: A Conference on Clinical and Social Issues) was held in 1985 in Canada. Several national self-help conferences have also been sponsored. Beginning in approximately 1984, many more professional conferences and continuing education workshops have been held on the topic of counseling the adult victim/survivor.

To date, the treatment literature is descriptive and impressionistic rather than empirically based. It consists primarily of case reports of individual and group therapy, including the strategies employed and the perceived outcome of treatment. In the absence of prescriptive guidelines, clinicians have had to develop and apply their own strategies and techniques in a trial-and-error fashion. Treatment reports and conceptualizations are only now appearing in the clinical literature. The material presented here on approaches and techniques is based on these clinical reports and on relevant theoretical formulations. With several exceptions these approaches and techniques have not yet been systematically evaluated to determine their effectiveness in treating the effects of incest. They have good face validity, are theoretically based, and appear to provide relief and recovery for the survivors in treatment; nevertheless, they require more extensive evaluation and development, work that is only now beginning. As has been stressed throughout this book, the choice of technique should be determined by the needs of the client, her personality characteristics, the phase and intensity of her stress response, and her most salient traumagenic dynamics and issues.

TREATMENT APPROACHES

Giarretto's (1976) comment on the treatment approach with incest victims remains pertinent: "A particular psychological school or discipline is not rigidly adhered to. . . . A variety of techniques is employed in implementing the therapeutic model. None is used for its own sake; instead, I try to tune into the client and the situation and try to apply a fitting technique" (p. 154). Many therapists have found that a very flexible, eclectic, multimodal therapy utilizing a broad range of techniques is most suitable. Whatever the technique used, the therapist must keep in mind that a shamed client is being treated. The therapist must take care to be very respectful and to avoid behaviors or techniques which reinforce the client's sense of unworthiness. Techniques should be introduced gradually, with extra attention given to the survivor's need for control and her tendency towards self-blame and punishment.

Treatment Modalities

Most frequently, incest therapy is conducted on an individual or group basis; couples/marital and family therapy are also utilized, particularly when the victim is still in the parental home. Family therapy is not recommended as the sole treatment, but rather as secondary to the treatment of every family member in individual, dyadic, and group formats (Giarretto, 1982). When applied to incest, the traditional family therapy models are inadequate, since they tend to rebalance the family in traditional roles (Brickman, 1984) and often treat interpersonal effects without adequate attention to the intrapsychic components which support incest transmission (Calof, 1987). Attempts to rebalance the family usually occur in the absence of adequate understanding of incest dynamics or consideration of the power differentials in the family which are conducive to incest.

Duration and Focus of Therapy

Incest therapy may be time-limited and strategic or time-unlimited, global and in-depth — or anything in between. However, most experts in the field agree that the dynamics of incest and the depth of the issues to be addressed in the recovery process generally require long-term treatment of one to several years' duration.

Some survivors need the security of time limits for specific goals, because time-unlimited, unfocused treatment is overly threatening. Others deliberately seek out time-limited work to allow them to get a feel for their incest issues, the therapist, and the therapy. Others seek time-unlimited work right from the start. They need the security of knowing that the therapist will be allied with them over the long term as they address past and current issues.

During the intake and assessment phase, the therapist should directly but sensitively present her observations to the survivor about her therapy needs and the likely course, intensity, and duration of treatment. All perceived areas of distress or dysfunction must be touched, although these may be difficult to assess and discuss due to client's shame, defenses, and hesitancies. My approach is to lay out options and then to work on a decision about the scope of treatment. The contract that results is sometimes for a specific goal within a specific time frame; at other times the contract sets up the possibility of exploring the issues within a set time with the decision for future treatment coming after the exploration; often the initial treatment contract provides for global exploratory therapy with no time limits.

I am also deliberately up front with the fact that incest therapy is usually lengthy because the issues are complex and a recovery process is involved. Firm time estimates are difficult to make because in all likelihood the range of therapy needs is not evident at intake, even when an in-depth assessment has been made. I try to temper my direct approach with sensitivity to the client's frustration about needing to devote more "life time" and therapy time to the incest. Comparing incest recovery to other recovery processes (e.g., recovery from a serious burn or accident or from alcoholism) provides a useful and understandable rationale for the length of treatment. Similarly, offering the perspective that the problem occurred and developed secondary manifestations over a long period may assist the survivor in understanding why time is needed to unravel its effects. Finally, time is needed for the survivor to develop a strong therapeutic alliance and to process her reactions at a pace that is tolerable to her. Therapy is counter-productive if it ends up further overwhelming her just to meet a time limitation.

Short-Term Treatment. Short-term work is, of necessity and by design, focused. It has several variations. When a client presents in crisis, immedi-ate intervention with stabilization as the goal is required. The therapist attempts to restore the client to the pre-crisis level of functioning as quickly as possible by offering support and the opportunity to ventilate. Specific strategies are pursued according to whether the client is experi-encing intrusive or numbing symptoms (these will be discussed below in the strategies section). In either case, when the person's normal coping ability and defenses are relatively debilitated, the therapist must intervene before maladaptive reorganization of the defenses takes place. The oppor-tunity to talk about the event(s) and personal reactions to it and to problem-solve with a supportive person who is not overwhelmed by hearing about the incest can be very reassuring for the client.

Another short-term variation is time-limited, goal-oriented counseling. On occasion, a survivor will seek counseling for a specific purpose having to do with the incest.

Jan, an 18-year-old college freshman, sought help at the campus counsel-ing center specifically to learn how to close her bedroom door at night. Her family rules dictated that no door in the house was to be closed, ostensibly for safety reasons (i.e., to insure that family members could get out quickly in the event of a fire or another emergency in the middle of the night). In reality, the rule allowed Jan's father unlimited and unimpeded access to her bedroom during the night. Jan believed that learning to close the door would prevent her father from abusing her any longer.

Following intake and assessment, the therapist suggested that learning to close the door of her bedroom would be the first order of business, but that additional treatment was advised. She also urged Jan to contact a local social service agency about her father's abusiveness, which Jan refused to do. Jan had a number of problems and symptoms, including serious faint-ing spells when she became anxious and specifically when she dared to speak about what her father did on his nightly visits.

Jan refused other treatment, stating that her only goal was to learn how to close her bedroom door at night. She and the therapist met for five sessions, which were devoted to discussing the problem, devising solutions, behavioral rehearsal, and offering her support in achieving her goal. Jan was elated when she was able to close the door. She then went even further and had a lock installed, despite her parents' protests. She stopped counsel-

ing once this goal was achieved and assured the therapist that she would consider returning at a later date.

This case illustrates the client's role in goal-setting, as well as non-crisis, short-term, focal intervention that supported the client's reality and her needs while respecting her boundaries.

Time-limited treatment must be focal rather than global. It is designed to prevent strong attachment and dependency from developing and to reinforce the client's strength. While time limits are used in both individual and group modalities, they have been reported most frequently for groups. In general, time-limited groups have been found to be very beneficial for the treatment of many incest-related issues, particularly when the treatment goals are spelled out as part of the therapy contract and when group work is done concurrent with or after individual work. As with individual therapy, longer-term work is needed for more wide-ranging exploration. Issues in time-limited and-unlimited groups are outlined in Chapter 12.

Long-term Treatment. Treatment of longer duration offers the opportunity for a more complete analysis of the full range of material at both the conscious and unconscious levels. The therapeutic relationship is critical to the success of the treatment. In order to move into and tolerate the intensity of treatment, the survivor may repeatedly test the therapist to ascertain strength, reliability, consistency, and trustworthiness. Horowitz (1986) had the following to say about the course of long-term work for compounded traumatic stress reactions:

> The longer the time is from the stressor event to the present therapy, the more likely it is that the stress event syndrome will involve complex problems of maladaptive interpersonal behavior patterns. There is a lock-in across levels of interpretative work, so that work at the surface levels will help maladaptive patterns based at the organizers of meaning at deeper levels. Early work in therapy may lead to improved interpersonal relationship patterns, even when present, without proceeding to interpretive work at the level of self-concepts, role relationship, models, and unconscious fantasy scenarios, scripts, and life agendas. Nonetheless, in complex cases this is often necessary. . . . Thus, in the middle phase of therapy, the therapist may reformulate the case in terms of what has been learned thus far and deepen the level of interpretative work. This will mean exploring the usually unconscious meaning structures involved in forming views of self and others, including self-critical functions and their derivatives from developmentally important relationships. (pp.145–146)

TECHNIQUES

Incest therapy benefits from the application of quite a variety of techniques drawn from the diverse theories of personality and psychotherapy. The techniques presented here have been grouped into four categories:

stress/coping techniques; experiential/expressive-cathartic techniques; exploratory/psychodynamic techniques; and cognitive/behavioral techniques. It is clear that overlap exists among these four categories; in fact, some techniques may even fit all four. Before discussing techniques it is essential to mention the timing, pacing, and choice of intervention. A repertoire of techniques is useful since incest survivors have such a wide range of symptoms and coping mechanisms. Careful attention must be paid to the needs of each survivor with therapy tailored accordingly. Survivor response to interventions must also be closely monitored. Joy (1987) offered the following observations in this regard:

> . . . Particular difficulties . . . when working with incest victims involve the issues of trust and commitment to the therapy process. Because of the difficulty these clients have in trusting others, simply maintaining rapport can be challenging and exhausting. In addition, dealing with the incest issue itself tends to be exquisitely painful for the client. Hence, the pacing of the therapeutic interventions becomes a critical counselor skill. The counselor must move gently and compassionately when encountering the issue, but also firmly and decisively so as not to promote avoidance of the topic. When I have pushed too hard to force an unready client to confront and deal with the incest, the client has "fled" and not returned for further counseling. To avoid this, I find that flexibility is critical. If Gestalt approaches are too intense for the client, then one needs to be able to shift quickly to another, more comfortable mode of processing. Sometimes it is beneficial to put the incest issue "on hold" and work on other concerns, such as an ongoing relationship or socialization skills. I have found that most often the core incest issue will resurface at a later time in the counseling process, when perhaps the client is better able to work towards its resolution. (p. 319)

Particular difficulty in gauging client reactions to interventions arises with those survivors who are unable to identify their reactions, who dissociate or otherwise defend against them, and who experience delayed or indirect reactions (e.g., through dreams and fantasy). The therapist is thus quite challenged to keep pace with the survivor's reactions. I have found several strategies to be useful. I encourage some clients to keep a therapy and dream journal which I read during or between sessions or to draw their reactions which we discuss together. I try to identify when a client tends to dissociate during sessions and the topics which lead to such splitting off or to delayed reactions. Once identified, I gently point them out to the survivor and encourage her to gradually deal with them more directly. Finally, I contract with clients that they not leave therapy without first having a session to discuss reasons for leaving and I encourage open discussion of the therapy process. Incest survivors need constant encouragement for the legitimacy of their emotions and need consistent reassurance that they will not be punished for expressing themselves. Even if the client ultimately chooses to leave therapy following such a discussion, she has had important modeling of communication skills and her right to decide for herself. Quite likely, such training was missing in her family.

Stress/Coping Techniques

These techniques are designed to help individuals cope with stress which is overwhelming and distressing. The incest client typically has had to deal with multiple stressors extending over a period of time, in addition to any coping techniques which have become dysfunctional and stressful in and of themselves. Techniques include those drawn from crisis intervention, trauma or victimization theory, stress management theory, and the interdisciplinary study of coping with aversive life events. Optimally, stress/coping techniques are geared to the phase of the client's stress response and her degree of distress.

Crisis Therapy. Crisis intervention techniques are called for when the client enters therapy in a crisis or when a crisis develops during the course of therapy due to additional stressors outside of the clinical setting (e.g., a client who is revictimized, involved in a serious accident or has a death in the family) or due to the stress of the therapy itself (e.g., client who becomes suicidal or homicidal while reworking the trauma). In an acute crisis, where lethal potential is high and the client is not capable of acting on her own behalf, psychological first aid with a directive stance on the part of the therapist is necessary and hospitalization may be advised. With low lethality and a client capable of acting on her own behalf, a more facilitative approach is recommended. According to Slaikeu (1984) the five components of psychological first aid are: (1) make psychological contact; (2) explore the dimensions of the problem; (3) examine possible solutions; (4) assist in taking concrete action; (5) follow up.

Crisis therapy or stress response therapy is the follow-up to psychological first aid and is more extensive in scope and duration. It is geared to helping the client integrate the crisis and its impact into the different areas of her life, namely, the behavioral, affective, somatic, interpersonal and cognitive, in a way that increases healthy rather than maladaptive reorganization. The client is helped to (a) physically survive the crisis experience, (b) identify and express feelings that accompany the crisis, (c) gain cognitive mastery over the crisis, and (d) make a range of behavioral and interpersonal adjustments necessitated by the crisis. It is multimodal, utilizing techniques from a variety of therapeutic orientations, and has been found to be most effective when enacted during the period of disorganization caused by the crisis (Slaikeu, 1984, pp. 117–118).

Slaikeu's crisis therapy model resembles Horowitz's (1986) stress response syndrome model, which is also multimodal but more psychodynamic in orientation. Horowitz emphasizes choosing techniques and ordering treatment priorities according to whether the client is in the numbing-denial or intrusive-repetitive phase of the stress response and according to the client's personality style.

Techniques for Intrusive Phase Symptoms. Rest, containment, and supportive techniques are used with intrusive phase symptoms to supplement weakened controls and reduce the intensity of the symptoms or the triggers for continued distress. Common intrusive symptoms include flashbacks; sleep disturbance including recurrent, distressing dreams of the event; hyperarousal and hypervigilance; exaggerated startle response; and mild to severe cognitive impairment. Because of the intensity of intrusive reactions, clients may be quite distraught when experiencing them. Further, these symptoms are often very uncomfortable and frightening, especially when they occur or recur suddenly and unexpectedly and seem to lack association to a stimulus. They are also distressing when they interrupt a sustained period of improved mood and functioning. Information about the normalcy of alternating symptoms and the likelihood of lessened intensity over time offers reassurance and hope.

Many standard stress management techniques can be applied during this phase. In particular, emotional ventilation, external structuring and problem-solving, stress inoculation training, social supports including self-help groups, desensitization and relaxation are useful. At times it may be necessary to advise the client against activities which require alertness and concentration, such as driving, because the intrusive symptoms interfere and make concentration difficult.

Sedatives or antianxiety medications may be prescribed in small doses for severe persistent sleep disturbance, which tends to exacerbate the stress response. Antidepressants are not generally recommended to relieve minor depressive episodes or the sadness associated with grieving, but may be considered when a major depressive disorder develops which does not respond to therapy alone. Alcohol should be recommended with caution. Occasionally, a drink may provide relief, but alcohol may also be used for self-medication and dependency may develop, especially for the incest survivor whose family history shows addictive/compulsive patterns. The client may be prone to use any type of substance or compulsive behavior to self-medicate or dissociate.

Horowitz provides what he describes as a preliminary listing of phase-specific techniques (see Table 4) and urges that each be selected and applied in a client-specific way. As can be seen, quite a number of techniques are available for intrusive symptoms.

Numbing-denial Phase Symptoms. Abreactive-cathartic methods are used initially to help the client process the event and her reactions to it. Denial is necessary and adaptive at times since it provides the individual

TABLE 4
Treatments for Stress Response Syndromes

STATES	
Denial-Numbing Phase	*Intrusive-Repetitive Phase*
Reduce controls — interpret defenses and attitudes that make controls necessary — suggest recollection	Supply structure externally — structure time and events for patient when essential — organize information Reduce external demands and stimulus levels Rest Provide identification models, group membership, good leadership, orienting values Permit temporary idealization, dependency
Encourage abreaction Encourage description — association — speech — use of images rather than just words in recollection and fantasy — conceptual enactments, possibly also role playing and art therapy Reconstructions to prime memory and associations	Work through and reorganize by clarifying and educative interpretive work Differentiate — reality from fantasy — past from current schemata — self-attributes from object attributes Remove environmental reminders and triggers, interpret their meaning and effect Teach "dosing," e.g., attention on and away from stress-related information
Encourage catharsis Explore emotional aspects of relationships and experiences of self during event Supply support and encourage emotional relationships to counteract numbness	Support Evoke other emotions, e.g., benevolent environment Suppress emotion, e.g., selective use of antianxiety agents Desensitization procedures and relaxation

with the means to reestablish psychological equilibrium. In the case of the abuse victims, denial originally provided the means to survive the abuse. However, denial-numbing mechanisms become maladaptive when used too extensively since they impede processing and resolution of the trauma. Table 4 contains a list of techniques for denial/numbing symptoms. A variety of experiential/expressive-cathartic techniques can be used to break through numbing-denial.

Horowitz has also outlined priorities of treatment for traumatic stress response as a guide to the clinician. His priorities are listed in Table 5.

Experiential/Expressive-Cathartic Techniques

Techniques from gestalt and other experiential/humanistic therapies, from psychodrama, and from art, movement, music, and writing therapies are those most useful in breaking through denial and promoting ventilation, catharsis, and abreaction of the trauma. Nevertheless, cathartic techniques should be introduced and applied with caution and only after careful preparation; also, they may need to be interspersed with containment techniques as noted above. Cathartic techniques are used to lower or dismantle defenses and to encourage the recollection and expression of memories and affect which have been warded off or forbidden. For some victims, relinquishing the control embodied by the defenses may be so anxiety-provoking as to be life-threatening or cause decompensation. Further, since many survivors were threatened into forced silence by the abuser, recollection and expression are highly emotionally charged, frequently arousing intense anxiety reactions. It is critical that the therapist respect the survivor's defenses and not move too quickly to dismantle them. The survivor's blocking mechanisms should be approached gently and slowly, except in those cases when an implosive or chemical technique is determined to be necessary or advantageous. (These will be discussed below.)

I have repeatedly stressed the importance of the therapeutic alliance to the success of incest treatment. The survivor must feel that she can trust the therapist to support her and not abandon or reject her as she breaks through her defenses and the threats of childhood. A fairly strong alliance should be developed before the introduction of expressive/cathartic techniques. These techniques vary in their demands and intensity; those which are least threatening and least intense should be applied first. The therapist should assess the client's reactions carefully to ensure that she is not emotionally flooded by the treatment. The therapist must also expect that, rather paradoxically, the survivor's reactions may be muted or masked, especially if she is feeling overwhelmed. Because of this, enough time should be allowed for assessing the reactions with the client and working through the material before introducing additional cathartic techniques.

I and a number of colleagues have treated several women who sought therapy in crisis or during severe anxiety reactions after having done intensive body or expressive work (e.g., body massage, acupressure, primal scream therapy, Rolfing) which was overstimulating and led to strong, frightening, and intrusive-repetitive symptoms. While these techniques can be extremely beneficial, they should be attempted carefully, within the context of therapy, with adequate time allowed for discussing and integrating reactions.

TABLE 5
Priorities of Treatment

Patient's Current State	Treatment Goal
Under continuing impact of external stress event.	— Terminate external event or remove patient from contiguity with it. — Provide temporary relationship. — Help with decisions, plans, or working-through.
Swings to intolerable levels: — Ideational-emotional attacks. — Paralyzing denial and numbness.	— Reduce amplitude of oscillations to swings of tolerable intensity of ideation and emotion. — Continue emotional and ideational support. — Selection of techniques cited for states of intrusion in Table 4.
Frozen in overcontrol state of denial and numbness with or without intrusive repetitions.	— Help patient "dose" reexperience of event and implications that help remember for a time, put out of mind for a time, remember for a time, and so on. Selection of denial techniques from Table 4. — During periods of recollection, help patient organize and express experience. Increase sense of safety in therapeutic relationship so patient can resume processing the event.
Able to experience and tolerate episodes of ideation and waves of emotion.	— Help patient work through associations: the conceptual, emotional, object relations, and self-image implications of the stress event. — Help patient relate this stress event to earlier threats, relationship models, self-concepts, and future plans.
Able to work through ideas and emotions on one's own.	— Work through loss of therapeutic relationship. — Terminate treatment.

Reprinted from *Stress Response Syndromes*, Mardi Jon Horowitz, Second Edition, Copyright 1986, Mardi Jon Horowitz. Used with permission of the publisher, Jason Aronson, Inc.

In my experience some clients spontaneously engage in expressive techniques in attempting to either communicate or understand their experiences. For example, some clients keep a personal or therapy journal, produce art, or seek books and articles on incest. Even when such activities are initiated by the client, caution is necessary, since the survivor may inadvertently overload herself or deliberately use the material and her reactions as self-punishment. The behavior of one of my clients illustrates this point.

Lorraine kept a detailed therapy journal right from the start of her intensive, three-times-a-week therapy. She supplemented this with draw-ings expressing her anger or illustrating the horror of her abuse. Both writing and drawing were extremely helpful in her therapy. Early in treat-ment, she purchased and read Prisoners of Childhood by Alice Miller, a book which outlines the narcissistic damage done to a child when the parents use the child for their own needs and do not respect the child as an individual. This thesis was so powerful for Lorraine that she experienced intense anxiety and depressive reactions, dissociated, and became suicidal. She was hospitalized at this time because she became so depressed she was unable to guarantee that she would not attempt suicide.

Later in Lorraine's therapy, a self-hurtful pattern emerged which in-volved her therapy journal and this book. After social outings when she was able to enjoy herself with friends, she would go home and read all of her therapy notes and Prisoners of Childhood to flood herself with painful material and emotions as self-punishment for having had a good time. At other times, she would compulsively overeat or go to movies which oversti-mulated her, also as self-punishment. The confrontation and management of these overstimulating, self-hurtful behaviors became part of the treat-ment.

Various expressive techniques have been found to be especially useful with the incest survivor. Gestalt techniques, such as empty chair, role play and role reversal, body awareness, saying goodbye, exaggeration, and top-dog-underdog, encourage self-awareness and self-management, aid the identification and expression of feelings, body states, and unfinished busi-ness, and foster the reconciliation of splits and the reclamation of dis-owned parts of the self. All of these techniques stress working in the "here and now" rather than ruminating over the past and accepting responsibility for feelings. The survivor often works with her "self splits"—she may en-gage in dialogue with her "little girl" or "child within," with her censor or protector self, with her self-persecutor or with various parts of her body. Using the empty chair, she is able to confront her abuser and talk to other family members.

Psychodrama provides a setting for exploring family patterns and rela-tions, identifying and reclaiming disowned or unacknowledged feelings, and acting out or rehearsing for confrontations. Sociograms, family sculpt-ing, body positioning, the use of the alter ego, and other techniques all increase awareness while encouraging emotional ventilation.

Expressive techniques drawn from art, movement, music, and writing therapies add a nonverbal, symbolic mode of communication, enabling the

exploration of feelings inaccessible through the conventional talk therapies. Since these therapies circumvent inhibitions arising from defense
mechanisms and injunctions to secrecy, they may be especially helpful for
survivors who experience vague or strong bodily sensations that *something*
happened to them or for survivors whose trauma resulted in such psychosomatic reactions as localized anesthesia or frozen pelvic movement.
Greenberg and van der Kolk (1987) offered a case description of this process in their chapter entitled "Retrieval and integration of traumatic memories with the 'painting cure.'" Yates and Pawley (1987) described the use of
art therapy in exploring and resolving the trauma of sexual abuse.

Kearney-Cooke (in press) has described specialized expressive techniques she uses in group treatment of bulimic women with a sexual abuse
history. Guided imagery is used to assist clients in remembering their
experiences because "imagery, unlike other modes of communication, usually has not been punished in the individual's past and is therefore less
susceptible to personal censorship in the present" (p. 6). Clients are then
encouraged to sculpt what they remember and are further encouraged to
reenact their abuse to facilitate catharsis, insight, and mastery. The clients
are then involved in discussions of how they repeat the victimization process and participate in a shame ritual to allow the alleviation of residual
shame from the abuse. The support of the therapist and other group
members is essential in this destigmatization process.

Frequently, survivors are asked to keep a general journal, a therapy
journal, or a structured journal or to respond in writing to stimulus statements or questions. Some group treatments are built around the sharing of
such writing (Butler, 1985). Writing a detailed autobiography can help the
survivor acknowledge details about the past and works against reforgetting,
a not uncommon occurrence. Even when repression is strong and memories sketchy, the survivor can be encouraged to write what she does remember. This can serve as a general framework for additional memories. It is
often useful for the survivor to ask relatives and friends to tell her what
they know about her childhood. Their information may jog her memory or,
at the very least, add to her information framework. Herman and Schatzow
(1987) have provided a case description of this process.

A detailed lifeline can supplement an autobiography or journal and be
useful in itself. With its graphic portrayal of important family and life
events, a lifeline can reveal a previously undetected pattern in the survivor's childhood, adolescence and adulthood. For instance, when one of my
clients did a personal and family event lifeline, she color-coded happy and
crisis times, important life events, her father's alcoholism and sexual and
physical abuse, and her mother's depression. The visual depiction helped
her understand the intensity of both her abuse and her severe reactions to
it. It further justified to her the length of therapy, which she had previously
assumed to be due to her incompetence.

The therapist may ask the client to bring in family photographs to assist her in her recollections. Photographs can make childhood less remote and hazy while making the reality of abuse more vivid. Additionally, they can provide valuable information about family lifestyle and relationships and about the survivor as a child. One of my clients brought in several pictures of a large, unkempt group of children surrounding a grim, overweight mother. As we looked at the placement of the children in relation to each other and the mother, as well as their facial expressions and body postures, and noted the absence of the father, we were able to analyze the family in new ways. This client had been physically and emotionally neglected. She was an attractive, but chubby and bedraggled child. Looking at her child-hood picture, she told me how much she had always hated herself as a child, blaming herself for the parental neglect and the fact that her brother sexually abused her for years. From the adult perspective, she was able to see that she was neither unattractive nor unlovable but that she came from a deeply troubled and dysfunctional family.

Many therapists recommend letter writing, whether the letter is to be sent or not. In a letter to her mother, her abuser, or any other family members or significant others, the survivor can cover a range of topics and freely express her emotions. The survivor should begin by writing an un-censored letter that she will not send, so that she is not encumbered by style, tone, emotional censorship, or guilt. If she decides that she wants to send it, then she can work on the letter until it is in suitable form. The initial intent, of course, is to get her to express herself fully and with a minimum of self-consciousness and censorship. (Family confrontation and disclosure are discussed in Chapter 15.)

According to Mayer (1983), sentence stems, rating scales, poetry therapy, sociograms, genograms, and checklists are also useful. Art techniques can be particularly effective in bringing repressed and suppressed material to the surface. Mayer recommends the Draw-A-Person test, which she has modified to a Kinetic Draw-A-Person test and a Draw-The-Assault or Draw-The-Abuser technique. Techniques can also be adapted from child thera-py; sculpting, play therapy, and the use of anatomically correct dolls are but a few examples. Art and play therapy allow for the symbolic expression of the survivor's conflicts and impulses, which may be otherwise inaccessible. Metaphors and symbols pave an indirect but rich road to the incest experi-ence and bypass injunctions not to tell.

Bibliotherapy and audiovisual material enable the survivor to learn about abuse and hear the stories and reactions of other survivors (see Appendix B for recommended books and audiovisual materials). However, overstimulation should be avoided. Clients should be prepared ahead of time for books, readings, TV shows, movies, videotapes, and audiotapes, and urged to stop or "dose" their exposure if they feel overwhelmed. Some of the available audiovisual presentations, while excellent in depicting abuse, are emotionally overwhelming for survivors. For bibliotherapy, I suggest to my clients that they begin with readings which are more general and less emotion-laden than autobiographical writings and then move to the first-person accounts and poetry as they feel ready. Often, clients benefit from finding the story of a survivor which matches their own. This is especially so when the abuse was not of the "standard variety." For instance, a client whose abusive father was a minister was greatly relieved to find a story similar to her own in an anthology of survivor stories. She was able to relate to the writer's additional confusion and shame engendered by the father's religious standing. Like the father in the story, her father had labeled the sexual abuse as punishment and purification from God because she was a bad child.

Some survivors express themselves by "going public." They may give community talks, organize self-help groups or hotlines, volunteer at counseling services or safe houses, conduct research, appear on television or radio shows, make artwork and audiovisual educational materials, or write autobiographical articles or books. Blank (1985) used the term "survivor mission" to describe activity of this sort. He advised clinicians that, although such activity is usually not seen as within the "normal" range of therapy and so may be discouraged, it is a normal response which may be crucial to the recovery of a subpopulation of traumatized individuals. Butler (1985) expressed similar sentiments concerning incest when she said that the victim-to-survivor process was not enough for everyone and that some survivors needed to become warriors as a means of working through their trauma. For some, this means unequivocally breaking the taboo and silence while giving meaning to their abuse experience by helping others.

While therapists need to understand the gains which can be derived from "survivor missions," they also need to be direct and honest with their clients about their psychological readiness to undertake them. Also, motivations must be carefully assessed. For example, survivor guilt motivates some activities which may be to the client's detriment, as illustrated by the following case.

Annette worked tirelessly and with little self-regard in a shelter for homeless and abused women and children. She was also a volunteer at the community rape crisis center, where she organized a self-help group for incest survivors. She had a long history of extensive caretaking of others, regardless of the cost to herself, dynamics which were addressed by two different therapists in concurrent individual and group treatment. Annette's work and volunteer activity resulted in a great deal of stress and strain, but she refused to leave them temporarily or until she had worked through caretaking issues in her therapy. She was even able to attribute her motivation to guilt, conditioned shame, and a need to put everyone else before herself. But she felt unable to change her behavior even though it was hurting her.

As part of therapy, clinicians can assist clients in assessing the gains, liabilities, and risks of engaging in such activities. It is particularly important to assess the family's possible reactions, especially if the survivor decides to use her real name rather than remaining anonymous or using a pseudonym. Assessing the range of expectable and possible reactions she will experience, including any loss of privacy and control, is also critical. The survivor can then make an informed decision about whether and how to go public. The therapist can serve as a support once the decision has been made to engage in some sort of public activity. The maintenance of roles and boundaries can be problematic if therapist and client choose to make joint public appearances. It is necessary to discuss these changes and their management before engaging in any activities of this sort. The experiences of two survivors offer perspectives on this matter.

Martha told me that she wanted to write a book about her incest experience in order to help others. She wrote an outline of the book and circulated it among several friends, one of whom forwarded it to a publishing agent. Martha began this process without having given any consideration to how writing and publishing her story would affect her or to possible repercussions in her family. At the time she wrote the outline, she still tended to get severely depressed and to dissociate when working directly with abuse memories and emotions. She is still in therapy and has deferred the decision to publish pending more complete working-through and resolution of her incest issues and further exploration of possible outcomes of publishing. She has also decided to attempt some other, less intensive kinds of public exposure before making a firm commitment to publish.

Maureen published her story in a magazine under her real name. Following publication, she was deluged with attention from friends and acquaintances, all of whom wanted to discuss or comment on what she had written. Her story led to multiple requests for interviews on TV and radio and for public talks at professional conferences. Maureen had expected her story to attract attention but was unprepared for the frightening lack of control she experienced as a consequence. She and her therapist then devised strategies for her to regain some control, privacy, and safety. Specifically, she decided to be very selective about further public appearances until she felt more safe and in control.

Exploratory/Psychodynamic Techniques

Exploratory and insight-oriented techniques derived primarily from the psychodynamic tradition resemble many of the expressive-cathartic techniques but have some differences as well. Their aim is to assist in the exploration of unconscious, as well as conscious, material. Although Miller (1981, 1984) has forcefully challenged classic analytic theory for concealing abuse and causing individuals to deny the trauma and blame themselves for it, she has nonetheless espoused the use of analytic techniques with survivors of childhood abuse within a modified theoretical framework. She urges a return to Freud's original discovery of the role of childhood trauma as etiologic to subsequent symptom formation and the repudiation of the drive theory which Freud substituted for his original seduction/trauma theory. Miller advocates the classic analytic position of the neutral therapist but stresses that the analyst is the advocate of the child and believes in her subjective experience above all else. The therapist uses such techniques as free association and dream analysis along with the analysis of transference and countertransference. In particular, through repetition compulsions and reenactments and the analysis of defense mechanisms, childhood experiences will be revealed. Miller believes that the abuse will be manifest in all of these forms and that the task of the therapist is to understand them as a symbolic communication about that which cannot be directly communicated or spoken. Only through strong therapeutic support and validation provided by the therapist can the adult face and integrate the previously repressed or otherwise warded-off memories and emotions from the past. Brickman (1985), Greer (1986), and Pasternak (1987) have also discussed the use of a modified psychoanalytic approach with incest survivors.

Hypnosis is used within the psychodynamic framework and within other frameworks as well. Recently it has been mentioned as the technique of choice for multiple personality disorder. The client's natural capacity to go into trance, often developed as part of the abuse scenario, is used by therapists who describe a "fight fire with fire" approach (Calof, 1987; Groves, 1987). These clinicians view trance as a response to the double-bind inherent in trauma (Speigel, 1986). Hypnosis can assist in the recapturing of lost memories, in the abreaction of the trauma, in the identification of and reconnection with disowned parts of the self, in pain management and substance control, and as a means of relaxation and self-management through autohypnosis. Formal hypnosis may at times prove useful and necessary, yet even hypnotists such as Calof describe following the client's lead and allowing material to reach consciousness in its own time and through a natural rather than induced trance. Groves utilizes a similar approach and stresses the use of tone and specific language to enable a free-flowing trance. With a more formal induction, the therapist should plan on allowing extra time and sessions to process the material to avoid flooding the survivor. I have used projective techniques such as the imagining of a scene on television which can be turned on or off at will to insure the client's sense of control. Herman (1987) described a similar strategy with the same rationale.

Cognitive/Behavioral Techniques

A broad spectrum of techniques fits within the cognitive/behavioral category, ranging from developmental skill-building and social learning approaches to behavior modification. Some are very useful in working with the denial-numbing phase of the traumatic stress response, while others are most effective with the intrusive-repetitive phase. The reader is referred back to Table 4 for a listing of techniques under each response phase. Cognitive and behavioral techniques are especially effective in reversing the developmental deficits and conditioned responses caused by the abuse and/or the dysfunctional family atmosphere and in challenging and correcting the faulty cognitions many survivors hold. These techniques, used to modify the "functional" behavioral and cognitive dysfunctions from the abuse and its aftermath, can be broken down into three subcategories: developmental, cognitive, and behavioral.

Developmental. Developmental techniques are designed to promote individual growth and differentiation through self-assessment and the development of new skills and abilities. Since developmental deficits and arrest often result from abuse, developmental techniques, sometimes incorporated in specialized training programs, address these problems and provide opportunities and exercises for their reversal or amelioration.

Helfer (1978) has designed a developmental program described in *Childhood Comes First: A Crash Course in Childhood for Adults.* The course includes a series of graduated exercises which a learner who has "missed childhood" completes with the guidance and support of a coach (who may be the therapist). Helfer begins this program with a description of the developmental tasks that are missed in conditions of abnormal child-rearing, which he labels "The World of Abnormal Rearing (W.A.R.)." His remedial course starts with exercises to get the client in touch with her five senses, which may have been undeveloped, underdeveloped, or overdeveloped due to poor parenting and abuse. For example, the survivor may have come to fear all touch because touch in her family was never safe. Helfer's exercises encourage the distinction between good touch and bad touch and teach the client to enjoy the benefits of soothing, supportive touch.

The development of the atrophied senses is followed by other exercises designed to develop a positive sense of self: learning to regard the self and feelings as good and "OK"; exercising positive self-control and positive responsibility; and recognizing the role of depression. Learning to interact positively with others and developing a variety of different types of relationships build upon self-development. These too are presented in a graduated fashion — from learning to distinguish between different types of relationships to developing intimacy, selecting a mate, pregnancy, and parenting. This program may be useful in part or in its entirety for incest survivors. Exercises may be formally done within the therapy or done adjunctively through a self-help network such as Parents Anonymous or Grown-Up Abused Children (Leehan & Wilson, 1985).

Incest therapy has been likened to reparenting. Of course the therapist can never restore the missed experiences with the real parents, make up for the abuse, be available as a real parent, or promise lifetime availability; however, it may be useful for the therapist to consider that s/he functions as a foster or surrogate parent or as a coach/trainer in relation to the client. Whatever the role conceptualization, the therapist serves as an important model of an authority figure. Cohen (1984) described the restorative nature of reparenting within the therapy:

> Reparenting is useful. It is a subtle learning for the client about the nature of an authority person who is basically consistent and predictable, but neither all bad nor all good. The use of the therapist as a model is a lengthy process in that the client will work hard at insisting that the therapist be all good or all bad. Additional problems result when a therapist tries to appear "perfect" for the client out of the therapist's own need. Modeling is rarely a sufficient technique in and of itself but is successful in the context of other therapeutic interventions. (p. 252)

Maintaining appropriate boundaries, being neither overly intrusive, withholding, gratifying, nor disclosing, also teaches important lessons usually absent in incestuous families. Although the therapist is in charge of maintaining clarity about boundaries and of setting limits throughout the process, the survivor can be expected to exercise more awareness and responsibility as the therapy progresses.

Self-nurturing exercises are developmental in that the survivor is encouraged to do things for herself that are relaxing, pleasurable, and positive. Many survivors are unaware of how hard they are on themselves and of how little they attend to their own needs. Self-nurturing may be as simple as complimenting herself on a job well done or as complicated as setting up a complete stress management program. Many survivors benefit from the therapist's suggestion that they create a safe and secure environment for themselves in their homes or their rooms. They may be encouraged to buy themselves things that bring them pleasure or to create a home atmosphere that is aesthetically pleasing as well as secure. Such a place may serve as a respite from the world and at times from the pain of recovery.

Although the survivor may feel unable to nurture her adult self, she may be able to nurture the little girl inside. Even well-defended clients respond positively, though often with tears and sadness, to the suggestion to get in touch with the child within. The client can be encouraged to be kind to her little girl, to nurture and care for her, to allow her to play and to rest, and to become more aware of her body state and bodily needs.

The development of religious faith or spirituality as defined by the 12-step programs modeled on Alcoholics Anonymous can be similarly therapeutic. "Letting go of self-will," detaching, believing in a higher power—all help the survivor give up overcontrolling and caretaking behavior.* Spiritual practice and belief can be a calming source of support and strength during times of stress. Many survivors balk at the idea of God or a higher power, feeling as though they were long ago abandoned by a cruel and uncaring God. The survivor can be helped to see that she need not turn to an organized religion or even believe in God in order to develop her spirituality. Rather, the emotions deriving from incest, particularly shame, block personal and spiritual growth. Fossum and Mason (1986), in their work with shame issues in families, use the "clogged drain" metaphor:

> We tell families that all the "gunky stuff" has to come out and float to the surface before the drain can again flow freely. Families find that the hurt, anger and rage known in shame, which were felt and never expressed over the years, are often buried under repression and denial. These built-up layers of accumulated pain so clog our "spiritual drains" that release is demanded by our internal systems. We refer to family therapy as "Drano." (p. 161)

This metaphor is very apt in working with incest survivors. Once they work through their "gunky stuff," they are much freer to develop emotionally and spiritually and to change their behaviors in ways that are in their best interest. Survivors can be encouraged to practice doing something calming and peaceful every day as a way to identify personal needs. They may further benefit from using self-affirmations to help them "center" or "ground" themselves when stressed and most prone to self-deprecating or self-defeating thoughts and behavior.

The development of more personalized and meaningful relations with others is also growth-enhancing. The negative experiences survivors have

---

*Swink and Leveille (1986) have noted problems that the AA philosophy may pose for incest survivors, especially the insistence that each member take responsibility for what happened to him/her and the necessity to forgive everyone to be free of anger and resentment. A 12-step program can be very useful if some of the teachings are modified for incest survivors.

had, along with the negative perceptions they frequently apply to themselves and others ("I am completely and totally unlovable"; "No one is to be trusted"; "Everyone is out to abuse you, to get all that they can"), impede their ability to develop close relationships and to learn about human goodness and trustworthiness. Improved interactions with others, beginning with the modeling in therapy (whether individual or group), help the client break out of isolation and learn the skills to develop mutual and satisfactory relationships. The survivor should be coached and encouraged in the gradual development of a support network of friends, acquaintances, and colleagues, and in involvement in community, civic, and recreational activities. The support of others increases her sense of self-worth and provides a lifeline as she separates and individuates from her family of origin. Herman (1981) has stressed the importance of encouraging a close relationship with an available female who can serve as a role model and support for the survivor.

Cognitive Techniques. Cognitive techniques are used to interrupt, correct, or restructure the survivor's belief system about herself and the abuse. According to Jehu, Klassen, and Gazan (1985):

> Cognitive restructuring is based on the premise that beliefs have a significant influence on feelings and actions. If the beliefs are distorted or unrealistic, then feelings and actions are likely to be distressing and inappropriate. In this way distorted beliefs may contribute to many emotional and behavioral problems. It follows that the correction of distorted beliefs is likely to be accompanied by the alleviation of such problems.
>
> In order to correct distorted beliefs it is necessary for clients (a) to become aware of their beliefs, (b) to recognize any distortions they contain, and (c) to substitute more accurate beliefs. (pp. 49–50)

These authors tested the efficacy of cognitive restructuring techniques in treating the distorted beliefs of 11 victims of childhood sexual abuse. Clinically and statistically significant improvements in both beliefs (as measured by an instrument being developed by the authors) and mood (as measured by the Beck Depression Inventory) were found. The following types of distortions were noted:

- all-or-nothing or dichotomous thinking;
- overgeneralization;
- mislabeling;
- mental filtering or selective abstraction;
- disqualifying the positive;
- jumping to conclusions;
- magnification and minimization;
- emotional reasoning;

- should statements; and
- personalization/misattribution.

Alternatives to distortions were provided by:

- provision of information;
- logical analysis — determining whether the evidence supports the conclusion that has been drawn and exploring alternative possibilities;
- decatastrophizing — helping the client demagnify the consequences of abuse so she can put herself in context;
- distancing — helping the client shift from a subjective to an objective perspective on her beliefs;
- reattribution — correcting the client's tendency to assume all responsibility for the abuse while not taking other factors into account; and
- assigned activities — specifically assigning activities to disconfirm distorted beliefs and/or confirm those which are more accurate.

Donaldson and Gardner (1985) also reported on the importance of cognitive reprocessing of the incest to allow reconceptualizations of the stress response. Their work was based on Horowitz's model (1976) of the ideal course for processing a stressful event. Horowitz contended that this processing must occur or the thoughts, feelings, and memories associated with the event will continue to occupy active memory storage, to push for release, and to be experienced as intrusive-repetitive thoughts and symptoms. Because they are so uncomfortable, an attempt is made to suppress them, thus setting up the cycle of intrusive repetitive thoughts alternating with denial-numbing. Donaldson and Gardner judged that 21 of 26 women they treated showed marked symptom relief by reworking beliefs. Table 6 illustrates their reconceptualization of typical stress responses.

Based on these studies and the findings of Gold (1986) which suggest that sexually victimized women's adult functioning is related most strongly to their attributional style for bad events, it appears that cognitive techniques show particular promise in providing incest survivors with alternatives to the beliefs they developed at the time of the abuse. These beliefs were formulated within the context and stress of the incest. Since they were not fully processed and corrected at that time, they continued uninterrupted into adulthood, where they strongly influenced mood and behavior.

Reattribution of blame and responsibility occurs only as the survivor develops more perspective on and reframes and reconceptualizes the abuse circumstances. Rieker and Carmen (1986), as well as other clinicians, stress the necessity of reconceptualizing the abuse — in other words countering

TABLE 6
Reconceptualizations of Stress Responses

Category	Stress Response	Reconceptualization
Fear and Anxiety	I'm afraid I will always be alone.	I can have close relationships. I need not be alone.
	I'm afraid of losing my mind.	I can control my emotional behavior, I won't go crazy.
	Other people will hurt me.	I can protect myself now.
Anger and Frustration	I hate myself—I let this happen.	I am not a bad person, I no longer blame myself.
	I hate my mother—she didn't protect me.	My mother disappointed me, but I no longer hate her.
	I hate my father—I want to hurt him.	My father is responsible for the sexual abuse, but I can stop hating him.
Guilt and Remorse	I am responsibile for the incest—I caused it.	I am not responsible for the incest—I was a victim.
	I am being punished for being a bad person.	I do not understand fully why the incest happened, but I was not being punished for being bad.
	I shouldn't feel so angry and hateful.	I have a right to feel angry.
Shame and Self-disgust	I will always be helpless. I cannot control my life.	I can exert control in many areas of my life, I need not be a victim in all areas.
	I am not confident in myself, I don't trust myself.	I feel confident in some areas of my life, I trust myself.
	I cannot trust anyone.	I can trust some people.
Sadness	I lost my childhood.	I lost a lot, but not everything. I can salvage some relationships.
	I cannot feel, I am empty.	I can feel, I'm not empty.

From Donaldson and Gardner, 1985, p. 372.

the denial and dissociation of the abuse and stressing its reality instead. The survivor must come to understand that as the child in a dysfunctional relationship or family she was not responsible for having been abused. Nor did she cause the abuse to occur because of something inherent in her personality or character. Although it would seem that reattribution should be a relatively straightforward process, it commonly takes time because it counters everything the survivor has been taught and believes about the causes of her abuse. Furthermore, reattribution counters her adaptation and her defensive system. She is used to blaming herself or something about herself ("characterological self-blame" and shame [Janoff-Bulman, 1979]) rather than her parents or other family members. Before the survivor is able to reattribute responsibility, the therapist may have to repeatedly reframe the abuse and interrupt negative self-concepts and shame binds. Confronting abuse experiences within a group format is particularly effective in this regard, since the survivor has to face the dissonance of how she responds to the experiences of others versus how she thinks about her own. She receives strong support for viewing the incest for what is was—abuse.

Helen had been incestuously abused by her stepfather for most of childhood and adolescence. When her mother and stepfather married she was seven and had not yet recovered from her parents' divorce. She overidealized her stepfather yet resented him for taking her father's place and her mother's attention. She initially enjoyed his sexual advances because they made her feel special and equal to her mother. She initiated the contact on some occasions and became very self-blaming about this when the abuse escalated and she wanted it to stop. Her stepfather would remind her how she would "seduce" him and taunt her that he would tell her mother if Helen ever disclosed.

Helen's greatest challenge in treatment was to see her stepfather as the responsible party, even though she approached him on occasion and even though she responded sexually to his stimulation. She had to intensively examine family dynamics and repeatedly be confronted about the incestuous circumstances before she was able to reframe her behavior as a conditioned response and as due in part to her vulnerability and neediness following her parents' divorce. Only then could she forgive herself and not base current behavior on guilt and shame.

Two other cognitive techniques are related to reattribution. The first is the normalization and legitimization of the incest experience, its aftereffects, and the coping mechanisms or survivor skills. Through normalization and legitimization, the survivor comes to understand her reactions as appropriate to the situation with its lack of options and assistance. She learns that her reactions allowed her to survive thus, they are not crazy. She now has the option to change or modify those which are maladaptive or contrary to her best interests. Lamb (1986) urged therapists to support their client's actions and personal power in having attempted to counter or escape the abuse. Through "unlearning learned helplessness" or counter-conditioning, the survivor learns about and is encouraged to try other cognitive and behavioral options. Because learned helplessness has been so ingrained and reinforced, repeated exposure to options, along with intensive support for new cognitions and behavior, is needed. The survivor needs to become aware of her cognitions or automatic thoughts and the schemata (silent assumptions) about herself which affect her behavioral repertoire and can in turn be influenced by behavioral changes. The therapist is constantly challenged to help the survivor learn alternative cognitions and behaviors to effectively break out of the double bind of the abuse.

Guided imagery and metaphor used alone or in conjunction with relaxation or hypnosis constitute a second set of behavioral techniques which assist the survivor to break through stereotyped thinking and to imagine alternatives. Metaphors may promote relaxation, contribute to the breakdown of defenses, allow memories to emerge, and enable the client to gain or maintain control. Incest survivors often use metaphors to describe themselves, their memories, and defenses since these devices may be the only way they can speak, at least initially. For example, many survivors describe being well-defended behind a wall or under the bed or in a closet or having their memories safely locked away in dusty attics or in strongboxes securely tied with heavy chains and locks. These same metaphors can be used in lowering defenses. The therapist can suggest lowering defenses by taking a brick out of the wall and looking out or letting someone from the outside in. Or the survivor can visualize what would happen if she unlocked the padlock and removed the chains. An illustration of how threatening the loosening of defenses can feel was given by one of my clients, who described feeling as though she would totally fall apart if she removed the chains from around the box. They were all that kept the box together. This particular client was very accurate—she had excessively strong compulsive defenses which allowed her to "stay together" and to function but which impeded her deriving any joy from life or developing close relationships.

Groves (1987) has developed a technique for the resolution of traumatic memories using the client's subjective experience of trauma, which he found most often to be expressed in metaphor. He urges the therapist to explore the client's idiosyncratic metaphors as described and not to reframe or redefine them as either feelings or behavior. Groves believes that trauma is embedded physiologically and that metaphors allow the client to describe the experience and to make changes in it; this changes its intra-psychic components, allowing for behavior change.

Metaphors can also be helpful in visualizing success in the therapy or imagining an extensive support network in confronting the incest. One of my clients conceptualized herself and her incest history very differently after being able to visualize herself on a bed surrounded by all of her friends, who were smiling at her and offering her support. This visualization helped to break down her sense of isolation and her negative self-perceptions. Another client visualized herself as a small child about to fall down a deep pit. I was standing next to her and had a firm grip on the suspenders of her overalls.

Veronen and Kilpatrick (1983) found that stress inoculation training was useful in assisting victims of rape who suffered fear, anxiety, and phobic avoidance reactions. This technique, with modifications, may be used with incest survivors suffering from these same responses. The goal is not the elimination of anxiety but its management. Stress inoculation training emphasizes an analysis of cognitions and internal dialogue and images, and encourages active participation of the client, allowing her broad latitude in her choice of coping skill. Six cognitive/behavioral coping skills are included: muscle relaxation, breath control, role-playing, covert modeling (imaginal role-playing), thought stoppage, and guided self-dialogue. Flannery (1987) also described the utility of a stress management approach in the treatment of learned helplessness associated with psychological trauma.

Implosive therapy (flooding), adapted from Stampfl and Levis (1967), has been described as a treatment of choice for combat-related PTSD by Keane, Fairbank, Caddell, Zimering, and Bender (1985). This technique, a variant of systematic desensitization, might be used with incest survivors as well; however, its use should be reserved as a last resort. It is a powerful technique directed towards eliminating avoidance of the memory of the trauma and through exposure reducing the anxiety associated with it. The purpose of the technique is not to change the trauma itself, but to decrease the victim's anxiety response to the memories. The technique includes two treatment phases: relaxation training followed by repeated presentation of the traumatic scenes. Anxiety, related stimuli, and disturbing cognitions are reduced through an extinction procedure; this promotes symptom reduction and improved psychological functioning. This technique might be countertherapeutic for incest survivors because it recreates conditions of the trauma, particularly lack of control and feelings of powerlessness. More research is needed to determine the usefulness of flooding.

Cupchik (1984) has described a reintrojection technique, that is, a clinical procedure oriented towards altering the client's parental introject. This technique could prove useful with incest survivors who have sufficiently worked through parental issues to be able to see their parents as people with their own problems, hurts, and disappointments, and to forgive them. The issue of forgiveness is a complex one, addressed in more detail in Chapter 15.

Behavioral Techniques. Such techniques as stress inoculation training, stress management training, desensitization, relaxation, assertiveness training, anger management training, problem-solving, goal-setting, decision-making, and sex therapy incorporate cognitive and behavioral components. The survivor's change in behavior then affects the way she thinks or feels. The therapist's orientation determines whether interventions will first be made with cognitions or behaviors or whether both will be addressed simultaneously.

The development of a full repertoire of stress management and coping skills includes such behavioral components as relaxation, breath control, exercise, assertiveness training, and social networking and support. Anger and aggression management often need particular attention. Anger presents a problem for a great number of survivors. They may reach a stage in therapy when they experience seemingly uncontrollable rage, including suicidal and homicidal impulses. Women's socialization typically does not allow the expression of anger or aggression, instead rewarding passivity, acquiescence, and "good girl" behavior, behavior reinforced by incest. Consequently, many females are uncomfortable with anger or feel they have no right to express it. It becomes repressed and stockpiled, expressed in disguised forms such as passive-aggressive behavior, depression, manipulativeness, anxiety, and somatic complaints. The victimized female often directs her rage inward, expressing it through self-blame, self-contempt, self-defeating and self-abusive behaviors.

As the survivor feels her anger and rage, it is necessary to introduce anger management techniques and activities geared towards positive and healthy discharge and, at times, containment. She must learn that feelings of anger and rage are appropriate considering what happened to her and that anger is not an inherently bad emotion. She is supported in her anger and her right to it but not supported for expression which is indirect or aggressive. She learns to "dose" her anger and to devise means to discharge it in healthy ways. A number of books on anger control and anger management are now available. Exercise and sports such as tennis, squash, jogging, and racquetball can be used to discharge the built-up emotion. Additionally, both therapist and survivor need to be creative in developing individualized techniques. For example, one of my clients likes to break pencils or shred magazines during sessions when she experiences a lot of anger. She selected these methods because she likes the sounds they make. Survivors frequently are assisted with standard anger expression techniques, such as hitting pillows or furniture with bats, pounding pillows or beds, or screaming or drawing.

Assertiveness techniques can be used to control and channel anger/aggression and to help the survivor with learned helplessness and passivity. The survivor learns to differentiate aggressive, assertive, and non-assertive behaviors, assesses blocks to assertive behavior, and engages in role rehearsal. The therapist serves as a model of appropriate assertiveness.

Wilderness therapy, a rather new technique applied to this population, is a variation on the Outward Bound experience where participants physically challenge themselves to build self-confidence, self-esteem, and trust. Sexual abuse survivors in these programs are physically challenged in ways which evoke the same feelings of helplessness and powerlessness experienced during the abuse. Through reexperiencing and reworking these emotions, survivors learn to master them and regain some of their personal efficacy and self-respect.

Learning self-defense strategies enables the survivor to be more confident and less vulnerable. Many survivors experience partial or total paralysis or revert to acute passivity when faced with any situation resembling the abuse or when in the company of men. They are thus extremely vulnerable and easy targets for revictimization. Self-defense training including behavioral rehearsal helps reduce learned helplessness.

Medication may be prescribed to manage or alleviate particular symptoms. Occasionally the clinician may opt to use heavy sedation or chemical abreaction (i.e., sodium amytal narcosynthesis) as part of the therapy. Such a technique is most often used when the client is a serious danger to herself or others or in cases where the abuse material is inaccessible or the therapy stalemated. In general, chemical abreaction is not recommended (Calof, 1987; Herman, 1987) because the client is not in control and the technique may inadvertently recreate aspects of the trauma. This is true in general but is even more the case when drugs were used to perpetrate the abuse. Other issues involved in medical examinations and procedures and in the prescription of medication are discussed in Chapter 14.

A behavioral intervention which deserves particular mention is physical contact between therapist and client or between group members and their therapist(s). When consistent with the clinician's therapeutic orientation, style, and comfort level and when not contraindicated by the client's status, touching can be helpful. It can express empathy, caring, affection, and comforting. With incest survivors, it can dramatically demonstrate the difference between positive and exploitive touch and can be conceptualized as healthy boundary and limit-setting as well as healthy reparenting.

Since physical contact is quite threatening for many incest survivors, it should not be made without careful exploration of whether the client will allow it and how she interprets it. She must be in control at all times. Touching may be similarly threatening for the therapist and should not be undertaken without self-assessment as to its meaning and purpose. Is the therapist comfortable with it? Can he or she maintain boundaries? Many therapists make it a point to never touch their clients because they believe physical contact destroys the neutrality of the therapeutic relationship or because they are fearful that such contact is untherapeutic and will be misinterpreted, possibly even provoking malpractice action. The therapist who is uncomfortable with or philosophically opposed to physical contact with a client should maintain a no-touch stance. Specific training programs incorporating positive touch, such as the Helfer program described earlier or adjunctive body therapies, offer opportunities for learning positive touching. Clients might further be instructed to deliberately engage in various types of touching activities, such as touching friends or animals, massage, or selected recreational activities, exercises or sports.

Any touching in the therapy should be solely for the benefit of the client. It should be made explicit that the touching will not be sexual and that sexualization will not be allowed. It is of crucial importance that the client's permission be requested prior to making any physical contact, even of the most limited sort, such as touching the client on the arm as she leaves a session. Asking communicates respect for her and her body; it says that her preference will be respected and that no intrusion (however slight) will occur against her will. At times, a survivor might initiate physical or sexualized contact to test the therapist's trustworthiness and ability to maintain boundaries. It is always incumbent upon the therapist to maintain the limits and to explore the meaning of the behavior. This is discussed more fully in Chapter 11.

I do not have a hard and fast rule about physical contact, although my training emphasized limited or no contact. I rely on my clinical judgment and intuition about individual clients as to whether and when to touch them, always with their permission. With the majority of the incest survivors I treat, physical contact is limited and serves to offer support or reassurance during times of stress or intense emotion. However, I have found it occasionally useful to regularly hold the hand of one of my clients or sit next to her and hold her during her most painful recollections. This client is especially shamed during the recollections of her most severe abuse and her emotions and actions; she expects to be abandoned and rejected for daring to tell me about what happened. Holding her during such a session or hugging her afterwards has communicated to her that her worth and lovability as an individual are separate from what happened to her. With this client, who had been severely touch deprived, particularly by her mother, physical contact has been extremely beneficial. She gave me the book *Hug Therapy* (Keating, 1983) and specifically marked the following quote to illustrate what hugs meant to her: "Hugging fosters a feeling of self-worth; it makes you more accepting of yourself. . . . By helping you realize that you are a good person—*a huggable person*—it makes you want to take better care of that good person . . . "

Limits and boundaries that are consistent and neither too rigid nor too permeable can be established behaviorally as well as cognitively. Some survivors who have learned intense self-control in order to adhere to the rules learned in childhood need to be challenged, their standards replaced with some which are less rigid and more individually determined. Survivors with little self-control need help in establishing boundaries and behavioral limits. The therapist may set limits with physical space, time, fees, and the use of office equipment, or in making distinctions between personal and professional time and availability.

Adjunctive Therapies

Because of the complexities of incest therapy and the wide variety of symptoms and issues involved, adjunctive therapies or self-help modalities are employed fairly regularly. Some of the most common of these therapies include either group therapy or an incest self-help group, other specialized treatment programs (e.g., for eating disorders, sexual dysfunction or sexual development, alcoholism or drug abuse), involvement in any of the 12-step programs for addictions or co-addictions, marital or family therapy, sex therapy, or psychoeducational groups and courses. While these may highlight a specific problem or set of problems, they have several important supplemental benefits: They provide sources of assistance and support to the survivor besides the therapist; they provide the survivor with contact and the support of others who have similar problems, thus reducing isolation and stigma; many stress self-help and offer models of individuals who have been successfully involved in the recovery process; and they provide information on the problem and strategies for overcoming it different from, although usually complementary to, those taught in therapy.

Considerable therapeutic gain can accrue from periodic involvement in problem-specific time-limited treatment or psychoeducational courses. Wilderness therapy or involvement in time-limited courses on sexuality, assertiveness training, self-defense, etc., may spur the work of the primary therapy.

Family members may need their own treatment or need to be included in the survivor's treatment on either an occasional or a regular basis. Because of the multigenerational patterns and problems in many incest families, it is common for other family members to have problems with addictions, co-addictions, depression, being victimized and victimizing others. In addition, family members and friends may have felt the impact of the survivor's past and present trauma reactions as well as her reactions to therapy. They may benefit from their own treatment or a support or self-help group specifically designed for the significant others of PTSD victims. Concerning family members, Scurfield (1985) wrote: "Clearly, it should be a routine part of the assessment and treatment planning process to give full consideration to the possible impact of PTSD on the family and appropriate inclusion of one or more other family members as part of the treatment, either concurrently, conjointly, or sequentially to PTSD treatment with the survivor" (p. 249).

I have found it useful on occasion to include a family member or friend in a session or to offer consultation by phone. At the very least, these individuals may need education about traumatic stress response and reactions to incest and guidance for how to offer empathy, support, and assistance. They too may need support. It may also be useful to apprise them of what the survivor is experiencing in the treatment and to make recommendations if an emergency develops. This may be especially true during periods of serious depressive, self-mutilating, and suicidal reactions, and during periods of strong intrusive symptomatology such as flashbacks and nightmares. Family members may also be able to provide the therapist with information about the survivor's functioning and symptoms. (See Chapter 15 for additional discussion of family involvement and issues.)

Many treatment techniques are useful in ameliorating the aftereffects of incest. This chapter reviewed stress/coping, experimental/expressive cathartic, exploratory/psychodynamic, and cognitive/behavioral techniques for incest treatment. Techniques are selected according to the therapist's orientation, the needs of the survivor, and the phase of her traumatic stress response. They are applied within the context of a therapeutic alliance whenever possible and with care given to respecting the client and not causing her further shame.

CHAPTER 11

The Effects of Abuse Dynamics
on the Therapy Process

T HE THERAPIST-CLIENT relationship is a crucial component of all therapy. Its importance is highlighted in incest therapy because of the nature of the incestuous injury: Not only was the victimization human-induced but it was perpetrated by a family member. Abuse at the hands of a relative intensifies rather than lessens its negative impact and compromises the child's ability to trust others and to develop a positive self-concept. The therapy relationship is instrumental in providing the survivor with the necessary support to address and work through the trauma while modeling a healthy, non-exploitative relationship.

Numerous intrapsychic and interpersonal effects of incest are manifest in the therapy process and relationship. These in turn stimulate and reinforce the therapist's reactions and biases. The transference and countertransference issues and reactions most typically related to child sexual victimization are discussed here. Although I have attempted a fairly inclusive approach in this discussion, the chapter certainly cannot address reactions of all types or the vagaries of each individual therapy. These more unique transference reactions must also be monitored and managed.

The therapist's orientation will determine the degree to which transference reactions are attended to and how they are addressed in the treatment. Short-term treatment by necessity offers less of an opportunity to analyze transference, although Horowitz (1986) has discussed the interpretation of transference within a time-limited stress treatment model. As a therapeutic rule of thumb, he urges that the interpretation of transference be included in the therapy, not as the focus of treatment but rather directed towards negative responses likely to impede therapy. Miller (1984) discusses transference as symbolic reenactment of the past and the means by which the survivor communicates about the past. Her psychoanalytic treatment model is lengthier and deeper than the model proposed by Horowitz and focus directly on the transference as coded communication on the part of the client.

TRANSFERENCE ISSUES

Many aspects of the incest, the family experience, and individual personality style and functioning are brought to therapy and projected onto the therapist. In this section, I identify the most common transference issues. They are not discrete, considerable overlap exists between them, and they may present in a somewhat layered or cascading fashion.

Betrayal, Disillusionment, and Mistrust

Incest survivors have experienced betrayal in their most significant relationships. As a result, their ability to trust others has been seriously compromised. Many describe intense disillusionment with the perpetrator(s), with non-offending but nonhelpful family members, and with others who were nonresponsive or revictimized them. Many survivors become totally mistrustful and suspicious of others, never learning to trust that other people will not harm them. Building basic trust is the earliest developmental task and the foundation on which all others are built (Erikson, 1980). Failure at this initial stage impairs identity development, the ability to form healthy and mutual relationships, and the ability to be intimate.

The survivor brings this lack of trust to the therapy relationship, making development of a therapeutic alliance a slow and often tedious task. She may fear the therapist, seeing him/her as parental or authority figure and thus as abusive, manipulative, unprotective, and/or rejecting. Or, more simply, the therapist may be seen as one other person who is untrustworthy and therefore suspect. This is especially true if the client has had previous negative experiences with anyone in a helping profession, particularly if the experiences involved attempted or actual sexual interaction.

Braun (1986a) had the following to say about trust issues in the treatment of multiple personality disorder. It is likewise applicable to incest survivors who are not multiples:

> The issue of trust will be called into question at each major point in therapy. The therapist must be careful not to react to this as an intentional affront. Multiple personality disorder patients have been abused in an inconsistent and unpredictable way. This partial reinforcement schedule for mistrust is very difficult to extinguish. Working on each major therapy issue is scary, and fear becomes the stimulus for the reactivation of mistrust. (p. 11)

The therapist must be consistent and reassuring and should not take trust for granted, even with a dependent or compliant client or one who professes trust, or even after a certain level of trust has developed. The therapist should be especially careful with any aspect of the therapy which causes a survivor to question the therapist's honesty and trustworthiness. For example, issues of confidentiality and privacy are critical to this population since they have had the experience of being so thoroughly violated.

Throughout the course of therapy, the client may engage in behavior to test the therapist's trustworthiness or to reinforce her belief that no one will be there for her. She fears allowing herself to trust because doing so makes her vulnerable to the influence of others and to possible criticism, abandonment, and rejection.

The therapist must do her best to not personalize this testing or any accusations the survivor might make. Survivors who have been repeatedly subjected to double-bind communication will repeat this communication style with the therapist (Braun, 1986a). The therapist is best advised to use the transference as communication about how family interactions were experienced by the survivor.

As the therapy progresses and the survivor delves more deeply into the abuse issues (especially those having to do with betrayal and coercion), or as crises develop, crises in trust are to be expected. Not infrequently, crises provide a singular opportunity for the therapist to prove trustworthiness by remaining available and consistent. Crises are the times when anxiety concerning abandonment is at a peak—even though the survivor's needs are the greatest her expectation is that once again she will be let down.

Some survivors have another trust problem—that of trusting their own perceptions and experience. As discussed in Chapters 2 and 3, when a child is betrayed repeatedly and when she lacks outside confirmation, she comes to disbelieve her experience and reactions and develops accommodation mechanisms to cope (Summit, 1983). This restructuring of reality and the disconfirmation of self are reflected in the therapy, where the survivor might constantly call her memories and emotions into question and question her sanity. The therapist's task is to assist the survivor in recontextualizing the abuse (Rieker & Carmen, 1986) and in encouraging the identification and development of the genuine self through the expression of previously unacknowledged parts of the self.

Traumatic Transference

Spiegel (1986) described a variation on trust transference, traumatic transference, which occurs when " . . . the patient unconsciously expects that the therapist, despite overt helpfulness and concern, will covertly exploit the patient for his or her own narcissistic gratification" (p. 72) in much the same way her parent(s) or other abusers did. The survivor fears and even expects to be abused by the therapist. Aspects of the treatment might be experienced as abuse and so must be undertaken gradually and with due consideration for the survivor, along with an understanding of this type of transference reaction.

Accessing the memory, even for the purpose of working it through in therapy, is experienced as a reinflicting of previously inflicted trauma, just as many rape victims experience police interrogation about the event as a repeat of the rape itself. Thus, the working through of transference is as difficult to resolve as it is critical. (p. 72)

The therapist must continuously strive to create a safe environment and to provide a reliable, trustworthy relationship. She must guard against allowing herself to be drawn into the role of sadistic abuser in reenactment of the abuse and should explain reasons for exploring painful material. When transference reactions of this sort arise, they must be used to explore and understand the past with the survivor.

Shame, Self-Hatred, and Low Self-Esteem

The ability to trust others allows for secure attachment. Such bonding sets the stage for healthy ego development and a positive self-concept. The experience of incest with its predominant message that love equals abuse has great potential to undermine a positive identity. The experience of abuse enters the self-concept; a significant number of incestuously abused children come to believe that something about them, something *inherently wrong with them,* caused the incest to occur. These beliefs, coupled with guilt and anxiety, result in a shamed sense of self—that the self is unlovable, deserving of abuse, and unworthy of care and good attention. In addition, children incorporate a sense of stigma from having been involved in a secret and forbidden activity, something so awful that it could not be discussed.

Not uncommonly, this and other aspects of incestuous abuse result in a self-concept grounded in alienation, self-hatred, and negative self-esteem. The child may come to hate her very being and especially her body for "having caused it all" and further blame herself for the fact that no one protected or assisted her. These feelings are expressed as variations of: "If your own father (brother/ uncle/ grandfather) did that (repeatedly) to you, then it must have been something about you and therefore your fault. You somehow *deserved it.* And, if your own mother (father/aunt/grandmother) didn't notice, care, or do anything about it, or blamed you, then you must be guilty and despicable. If your own family didn't care about you, then who will?"

Survivors project their shame onto their therapists, expecting them to hold them in the same contempt they have for themselves and to behave disrespectfully as their family did. They feel undeserving of the therapist's positive attention and suffer anxiety that sooner or later the therapist will discover their secret—that the incest occurred *because of something about them.* They further expect a reenactment of any nonprotection or blame experienced during their childhood. *Because of who they are* and because of the incest, they fear the therapist will shun and castigate them. One survivor described her fear:

I'm on familiar terms with feelings of blame and shame. I always thought I'd be blamed if anyone found out. Even when I started seeing my therapist, I had that "edge of the chair" feeling that she would surely blame me. Obviously, she never did. I'm sure I would have accepted it, maybe angry as hell, but nonetheless accepted it. I've always believed that I was guilty, that it was all my fault.

Interpersonal/Intimacy Difficulties

As suggested by the previous problem areas, many survivors experience serious difficulty with interpersonal and intimate relationships; yet, another group of survivors are able to successfully overcome their negative self-concept by developing friendships and love relationships that are reparative in that they contradict the feelings and learnings of the earlier experiences. The therapy relationship holds the potential to be such a reparative experience, possibly the survivor's first.

It is easy to see how negative self-perceptions are projected onto others. The survivor's self-denigration often makes positive regard from anyone, including the therapist, impossible to accept. This pattern may have developed from a very young age, resulting in a lack of friends and social skills and later in nonexistent or failed intimate relationships. Some survivors defend against the possibility of any more hurt or betrayal by cutting themselves off from most contact with others. Their attitude may be expressed as "nobody/nothing will hurt me because I'm not going to put myself in the position of allowing anyone in." These individuals are typically isolated and withdrawn or aggressive and abrasive in their interactions.

When positive regard is forthcoming, a survivor may do everything in her power to sabotage the relationship, reverse it, or flee from it. Westerlund (1983) addressed this anxiety and urged therapists to be aware that the intimacy of a one-to-one contact with a supportive helping person in an enclosed space may be too overwhelming for some survivors. The therapist should maintain an initial stance that is somewhat neutral, rather than being overly supportive or abstinent, in order to engage and not frighten the survivor. Some women initially do better in a group therapy format, where the intensity of an individual relationship is "watered down" and therefore not as threatening.

Many survivors who can tolerate a one-on-one relationship and who allow one or more to develop find themselves constantly fearful of rejection and disappointment. Leehan and Wilson (1985), paraphrasing one of their clients, called this the "waiting for the other shoe to drop" phenomenon. Survivors fear and expect that after they receive positive regard and attention something bad will happen. They will be found out for what they really are and rejected. One of my clients repeatedly asks, "I didn't do anything wrong?" and another "Do you hate me? Are you going to get rid of me?" when they dare to divulge some of their more negative feelings or most closely guarded secrets. Their innermost fear is that the therapist will, at some point, use these disclosures as cause for rejection.

In order to ease the anxiety of waiting for the "bad" to happen, some clients engage in self-defeating behavior or manipulate the situation to bring about the expected rejection. Self-sabotage may occur in many areas of the individual's life. She may be unable to function successfully inter-personally, in school, or at work due to fear of failure and debilitating anxiety. Or self-sabotage may be a way of defending against the anxiety associated with doing well. Even when successful, she may not believe success was due to her efforts or abilities and so may discount the positive. Because of her ingrained belief that she doesn't deserve good attention or her fear of being selfish, she may respond to complimentary feedback with guilt and anxiety. She may diminish or externalize credit for all of her accomplishments so as not to draw attention to herself. A self-sabotaging pattern is likely to be evident within the therapy where the survivor resists efforts to help her or resists all efforts to change. Another complication is that many survivors have learned to be superficially compliant or to devel-op a false self to safeguard themselves. Thus, a survivor may appear to be engaged in the treatment when in fact she is only working on surface issues without actually changing.

An opposite pattern is sometimes observed, that of exaggerated compe-tence and grandiosity. Some survivors inflate their sense of self and their abilities in order to defend against their badness and their depression. Or they express intense anger and bitterness that their skills and talents have not been recognized or nurtured. They may even use this fact to rational-ize any lack of success or inability to achieve goals. Miller (1981, p. 56) described such a tendency when she wrote that "Grandiosity is the coun-terpart of depression *within* the narcissistic disturbance." An inflated sense of self further defends against the fear associated with developing relation-ships with others, as a type of self-fulfilling prophecy. Grandiosity can be used to set the self apart in a superior way that alienates or intimidates others. This reinforces the sense of being different while intensifying lone-liness and isolation.

These same feelings make most survivors extremely needy of affection, nurturance, and attention. Thus, the therapist is faced with the challenge of a client who does not trust or feel she deserves a good relationship and who attempts to sabotage one as it develops, and yet needs exactly those things she fears and feels she doesn't deserve. Moreover, the intensity and sometimes instability of the survivor's engagement with the therapist pro-voke intense reactions on the part of the therapist. The survivor is faced with a painful dilemma. In order to recover from the injury of incest she must tolerate and allow the development of a reparative human relation-ship. The therapist must understand this dilemma and offer patience, respect, reliability and consistency, while monitoring the relationship and offering interpretations about the process.

Complicating the dynamic further is the fact that a substantial number of survivors possess an overdeveloped awareness of the reactions and feelings of others, originally learned as a survival mechanism. Some describe themselves as radars and chameleons, constantly scanning for problems and changing their own behavior to accommodate the needs of others or to escape danger or interpersonal conflict. Minor mood or behavioral changes in others are registered, often unconsciously, so that the survivor can change her own behavior in response. Further, changes in others which in reality have nothing to do with her may be personalized or misattributed to some fault or badness on her part. In therapy, she has the opportunity to learn to first become aware of her perceptions and conclusions, to test their accuracy, and then to change them when inaccurate. She also learns that it is not necessary for her to constantly respond to the mood state or needs of others.

Finally, since the survivor experienced many forms of double-bind in her family of origin, it is likely that she will use similar forms of communication with the therapist, who may experience confusion, frustration and rage as a result. Again, this situation calls for the therapist's stepping back from the interaction and not taking it personally but rather analyzing it and working on alternative cognitions and behaviors with the survivor.

Guilt, Complicity, and Responsibility

In a similar fashion, feelings of guilt, responsibility, and complicity related to the incest negatively affect feelings about the self and intensify anxiety about relations with others. Many survivors do not realize the extent to which they make themselves the guilty party (and usually the only guilty party) for the abuse. Their guilt is often so strong that it is generalized to their very existence. They may find themselves feeling guilty and apologizing for themselves almost continuously, a stance they demonstrate in therapy.

Women who have ambivalent feelings regarding their own responsibility (as is often found in father-daughter cases where the mother directly or indirectly blames the child, in close-in-age sibling contact where responsibility for initiation or maintenance of the behavior is unclear, or in cases where the child wanted, initiated or enjoyed the contact), seem to be the most confused about their own guilt. Additionally, many survivors blame themselves for not having been able to say no, believing that not doing so was equivalent to wanting or pursuing the contact. They may also feel guilty for not having been able to prevent the abuse of siblings. Finally, their guilt may result from having been blamed and scapegoated within the family.

Another complicating factor in assessing responsibility and resolving guilt is that the survivor may feel a combination of love and hate towards the abuser and other family members. This is particularly likely in the case of the abuser who provided nurturance and affection she otherwise lacked. She may fear losing the good parts of the relationship if she places the responsibility for the incest squarely on him. A survivor's protectiveness of the perpetrator may also be due to the role reversal or "parentification" she experienced, coupled with her overdeveloped sense of responsibility and protection. Giving up her role as "protector of the family secrets" can produce a great deal of anxiety and a different kind of guilt, that of being disloyal. She may have anxious feelings about exposing all that she worked so hard to disguise. The therapist must guard against scapegoating the abuser and the entire family while not condoning the abuse.

Further confusion about the issues of guilt and responsibility develop if the child experienced *sexual pleasure* or *personal power* as part of the incest or if she sought revenge through the incestuous contact. These two aspects are sometimes referred to as the secondary secrets or the "secrets within the incest secret" and are among the most difficult to disclose. They may cause the victim great consternation, guilt, anxiety, and additional self-blame, self-hatred and self-alienation.

Sexual Issues. Bass and Thornton (1983) offered a very concrete explanation and example of the sexual pleasure dimension:

> In some instances the abused child's body may respond to the sexual stimulation even as her consciousness is horrified.
> Because she does not know that her body can respond without her consent, or even that it can respond in such a way at all, the abused child feels that she must have wanted the abuse, must have asked for it in some way. It is this betrayal of herself by her body that she sometimes finds the hardest to forgive. And again, she does not tell; she fears that anyone she tells would surely blame her as much as she blames herself. (pp. 18, 19)

As is evident from this example, some abusers take great pleasure in the child's sexual response, even when involuntary. It may be used to support the rationalization that the child enjoys and benefits from the activity and may also be a means by which the child is further coerced and confused along the lines of "See, you climaxed. That means that you really wanted it and enjoyed it." As adults, survivors may remember the lust in their perpetrator's eyes and use it as conclusive proof of their malignant sexuality.

Of course, some children enjoyed the sexual sensations without conflict or resistance and may have sought the contact or even initiated it. Brooks (1983) discussed this latter circumstance as due in part to a mother's hostile-dependent stance towards the child pre-incest; this causes the child to seek out nurturance from the father, who unfortunately sexualizes the contact. The child may initially find pleasure and comfort in the sexual behavior, as well as a way to revenge the mother for her lack of nurturance. This child may later feel guilty for her behavior as well as for her enjoyment and her anger. Further blaming or scapegoating by the mother for the incest often brings about an intensification of these feelings and corresponding guilt.

Power Issues. Guilt feelings may also be stimulated by enjoyment of a power position in relation to the abuser and to the family at large. A number of survivors used their ability to manipulate the situation or the abuser to get what they needed (cessation of abuse of their mother or siblings, lunch money or other necessities) or what they wanted (special favors or privileges, money, gifts, clothes, revenge) and in fact may have exchanged sexual favors in return for special attention. They may later feel as though they prostituted themselves.

Some women come to believe that they are sexually powerful and irresistible to any man, usually in a malignant way. They derive special pleasure or satisfaction from demeaning or getting back at men by having them pay for sexual services. They set out to seduce men who are authority figures and/or are supposed to be "unseducible," e.g., other family members, members of the clergy, therapists. Whereas they are initially pleased with a "successful conquest," later they feel great disillusionment and anger at the individual man and at men in general for being so acquiescent and dishonorable.

Another seduction pattern has also been observed where the survivor is indiscriminate in sex of partner—a conquest is a conquest. These individuals are sometimes also similarly indiscriminate in the type of sexual activity they engage in. The motivations of self-contempt and of anger, revenge, and contempt towards the abuser and the non-offending parent are usually at the core of this type of behavior. The survivor may have come to view herself as malignantly powerful both within and outside of the family, a belief she brings to and may act out in therapy.

In incestuous abuse, the child often learns that sex and affection are synonymous and that sexual behavior is involved in all close interpersonal interactions. She may have learned to be pleasing sexually or to come on to others as a means of establishing a relationship with them. She may do the same with the therapy relationship. De Young (1981a) and other clinicians have noted that some patients use the transference to work through the sexual aspects of the incestuous relationship and that a therapist who is insensitive to or ignorant of this process may sexualize rather than understand what is transpiring. A trusting, protective therapeutic environment is imperative for the survivor to develop a relationship not based on sexual interaction or sexual favors and to be able to explore feelings without fear of exploitation. A sexual encounter between a therapist and client has great negative potential for any client because such contacts are "symbolically incestuous" (Barnhouse, 1978), but they hold special potential for harm for the incest survivor since they reenact the exploitation of the abuse with another authority figure who is supposed to be trustworthy and nurturing. (This situation is discussed in more detail below in the section on countertransference reactions and therapist gender.)

Guilt, responsibility, and the secondary secrets may cause the survivor to be extremely cautious and secretive in the therapy relationship. She may allow only limited discussion of the incest and conceal a great deal of information. She may respond with strong denial, intense anger, or aggression towards herself or others if the therapist suggests that the perpetrator was responsible for the incest or that the family atmosphere was conducive to its development, or when the therapist asks about the possibility of positive feelings or enjoyment or about contempt and the wish for revenge. Clearly, the clinician does well to avoid probing these issues early in the therapy and does so only within the context of a fairly well established relationship. Strong feelings of guilt resolve only gradually with repeated exposure to new and disconfirming information and with a supportive ally.

Defenses, Survivor Skills, and Accommodation Mechanisms

The defenses used to cope during the abuse and afterwards come into play in the therapy. It is crucial that the therapist conceptualize and understand these defenses as coping strategies which were necessary at the time of the incest but have outlived their usefulness and become problematic in the post-abuse period. According to Summit (1983, p.184), "In dealing with the accommodation mechanisms of the child or the vestigial scars of the adult survivor, the therapist must take care to avoid reinforcing a sense of badness, inadequacy or craziness by condemning or stigmatizing the symptoms." The variety and intensity of defenses and the fact that they mimic symptoms of mental illness quite often make them terrifying for the survivor. Survivors frequently point to their symptoms as the obvious proof of their insanity. Before the survivor can change her perspective the therapist must repeatedly depathologize them and place them in the context of the abuse as stress responses to traumatic episodes.

The therapist has the opportunity to observe many of these defenses and accommodation mechanisms within the therapy hour. Such prominent defenses as repression and amnesia, dissociation, splitting, repetition compulsion, projection, and reaction formation come into play in defending against the anxiety of the content and process of the therapy. Florid intrusive/reexperiencing symptoms (flashbacks, frightening images, hypervigilance, and anxiety states) and similarly florid numbing symptoms (fainting, derealization, detachment, and dissociation) are very frightening for the therapist and survivor alike. The necessity for these defenses lessens over the course of therapy as the traumatic material is resolved.

Caretaking and Learned Responsibility

The "parentified" child has learned to be responsible for the family functioning with little or no expectation that her needs will be noticed or responded to. She usually has learned her role so well that she has difficulty distinguishing between caring about and taking care of others. She almost automatically takes care of others, often to an extreme degree and with disregard to her own needs. This woman often fits the label of superwoman — she tries and often succeeds at being all things to all people and is used to juggling multiple roles and responsibilities. It is not uncommon for her to become involved with dependent, immature individuals who want someone to take care of them or with cold, indifferent, and/or abusive individuals who take much but give little in return. Her ingrained hyperattunement to the needs of others interacts with her guilt and low self-esteem to hold her in a caretaking role. She has not learned that she deserves anything more and does not know how to ask for or demand it. In fact, her caretaking of others can likewise serve as a learned way for her to control and limit intimacy or to prevent anyone from getting too close to her. Women in this pattern may only seek help when they are totally overwhelmed and desperate, usually when faced with multiple crises. It takes severe stress to get through their superior coping ability and to surface their underlying depression. They may be very embarrassed and ashamed because they feel like failures — seeking help puts them in an uncomfortable and unaccustomed position vis-à-vis the helper.

In conjunction with the learned responsibility for others, some survivors learn to never ask for or expect anything for themselves. This counterdependent style is frequently related to having depriving, neglectful, or unavailable parents or family circumstance. These girls learned to cope by being self-sufficient. They pride themselves on their independence and their ability to care for themselves and other family members without assistance from anyone; furthermore, their guilt and low self-esteem may make it very difficult for them to allow anything for themselves.

Both of these styles may be challenging to manage in the therapeutic context. The therapist must work against being trapped by the overly considerate and conscientious client and must constantly point out when she places the needs of others, including those of the therapist, before her own. This behavior might be difficult to catch because it is so ingrained and is designed to gratify and please others. The therapist is no exception and must pay special attention to this dynamic in order not to be lulled by the client's pleasantness and caretaking. One of my clients exemplified this behavior.

Two years into therapy, Ann began to discuss how she tried to be the perfect client for me. She was used to taking care of others and used her caretaking to insure that I would continue to work with her. Her most flagrant example of caretaking occurred when she drove about 10 miles out of her way on a day when she did not have an appointment in order to pay me because it was the end of the month and my "payday."

A variation of this transference pattern occurs when the survivor idealizes the therapist and treats her with undue consideration. The survivor may be very envious of the therapist but masks this reaction with her concern about losing her. So she treats the therapist with "kid gloves" in hopes of keeping her.

The counterdependent client presents a different sort of challenge. Because of her self-sufficiency, she may actively work against or sabotage any dependency or unconsciously do something to demonstrate her independence from the therapist when dependency is developing. Here again an overlap of issues is seen. This client fears rejection by the therapist, whom she does not believe is trustworthy. Counterdependence provides the defense against the fear and offers a means to maintain control and limit vulnerability. Another survivor serves as an example.

Bonnie, a survivor of father-daughter incest, came from a very under-privileged background. Her mother kicked her father out of the house when she learned of the abuse and kept the family together by sheer force of will and hard work. Bonnie learned the work ethic well—she coped with her guilt and shame in the aftermath of the abuse by becoming a super-achiever at whatever she undertook.

Bonnie sought treatment for a major depressive disorder which developed when she suffered some personal and career setbacks which did not reverse with her usual compulsive effort. Although part of the therapy was geared towards stress management, Bonnie sabotaged almost all efforts to learn to relax and to positively care for herself and avoided addressing the incest and family issues. She fled treatment when she felt back in control of her life and returned to her compulsive workaholism. She reinitiated treatment when she again became clinically depressed. Her defensive over-work was no longer enough to keep the underlying depression from surfacing.

Whether the client is caretaking and/or counterdependent, it is likely that she wants the therapist to care about her and take care of her. She either does not know how to ask for this directly or may be prevented from asking by past experiences of having been abandoned or punished. She may become furious with the therapist if she feels a lack of responsiveness or if she feels the therapist ought to be able to "read her mind" and know her needs, as she is able to do with others. Due to the propensity to blame herself or to turn things against herself, she may engage in self-punishing behavior for wanting to be cared for and in order to express anger towards the therapist while testing his/her responsiveness.

When the survivor becomes aware of her own needs and her caretaking pattern with others, she may feel overwhelmed or frightened by her neediness as well as furious at past neglect. These issues need to be addressed carefully and in doses. Where warranted, the imbalance of past and current relationships needs to be analyzed and changed. Some relationships will no longer be satisfactory, leaving the survivor feeling alone and unsupported when a support system is most needed. She is apt to be very dependent on therapy during this time, until she is able to develop mutually satisfying relationships. Those family members and friends who remain supportive should be mobilized. A therapy group or self-help group is useful in providing another source of support.

Loss and Grief

During therapy, it is necessary for the survivor to confront and grieve for what was lost due to the abuse experience and any related individual and family problems. The most common losses include lost childhood, lost innocence and trust, lost identity (i.e., I am not the person I might have been), lost potential (with family members, interpersonally, sexually, and occupationally), and lost good family and good parenting. Victims may have more idiosyncratic losses to mourn as well. Grieving, a necessary therapy component, brings to the surface feelings of sadness, depression, and anger which must be encouraged and supported by the therapist. A therapy or self-help group, as well as the individual therapy, are instrumental to the mourning process, since the survivor is often able to acknowledge and accept her own losses only after she has identified and empathized with the losses suffered by others. The support and empathy of other group members and the therapist help her to address and mourn for herself.

The reality of past losses, past neglect, and past deprivation may transfer to the present. The survivor may become fearful of losing current relationships, especially the one with the therapist. Because of this, special attention must be paid to any changes or leavetakings, such as absences, vacations, and termination. The client's tendency to blame herself, to project negative self-esteem, and to find proof of her own unworthiness and the untrustworthiness of others are activated during changes and interact with fear of abandonment or rejection.

Separations for such events as professional conferences, vacations, holidays, or childbirth should be announced and prepared for well in advance. The survivor needs repeated encouragement to identify and express how she feels about the therapist's planned absence. Quite often, she uses her understanding of the need for or legitimacy of a separation to dismiss any negative or needy feelings she might have. Instead, she may castigate herself for her feelings (e.g., for feeling like a baby, for being dependent or scared, for being ridiculous), use familiar defenses and behaviors to deny any emotions or to take care of the therapist (e.g., to show no emotion so as not to cause problems for the therapist, to use anger as a means of distancing from or annoying the therapist), and resort to self-sufficiency as counterdependence (to deny that the therapist's absence has any impact).

The client clearly needs support and validation for whatever emotions are generated by absences and leavetakings. This is particularly true with respect to anger, which might be denied or displaced. In order to correct faulty assumptions, the therapist must first ferret out the client's reactions and attributions. If it seems appropriate, the therapist might counter misattributions by being factual about the reasons for an absence and sharing her own emotions about the separation. Due to their rejection/abandonment fears, survivors frequently benefit from knowing that the therapist's absence does not mean a cessation of caring, nor is it due to personal dislike or hostility.

Fear of abandonment and of punishment is reflected in the extreme concern some survivors voice about the therapist's safety during a separation. Survivors might be highly superstitious that something bad will befall the therapist as punishment for their developing trust and making disclosures or for daring to express anger at the therapist for leaving. Such a mishap would conclusively prove their malignant power and reenact the loss of a significant relationship. Again, exploration of these fears is warranted. The therapist can offer the reassurance that she fully intends to return; however, if something beyond her control were to happen, it would not be the client's fault nor would it be punishment of her. Adequate backup coverage should be planned for each separation, even if the survivor scoffs at such a plan or indicates that she would never use it or be comfortable seeing another therapist. Backup planning communicates through appropriate caretaking and professional responsibility that the client and her concerns are taken seriously and that she is not being abandoned in the therapist's absence.

Particular survivors may require individualized strategies during separations. When I am away in a professional capacity, I maintain regular and often daily phone contact with clients who are in crisis or are otherwise in need of reassurance or object constancy. I also encourage them to use whatever additional supports they have available during separations. I have a different policy during my vacation time, when I maintain complete separation with no contact. In some cases, I have written a letter or shared a possession from my office preseparation to encourage object constancy. Some colleagues send a note or postcard or make phone contact during vacation or other absences.

It is certainly necessary for the therapist to avoid overly solicitous behaviors or those that play into any client manipulation. Similarly, the client should not be encouraged to be overattached or overdependent and boundaries should be clearly delineated about the therapist's personal time. On the other hand, the stress associated with separations should not be minimized or ignored. Actions must be selected in response to client needs and the therapist's judgment about what would be most therapeutic. And the development and maintenance of clear boundaries are in and of themselves therapeutic for this population. Clarity and consistency contribute to the development of trust and counter the inconsistency found in many incestuous families.

On occasion, separations will be so difficult that hospitalization or another type of placement is necessary to assure the client's well-being and security. While not necessarily the treatment of choice, hospitalization may be considered when the client has little or no support system or when she cannot function or insure her safety during the period of separation from the therapist.

In a similar vein, any leave-taking should be carefully prepared for. It will be most difficult when the therapeutic work is incomplete, a situation most likely to occur when the therapist is leaving a training placement, when an agency imposes time limits on therapy, or when the therapist or client moves. When the client transfers to a new therapist, overlapping or joint sessions with old and new therapists can ease the transition.

Termination, whether due to the formal end of treatment or some other reason, should be announced as early as is feasible to leave time for processing and preparation. The survivor may initially deny the termination and its impact, refuse to discuss it, or attempt to change the terms of the relationship with the therapist by making him or her a friend. As the boundaries of the relationship are maintained and termination occurs, a wide range of emotions is to be expected. The survivor mourns the loss of the present relationship, which serves as a reminder of past losses or abandonments. Rage reactions are not uncommon nor are strong depressive and dissociative reactions to abandonment by the therapist. Separation, individuation, and independence, as stated goals of treatment, should be referred to periodically to prepare the client for their eventuality. Termination should include a recognition of the client's growth and gains as well as loss issues.

Rage and Anger

Although anger may be an emotion the survivor expresses right from the start of therapy, it is common for feelings of rage to occur during the course of treatment in conjunction with feelings of loss and sorrow. The chronicling and recognition of the losses cause anger about what was lost, as well as about having been abused, betrayed, and neglected. The rage may further be expressed as part of the therapy and directed at the therapist. Especially for those survivors diagnosed as having borderline personality disorder, the relationship may be conflictual, alternating between periods of attachment to and idealization of the therapist and periods of withdrawal and hostility when the relationship fails to meet the survivor's expectations. The therapist's equanimity is severely challenged by the intensity and instability demonstrated by these clients.

Because women are more likely than men to inwardly focus their anger, it is commonly expressed in disguised forms, such as passive-aggressive behavior, depression, manipulativeness, anxiety, and somatic complaints. Quite often, the survivor vents it against herself through self-blame, self-contempt, and self-defeating and self-abusive behavior. This containment and misdirection of anger can lead to frighteningly intense rage with explosive potential, accompanied by anxiety and panic about discharging and controlling the feelings. Rage of explosive proportions is frightening for the therapist, who might respond with distancing and rejection. A more therapeutic strategy is first to accept and legitimize the anger and then to assist the survivor to regain some control and to discharge the anger in nonharmful ways. This topic receives additional discussion in Chapters 10 and 14.

COUNTERTRANSFERENCE REACTIONS

Professionals have no immunity to the dominant societal attitudes concerning incest. These may be projected, along with more personal reactions, whether positive or negative, onto the client and onto the therapeutic process. In this section, countertransference reactions are discussed, along with therapeutic and non-therapeutic behaviors which derive from them. These reactions are drawn from the major themes in the clinical literature, since only one study of countertransference reactions to incest therapy and incest survivors have been completed to date (Johns, 1987).

Renshaw (1982) discussed three types of countertransference reactions to incest: avoidance, attraction, and attack. All of the therapist's emotional and behavioral reactions discussed in this section can be listed in one or more of these categories. Avoidance refers to the desire to deny, escape from, or not see the situation as it really is. Incest avoidance is generally based on such emotions as anxiety, discomfort, repugnance, dread, and horror. Attraction connotes a moving towards or an arousal, a desire to become involved in or stimulated by the situation. Attack is motivated by anger and condemnation of the activity and connotes aggressive responses to those involved in it.

Interestingly, many of the countertranference themes found by Danieli (1984) in her study of emotional responses experienced by psychotherapists working with Holocaust survivors are consistent with the dominant reactions of therapists working with incest survivors.*   As discussed in Chapter 7, the conditions of incestuous abuse often markedly resemble conditions found in concentration camps: a prolonged internment involving chronic trauma and total dependence on a sadistic authority figure. Incest, like the Holocaust, has been surrounded by a conspiracy of silence. Since both types of victimization are human-induced, they are more repugnant and more likely to cause an intense reaction in the victim and an avoidant reaction in the helper than a victimization brought on by natural forces. Danieli found that the therapy experiences of Holocaust survivors rarely included more than cursory mention of the concentration camp experiences, a situation very akin to that of incest survivors until just recently. The failure of therapists to listen, explore, and understand each type of trauma has contributed to compounded effects and secondary injuries (Butler, 1978; Symonds, 1980).

Dread and Horror

Many therapists find themselves horrified when a client discloses incest because of the deviance it implies. The thought of a child being sexually coerced by and involved with a parent, in and of itself, is enough to be totally shocking. The details of the abuse are even more shocking, and those involving pleasurable, sadistic or violent aspects even more so. Thus, the most traumatic aspects of the incest and those most in need of ventilation and validation are the ones that cause the therapist the greatest degree of discomfort. Therapist discomfort often leads to defensive behavior, such as the therapist's changing the subject, subtly denying that the situation could have been that bad (even though doing so contradicts the therapist's emotional response), and encouraging the client to forget it and get on with her life. Meiselman (1978) had this to say about incest horror:

> Incest horror is unfortunate, not because it expresses disapproval of incest but because its intensity impairs our ability to think about incestuous behavior in a calm and rational way. . . . A horrified attitude prevents us from recognizing the true scope of the problem by relegating incest to the realm of events that are so bizarre that they occur only among the scum of society or in the context of extreme psychopathology. We need to adopt the attitude, as professionals, that incest is an unfortunate event that is preventable, detectable, and treatable. (pp. 331–332)

Furthermore, incest occurrence needs to be acknowledged as widespread and not as deviant from the norms of society as has been believed.

*In noting the similarities of response to the Holocaust and incest, I am not trying to equate the two, nor am I diminishing their differences.

Denial and Avoidance

Incest horror is directly related to the tendency to deny and avoid its very occurrence. Therapists' propensity to deny incest has long been buttressed by Freud's replacement of his original formulation, the seduction theory, which accepted the reality of adult-child sexual abuse, with the drive theory, which negated its reality by ascribing it to the child's fantasy. Miller (1984) has eloquently described how the truth about the trauma of childhood sexual abuse was so threatening that a theory was constructed to defend against it:

> ... The link between parents' need for erotic fulfillment and their right to use and punish the child is such an inherent feature of our culture that until recently its legitimacy had been questioned by very few.
>
> Now, however, the psychoanalytic method has brought us face to face with the consequences of this phenomenon—with repression and the related loss of vitality that occurs in neurosis. This revelation has apparently severely strained the limits of what people can accept. The shock, confusion, and dismay it caused could be mastered (warded off) only by denying the facts or, if this was no longer possible, by constructing various theories. The more complicated, incomprehensible, and rigid these theories, the better guarantee they provided that the actually very obvious but painful situation remained concealed. (p. 109)

In order to conduct effective incest therapy, the therapist must absolutely accept that incest occurs and that children are used and exploited by their adult caretakers. They must continuously counter the personal tendency to defend the adults at the expense of the child or to otherwise deny, discount, or dismiss the survivor's story. They must also abandon those theoretical formulations and positions which reinforce denial and work through any of their own childhood traumas to be able to adequately address those of their clients (Miller, 1984). Only through acceptance of the abuse experiences and their abreaction can the trauma be mastered and the incest wound healed.

Therapists must also guard against denying the less common forms of incest and any incest which is excessively violent, gruesome, or bizarre. Survivors with such experiences are more fearful and reluctant to disclose and may demonstrate a more severe pathology which impedes disclosure. For example, it is now recognized that the most fragmented multiple personalities often develop due to prolonged, tortuous abuse sometimes involving satanic cult rituals, child pornography, druggings, human sacrifice or other murder, and even episodes of cannibalism. Survivors of tortuous abuse are in need of therapists who accept rather than disbelieve what they so painfully experienced and must discharge.

Shame, Pity and Disgust

Incest horror and denial can lead to related emotions of shame, pity, and disgust projected onto the survivor, contributing to and reinforcing her own negative feelings. The therapist might convey to the survivor that she was irreparably tainted for having had incest experience, attitudes which correspond to those the survivor might already feel about herself. De Young (1981a) has explained that the therapist finds ample reinforcement for the assumption that the child seduced, encouraged, or otherwise brought on the victimization from three different sources: the accusations of seduction made against incest victims by professional researchers; the documentation of the passivity of many victims during the abuse; and the rationalizations of incest offenders. Survivors may be blamed for their "acquiescence and compliance" and "charming and seductive personalities," and hence doubly victimized by therapists who do not understand the dynamics of sexual victimization and the child's accommodation mechanisms.

These negative feelings can directly contribute to therapist attempts to deny the incest and its etiological significance or to avoid hearing details or feelings about it. Some therapists defend by distancing from the survivor and her story and by maintaining a strong and largely abstinent professional role. In some cases, therapists will go so far as to refer clients out to sexual assault centers or therapists who have expertise in sexual abuse so that "they can handle the incest part," while the therapist continues to work with other parts of the personality. Such a strategy is sometimes justified, for example, when the client joins an incest therapy group to supplement her individual work or to stimulate her to work on incest issues. In most cases, however, the partitioning of the incest from the main therapy to assuage the therapist's discomfort is a disservice to the survivor and communicates negative attitudes on the therapist's part. When the therapist cannot get his or her negative reactions neutralized or under control, or is unwilling to do research and get training on treating sexual abuse, referral to another therapist is indicated.

Guilt

Therapist guilt about the incest survivor is evoked in many ways. Therapists who had reasonably happy, nonabusive childhoods often feel guilty when they hear of their client's incestuous experiences and the aftereffects. The client might be viewed as having suffered enough and as being fragile. In an attempt to protect her against further pain and to relieve guilt, the therapist might discourage discussion of the incest or engage in behavior which rescues and overprotects. Thus, the therapist might over-give and not maintain reasonable professional boundaries. In this circumstance, the survivor is treated as fragile, overly special, and in need of constant special arrangements, e.g., phone contact at any time of the day or night without regard for the therapist's personal time, regularly extended or extra sessions, late or nonpayment of fees, and so on. This stance may later boomerang by causing feelings of rage towards the client for being overdependent and overdemanding. In cyclical fashion, feelings of rage result in more guilt.

Therapist guilt might also result from feeling helpless to undo the client's experience, from not having "magic answers" to make it all go away, and from stimulating pain as part of the therapy. As a consequence, the therapist avoids encouraging the abreaction of the incest material to spare the survivor and as self-protection. The therapist's task is not to undo the past and not to deny the pain but rather to assist the survivor to work it through until it no longer interferes with her ability to function. Both Pasternak (1987) and Miller (1984) have discussed the need for the therapist to learn the details of the abuse, no matter how gruesome, in order to understand reactions and symptoms. The stages and tasks of therapy provided by the traumatic stress model (see Chapter 9) and the "cleaning of an infected wound" analogy provide a rationale for direct treatment of the incest and its attendant pain. Both the structure and rationale counterbalance the therapist's tendency to back away from details, the pain and associated fear of further injuring the survivor.

Therapists may have more personal types of guilt emanating from their own incestuous experiences or feelings, particularly those which are unacknowledged or unresolved. These experiences include having been directly involved in incest, having knowledge of its occurrence between other members of her/his family (having been envious or desirous of the relationship or relieved at not having been included), or having known and done nothing to prevent or stop incest in the family of origin. Furthermore, the therapist might feel guilty for not responding to previous disclosures of incest by family members, friends, or other clients. The therapist might shy away from learning about the survivor's incest as self-protection from her/his own unresolved feelings associated with both survivor and bystander guilt.

Rage

Details of incestuous abuse often stimulate indignation and rage reactions in helpers. They become angry at the abuse, the perpetrator(s), the other family members, the circumstances, sexism and the status of women, "the system," and colleagues who are not helpful or supportive. Because these "others" are usually unavailable during treatment, the anger may be displaced onto the survivor, who is then blamed for bringing it on herself, for her helplessness in the situation and later, and for causing the therapist to feel such pain, guilt, and helplessness.

While it can be therapeutic for the survivor to experience that someone is angry about what happened to her, the therapist must own her anger and explore how the client responds to hearing that somone has angry feelings about her experience. Care is needed not to force anger on the client or to express it before the client is ready to hear and accept it. When the therapist feels intense rage, it should be processed outside of the therapy, optimally in supervision or otherwise with professional colleagues.

Any projection of rage and other negative emotions onto the therapist, either through the transference or as a challenge to the therapist's caring, may elicit fear and rage reactions in response. She may be enraged at being identified as an authority figure to be challenged and as a potential abuser to be feared, especially if she has made exceptional efforts to engage the client and to prove trustworthiness. In some instances, the intensity of the survivor's rage may be overwhelming for both client and therapist. The therapist's inability to tolerate the client's projected rage and negative transference reactions or to understand and cope with his/her own can ultimately lead to a distancing from and rejection of the client and a premature termination of the therapy.

Grief and Mourning

It is common for the therapist to experience strong feelings of sadness and grief when the survivor recounts what happened to her. Details of the abuse, what the child experienced, and what she had to do in order to accommodate to it are all especially distressing. Recognition that the pain and suffering were caused by a closely related individual who violated the child's innocence to satisfy his needs also evokes sorrowful feelings. Therapists sometimes avoid hearing about the pain by deflecting or shifting the subject when the survivor tries to discuss it in any detail. Again, this tendency is likely to be more pronounced the more gruesome the type of abuse and its details.

Victim as Needy; Survivor as Self-Sufficient

The therapist might hold an overly rigid view of the client as *either* victim or survivor and project ascribed characteristics of either role onto her. When viewed only as a victim, she is seen as fragile and helpless and in need of someone to take care of her. The therapist with this perspective overprotects in an attempt to spare the survivor further pain. The potential exists for the therapist to try to become the survivor's good parent and to make up for what has been missed or lost, even though this is impossible. Danieli (1984) used the term "therapist as liberator" to describe another facet of this tendency—the therapist seeks to rescue or liberate the survivor from the horrors of her past, from her bad family and bad experiences. The focus on the client's fragility ignores her capabilities and may short-circuit the experiencing of emotions and trauma mastery. The injured child is overemphasized in this position as the therapist takes on an overresponsible, compensatory role.

The opposite position is to view the client/survivor as a heroine who accomplished the extraordinary through her superior resources, coping abilities, and self-sufficiency. Her adult is overemphasized at the expense of her "child within." Taken to the extreme, this position discounts the client's past and present suffering by unrealistically glorifying her survival capabilities. It does not provide adequate recognition of the reasons she had to develop these capabilities or the price she paid for being so "brave." The therapist with this perspective tends to reinforce rather than interpret defenses while discouraging exploration and abreaction of the trauma.

Everyone Is a Victim

A related reaction is to minimize or trivialize the client's unique experience by emphasizing that most women are victims and that victimization of some sort is a common experience in society. This type of response assumes that all victimization experiences are the same, ignoring differences in degree or severity. The therapist prematurely forecloses discussion of the details of the survivor's past or its individual meaning when she assumes that her response match those experienced by other victims.

Therapists who were sexually abused as children may find that their experiences enable them to empathize, understand, and connect with their clients in a way that fosters the therapeutic alliance. However, this situation can be problematic when used defensively to inhibit exploration of the client's experience or when overidentification occurs. The therapist might discourage discussion to avoid having personal memories and pain stirred up or might assume knowledge of the client's reality through her own abuse experience. Maintenance of the professional role and boundaries may be particularly difficult for the formerly abused therapist if she overidentifies with the client's experience and position or avoids taking an authority position because of fear of either abusing the power of the position or possibly failing the client. She may also fear experiencing negative transference reactions directed towards her as an authority figure.

Language Muting

Both therapist and client may defend against the reality of incest and their reactions to it by using muted, indirect language to describe the abuse. Such terms as "contact," "sexual experience," "seduction," and "sexu-

al affair" minimize the coercion, abuse, assault, and rape inherent in incest.* Some survivors resist using the word "incest" and are unable to
describe what happened to them with any directiveness or precision. It is
initially advisable for the therapist to use the client's terminology as a
means of developing the relationship and not frightening her by being
more direct. Or the therapist can choose to use stronger, more descriptive
words, while acknowledging they might be threatening for the client to
hear and that she might choose not to use them. Over time, as defenses are
lowered, feelings are processed, and the therapy relationship develops,
both survivor and therapist should strive to use direct rather than indirect
terminology.

A contrary situation arises with the survivor who uses direct words like
"rape" and "father-fuck," whose abuse experience included aberrant forms
of sex, and/or who is able to graphically describe what happened to her.
The therapist may find direct wording and graphic recounting so uncomfortable that language muting is used to defend against the discomfort.
The therapist would do better to use the survivor's terms and to share any
uncomfortable feelings with her or to ventilate those feelings outside of
the session with supervisors and colleagues. Sharing personal reactions
judiciously can provide a powerful way of relating to and empathizing with
the survivor.

"Contact Victimization"

In working with incest survivors, the therapist can expect to experience
contact or secondary victimization and not infrequently to develop symptoms of post-traumatic stress disorder. Therapists report experiencing intrusive reactions (intense fear, startle responses, hyperalertness, nightmares
and night terrors) alternating with numbing and denying responses (withdrawal, avoidance, distancing, exhaustion). Both types of reactions surface
when the therapist feels overwhelmed and horrified by the details of the
survivor's experience and/or by other personal or professional factors (such
as a personal experience of victimization or a heavy caseload).

According to Janoff-Bulman and Frieze (1983), much of the psychological distress associated with all forms of victimization is due to the shattering of basic assumptions about the self and the world. As part of contact
victimization, the therapist might be especially prone to lose faith in the
world as safe and meaningful and in women and children as being personally invulnerable. Not only does incestuous abuse violate the just world
theory (Lerner, 1980), which holds that bad things don't happen to good

---

*Ward (1985) and others argue that even the term "incest" minimizes the reality of
the violation and exploitation. The term "father rape" has been coined by Ward as
the most explicit and accurate. See Chapter 2 for a discussion of terminology.

and worthy people, but beyond that it violates beliefs about the sanctity and safety of the family, the role of parents, and the innocence of children.

The shattering of basic assumptions generates such feelings and defenses as callousness, detachment, vulnerability, and loss of faith. In turn these can cause anger and resentment in the therapist who has lost innocence by virtue of having worked with incest issues. Care must be taken not to displace anger and loss feelings onto the survivor.

Many of these reactions resemble those found in "burnout." In fact, the therapist who carries a large number of victims in her caseload, who is personally unsettled by working with severe victimization, who does not have adequate support, and/or who does not closely monitor personal reactions to incest and other forms of victimization is at risk of burnout. Remedial strategies include carrying mixed caseloads, making time for rest and recreation, keeping personal and professional time as separate as possible, taking regular and frequent vacations or mental health days, developing and using a support network, engaging in other professional activities besides therapy, and engaging in ongoing supervision or therapy.

Privileged Voyeurism

Privileged voyeurism connotes an attraction to and an excessive inquisitiveness about the incest. This can occur in a general way but usually involves an excessive focus on sexual details. In either case, lack of consideration of the individual client or of other concerns and issues besides the incest characterizes this type of response.

In the more general form of privileged voyeurism, the therapist regards the survivor as an object of curiosity due to having been involved in the deviant, abnormal or forbidden. This therapist obviously does not know much about incestuous exploitation and uses the survivor to gain information or satisfy curiosity. The survivor subjected to this type of voyeurism describes being made to feel like a case study or a side show. Additionally, survivors describe being used as the therapist's "test case" as the therapist learns to conduct incest treatment. Comments such as "you're such a good case study" or "I've learned how to do incest therapy from working with you" or "You taught me everything I know about incest" are disrespectful of the survivor and make her feel used. This perspective is dangerous because it encourages the "survivor as heroine" aspect of the incest, minimizes its harmfulness, and recreates the dynamic of the survivor taking care of others, this time the therapist. As one survivor put it: "I parented my parents and thought that was enough. I didn't want to have to teach or take care of my therapist. Her job was to take care of me."

In the second type of privileged voyeurism, the therapist focuses on the sexual aspects and details of the abuse to the exclusion of other issues. Survivors who have experienced this therapist reaction tell of feeling pres-

sured to describe in detail the most intimate and often the most humiliat-
ing sexual aspects of the abuse early in treatment to satisfy the therapist's
prurient interests. They also describe being made to feel like they are on
the witness stand and are constantly redirected from other issues back to
the sexual details. The therapist often appears spellbound or tantalized by
the survivor's incest history. Clearly, such behavior is another experience of
victimization. The therapist who finds himself unduly stimulated or excessively curious about sexual details of abuse is in need of outside consultation and supervision. It is the therapist's ethical and professional responsibility to gain knowledge and understanding of incest outside of the
therapeutic situation. The client enters therapy for professional help, not
to be used as the therapist's case study, resource or turn-on.

Sexualization of the Relationship

Sexualization of the relationship is certainly related to privileged voyeurism, although voyeurism does not always lead to direct sexual contact.
De Young (1981a, p. 98) found that the disclosure of incest in therapy has
the potential to create "a new identity for the patient in the eyes of the
therapist," that of a sexual being, someone exciting and arousing by virtue
of having been involved in the forbidden." She may also be viewed as
having been to blame for seducing her father/brother/grandfather or
whomever, as being "spoiled goods" and undeserving of respect. This position is reinforced by any subsequent sexual revictimization or sexual acting-out, promiscuity or maladjustment. Sexualized behavior or traumatic
reenactment in the transference contributes to these therapist perceptions, although these perceptions need not be based on any present behavior to be activated. In addition to these factors, the learned helplessness of
incest and its contribution to revictimization unfortunately make incest
survivors the likely targets of sexual abuse by therapists, individuals who
are in positions of authority with them.

Without understanding and management of both the transference and
countertransference reactions, the therapist might sexualize the relationship and find rationalizations for doing so, e.g., a sexual encounter facilitates the therapy, sexual intercourse with the therapist is a corrective emotional experience because it demonstrates love and tenderness rather than
abuse, sexual intercourse with the therapist constitutes *in vivo* sex therapy,
the client is needy of good attention, the client wants a sexual encounter
because she engages in behavior and dresses in seductive ways, etc. These
therapist rationalizations resemble those used by incest perpetrators. As
with the sexualization of therapy relationships in general, it appears that
male therapists tend to abuse with much greater frequency than female
therapists and to abuse female clients in much higher proportions than

males; nevertheless, same-sex abuse has been documented and found to have many of the same rationalizations as found in opposite-sex abuse. Sexualization is discussed in the following section on therapist gender.

Therapist Gender as a Special Transferential Issue

Considerable debate has surrounded the issue of whether male therapists should treat female incest survivors. The predominant question has to do with whether male therapists can overcome their socialization to disengage from a position of power with females and to adequately identify and empathize with the incest victim/survivor and her experience. Many feminist authors and clinicians believe that male therapists consciously or unconsciously tend to identify with the male perpetrator's position and deny, excuse, or minimize his behavior, while ascribing blame to the victim and denying or minimizing the effects of the incest. In general, I concur with the position that the female therapist has a greater ability to understand the victimization of the abuse without excusing or rationalizing it. However, I also feel that some male therapists, with adequate attention to abuse issues and countertransference, can productively treat incest survivors. Male therapists have treated incest cases, do so currently, and will continue to do so in the future, if only because of the enormity of the incest problem. Even more important than therapist gender is therapist sensitivity and knowledge about incest and its therapeutic management, as well as awareness of potential problems due to gender issues. Sensitive and competent handling of cases by a man can be therapeutic in directly countering the male role and image that the child received.

The choice of therapist and therapist gender is the survivor's and should not be made for her. Most female survivors seem to prefer female therapists, basing their preference on the belief they will be better understood by a female. Correspondingly, many survivors choose females because they are terrified of men, do not believe men can understand incest, and are concerned about being revictimized. Yet some survivors deliberately choose a male therapist and a father figure. Some choose him because he is of the same gender as the person in their past who was least abusive and most nurturing and who is now the least threatening. The survivor needs to be in control of this choice and to have her choice respected. Her self-control was severely limited during the abuse, and an underlying goal of treatment is for her to regain control and overcome helplessness. This notwithstanding, careful analysis of the reasons for the choice both at the beginning of therapy and during the course of treatment is necessary. Similarly, transference and countertransference between male therapist and female survivor must be handled with additional care.

Other useful treatment models to be considered involve male and female therapists at different stages of the therapy, according to the survivor's needs, and concurrent treatment by a male/female team, as found in some incest groups and consultative relationships.

The Male Therapist. In general, retrospective incest therapy is likely to be more complicated for male therapists due to socialization and power issues. The male therapist has to work through his socialization as more powerful in relation to females and the tendency to identify with the offender before he can identify with the victim (Herman, 1981). This identification with the offender and/or defensiveness about abuse may lead to a number of countertransference issues. The male therapist may be more prone to excuse or rationalize the behavior of the perpetrator. The survivor's feelings of rage and pain may be deemphasized while behaviors which imply her possible complicity and enjoyment are stressed. In this situation, the client does not receive the validation and support she needs; instead she is made to feel the way she did during the incest. She will likely feel blamed, guilty, and unsupported ("so, what's your problem?") in her legitimate feelings of insult and anger by another male in a position of authority.

The therapist, as a man, may find that he's fearful of being rejected by the client or of having her rage displaced onto him; consequently, he may modify his technique to prove that he is not like other men and try to make up for what was done by them. This therapist is prone to overcompensate and might take an indulgent, overprotective stance with the survivor. The overprotective stance reinforces the survivor's helplessness and recreates another situation in which "daddy" or the male authority figure is in charge and knows what is best for her. Alternatively, he may stay distant and detached from her due to fear of developing a therapeutic relationship and fear of being sexually stimulated. The overly detached male therapist can reinforce the survivor's sense of shame, isolation, and mistrust. She may perceive the lack of involvement as due to her badness and malignant sexuality and may feel unworthy of positive and satisfying relationships with others, particularly men.

As previously discussed, excessive and voyeuristic interest in the sexual details of the abuse often occurs in conjunction with a lack of adequate attention to the dynamics of the abuse or its coercive elements. The male therapist may be overly fascinated and aroused by the survivor's discussion of being involved in such taboo behavior. His reactions, even when not acted upon, cause the survivor to reexperience feelings of shame, guilt, and disillusionment. Sexual aftereffects and sexualized transference reactions may also titillate the male therapist. As discussed in Chapter 6, sexual aftereffects range from a total blunting of sexual response and a lack of sexual involvement to promiscuous, compulsive sexual behavior. Some survivors are very sexually naive and inexperienced; some are highly sexual and seductive, conditioned to use sex as a means of developing and maintaining relationships. Both extremes may be compelling to the therapist. The sexually naive and inexperienced client may evoke the male's protective and teaching tendencies. Like the incest father, he may rationalize any sexual contact as sex education and a positive learning experience. The sexualized incest survivor may "lead with her sexuality," confusing sex with affection and eroticizing all contacts she has with men, the therapist included. Because of her low self-esteem, she may feel that the only way she deserves a relationship with a man is if she offers sexual involvement. An additional motivation is to use the involvement to confirm her belief that "men only want one thing" and that no man is trustworthy. The therapist may rationalize sexual behavior with the sexualized client by telling himself "she asked for/deserved it," that "she wanted it," or that she could not possibly be harmed by it because of her past experience.

Sexual involvement between male therapists and female clients has been found to occur quite regularly, despite the fact that it constitutes a serious ethical and professional violation. Research is beginning to establish that incest survivors may be sexually abused in therapy in disproportionate numbers to other female clients (Armsworth, 1987; De Young, 1981a). As discussed above, incest survivors have special vulnerabilities which they bring to their therapy. By virtue of the power differential involved and the violation of trust inherent in such a relationship, it recapitulates the original incest trauma and thus counters trauma mastery, the goal of treatment. The client suffers another betrayal and receives additional proof of the untrustworthiness of men and her own "evil eroticism."

Male therapists who are secure in their sexuality and who address and work through power issues and their tendency to identify with the perpetrator can then identify with the victim and model appropriate behavior. With them, the survivor truly has the opportunity to experience a caring relationship with a man with whom appropriate sexual boundaries are maintained and to learn to distinguish sex from affection. Past learning and mistrust can be countered by an experience with a man who draws clear distinctions between caring about her and exploiting her.

The Female Therapist. Female therapists err when they become overly identified with the victim and enmeshed in feelings of powerlessness and hopelessness (Herman, 1981). Hearing details of the abuse may elicit strong panic and anxiety reactions in the woman therapist. These are intensified if she comes to recognize or be reminded of incestuous events in her own background. In order to protect herself from being further threatened by her feelings and those of the survivor, she may subtly or overtly communicate that she does not want to hear about the incest experience, especially its sexual details. This avoidance replicates the denial the survivor experienced with her mother or other family members and reinforces her sense of stigma and isolation, as well as her previous training that incestuous abuse is unspeakable. She misses the opportunity to discuss the sexual aspects of the abuse with a supportive ally who can help her sort out the residuals. She may conclude that no one is willing or able to listen to her story or provide the help and support she seeks. As a result she may terminate therapy.

In working with a survivor of father-daughter incest, the female therapist commonly has to contend with displaced anger and rage that the survivor feels towards her mother for past deprivation/abandonment/betrayal. Anger with the mother often precedes anger directed towards the father. The analysis of the mother-daughter relationship is an important aspect of the therapy. According to Brooks (1983, p. 131), "The female therapist-female patient dyad more readily permits a reactivation of the unconscious pre-oedipal conflicts within the transference and provides the opportunity for the analysis of guilt, the making of reparation, and the development of higher levels of object relations." The female therapist who does not understand these transference reactions may defensively minimize and dismiss the anger towards the mother rather than exploring it with the client. She may attempt to get the client to redirect it prematurely from the mother to the father by sharing her own feelings of rage towards him. Herman (1981) discussed the outcome of this situation:

> When the therapist expresses rage at the father, the patient may feel that the therapist is trying to rob her of a relationship which is special and precious to her. She may assume that the therapist is motivated by spite or jealousy, and this simply confirms her belief that all women are potential rivals. The relationship with the therapist then becomes hostile and competitive instead of cooperative. (p. 184)

Many survivors hold a range of feelings towards the perpetrator. The therapist who does not understand the possibility of non-angry, ambivalent, and even tender feelings towards him may subtly or directly convey to the survivor that such feelings are unacceptable, leaving her further confused, shamed, and guilty. The opportunity for exploration of the mixed feelings is lost.

Just as the female therapist is less likely than her male counterpart to focus on sexual details of the abuse she is also less likely to sexualize the relationship with the survivor (although sporadic reports have surfaced of female therapists becoming sexually involved with survivors). Instead, her strong identification with the victim, survivor and bystander guilt, and guilt about inadequate mothering may foster overprotection, overgratification, and difficulty maintaining professional boundaries. Any sexualization with a client is likely to be due to these motivations rather than the power motivations more often at work for males.

In summary, many issues are brought to the therapy process by both the survivor and therapist. Incest inspires strong emotions in society at large, emotions which neither survivor and therapist can avoid. The therapist must strive to arrive at a balanced perspective within the treatment. The survivor must be encouraged to present information about her past; then both the survivor and what she divulges must be accepted. Miller (1984) summarized what is necessary:

> Thus, therapists' adequate support must be reinforced by their knowledge and emotional experience. I have made every effort to call attention to that aspect of knowledge having to do with the actual situation of the child in our society because I think it is a necessary (although not sufficient) condition if therapy is to be successful. . . . But theoretical understanding alone is still not enough. Only therapists who have had the opportunity to experience and work through their own traumatic past will be able to accompany patients on the path to truth about themselves and not hinder them on their way. Such therapists will not confuse their patients, make them anxious, or educate, instruct, misuse, or seduce them, for they no longer have to fear the eruption in themselves of feelings that were stifled long ago, and they know from experience the healing power of these feelings. (p. 314)

CHAPTER 12

Group Treatment

GROUP TREATMENT, either alone or in combination with individual treat-ment, is helpful for the survivor reworking the afteraffects of incest. In fact, combined individual and group therapy, conducted concurrently or consecutively, provides the most effective treatment for incest trauma. This chapter describes the rationale and specific benefits of group. Differ-ent treatment models are discussed as to their structure and goals; this is followed by a discussion of indications and contraindications for group participation, ground rules, and process issues. Transference issues and treatment complications as they present in group are also reviewed. Finally, several techniques found useful in incest therapy groups are presented, along with a short discussion of the differences between self-help and formal therapy group formats.

RATIONALE FOR AND ADVANTAGES OF
GROUP TREATMENT

The obvious rationale for group treatment is its potential for countering and alleviating the most insidious characteristics and effects of incest. The impaired interpersonal functioning and mistrust which result from this human-induced trauma are reworked in a context that requires interper-sonal engagement. Group allows for the breaking of the secrecy, isolation, and stigma resulting from the abuse and fosters exploration and resolution of the trauma and its aftermath. The sharing and empathy derived from common experiences and reactions, as well as the analysis of the interac-tions between members, are of great therapeutic value. Together group members build an environment of safety and consistency within which to explore the effect incest has had on their lives and to help each other undo its damage by developing trust and by practicing new skills and behaviors.

Most commonly, survivors participate first in individual therapy followed by group therapy or with group work undertaken simultaneously. Van der Kolk (1987b) discussed both the strength and the limitations of individual therapy for the trauma victim:

> Most trauma victims benefit initially from individual therapy. It allows disclo-sure of the trauma, the safe expression of related feelings, and the reestab-lishment of a trusting relationship with at least one other person. Patients can explore and validate perceptions and emotions and experience consis-tent and undivided attention from one other individual. Provided that a degree of safety can be established in the individual therapy relationship, a trauma victim can begin dealing with both the sense of shame and the vulnerability. . . . Individual therapy allows for a detailed examination of a patient's mental processes and memories that cannot be replicated in a group therapy setting.
>
> In individual therapy there is an inherent inequality: it is a relationship between a therapist, the "helper," who implicitly has answers and is not helpless, and the patient or client, who needs help and who may experience at least some passivity and possibly some sense of helplessness. . . . Support-ive individual therapy tends to reinforce dependency on the therapist and may decrease the subjective sense of mastery. (pp. 162–163)

Group participation provides a number of specific advantages which support and enhance the goals of incest therapy. According to Sprei (with Unger, 1986, p. 3): "There are many benefits derived from a group setting that are rarely achieved as quickly or as thoroughly in an individual setting" (p. 3). Van der Kolk elaborated on this point:

> In a group patients can start reexperiencing themselves as being useful to other people. Ventilation and sharing of feelings and experiences in groups of people who have gone through similar experiences promotes the experi-ence of being both victim and helper. Even a trusting and secure relationship with a therapist who serves as a parental substitute does not necessarily enable the patient to assess his or her relationships with others accurately. In a group, the therapist can facilitate reempowerment by encouraging mutual support and by exploring the patient's resistances to taking an active role.
>
> Although no controlled studies exist, group therapy is widely regarded as a treatment of choice for many patients with PTSD, either as the sole form of therapy or as an adjunct to individual psychotherapy. (1987b, pp. 163–164)

The specific benefits of group treatment for incest survivors are the follow-ing, adapted from those identified by Sprei (with Unger, 1986):

Identification with Other Members and Establishing a Therapeutic Alliance with Them

Involvement in a group with other survivors challenges the individual's shamed and stigmatized sense of self. Cognitive dissonance ensues when group members who believe they and other survivors are reprehensible and unlovable meet in a group and discover that other survivors look and act like "normal people." The group provides a unique opportunity to challenge the double standard survivors use to judge themselves. Negative self-concept does not change immediately, however. The survivor may persist in her negative views of herself by finding ways in which she differs from others in the group and by distancing herself from them. She may also continue to project these same negative perceptions onto other group members in order to maintain her belief that all incest victims are irreparably flawed. This was exemplified by a client who wanted to join a group to be with "other lepers."

For the group to be effective, trust must develop among the members. As in individual treatment, trust must never be rushed or taken for granted; it usually evolves slowly, with a great deal of testing. Stability of group membership, consistent attendance, and individual reliability are important in the development of group cohesion and trust. Over time, with this interpersonal support and the provision of a new framework for understanding their experience, survivors develop a more positive self-concept and sense of identification. Moreover, members frequently develop a sense of pride in themselves and other survivors for having gotten through the incest experience and for their work at resolution.

Recognition of Commonalities Among Members

The group setting, by its very nature, serves to raise members' consciousness about incest; it assists them in developing a less individual and more interpersonal and sociocultural perspective. As a consequence, the incest becomes more normalized. Leehan and Wilson (1985) labeled the recognition of the commonality of the experience "the reality factor" of group treatment. Members come to recognize that they are not alone and that they share commonalities of the experience, its immediate and long-term aftereffects, and coping mechanisms. This normalization extends to some of the less typical or more bizarre forms of incest or aftereffects as well. Group members have great capacity to understand different forms of exploitation and their likely emotional consequences.

In group such problems as low self-esteem, guilt, excessive responsibility, addictive and self-destructive behaviors, dissociative responses, and problems with intimacy and sexuality come to be viewed less as character defects and more as common reactions to incestuous abuse. This new perspective helps group members understand their symptoms differently. They can congratulate and support each other for having coped and can receive the same support from others for their coping abilities.

Members develop a different perspective when listening to others tell their stories. This cannot be achieved in quite the same way by reading books, viewing a film, or listening to a lecture about incest. Morrissey (1982, p. 5) noted, "A survivor can hear another person's story with the perspective that her distance from the events of another's life affords her." This distance enables the development of a new understanding of family problems, dynamics, and messages which supported and maintained the occurrence of incest in the family.

Breaking Secrecy and Acknowledging the Abuse

Even when the secret is broached in individual therapy, it is still done in a private and confidential context, which inadvertently serves to maintain secrecy. In contrast, the act of attending a specialized group is in and of itself a public acknowledgment of the abuse as well as an act of disclosure. Furthermore, the abuse experience and its aftermath are processed and discussed repeatedly during the course of the group, simply by virtue of the fact that each member tells her story. The recounting of incest by one group member almost never fails to elicit reactions and expanded reworkings of their own experience by other members. Repetition and reworking serve to counter denial, minimization, and repression, and instead make the incest more real.

Group attendance and disclosure often make it easier for the survivor to discuss her experience "on the outside" with her partner or spouse, other family members, and/or close friends. Preparation and rehearsal for disclosures, along with anticipation of possible outcomes, can be undertaken in the group. Whether outside disclosures go well or not, the group provides support and processing of the experience for the survivor. (Disclosure and confrontation are discussed in Chapter 15.)

The Group as Support Network and New or Surrogate "Family"

The group allows for the reparation of interpersonal injuries, especially betrayal and mistrust. It provides its members with the experience of a safe, supportive, and consistent environment in which to develop trust in others. The group further provides a practice environment in which survivors learn new modes of communicating, interacting, and problem-solving without the threat of further abuse or retaliation. Many survivors come to view the group as a new family in which they are reparented as they help to reparent others.

Context and Catalyst for the Exploration of Emotions and Beliefs

The group is both a unique context and a catalyst for breaking through denial and allowing the exploration and ventilation of feelings and beliefs. A "chaining effect" occurs repeatedly: The disclosures of some members and group discussion enable others to focus on aspects of the abuse which were previously unavailable to them due to repression or some other defense. Group can be very powerful in this regard and the client flooded if her defenses and survivor mechanisms dismantled too rapidly. At times, it is necessary for the group leaders to intervene and "to slow the process, in order to allow time for some measure of defensive reintegration" (Herman & Schatzow, 1987).

As in individual incest therapy, the emotions the client explores and reconnects with are often negative and painful. The group provides a uniquely supportive atmosphere in which members can identify with each others' emotions based on their personal experience and understanding. The exploration of ambivalent feelings, the resolution of feelings of guilt and responsibility, the experiencing of rage and anger, and the grieving of losses are major emotional issues.

The Context and Catalyst for the Challenging of Beliefs and Childhood Messages

Distorted beliefs and childhood rules and messages fostered within the abusive environment are optimally challenged in the group context. Initially, the focus is on uncovering beliefs and family messages to determine how they continue to influence the survivor's view of herself and her behavioral repertoire. Once these are identified, group members differentiate messages and beliefs from facts. These are challenged and replaced with beliefs and messages which are less distorted and more self-accepting and self-nurturing. The specific belief is explored to determine its origin and then is challenged with new information. Once the survivor identifies faulty internalized perceptions, she is free to choose which beliefs to maintain and which to replace. For example, the belief of badness, malignancy, or ugliness on the part of one member is directly challenged when others do not share the same perception.

Similarly, the group explores and challenges those beliefs and family rules which have served to maintain and reinforce learned powerlessness and helplessness. Double-bind communications and situations are discussed and alternative actions proposed. The group encourages members to learn problem-solving and assertive behaviors. As beliefs and behaviors change, survivors are no longer caught in the double-bind situation engendered by their childhood experiences. They have more personal freedom and more opportunities for self-development as they separate from the family of origin.

A Unique Forum for Grieving

The group provides a unique forum for exploring and grieving the multitude of losses resulting from incest. At times, whole sessions will be devoted to feeling angry, cheated, and resentful for one's own losses and those suffered by others in the group. Similarly, some sessions will be devoted to hurt and sadness, with members comforting and supporting each other in their expressions of pain and sorrow.

Observation and Exploration of Interactional Patterns and Client Dynamics

Group presents an opportunity unavailable in individual therapy for the therapists' and members' firsthand observation of the client's interactional patterns, dynamics, and defense mechanisms. Some familiar patterns include the caretaking of others coupled with the denial of self, patterns conducive to revictimization or the victimization of others, and setting the self apart from the group out of mistrust or habit or to maintain the image of being different (these are discussed in greater detail below). Group members give and receive feedback about their interactive style and practice new behaviors within the group.

GROUP STRUCTURE AND ORGANIZATION

At present, the literature on incest treatment contains mostly reports of time-limited groups. The reports show high consistency in recommended format and organization, themes, leadership issues, and process issues. The recommendations made here are based on these reports and my experience with both time-limited and time-unlimited incest groups. To date the longest group I have conducted was of four years' duration.

Time-limited Incest Groups

Reports of time-limited groups for incest survivors show them ranging in duration from 4 to 20 sessions (Bergart, 1986; Cole, 1985; Gordy, 1983; Herman & Schatzow, 1984, 1987; Sprei, 1986, 1987; Tsai & Wagner, 1978). These authors recommend between 10 and 20 sessions as optimal for a time-limited group. Groups of less than 10 sessions have been found to have only limited utility. The goals of time-limited groups are deliberately focused and the format generally more structured than found in a time-unlimited group. The time-limited format touches on dynamics, defenses, and interaction patterns between members; however, it does not allow for an in-depth exploration or resolution of these issues. Several authors have argued that a short-term format is the treatment of choice with trauma victims to avoid the development of an "us victims against a dangerous world" stance, to discourage long-term dependency on an authority figure and a continuance of the helplessness associated with victimization, and to encourage reliance upon and interaction with others (van der Kolk, 1987b). Herman and Schatzow (1984) recommend time-limited homogeneous groups for incest survivors followed by therapy in groups of people with mixed problems and diagnoses.

According to Sprei (1986), time limits offer the following advantages:

(1) They make it easier for members who are only willing to make a time-limited commitment to treatment.
(2) They promote goal-oriented work.
(3) They focus attention on common themes of sexual abuse and in so doing minimize the focus on interpersonal relations within the group.
(4) They limit the level of anxiety experienced by a survivor considering joining a group.
(5) They deliberately decrease the level of dependency survivors can develop.
(6) They provide a hopeful, optimistic outlook for survivors.
(7) They encourage bonding and minimize resistance to sharing by virtue of the time limit.
(8) They provide a clear structure during the intense and disorganizing aspects of the treatment.
(9) They encourage the emergence of feelings and issues that can be further explored in individual or long-term group treatment.
(10) They fit the needs and organizational structure of most sexual assault centers, mental health centers, and other crisis service agencies.

The process in these time-limited groups strongly resembles Mann's (1973) 12-session model of time-limited individual therapy. He articulated four stages of approximately three sessions' duration each with the following characteristics: (1) rapid symptomatic improvement; (2) the return and worsening of symptoms; (3) the development of resistance to change and negative transference; and (4) progress on presenting concerns and termination. The descriptions of time-limited incest treatment groups provided by Sprei (1986) and Herman and Schatzow (1984) are consistent with this model. The groups further follow the course of treatment outlined for individual incest treatment in Chapter 8.

Stage 1: Rapid Symptomatic Improvement. In the first few sessions, once anxiety has allayed somewhat by meeting other survivors, members bond quickly as they share their goals and expectations and begin to share their incest histories. This stage is analogous to the "building the adult relationship" stage in individual treatment. The following types of goals are usually articulated: the exploration of the incest and its past and current effects with others who had similar experiences; the recovery of memories; improved current functioning, especially in terms of interpersonal relationships and improved self-esteem; and disclosure of the incest to significant friend(s) or family member(s) (Herman & Schatzow, 1984).

As sometimes happens in individual treatment, intense relief at letting go of the secret and meeting others who have had similar experiences sometimes leads to immediate symptomatic improvement and a "flight into health" without working through the issues (Forward & Buck, 1978).

Stage 2: The Return and Worsening of Symptoms. In many groups, the initial opening-up is followed by the return and worsening of symptoms and a closing-down. The intrusive or numbing symptoms of post-traumatic stress disorder return as clients regress and appear to get worse. Sprei (1986) has this to say about reasons survivors have for "putting the walls back up" after the relief of sharing:

> It may be a fear reaction to the intimacy and intensity that has developed. Some members need to test their defenses to ensure they are still working. Others fear opening up further. All these reactions are ways of maintaining control. In leading this session, the therapists need to be supportive, non-punitive, and respectful of the client's rights to maintain boundaries while also reassuring members that it is safe to gradually let go of past survival mechanisms. (p. 39)

Of particular significance is that both the sharing and reliving of the trauma and the experiencing of symptoms occur in the group with individuals who have had similar experiences and who can mirror the trauma. This further breaks the isolation of the past and allows hopefulness about the future.

Stage 3: Working on Goals and Developing a New Perspective on Incest. During these sessions, the focus is on issues of responsibility, self-blame, and trust and on working with the "child within." Grief work also characterizes this stage. Members help one another to reevaluate the entrapping nature of their childhood abuse and the accommodation mechanisms they utilized to cope. They begin to place responsibility on the involved adult(s) and thus to be less self-blaming and ashamed. Members are encouraged to attempt new behaviors and to work on their goals, using group support and their new "adult" perspective on incest and improved self-concept. Herman and Schatzow (1984) succinctly discussed the activity at this stage of the group:

> The orientation toward action in the present during the second half of the sessions generally helped group members develop a sense of competence and strength. The feeling of shared terror of the early sessions gradually gave way to expressions of courage; the hurt gave way to anger, and the feeling of helplessness gave way to explorations of intiative. In this way, the stages of the group recapitulated in brief a maturational sequence for each individual,

and many group members came to recognize that though they had been defenseless as children, they were no longer defenseless as adults. (p. 612)

At this stage, members also begin to focus more on their relationships and reactions to other group members, so that transference issues are more noticeable. It is advisable to spend some group time processing the most obvious interactional patterns and issues but to maintain the primary focus on the treatment of the trauma and the achievement of personal goals.

Stage 4: Termination and Future Plans. During the last several sessions members are reminded of the impending ending of the group to counter denial, a fairly common reaction. The reminder and the concreteness of time limits stimulate feelings of anxiety and sadness about separation and loss but also have the effect of spurring additional efforts towards goal accomplishment. A formal termination with plans for future actions completes the short-term treatment cycle.

Time-Unlimited Incest Groups

Time-unlimited incest groups have been reported in two formats: massed, intensive treatment, several hours a day and of several weeks' duration, with open-ended aftercare (Wise, 1985); and groups of open-ended duration, from six months' to several years' duration. These can be organized on either an inpatient or an outpatient basis and involve a stable membership which only changes if a vacancy occurs and the group re-opens. Time-unlimited therapy groups allow for more in-depth treatment of issues in a family-like context, the process resembling that of long-term individual therapy as discussed in Chapters 9 through 11.

A group of longer-term duration is advantageous for several important reasons. By virtue of the extended time format and the opportunity for long-term observation of patterns of interaction between group members, it facilitates greater understanding of each client's dynamics. It allows for more development of the transference, especially negative transference, which can then be analyzed. Patterns of interaction often reenact those from the family of origin, which are particularly stimulated by the group/ family setting. Some of the more common transference issues are discussed later in this chapter.

As van der Kolk (1987b) noted, groups uniquely give the opportunity for traumatized persons to give up their identity as victim. This requires that they involve themselves in interacting and working with others. Long-term treatment encourages repeated and diversified presentations of problematic issues directly or through the transference, as well as providing more opportunities for role play and practice of new behaviors. It further allows more extensive working-through of the trauma and its secondary elaborations.

Over time members work on issues of trust differently from the way they do in a time-limited setting. Although the bonding that occurs in time-limited groups is genuine, stimulated by shared experiences of exploitation and the discussion of common themes, survivors do not have enough time to work on a deeper level of trust. In a long-term group members have the opportunity to repeatedly test for the trustworthiness and consistency of other members and the leaders and to have their trustworthiness identified in return. Because trust was repeatedly violated in the family over a long period of time, extended periods of testing might be necessary for a survivor to be able to trust again.

An example of this emerged in a long-term group I co-led. Three years into this group, most members continued to be guarded and disclosed they could not completely trust one another despite extensive work on both the incest and group process issues. My co-leader and I were somewhat surprised at this admission because the group had functioned quite well over its duration and relationship issues within and outside of the group had received considerable attention. Also, group members had shown marked improvement in interpersonal functioning during the course of the group. An additional year's work on trust and relationship issues was needed before members could let down their guards and admit to trusting one another. We came to understand that members of this group needed massive validation, support, and consistency to delve into incest issues. During the last year, they were increasingly disclosing and confrontive with one another because they trusted that they would be understood and supported.

The Selection of Group Members

Group is the preferred treatment of many incest survivors. The intimacy, focused attention, and intense transference with an authority figure in individual therapy, as well as previous negative experiences (including sexual abuse by therapists), may make individual treatment far too threatening. Many survivors feel that the only people whom they can completely trust and rely on for understanding are those who have had similar experiences. Some survivors may need the validating work of group treatment, accomplished in either self-help or therapy groups, before they can engage in individual therapy.

On the other hand, some survivors are unable to function in a group due to severe interpersonal deficits and difficulties, the severity and constancy of their symptomatology, and/or an inability to hear or react to the incest experiences of others. Some find a group too threatening because of the shame, secrecy, and denial surrounding the incest or because of the projection of feelings of self-revulsion and powerlessness onto other group members. The latter reaction may inhibit them from believing they can receive any kind of support or assistance from their peers. Other survivors are too afraid of losing the control they have achieved and "going crazy" if they join a group. For many of these women, individual therapy to address these and other incest issues is a necessary precursor to group participation. Some survivors never get to a point where they can comfortably or productively participate in a group. This limitation, though unfortunate, should be respected by the therapist.

Group participation is not advisable or recommended for all incest survivors. A careful assessment of the woman's appropriateness for a group experience, including her ego strength, motivation, needs, interpersonal skills, current life circumstances and functioning, is necessary to insure that she and other group members will benefit from her inclusion and that she is able to deal with group process and content. Despite its obvious advantages, group treatment does have disadvantages for some survivors and should not be assumed as therapeutic for all. The severity of the survivor's traumatic responses and their secondary elaborations, her progress in therapy, and her expressed readiness for a group experience all determine whether group treatment is appropriate.

The contraindications listed for group treatment in general are applicable to incest groups. The following personality characteristics and behaviors are contraindicated: acute psychosis, active homicidal or suicidal behavior, active, severe substance abuse, lack of motivation to change, dread of self-disclosure, a high degree of denial, paranoid, sociopathic, and strongly narcissistic or borderline personalities.

Rieth (n.d.) mentioned the special difficulties inherent in assessing the group suitability of survivors diagnosed as borderline personality disorder. She stated:

> Because many women with a diagnosis of Borderline Personality Disorder were sexually abused in their childhoods, extra care must be taken to assess the ego strength and history of acting out behaviors with these clients. The primary therapist is invaluable in assisting the group therapist with this assessment; the strength and resilience of the client's relationship with the primary therapist can be a good predictor of her ability to gain from and contribute to the group (pp. 9–10).

In general, those survivors who are unable to control strong impulsive and aggressive tendencies or who can tolerate neither the painful feelings arising in treatment nor the interpersonal demands of group participation should be excluded.

A number of other assessment criteria pertain specifically to the incest experience. A woman's ability to acknowledge the incest as real for herself and for others and her motivation for joining a group with other survivors are important factors to assess. The woman who disbelieves the reality of abuse in her life or in others' lives is not a good group candidate. Some survivors decide to join a group or are encouraged to join one by their individual therapists soon after incest is revealed, but before its reality is fully accepted or acknowledged. Since the reality factor in group is so powerful, potential members benefit from working on issues of acknowledgment in individual treatment prior to group participation.

Similarly, the client who cannot discuss her own incest experience without an intense, uncontrollable anxiety, dissociative or depressive reaction (as opposed to the more occasional or moderate reaction) may not be ready for a group experience. This client is likely to need such constant monitoring and attention that group process would be impeded and attention to other group members short-circuited. Reactions of this sort can be frightening to all members of the group and can also lead to feelings of resentment. Clients with multiple personality disorder should also be carefully assessed: Can they tolerate the strong emotional content and interpersonal contact of the group, and can the group members understand and work with personality switches if and when they occur?

Reasons for wanting to join a group are important to assess. Group members should, in general, be positively oriented towards a group experience and group process rather than ambivalent or resistant. I and other therapists have had the experience of including women who were not well motivated in our zeal to have enough members to get a group started. We have learned to be more cautious and exercise more clinical judgment in screening potential members.

It is recommended that the client function reasonably well on a day-to-day basis and not be in personal crisis at the time she joins a group. The experience of group can be disorganizing and has the potential to compound or exacerbate other destabilizing life events. If possible, the potential group member should also have an identified support system outside of the group to call on if needed.

Many therapists conducting incest groups require that group members be in concurrent individual treatment. There are good reasons for this, since individual therapy provides the survivor with a supportive relationship within which to process and reintegrate the memories and emotions generated in the group. Difficulty arises, however, for those survivors who are unable to tolerate the one-to-one contact and intimacy of individual therapy or those who have completed individual therapy. In such a situation, the group therapist must use clinical judgment and understanding of the interpersonal effects of incest in deciding to include or exclude a woman. While I feel it is preferable for group members to have simultaneous individual therapy or to have had therapy experience, this is not always possible or desirable.

For those group members in individual and/or simultaneous treatment, I require that they give permission for their primary therapist to be contacted prior to the initiation of group therapy and during the course of therapy as the need arises. Such contact impedes secrecy and splitting between therapists and treatments, while allowing for coordinated treatment planning and the enlistment of the primary therapist's support if the client becomes distressed and disorganized. Herman and Schatzow (1984) discussed another less obvious reason for contact with group members' individual therapists: to evaluate the quality of the individual therapy relationship. They wrote: "In several cases, we found that the client had become involved in a therapy relationship that we considered inappropriate and incompatible with successful participation in a group. Most of these situations involved boundary violations on the part of the therapist" (p. 607). All involved dual relationships, the most serious being sexual involvement between the therapist and client, an explicit reenactment of the childhood abuse. In such cases, the group therapist must challenge the relationship on professional and ethical grounds and assist the client by referring her to a more ethical therapist (and possibly by helping her to file an ethical or legal complaint).

Preliminary or concurrent treatment is a definite requirement when a survivor suffers from any type of active, serious addiction. Support group membership and participation (i.e., any of the "Anonymous" group programs) is also either strongly suggested or required.

Screening Potential Members: The Intake Interview

During the intake interview the therapist or co-therapists meet individually with each potential member to assess her motivation, dynamics, issues, interpersonal skills, and general suitability for the group. The intake interview has several other purposes, including introducing the survivor to the goals, structure, and functioning of the group, and serving as a preliminary forum in which she acknowledges and talks about the abuse and her reasons for wanting a group experience.

If the group is to have two leaders, it is advisable for both therapists to jointly conduct the screening session. Doing so may be stressful for the potential member, yet it offers an initial opportunity for her to "publicly" discuss the abuse and as a result may have a desensitizing effect for later group discussion. The jointly conducted intake also decreases the possible formation of a pre-group alliance between the client and one of the therapists. Suggested questions for group membership screening are contained in Table 7. These can be used within a standard intake format and may be supplemented with the incest questionnaires or symptom checklists described in Chapter 8. During the intake the client also has the opportunity

TABLE 7
Suggested Questions for Screening Potential Group Members

- What are your reasons for wanting to join this group? What do you want to get out of the group?
- How did you hear about the group? Have you ever had a group experience of this sort or do you know of anyone who has? How was it?
- How do you feel being here today?
- Tell us about yourself, your current life—family, school, work, friends. How are things going in your life at the present time?
- What was it like to grow up in your family? Are you in contact with your family at present? How do you feel about your family?
- How do you think it will be for you to disclose your incest experience in a group and to hear others discuss theirs?
- Have you ever discussed the abuse with anyone before? What happened? What were the reactions? How did you react?
- Tell us, in general, about your incest experience. Who abused you? How did the abuse begin and end? How old were you? What kinds of activities were involved? What were you told by the perpetrator? Was force used? How did you cope? Did you ever tell anyone or did anyone find out about the incest? Their reactions? Your reactions?
- How has it been to have us ask about these things and to be talking to us about them?
- How do you think the incest affected you at the time it occurred and since then? How do you think it affects you today?
- What are your feelings about being in a group with other incest survivors? What are your fears/concerns about dealing with the incest?
- Have you been in or are you currently in individual or group therapy? Tell us about that therapy—what is/was worked on, the therapy relationship, how you feel/felt about the therapy and the relationship, etc.
- Tell us about your medical history and any substance abuse problems. Are you currently in treatment for any medical/addiction problems and are you currently on any medications?

---

to ask questions about the group. Most often, questions concern the structure, functioning, and effectiveness of the group, the therapists' experience with incest survivors and previous incest groups, assurances of safety in the group, etc. Ground rules and the requirements of participation are discussed at this time.

The client's suitability for the group and recommendations for inclusion or exclusion are discussed at the time of the intake. The therapists need to carefully balance the group membership. It is preferable that members be at similar points in their therapy and their incest resolution or, at the very least, that they not be widely divergent. Optimally, commonalities should exist between the members of each group. No member should be a "minority" or "isolate" in any of the following characteristics: age and life stage, race, sexual preference, incest experience, class or occupational status.

The feelings of being different from others, so often a consequence of incest, are reinforced if a survivor is substantially different from all other members of the group. If a woman would be in a minority on some characteristic, yet seems suitable for the group, she can be given the choice of joining or of waiting for a more compatible group.

Of course, special care needs to be taken with the woman for whom the group is unsuitable, whatever the reason. The therapists should be clear about their reasons for recommending that she not participate, while supporting her in finding more appropriate resources. Whatever the outcome of the screening interview, each woman should be prepared for the possibility that she will experience some emotional reactions to the intake discussion and should be encouraged to recontact the therapists as needed or with additional questions or concerns.

Ground Rules

Ground rules, especially those concerning confidentiality, safety, and attendance, are introduced during the intake interview and reintroduced during the first group session. Ground rules communicate that the group will have a structure and that attention will be paid to issues of safety and trust. Although certain ground rules are predetermined, group members optimally decide on guidelines and then monitor themselves about issues such as absenteeism, tardiness, and socializing outside meetings. By making their own decisions, members learn that they are in charge of what happens in their group and that their opinions are valued (Rieth, n.d.). The following ground rules are standard in all therapy groups. They are discussed here as they pertain to incest issues.

Confidentiality. Due to the prominence of secrecy, shame, and trust issues, confidentiality takes on special importance in incest groups. Group members must arrive at a clear mutual understanding of bounds of confidentiality to insure the privacy and comfort necessary for trust to develop.

Attendance. Attendance fosters group stability and consistency, which in turn promote the development of reliability and trust among members. In most time-limited groups, a commitment to attend all meetings is a prerequisite to membership. In open-ended groups, members are asked to commit to attend as many meetings as possible and to give the group early notice of planned absences. Members are discouraged from skipping sessions or dropping out of the group altogether when the content or process is painful or intense. Instead, they are asked to return to the group to discuss their responses and fears so they can receive support and work through conflict.

Absenteeism is disruptive to group process and stability, since it stimulates feelings of abandonment in the group members who attend regularly. When a member is habitually absent, it is necessary for her to explore the reasons and meaning of her nonattendance and for the group to discuss reactions. Some groups may decide they can tolerate occasional absences and set guidelines as to how they should be handled. Other groups may find repeated absences too disruptive and suggest that the absent member terminate until she is ready to attend regularly. Group members are also asked to arrive on time and to call, if possible, when detained or running late. Further ground rules concerning tardiness sometimes have to be developed.

Emotional Discharge. The expression of feeling is encouraged since it is an instrumental element of the recovery process. Any expression of feeling is legitimate. Ground rules govern the means of discharging emotions, however—being physically violent and hurting oneself, others, and furnishings are not allowed. Emotional aggression is also not allowed. The cotherapists own the responsibility for stopping any interaction betwen members that they judge to be aggressive or otherwise emotionally harmful. Group members are encouraged to express their emotions, particularly anger and rage, in constructive, safe, and nonthreatening ways. These skills may need to be taught and reinforced repeatedly.

A special circumstance arises for the survivor who experiences intrusive or numbing symptoms in a session to such an excessive or uncomfortable degree that a time-out period is required. A ground rule concerning this issue provides a measure of preparation and safety for the members. Generally, members are encouraged to tell the group of her reaction, not to leave impulsively and not to leave the immediate vicinity of the group session. She can choose whether to be alone or accompanied by one of the leaders. Once she feels more settled, she is asked to rejoin the group. Time-outs and the emotions which give rise to them must be fully discussed in session for both closure and reassurance. Members then have the opportunity to share similar experiences and suggest coping strategies or to clear up any miscommunication which may have resulted in the leave-taking.

Group Process. Members begin group with an agreement to be active participants to the degree that they can. This means being as participatory and open as possible while encouraging and supporting other group members to do the same. Activity level and ability to interact vary markedly among members. Some verbalize easily while others are unable to talk even though they may be desperate to do so. A group atmosphere of patience, support, encouragement, consistency, and empathy assists withdrawn and scared member(s) to interact.

Several group formats have been tried and found to be useful. Each has a particular rationale. Some groups divide up the available time into equal

segments, with each member having an alotted time; this insures the interaction of all members, even the quietest. Another strategy is to have members ask for the time they need at the beginning of each session and to
negotiate time so that the needs of all members fit within the session's
timeframe. This approach promotes members' learning to ask for attention
for themselves and to negotiate with one another. Some groups leave the
issue of time-sharing open-ended, so that issues of sharing and asking for
time can be discussed as they develop over the course of the group. A more
structured approach is used in those groups that organize each session
around a particular theme or topic for discussion. Decision-making about
group format encourages members to have input into how the group functions, to have their preferences taken seriously, and to negotiate with one
another. It is likely that they did not have these same opportunities in their
families.

Whatever the prevailing norm about the use of group time, it is recommended that time boundaries be maintained, particularly concerning ending time. Many therapists have reported a tendency for these groups to run
overtime due to presentation of individual crises right at the end of the
session. Often such a situation constitutes a manipulation designed to test
the caring and commitment of the group — it may be the only way a survivor knows to get attention. The therapists must address individual and
group process issues which work against the time boundaries while encouraging members to negotiate how to share the available time.

Each individual needs the assurance that she will be taken "where she
is." Even though each group member suffered incest, the experiences and
families of origin vary markedly. Each individual will work through her own
issues at her own pace and in her own way. There is no right way for a
member to proceed.

It is also helpful to underscore that a member's experience and her
reactions will be accepted without condemnation. Survivors who have
experienced bizarre forms of incest and/or reactions have additional fears
about disclosure and about being believed and accepted. These individuals
will likely put the group through some testing before daring to disclose.
Alternatively, they may disclose their most unusual experience or reaction
"up front" as a means of testing.

Because issues of control and boundaries are such salient ones for incest
survivors, group process must offer maximum control to each member.
Members are encouraged to tell the group if they need space or time-out
when the material under discussion is overly frightening, threatening, or
painful, or when they have an intense and/or adverse reaction. The group
can then back off and offer the distressed member support. At times it will
be appropriate for the group to ask a member to continue despite her
discomfort. The member should be the one to decide whether she wants to
continue or not. In a similar vein, some survivors need to learn to ask for

things for themselves, such as attention or response from others. Others need to learn to hold back from initiating, caretaking or other behavior which is intrusive and disrespectful of the strength or individuality of others.

A related issue has to do with opinion and advice-giving. Members are responsible for carefully listening to one another but are not responsible for each others' actions or decisions. Stating opinions and giving advice run counter to allowing each member control and should be avoided. Similarly, although disagreements and conflict surface in every group, blaming and arguing are discouraged. Negotiation, feedback skills, and conflict resolution are encouraged and taught as preferable to fighting, arguing, and blaming.

A group norm of survival appreciation is encouraged. Low self-esteem and self-criticism are countered in an atmosphere where coping skills are reinforced as positive and as the means of surviving a self-destructive atmosphere. Members are encouraged to draw upon their survival strengths and instincts in working through the trauma and finding different alternatives for themselves.

Finally, group process is enhanced and pain and despair are countered when hope is offered and lightness is allowed. The potential to recover from incest injuries and to live a less encumbered life is stressed. Members are encouraged to be hopeful and to engage in health-promoting and positive activities. Even though they are still dealing with its aftermath, the abuse is over and members can make healthy choices for themselves. Humor (even gallows humor) is useful in breaking the tension and in offering support and, sometimes, distraction.

Leehan and Wilson (1985) have pointed out that positive emotions, such as happiness or satisfaction, may be as difficult to express as negative ones. Because of past negative reactions to positive feelings, survivors are often reluctant to have or share anything positive. These authors had the following to say about positive feelings:

> . . . it is important for the group leaders to program into meetings some time when the members can share some of the good things that happen to them. They must make sure that the sessions do not simply become heavy and depressing problem sessions. Sometimes we have begun sessions by asking members to share one good thing that has happened to them during the week or to share one accomplishment from the past week of which they are proud. For many this is extremely difficult.
>
> When members share their accomplishments, the leaders must respond honestly and enthusiastically. They must show true appreciation for what has been done and let the group member know when success is recognized. They should elicit responses from the other members so that the member who is sharing can feel the full extent of that recognition. This process also enables all members to experience the feelings associated with giving praise. Such acts of positive reinforcement were not common in their families.

The group leader also must not let the group members negate their own accomplishments. Too often, after someone's success has been acknowledged by group members, that person will be the first to denigrate it with an: "It was easy." or "I was lucky." Leaders must confront such remarks and reinforce the true value of the accomplishments. It should be made clear that there is no need to negate or deny what one has accomplished. (pp. 88–89)

Contact Outside of Group. A policy for contact between members outside of group for socializing, support, and/or the resolution of issues between them must be decided by the group. Contrary to the norm of most therapy groups, where outside contact is discouraged, in most incest therapy groups contact between members for support is allowed. Nonetheless, members are asked not to discuss other members or group issues on the outside. They are asked to be open about outside contacts to prevent secret relationships, alliances, and jealousy from developing. In deciding whether to allow outside contact, the group must be sensitive to the needs of all members. Some members require a lot of distance and want little or no outside contact; some want to learn to transfer the relationships from "inside" to their "outside" lives and request contact. Group members are encouraged to negotiate their needs and to share whatever amount of contact feels comfortable.

Termination. If a member decides to terminate, she is asked to tell the group of her decision during one session and to return for an additional session; this allows time to discuss reasons for leaving, to uncover any miscommunications, to share reactions, to give and receive feedback, to gain some closure, and to say goodbye. Not infrequently, this "last session" results in the member's deciding to continue, especially if her decision to leave was based on individual sensitivity and hypervigilance, erroneous communication, or distorted beliefs, such as "No one in the group likes me"; "I have nothing in common with this group"; "This is too painful and it doesn't make a difference anyway"; "My life is hopeless and is not going to get any better." The "one last session rule" often allows feedback that contradicts these messages.

Group Leadership

Experience and Knowledge Base. The obvious requirement for cotherapists conducting incest groups is training in group process and leadership along with knowledge of traumatic stress and incest. In particular, leaders must have a working knowledge of how the dynamics of child sexual abuse and family dynamics affect the group process. Just as it is not acceptable for individual therapists to learn about incest from their survivor clients, it is not acceptable for group leaders to use groups as their *in vivo* source of training. I mention this here because I have been repeatedly told of just this situation by survivors. The therapist must guard against playing the role of the incompetent/passive/needy authority figure who relies on the survivor for assistance, since this directly recreates the childhood scenario of many. It places the survivor in the position of again taking on a care-taking role rather than allowing for the identification and modification of this role.

The therapists function in a variety of different roles in group — as process facilitators, observer-participants, educators, female and parental role models, alter egos, and limit-setters. They will be called upon to be patient, gentle, understanding, reliable, and responsive to group members, and to simultaneously exercise the firmness necessary to maintain boundaries and insure safety in the group. Their major task is to be group facilitators and processors and to create a safe enough environment for group members to explore relationships among themselves and with the leaders. The development of trust is a major issue, as discussed earlier in this chapter. The development of some dependency on other group members and on the leader is positive to counter past experience but, as van der Kolk (1987b) has cautioned, therapists must be aware of a potential major pitfall in these groups:

> The initial force binding the group together is the sharing of the trauma. The intense feelings generated by disclosure at first promote idealization of the leader, who is often credited with much greater power than the leader of other therapy groups. This idealization may seem gratifying for both thera-pist and members, but ultimately it operates as a resistance to overcoming the helplessness generated by the trauma because it keeps the locus of control outside the individual. Traumatized individuals sometimes elevate group leaders into cult heroes, perpetuating an illusion of the group's omnip-otence through identification with a leader who is regarded without ambiva-lence. Idealization must be vigorously addressed and interpreted. Only after the group starts tackling the leader's real and imagined shortcomings can it really start to see itself as useful and powerful, and only then do group members regain a sense of individual effectiveness. (p. 165)

Co-leadership and Sex of Therapists. The available literature on incest group therapy is unanimous in recommending that groups be co-led. The intensity of the group process and emotional content places great demands on the therapist. A co-therapy model allows for mutual therapist support and shared observation and processing of group interaction patterns and issues. It has the potential for lessening the intensity of transference, par-ticularly the idealization of the therapist. Additionally, formal supervision and/or the support of professional colleagues is advisable to assist leaders in analyzing and maintaining control of group process and in identifying and ventilating their own emotions.

Strong justification exists for a female co-therapist team, the model most widely reported in use with these groups. Many survivors will not join a group which includes either male members or leaders. With some exceptions, incest survivors perceive females as being safer and more trustworthy than males as well as more understanding of victimization issues; nevertheless, they may not perceive them as powerful, competent, able to offer protection, or capable of being persons in their own right. This can provide a direct lead to the exploration of issues concerning their mothers. Many survivors have unexpressed feelings of anger and disappointment in weak and/or nonprotective mothers, mothers they often had to take care of rather than vice versa. The expression of these feelings is often a necessary precursor to anger towards the perpetrator. Survivors may only be able to express these feelings in an atmosphere where they are not triangulated with a male authority figure and receive the support of a female authority figure. Female therapists can further provide group members with positive role models of strong, competent, and responsive women.

Despite the strong rationale for the same-sex therapy team, some therapists believe that an equally strong rationale exists for the use of opposite-sex cotherapists. A number of such groups specifically for incest treatment are now being conducted, but at present which type of leadership is the most beneficial has not been established. Mixed-sex groups for grownup abused children (including incest survivors) utilizing a male-female cotherapy team have been reported by Courtois and Leehan (1982) and Leehan and Wilson (1985). These groups were successful in working with abuse survivors and deliberately used opposite-sex therapists to allow for the development and working-through of the different transferences. Leehan and Wilson wrote:

> It is easy to understand and even expected that the leader who is the same sex as the abusive parent will receive negative tranference and testing. However, testing will not be limited to that leader. As much, if not more, testing and hostility will be directed at the leader representing the nonabusive parent. Victims feel a great deal of anger and distrust toward the parent who did not protect them.
>
> This problem becomes even more difficult if the nonabusive parent was also victimized. In such a case, that parent may be idealized. Even though he or she did not protect the child, the parent is seen as a fellow victim and even a martyr. That ideal image is then transferred to the same-sex leader, with the result that this leader can do or say nothing wrong and the other nothing right. (pp. 82–83)

Cole's (1985) statement regarding sex of therapist reflects the prevailing view and suggests the possibility of therapy with a mixed-sex team subsequent to therapy with female cotherapists:

> The frequently used male and female group leadership team, with its assumption of two positive sex role models, is well beyond the needs of these

groups. A pivotal task of these groups centers around creation of trust. The least threatening place to start seems to be trust building with women. Trust in men seems to come later. (p. 81)

Clearly, different models should be attempted and their effectiveness assessed, with the goal of providing group treatment geared to the unique needs and preferences of each survivor.

The Therapist With an Incest History. Debate exists as to whether therapists need to have had incest experience themselves to be effective as group leaders or whether a history of incest can impede effectiveness. The situation is not clear-cut. The former victim certainly has a fuller understanding of survivor experiences, reactions, and difficulties in overcoming a history of incest; yet as in individual therapy she must have resolved her own issues and experience. She must be able to work objectively with the group without her own issues constantly being stimulated and getting in the way. While her past provides a powerful aid to understanding, she needs to be able to separate it from client issues. Both she and her cotherapist may need to monitor how well she is able to do this.

Whether the cotherapists have personal experience of sexual abuse or not, they can expect to be questioned about it by group members, either during the screening interview or during the course of the group. Each cotherapy team should decide ahead of time whether to self-disclose in response to such an inquiry and how much to question its motivation. Each type of disclosure causes reactions. Formerly abused therapists usually receive empathy and expressions of sadness and hurt. They may be sought out as the only people who could possibly understand and empathize with the incest experience. Nonabused therapists are greeted with relief, envy, anger, and sometimes confusion about why they are doing incest work. Some survivors feel that nonvictimized therapists cannot empathize or understand. Others tend to seek such a therapist, since she is perceived as having has a "normal" childhood and as not being stigmatized. Negative self-perceptions are not so easily projected onto the nonvictimized therapist. She may be idealized as having greater insight and fewer problems than her formerly abused counterpart and as therefore potentially more effective. Over time, issues of abuse/nonabuse lessen in importance; nevertheless, the initial perceptions and how they affect group interactions should be taken into consideration. Group members should be encouraged to discuss these perceptions during the course of the group.

Leadership Style and Compatibility. The theoretical orientation of the leaders and the group format determine leadership style. Some groups focus on the "here and now" of group interaction patterns and current effects of the past abuse and family dysfunction, some on the abuse experi-

ence itself and its aftermath, and some alternate between the two empha-
ses. A number of alternative treatment styles may be employed. Some
therapists work one-on-one with each individual member, as other members observe the interaction. This is the less preferred style since it puts the
therapist in the position of powerful authority figure who has all the answers. It's far better for therapists to function as content and process
observers. Their less active interaction can encourage group members to
take more control, to engage with one another, and to function essentially
as cotherapists. Some therapists use a fairly structured format with a set
series of exercises, while others suggest exercises or activities spontaneously (e.g., role play, body sculpting, family sculpting, gestalt and psychodrama exercises, bibliotherapy).

Whatever their preferred style, both therapists must coordinate their
approach to the treatment so that they are relatively compatible and support one another. They must function as a team to guard against being
split into good and bad parents, but their individuality should come
through as they engage with the group and its members. As in individual
work, they should maintain an empathic, encouraging stance and not function only as observers. They must be actively involved in the group so as
not to be perceived by group members as disengaged, disinterested critics.

PROCESS ISSUES

Group Transference Issues

The most common transference and countertransference issues arising
in incest therapy were addressed in Chapter 11. These same issues arise in
group therapy, supplemented by transference associated with the group
process. Group offers a closer approximation of a family than does individual treatment and thus provides an atmosphere that stimulates the emergence of family transference issues. Although these issues arise in time-
limited groups, they are more in evidence when the group is open-ended or
long-term. Groups of longer duration offer additional therapy time to identify these issues, to work them through, and to modify them as needed.
Five of the most common group transference issues are discussed below.
Others arise according to the individual group and its unique dynamics.

Boundary and Communications. Incest families typically have boundaries which are either too rigid or too permeable, or some combination of
each. An example of the combination is the family which is socially isolated from the outside community (rigid boundaries) but has enmeshed
roles among members and generations inside the family (diffuse boundaries). As a result of the lack of clear boundaries, family members have

difficulty with self-definition and self-regulation. The task of the group is to identify learned patterns of interaction and to address problems of self-definition and self-regulation, in order to offer opportunities for identity development and differentiation and new modes of interaction.

Usually the survivor's interaction and communication patterns in the group closely parallel those she learned in her family of origin. The development of trust is a major issue even when the group becomes cohesive. Continuous testing of the genuineness and caring of others is common. Double-bind communication is typically in evidence since "incest victims have learned to approach the world as a continuous double bind in which their responses are not effective. In order for separation/individuation to take place, the woman must learn to extricate herself from double bind situations and avoid setting up similar situations in the future" (Wooley & Vigilanti, 1984, p. 348). In group, survivors learn to identify double-bind communications and to express emotions which normally would have been suppressed by the double-bind. Group members support one another in this expression and thus break the pattern of isolation and denied affect.

Patterns of giving and receiving attention (asking for and sharing time) from other members and from group leaders offer valuable information about family patterns and the survivor's predominant style. Survivors exhibit their habitual patterns, ranging from overcontrol, protection, and caretaking (putting the needs of others first) to undercontrol, passivity, and withdrawal (never asking for or expecting anything from anyone). Verbal and nonverbal communications similarly offer cues to family functioning and survival behavior. These may range from an aggressive, expansive, domineering style to an unassertive, camouflaging, "don't notice me/I won't challenge you" stance. Since the fear of rejection and abandonment is so prominent in incest families, members test the "staying power" of the group. Some members threaten to leave to test whether the group cares enough about them to want them to stay; others keep group members at a distance.

Parental Transference Issues with the Cotherapists. Cotherapists may find themselves being treated in a wide variety of ways due to clients' projections. A common occurrence is for therapists to be split. The "good parent" therapist is idealized and treated as though she can do no wrong—behavior directed towards her may be pleasing, ingratiating, compliant, and protective. The "bad parent" is feared and so the survivor is hostile, wary or ingratiating in interacting with her. This therapist may also be treated with contempt, resentment, lack of cooperation, and an unwillingness to engage with her.

As discussed above, female therapists may evoke feelings about nonprotective, absent mothering. As a result, the survivor may distance to protect herself from further disappointment, may cling and attempt to merge with the therapist or may compete with her. Male therapists may be distanced as too threatening or approached for nurturance as a reenactment of previous behavior with the father.

Parental Issues Between Members. Parent-child issues may be played out between the members themselves, particularly when a wide age disparity exists between them. Older members may project feelings about their children onto younger members, for example, feeling jealous, protective or loving of them, scared for them, or resentful of their needs and their feelings. Often they are envious, and yet pleased, that younger members have the opportunity earlier in life to confront and work through incest experiences. As a group they tend to support younger members in getting their incest work done early in life.

Younger members may transfer feelings toward their mothers onto older members, including rage and hurt at the lack of attention or protection, love, neediness, a desire for closeness and protection, and contempt towards the mother's helplessness and passivity. These feelings are especially pronounced if the older survivor is also a mother in an incestuous family, a not infrequent occurrence.

Younger members also tend to empathize with the struggles of older members as they recognize that these women were abused at a time when incest and child sexual abuse were even more suppressed than when they were abused. Younger members assist in the mourning process through their support. Older members may themselves feel that their experience gets put to good use and thus has meaning when it provides encouragement to younger members.

Sibling Transference Between Members. Insight can be gained into the survivor's family role by observing her interactions with and reactions to other group members. Sprei (1986) has listed some of the most commonly manifested sibling transference reactions:

- jealousy/rivalry at attention directed towards other group members from the cotherapists (parents) or other members (siblings). This is additionally stimulated when a cotherapist is also the individual therapist of one or more members;
- strong attachment to or identification with other group members;
- protection of or taking care of other members (acting the part of the older sister or parent surrogate);
- the desire for other members to take care of her or to stand up to their own abuser (acting the part of the younger sister);
- resentment that other members can't provide her with protection or seeing other members as controlling;
- competition for the therapists' attention through a variety of differ-

ent strategies, including compliant "good girl" behavior or acting-out "bad girl" provocation or seduction attempts;
- feelings of isolation, disapproval, or rejection from other group members; and
- the negative comparison of herself to other group members.

Self-Projection onto Other Group Members. Members may project their own self-concept or disowned parts of themselves in a selective way onto certain group members or collectively onto the entire group. For example, one member projected her "bad, dirty, unlovable child" onto another member. She disliked her as a result and resisted interacting with her. Working out the relationship in the group allowed this client to discover a disowned part of herself and to address self-concept issues. The other client began to address how she played out her negative self-concept in the group and how she had disowned positive aspects of herself.

In a similar fashion group members project aspects of themselves onto the group as a whole. These members may perceive group as a meeting of contaminated losers who deserve one another. These perceptions may be openly shared with other members or closely guarded as a secret. The task of the group is to make these self-perceptions and distortions explicit and to explore their origins so that they can be challenged and modified.

The Interface between Individual and Group Treatment

Concurrent or sequential individual and group treatment with the same therapist has some clear advantages. The survivor usually feels a sense of security and continuity in having the same therapist in both settings. The therapist has the opportunity to observe the survivor in interaction with others (including another therapist) and to observe how the abuse dynamics are played out differently in each setting. Additionally, the therapist receives feedback about the client from the other group members and the other clinician. A preexisting individual therapy relationship or one that begins during the course of the group must be disclosed to other group members. Doing so communicates that secret relationships will not be maintained and encourages open discussion of reactions.

Group changes or waters down the transference developed in the individual work. The survivor has the opportunity to observe the therapist interacting with others just as the therapist does with her. She will come to see different facets of the therapist not available to her during individual sessions. The survivor needs to adjust to the non-exclusive nature of the therapy relationship and to sharing her therapist's attention with others. When she engages in behavior to draw special attention from her primary therapist or treats the therapist as the only one who can really understand her, the group can challenge her and offer additional sources of support. Other group members may have reactions which resemble sibling rivalry to the existence of an exclusive, confidential relationship outside the group. They are encouraged to identify and explore these reactions.

The vacillations of the individual relationship will surface in group, but in general a stronger bond with the individual therapist than with the cotherapist is to be expected. Some survivors initially have difficulty engaging with the cotherapist because they do not perceive her to be their "real therapist." Over time they usually come to accept her as powerful in her own right, although the individual therapeutic relationship usually continues to be primary.

I have found it particularly useful to observe how the survivor presents herself and what she tells or does not tell in group versus individual treatment. The survivor may be able to risk sharing more fully in individual treatment and may tend to deny or minimize her reactions and keep certain things secret in group. The therapist must decide when it is useful to comment on the differences in presentation and confront the survivor. Often the survivor is unconsciously reenacting family patterns and defenses. One of my clients would smile and joke in the group when something made her angry or when she was depressed. Only with repeated individual and group feedback of her dissonant self-presentation was she able to show her anger or depression. She had developed her smiling defense because anger was unacceptable in her family and was likely to precipitate more abuse. She learned how this defense became maladaptive because it prevented others from knowing her feelings and being able to respond to her.

When group and individual therapies are concurrent but involve different therapists, every effort must be made to insure communication between them. The aim is coordinated treatment designed to reduce splitting and manipulation of the therapists and the two therapies. The two treatments can certainly be complementary and to the advantage of the client, or at odds, to her disadvantage. Both therapists should communicate at the beginning of either treatment and later on a regular or an "as needed" basis. The outside therapist can play a crucial role by staying informed about what is happening in the group but refusing to be drawn into group issues or to rescue the client. The therapist may need to work hard to keep boundaries intact between group and individual treatment and can do so by referring the survivor back to group to deal with issues arising within it.

Two different therapists can result in sabotage of the group work, divided loyalties, and the reenactment of incestuous dynamics. Rieth (n.d) described such a group situation: During the time of an important interaction concerning a client's rage at her female group therapist for not protecting her, her male individual therapist began to tell her that she was not getting her needs met in group. The client was symbolically caught between "mother" and "father." She left the group to go to "father." A different outcome might have ensued if the therapists had communicated and conceptualized the interaction in terms of a reenactment of incestuous family dynamics.

Frequently Used Exercises and Techniques

Several exercises and techniques have been described as particularly useful in incest groups. These can be used with and supplemented by standard group therapy exercises and techniques and strategies adapted for incest treatment, as outlined in Chapter 10.

Group Go-Around. This exercise is used at the beginning of each session. It gives each member the chance to briefly present (1) significant events that occurred since the last group meeting, (2) reactions to or unfinished business from previous sessions, and (3) issues she would like to discuss and the amount of time she needs. The go-around provides a rather quick means of finding out how each member is doing, provides structure and consistency, and offers a mechanism for negotiating time.

While the advantages of this technique outweigh its drawbacks, certain problems may be anticipated. Some survivors cannot present their concerns briefly or find that once they begin to talk they do not want to stop as the go-around continues. The therapists can curtail a lengthy initial discussion by carefully outlining the structure of the go-around and by asking the client to return to her presented topic later in the session. There are times, however, when a client may find this too difficult because of the strong affect involved in what she is presenting. Although consistency is important, so is flexibility. Sometimes it is necessary for the therapist to call attention to the client's immediate need or distress and to ask members whether they will agree to give her time "up front" before proceeding with the exercise. Such an exception should be monitored and brought up for discussion if the same behavior recurs.

The therapist must also closely monitor whether members feel that they must be in crisis or greatly agitated in order to receive group attention. Consistently bringing up a crisis at either the beginning or the end of the session may be a means of gaining attention or special status as a reenactment of how the survivor received attention in her family. In group she has the opportunity to learn how constant crises can alienate others and be maladaptive. She learns other more assertive and less dramatic ways to get her needs met.

A further disadvantage of the go-around exercise is that it may subtly encourage clients to focus on current issues and concerns at the expense of deeper issues or discussion of the incest. Particularly at the beginning of the group, the therapists can encourage the examination of common themes, issues, feelings, defenses, and behavior patterns underlying current concerns, and can make connections between them and the abuse. Focusing on common issues encourages group discussion, which is preferable to a series of individual therapist-member interactions.

Closing Exercise. The group should consistently end on time to demonstrate and maintain clear boundaries. Group members can rotate in the role of timekeeper. It is useful to have a short ending exercise to assist in wrapping up the session. A closing exercise is especially important when the session has been marked by a high degree of emotionality, conflict, and/or strong numbing or intrusive symptom manifestation, or if there has been a tendency for members to bring up crisis concerns right at session's end. Setting aside time to end the group assists members to work within boundaries, to ground themselves in the present, and to focus on leaving the group setting and returning to the "real world." Many different exercises can be used. Some of the most commonly mentioned include self-affirmations, group affirmations, support for positive achievements during the past week, planning to do something assertive or self-nurturing during the coming week, planning to take action on something discussed during the session, specific homework exercises, etc.

Between Session Assignments. Some of the more structured groups regularly give homework assignments while less structured groups may give them occasionally. The most frequently reported include reading assignments, completion of incest questionnaires or other psychological instruments, keeping a journal, writing letters, or planning a disclosure or confrontation. Between-session assignments may foster more concrete planning or expression of feelings, leading to increased group interaction and more detailed discussion of the incest and the family.

Group Rituals. Many groups come to represent surrogate families for their members, a dynamic which can become especially pronounced in incest therapy. It is not unusual for members' families of origin to be alienated or unavailable or for the member to be working on distancing from an abusive or dysfunctional family. Issues of family contact and involvement are worked on throughout the course of the group but predictably become more pronounced around special events (e.g., graduation, marriage, divorce, childbirth) and holidays (e.g., Jewish Holy Days, Thanksgiving, Christmas, Mother's Day, Father's Day).

Swink and Leveille (1986) discussed how the process of "orphanization" is a component of incest therapy. The survivor must break old patterns of interacting with the family, a process most effectively conducted in group treatment. In some cases this means a complete break with the family of origin, a process that naturally evokes strong feelings of sadness and guilt.

Group members encourage one another to exercise self-care apart from their families.

Some groups, as surrogate families, devise rituals or celebrate special events. For example, outside activities, such as potluck dinners for all past or current group members, may be organized. Food or a special belonging is occasionally brought to group to mark special occasions. One group held a barbeque for a member who graduated from college after a long struggle. The group decided to celebrate this event after the family of origin failed to do so. Another group, after three years of working together and mourning together at holiday time, planned a special Christmas session. The session was loosely organized around the agreement that each member would contribute something personal and meaningful. The session was truly touching. Members left commenting that they felt better able to face the holidays because of the group commemoration. As in individual therapy, there needs to be the recognition that a group can never undo nor make up for the past. But it can be instrumental in offering meaningful contact and interactions in the present.

SELF-HELP VERSUS THERAPY GROUPS

Numerous self-help groups have been organized in the last two decades to provide individuals with shared problems a forum for meeting one another and gaining support. Herman (1981) has described the obvious advantages of such groups for incest victims:

> The advantages of self-help groups for incest victims are numerous. First of all, most self-help groups are free and therefore available to many more people than psychotherapy is. Second, such groups foster a sense of health and competence, because participants do not identify themselves as patients in need of treatment. Third, since incest victims run such a high risk of insensitive or destructive treatment in the traditional mental health system, a self-help group may offer a safer and more therapeutic environment than the available professional services. The victim may find more comfort, understanding, and emotional support with her peers than in a therapist's office. Finally, self-help groups, in contrast to psychotherapy, develop a social analysis of personal problems, and sometimes offer the opportunity of collective action. (p. 197)

Despite their obvious advantages and benefits, self-help groups have some potential limitations and disadvantages. In general, they are not recommended for women in acute distress, for those who find it impossible to interact with others, and especially for women who have difficulty controlling aggressive or impulsive tendencies or who seek to solve incest issues through merger with others and overdependence. Nor are they appropriate for the survivor who is actively suicidal, homicidal, substance-dependent, or suffering a life-threatening eating disorder. A self-help group also does not have the built-in safety mechanism provided by professionally trained cotherapists. In recognition of the high potential for distress in these groups, many are engaging mental health professionals experienced in incest treatment as backup for emergencies and referrals. Many are also conducting screening interviews. Again, to quote Herman:

> Establishment of a safe, nurturing atmosphere in a group necessitates some degree of prior screening, so that women who cannot benefit from the group do not disrupt it. Self-help groups also present the danger, inherent in any small group process, that the necessary atmosphere of cooperation and mutual support may be jeopardized by suspicion and conflict among their members. A successful self-help group does not form spontaneously; it requires as careful organization and structuring as a therapy group. (p. 198)

At this writing, many varieties of self-help groups for incest survivors have been developed. Some are designed to assist or educate the individual survivor, while others are organized around public education and advocacy activities. They range from drop-in meetings organized around a theme, to a regularly scheduled group with either an open or closed membership, to national and regional conferences and seminars organized by national incest organizations. At least one group, Incest Survivors Anonymous, is organized around the Alcoholics Anonymous model, with members engaged in recovery in the 12-step tradition. Some groups are free-standing; some are part of comprehensive incest family treatment programs; others are organized under the auspices of rape crisis centers, women's centers, church groups, or victim assistance organizations.

With the variety of self-help formats now available, incest survivors have more options than ever before and the opportunity to join or engage in activities matching their level of functioning. Involvement in self-help activities may enable later engagement in formal therapy for some survivors, while the reverse process may hold for others. The availability of these different groups communicates to survivors that they no longer have to be alone in contending with prior incest. The silence and secrecy have been broken.

Group therapy holds special potential for treating the aftereffects of incest. The rationale for and advantages of group treatment were presented in this chapter along with a discussion of treatment models, the structure and organization of these groups, and special process issues.

CHAPTER 13

Special Populations

SURVIVORS WHO ARE members of minority populations by virtue of their ethnicity, sexual orientation, gender, or physical limitations, who are mothers as a result of incest, who are children of military and foreign service families, or who are members of religious groups bring special concerns and issues to treatment. It is not uncommon for these individuals to have been doubly oppressed and/or victimized and for their group status to have had a strong effect on their traumatic stress reactions.

The therapist working with a client belonging to any of these groups (and some belong to more than one) walks a fine line. On one hand, awareness of and sensitivity to the unique qualities of the particular group are needed; on the other, differences must not be accentuated to the point that the client is stereotyped or stigmatized due to group membership. Additionally, the therapist must understand that traumatic stress reactions and minority status interact, the interaction possibly causing an intensification of certain aftereffects (Parson, 1985).

ETHNICITY

A popular stereotype about incest is that it occurs more frequently in lower-class economic groups and particularly in the black community and among various ethnic groups. Unfortunately, distorted and unrepresentative sampling in past incest research yielded findings which reinforced these class and ethnic stereotypes. Recent, better quality research has not found these same differences; nevertheless, at the present time a broad enough research base is not available to conclude definitively that incest occurs with equal frequency in all social classes, racial categories, or ethnic subgroups.

Studies by Peters (1984), Russell (1986), and Wyatt (1985) all show similarities in prevalence rates of child sexual abuse in the black and white communities. At least two studies hint at possible differences for other ethnic groups. Russell's study, the largest and most representative incest sample drawn to date, found lower prevalence rates for Asian and Jewish women and higher prevalence rates for Hispanics. The latter finding is consistent with data reported by Kersher and McShane (1984). Russell also reported that incest occurs more frequently to girls from high-income backgrounds than to those from low-income families, a finding at odds with what were until just recently the prevailing estimates. In her analysis, Russell mentioned the sparsity of research on racial, ethnic, and socioeconomic differences in the prevalence of incestuous abuse and concluded that such research is urgently needed, echoing similar recommendations made by Finkelhor and Baron (1986) in their review of high-risk children and by Kelly and Scott (1986) in their review of sociocultural considerations in child sexual abuse.

The studies mentioned above also analyzed severity of aftereffects and degree of trauma by ethnic group and found significant differences between groups. These data are of particular clinical interest and importance. Russell found that Hispanic victims reported the highest severity of aftereffects, followed by Afro-Americans, other racial and ethnic groups, Asians, and whites. Wyatt found no difference in short-term effects of child sexual abuse for white and Afro-American women, but a difference in long-term response, with Afro-Americans reporting greater lasting effects. The reasons for these differences are unclear and need further study; however, at the very least these findings suggest that clinicians must take ethnic and cultural background into consideration when working with minority clients. At present, although there is not enough research to support the notion that membership in a particular ethnic group is predictive of severity of aftereffects, ethnicity is bound to interact with traumatic stress. Parson (1985) has this to say about the interaction:

> Ethnic identification is an irreducible entity, central to how persons organize experience, and to an understanding of the unique "cultural prism" they use in perception and evaluation of reality. Ethnicity is thus central to how the patient or client seeks assistance (help-seeking behavior), what he or she defines as a "problem," what he or she understands as the causes of psychological difficulties, and the unique, subjective experience of traumatic stress symptoms. Ethnicity also shapes how the client views his or her symptoms, and the degree of hopefulness or pessimism toward recovery. Ethnic identification, additionally, determines the patient's attitudes about sharing troublesome emotional problems with therapists, attitudes toward his or her pain, expectations of the treatment, and what the client perceives as the best method of addressing the presenting difficulties.
>
> Unless ethnic variables are taken into account, interventions are bound to fail ... though degree of assimilation and socioeconomic status are important qualifiers. (p. 315)

Parson suggests that therapists make a special attempt to become "trans-ethnically competent" through self-evaluation, study, supervision, and consultation. To begin they must examine their own ethnocentrism—their feelings, beliefs, and stereotypes about different ethnic groups. According to Kelly and Scott (1986, p. 159), doing so " . . . will minimize the risk of overpathologizing behavior that is socioculturally appropriate or of minimizing significant events that on the surface may seem socioculturally related but in fact are inappropriate. This process can be facilitated by seeking consultation with a professional who is familiar with the sociocultural background of a client."

Clinicians must become knowledgeable of both the individual culture's perspective (intracultural) and the intercultural perspective, according to Korbin (1981). The intracultural perspective would include culture-specific norms, values, and practices as related to the child's sexuality. The intercultural perspective would involve a broader, external frame of reference which encourages the development of sexual norms and values promoting child welfare and impedes extreme cultural variations. In this regard, Kelly and Scott (1986, p. 158) noted, "The crucial conceptual dilemma involves how sociocultural factors as they relate to the problem of child sexual abuse can be incorporated into a clinical approach without adopting either an ethnocentric bias, which neglects appropriate cultural variability, or a purely culturally relativistic position, which overlooks universal humane standards."

The therapist working with an incest survivor who is a member of an ethnic minority group must take the ethnicity into consideration right from the beginning of treatment. Sociocultural issues may make it even more difficult for incest experiences to be admitted to and discussed and for mental health services to be utilized.*

At the very least, the therapist who is not a member of the same ethnic group must begin by showing awareness of and sensitivity to social and cultural differences and indicating willingness to learn about the client's background. Such sensitivity helps alleviate anxiety and begin trust-building between therapist and client; alternatively, it allows the client to make an informed decision about whether to continue in treatment with the therapist or to seek a referral to someone who already possesses knowledge of her culture.

Merely seeking mental health services may be contrary to the client's cultural norms and expectations. Many ethnic groups stress reliance on the

*At a recent National Organization of Victim Assistance conference on racial minorities, Dr. Jane Delgado, an expert on Hispanic mental health, highlighted the special problems Spanish-speaking women crime victims have in seeking assistance. This problem is especially marked with respect to sex crimes, including incest.

family network to the exclusion of all outsiders. Thus, the client may feel very discomforted and disloyal for going outside of the family to seek help for such a family-oriented problem as incest. The therapist can offer both understanding of her discomfort (which may persist throughout the therapy) and support for her actions. At some point in the course of treatment, it may prove necessary to consult with or include other members of the family network, especially those who can provide support.

Since therapy contradicts the cultural traditions of many ethnic minorities and these minorities often underutilize mental health services, the client may have little or no understanding of the therapeutic process. It is therefore necessary for the therapist to prepare the client by teaching her about the process, what she can expect from it and the therapist, and what is expected of her.

The therapist must learn about the cultural meanings, constraints, and traditions in general, and then those specifically having to do with sexual terminology, sexuality, and incest. The client may have culture-specific words or expressions for sexual terms and beliefs about sexuality. The therapist should use the client's sexual terminology and respect the client's identification with cultural perspectives on sexuality and incest. During the course of therapy, the therapist can present alternative perspectives (including the intercultural perspective discussed above) as needed. The therapist may also have to be creative in making strategic and therapeutic modifications to accomodate sociocultural considerations.

Louisa's parents, immigrants from Central America, were married when her mother became pregnant by her father. To spare her family disgrace and embarrassment, her mother chose to marry her father, even though in their home town he had a reputation for molesting young girls.

Louisa came to the attention of child protective services when she was molested by a school janitor. Louisa's father seemed very concerned and was cooperative with CPS workers, saying that he wanted to ensure Louisa's safety. Louisa's mother disclosed that she also had been abused as a child. She then added that her husband's concern for Louisa was due, at least in part, to his wanting her all to himself. He had been molesting her since she was a baby. The mother, feeling totally helpless, said that family would be shamed and shunned in the community if the story got out. In their culture, families did not interfere with one another and men held all the prerogatives.

SEXUAL ORIENTATION

In Chapter 6, we reported that incest may affect sexual preference in numerous ways. According to Meiselman (1978) and Russell (1986), some research data and clinical evidence suggest that one response to the trauma of incest is for a woman to turn away from heterosexuality and embrace a lesbian orientation and lifestyle. To quote Meiselman: "Apparently, father-daughter incest as a traumatic, conflict-inducing heterosexual experience in early life is associated with an increased incidence of lesbian feelings and behavior in maturity, although the majority of postincest daughters remain heterosexual" (p. 259). Some women admit that their same-sex preference is the direct result of their incest experience and its aftereffects, particularly a fear and mistrust of men and an aversion to heterosexual sex. In involvement with other women, they seek safety and security they believe to be unachievable with men. Others report knowing they were lesbian before the abuse and not as its result. Still other women are confused about their sexual identity, unsure whether they are homosexual by nature or as the result of heterosexual trauma. Westerlund (1983, p. 23) remarked that "Confusion about sexual orientation is not uncommonly a complaint although the majority of women with incest histories maintain heterosexual relationships." Male victims of homosexual incest also express confusion, wondering if the sexual abuse resulted from their being perceived as gay or whether they were made homosexual by abuse perpetrated by another man.

Maltz and Holman (1987) divided the women in their study who had sexual relations with other women into two groups: (1) heterosexual or bisexual women open to experimentation with female partners as part of either their prerecovery coping efforts or their incest recovery process, and (2) lesbians who are also incest survivors. In discussing these two groups, they wrote:

> There are many reasons why a heterosexual female survivor might choose female partners. Female partners may be less pressuring than males for sexual contact, and more understanding and supportive of the survivor's anxieties about sex. Some survivors may feel safer and more comfortable with females because their bodies lack many of the reminders of the abuse, such as a penis, semen, and body hair, and because their voices do not remind them of the low voice of the offender. Resolving incest issues can lead these women to overcome their old fears and can give them the option of relating to men, sometimes, much to the dismay of their woman-oriented friends. For these women, the incest may have blocked the recognition of their underlying heterosexual orientation.
>
> In contrast, women who are lesbian from early childhood may find that the incest—forced sexual contact with males—blocks their awareness of their preference for female partners. Anger at women, encouraged by anger at a mother who failed to protect, can also block recognition of attraction to women. These women may have spent years assuming they were heterosexual. (pp. 72–73)

Clearly, a same-sex preference can be blocked by other factors as well: societal discrimination and stereotyping, religious nonacceptance and condemnation, a survivor's preference for celibacy as a direct consequence of incest, etc.

We should also note other reasons accounting for lesbians becoming uncomfortable with other females. The nonprotection of the mother may have antedated the incest and been characterized by hostility and estrangement between mother and daughter, the preoedipal issues discussed by Brooks (1983). This coldness usually continues during and after the incest, causing additional feelings of guilt, anxiety, and remorse. The discomfort of some lesbians with other women is due to the fact that their abuse was perpetrated by female relatives. Their same-sex orientation might have been impeded due to unresolved effects of same-sex incest in much the same way that the opposite-sex orientation of heterosexual women is impeded by having been abused by a man.

Questions about sexuality and sexual orientation might cause a survivor to seek treatment or they might emerge gradually during therapy as incest issues are resolved. Although discussion of sexual functioning and sexual aftereffects is an important component of incest resolution, the exploration of sexual identity should not be undertaken unless the client seems confused about sexual preference and/or has exploration as a goal. Obviously, it is essential that the therapist be open and accepting of sexual preference and encourage exploration of the issues having to do with preference. The survivor may be very relieved at confiding confusion about sexual aftereffects and sexual orientation and benefit from talking about it with an accepting, noncondemnatory therapist.

On the other hand, the therapist must take care not to stereotype the lesbian, gay, or bisexual client by assuming that his or her sexual orientation results from incest and only problems have to do with sexuality. Lesbian women and gay men, like their heterosexual counterparts, have a full range of incest aftereffects to contend with, as well as other issues unrelated to sexual abuse. The stigmatization and oppression associated with homosexuality in the society at large may have intensified these effects. An exploration of the incest experience and its associated feelings is in order. Some incest experiences, whether homosexual or heterosexual, result in serious, negative aftereffects for the homosexual victim. Other experiences, particularly homosexual contacts involving peers or members of the extended family which were consensual, voluntary, and/or exploratory, have more benign and even positive aftereffects (Simari & Baskin, 1982).

In group treatment therapists should try to insure that survivors who are members of any minority population, including homosexuals, are not isolated. Nor should lesbian survivors be asked to explain or justify their sexual preference to other group members. Therapists must constantly monitor group process and issues revolving around sexual orientation. If some members cannot accept homosexuality or homosexual members, their position should be made overt and a group decision made as to whether productive functioning of the group as constituted is possible. It may be necessary for a member(s) to seek out another more compatible group or for the group to establish ground rules governing the discussion of sexual orientation.

Because of the oppression and misunderstanding they face in the society at large, some lesbian women and gay men have developed a separatist position and will work only with others of their same sexual preference. They specifically seek out a lesbian/gay therapist or a group comprised of other lesbian/gay survivors as the only context in which they will be able to receive full support and understanding. Maltz and Holman (1987) indicated that a survivors' group made up of other lesbians may be helpful in identifying and validating common concerns in ways they are not understood or validated in a group of mixed sexual preference. They quoted the following from one lesbian survivor:

> I know it was very important for me to get into a group with other lesbian incest survivors. The reason I changed groups was because I was in a group without any other lesbians. I never felt any discrimination, but I just didn't feel I could connect on that with anyone else in the group. I felt on the outside, and you tend to feel on the outside anyway. That's another thing, that as an incest victim, when you're going through it, you always feel separate and different from other people, and that's reinforced, being a lesbian. (p. 120)

PHYSICAL AND EMOTIONAL DISABILITIES AND LIMITATIONS

To date little if any research has specifically addressed the relation of incest occurrence and physical and emotional difference, limitation, or disability on the part of either the victim or perpetrator. Browning and Boatman (1977) were among the first clinical researchers to note that children with disabilities were more vulnerable to incest. Interestingly, at this point, it is the risk introduced by the mother's unavailability or disability that has received the most research attention.

Recent school and clinical reports substantiate that children and adults with limitations constitute a population at risk for sexual abuse and are thus another minority population of incest victims. In fact, physical or emotional differences and disabilities often make these individuals more vulnerable to victimization, less able to protect themselves, and less likely to receive adequate social services. Children and adults who do not have full physical or emotional capacity make easy targets because of their vulnerabilities. They may be even more entrapped in the victimization than their able-bodied counterparts.

From a young age, disabled children are taught to rely upon and obey their adult caretakers. By adolescence they have usually learned that passivity and cooperation gain them a measure of independence and survival. They are usually not taught assertiveness and self-protection skills, nor do they usually receive sex education. Thus, they may be easier to engage, intimidate, confuse, or silence. In some cases, disability or damage may have resulted either directly or indirectly from the abuse or the abuse may have caused additional disability. Issues of dependence, vulnerability, powerlessness, stigma, betrayal, self-blame, guilt, and confusion are salient for many disabled individuals and are likely to be compounded by any type of sexual victimization, particularly incest.

> Confusion is a common reaction of disabled victims to sexual exploitation. Disabled victims may feel that their fright or anger results from their disability, that people without their disability might feel differently, and that the problem is essentially theirs. Feelings of guilt and self-incrimination are compounded by their learned trust of others and their lack of self esteem, partially a result of internalized social myths and negative stereotypes about disabled people. Even if a disabled person feels that she is being abused or hurt, she may be reluctant to report her experiences, fearing that she will be blamed or will disrupt the family on which she is so dependent. (Staff, 1984, p. 8)

The therapist must be sensitive to these issues as well as those related to the client's particular disability. Depending upon the disability or limitation, the client may need treatment with therapists possessing special skills, knowledge, or training, and/or group treatment with similarly disabled individuals. For example, groups led by clinicians who have sign-language skills and specialized knowledge of the hearing impaired have been organized for deaf survivors. The type of disability may also dictate what can be addressed in treatment. A retarded survivor, for example, may not benefit from exploring past victimization; however, strong social service support specifically directed at keeping her safe from revictimization can be crucial.

MALE VICTIM/SURVIVORS

The male incest victim has not as yet been the subject of adequate investigation (as discussed in Chapters 4 and 5), leading Kelly, MacDonald, and Waterman (1987, p. 3) to observe that: "One of the most underresearched and clinically underserved populations is that of adult males who were sexually abused during childhood." Research and clinical information is only now accumulating since the male victim has been even more reluctant than the female victim to report the incest at the time of its occurrence or later or to seek treatment. His shame at having been victimized and not having been able to protect himself or having been aroused, his belief that the incest was not victimizing or had no effect, his fear that he will not be believed or will be blamed, and his belief that no help is available — all contribute to nonreporting.

Urquiza and Crowley (1986) suggest that the dearth of information is also due to the fact that relatively fewer males than females are victimized (with a frequency estimate in the range of 2.5 to 8.7% of men sexually victimized as children according to Finkelhor, 1984). The lower prevalence impedes disclosure because male victims lack the knowledge that males are sexually abused both inside and outside of the family. Maltz and Holman (1987) offered this comment on disclosure:

> Incest disclosure may be a particularly difficult challenge for men. Few men have publicly identified themselves as incest victims. As a consequence, there exists little social precedence for male survivors to share the secret of the abuse. Disclosure seems to threaten a boy's masculine identity. He may fear that if he makes such an admission, he will be labeled by others as a submissive victim or a homosexual. . . .
>
> In general, male survivors seem to consistently discount or minimize early sexual abuse. . . . It may be difficult for a male survivor to accept the notion that the sexual activity was both abusive and coercive. (p. 144)

Nondisclosure is just beginning to give way to disclosure, as attested to by a recent Oprah Winfrey show devoted to the topic of male incest survivors. This particular show was a first and resulted in this less common form of incest coming to the surface and being publicly discussed.

The available information about male survivors suggests that the aftereffects of incest are similar as well as dissimilar to those reported by females. In general, many of the aftereffects are the same. Kelly et al. (1987) reported on the problems of men in a small clinical sample using Browne and Finkelhor's (1986) categories for females. In terms of *emotional reactions and self-perceptions*, low self-esteem and feeling of being different and isolated were the most prominent. Other similarities included self-destructive ideation and behaviors and emotional reactions of extreme anxiety, extreme guilt or shame, extreme anger, nightmares, sleep problems and flashbacks of the abuse. Considering *impact on interpersonal relating*, males reported a higher frequency of difficulty relating to men as compared with women and feelings of betrayal generalized to their ability to develop and maintain intimate relationships. The men reported a number of *effects on sexual functioning*, including problems with sexual preoccupations, confusion about sexual identity, aversion to sexual intimacy, compulsive sexual behaviors, and difficulties in sexual performance. The survivor might cope through sexual withdrawal, on one hand, or through identification with the traditional male stereotype and macho sexual behavior, on the other. Finally, *effects on social functioning* were marked by discomfort in social situations, drug and alcohol abuse and employment problems.

The most outstanding differences are seen in the tendency of some male survivors to reestablish control and reassert masculinity through aggressive, hyper-masculine behavior and to recapitulate the abuse experience by becoming a perpetrator. Urquiza and Crowley (1986), in reporting on sex differences in the survivors of childhood sexual abuse, found differences in how males and females perceive the abuse both at the time of the abuse and later. Their data suggest that males tend to cope with abuse through externalized behavior (e.g., a desire to hurt others), while females cope through internalization (e.g., depressive symptomatology or revictimization). A similar finding was reported by Carmen, Rieker, and Mills (1984).

Other dissimilarities have to do with the differential socialization of males and females, including what the male victim has learned about the male role. He may take on greater responsibility and self-blame for the abuse due to having learned that boys are supposed to be strong and able to protect themselves. These feelings are reinforced when the boy is not believed or is castigated for allowing incest to occur (Rogers & Tremaine, 1984). Furthermore, the boy may misinterpret any physical arousal as signifying that he secretly enjoyed what happened or that he wanted it to happen.

Additional feelings of shame and stigma may be generated by the identity and sex of his abuser and the particular circumstances of his abuse. Abuse by a male perpetrator often results in confusion about sexual orientation, with fear that the abuse and any arousal he experienced made him homosexual or that something effiminate about him caused him to be abused. When the abuse is perpetrated by a significant person in his life, such as a father or stepfather, considerable self-hatred may result due to his identification with and reliance on this individual.

Abuse by a female perpetrator causes confusion of a different sort. On the one hand, in this culture, sexual contact between an older female and a younger male is often labeled as seduction and as desirable. The abuse is typically perpetrated differently by a female and involves physical tenderness and physical and emotional seduction. The victim, therefore, may not be aware that what transpired was abusive. On the other hand, when the male is aware that he was abused, increased feelings of shame and self-blame at not having been able to protect himself, especially from a female, often result. Males in this type of situation feel that they should have been able to do something, no matter what their age or what the circumstances of the abuse. I'm reminded of the man I interviewed for my research who was abused by an aunt when he was six. As an adult, he continued to believe that he should have been able to stop her. He carried considerable guilt and shame for not having been able to do so.

Males, more than females, are apt to make a disguised presentation in therapy, even when memories of incest are consciously available to them. The reluctance to disclose is due to shame and fear coupled with difficulty asking for help. It is therefore of the utmost importance that therapists be knowledgeable about the incestuous abuse of males and its predominant dynamics so that they know to ask about the possibility of its occurrence. As with the female victim, the therapist should probe gently and not insistently to prevent the client's being overwhelmed by his emotions. Male therapists should be aware that the male survivor might have a great deal of difficulty in working with another man if his abuse was same-sex. Similarly, female therapists might be threatening for the male abused by a female.

Once the abuse is acknowledged, the therapy process for the male victim resembles that outlined for the female. Many of the same issues dominate the clinical picture; however, as discussed above, males may have to work on variations of the issues of shame, fear, confusion, anger, sexual identity, and self-hatred/self-esteem. They will also need to understand male sex-role socialization and how it contributed to both their victimization and their response. In particular, the therapist must communicate uneqivocally that males can be incestuously victimized and that the client will be believed and will not be blamed as the initiator or as a willing participant even if he achieved an erection or ejaculated. The male victim must be reassured that he is taken seriously and not ridiculed or rejected due to his abuse experience.

The therapy of male victims must include another component not as necessary in the therapy of females: exploration of whether the survivor has externalized his feelings and sexually molested others. Available evidence shows that sex offenders most often were themselves sexually victimized and that molesting others occurs as the traumatic reenactment of past abuse (although not all male incest survivors become abusers, a point Kelly et al., 1987, have emphasized. They have developed a treatment group for male survivors who have not offended against others). If the survivor has sexually victimized others, his treatment must take that into account.

THE INCEST PREGNANCY AND CHILDBIRTH: THE VICTIM MOTHER AND CHILD

According to Roybal and Goodwin (1982), pregnancy occurs in 10–20% of all cases of incest. Its frequency seems to be declining and can be expected to continue to do so with the widespread availability of contraceptives and the increased reporting, intervention, and treatment to stop child sexual abuse. The percentage of actual childbirths is lower due to abortion, miscarriage, or other fetal loss. Furthermore, mortality rates and malformations are higher for offspring of consanguineous matings. Children born of incest are more likely to succumb in infancy or to have major defects which may later prove fatal than are children of nonincestuous unions (Adams & Neel, 1967; Baird & McGillivray, 1982). These pregnancies are reported most frequently in father-daughter or sibling incest, although they also occur between less closely related individuals.

The incest pregnancy and childbirth create two special clinical populations, each with unique needs—the incest victim-mother and the child born of incest. While it is obvious that major psychological issues would surround such a pregnancy and birth status, especially within the nuclear family, little is available in the literature on these populations, despite the fact that pregnancy is frequently mentioned as causing the disclosure or cessation of incest. Incest is sometimes disclosed by adolescent victims because they fear they are pregnant or will become pregnant. Additionally, pseudo-pregnancy has occurred where the victim had inadequate or faulty sexual information or became delusional.

The discussion here is based almost exclusively on observations from clinical practice. The following quote from Roybal and Goodwin serves to introduce the intensity of family role conflicts deriving from the incest pregnancy:

> The incongruity between behaving as a daughter to the father and behaving as mother to the father's child strains even our culture's streamlined kinship terminology. The incestuous father would be both father and grandfather to such a child; the incest victim's brothers are uncles to the child and also half-brothers; the infant's mother is also its half-sibling. Anthropologists argue that the incest taboo is designed to prevent such conflicting and incongruous situations which are psychologically intolerable. (1982, p. 126)

These same conflicts occur in less intense but no less dramatic form in sibling incest and with less intensity as the degree of relatedness between victim and perpetrator decreases; that is, incest between first-degree relatives results in more role strain and conflict than incest between second- or third-degree relatives.

Roybal and Goodwin discuss three family types in which they found father-daughter incest to result in pregnancy, each with particular characteristics and likely outcomes for the pregnancy. These same types are applicable in other forms of incest as well and are not mutually exclusive.

In the *intensely patriarchal family*, the pregnancy can be seen as but one more example of the father's tyranny. Cooper and Cormier (1982) note that such a father may have omnipotence and self-perpetuation as his motivation. He and his daughter produce a child with whom he can also have intercourse, as a means of reproducing himself again. This father is usually proud of conception and expects to raise the child within the family, although his paternity is often kept secret. The identity of the child's real mother may also be denied, with the child raised as the victim-mother's sibling instead of as her child. The victim has less chance to exit the family when its orientation is so endogenous. Family loyalty and fear of abandonment are paramount, and the father's demands and desires are obeyed without question. The father may even impregnate more than one daughter or encourage sex between siblings, thus causing additional relationship confusion and conflict.

In the *chaotic family*, the incest is only one in a multitude of serious family problems. As such it and any resultant pregnancy may go undetected and/or be denied until the actual time of childbirth. It is not uncommon for the child to be raised within the family and for the true identity of the parents to be guarded or unknown; however, there is a somewhat greater likelihood in the chaotic family than in the patriarchal family that the pregnancy will be aborted or the child given up for adoption or placed in foster care. Since many of these families come to the attention of social services, interventions may be suggested or forced from the outside. Because of this, the victim-mother has a somewhat better chance of escaping from this type of family situation than does the daugher in the patriarchal family.

Incest sometimes *accidentally* results in pregnancy, *independent of family type*. In this situation, the prognosis is improved since the victim-mother likely receives more assistance, has more options, and is less compromised. If the pregnancy is discovered early enough, abortion is offered as a means of alleviating the crisis. With later discovery or when the victim-mother chooses not to abort, placing the child for adoption is considered. Both of these options reduce the degree of interference of the incest and its resultant pregnancy on the victim-mother's growth and development.

Incest Victim/Mothers

According to Roybal and Goodwin, victim/mothers have been found to cope with the reality of pregnancy, whatever the family circumstance, in some rather dramatic ways. It is not uncommon for the victim-mother to dissociate from or deny the occurrence of the incest ("that didn't happen to me"), the pregnancy itself (to "not notice" the pregnancy until its reality is unavoidable — in some cases this only occurs at the time of delivery; the family may also buy into the denial by "not noticing" the obvious signs and changes of pregnancy), or the child (the baby is neglected, abandoned, given away, or otherwise left to the care of others).

Victim-mothers in patriarchal families sometimes show a different type of denial and an acquiescence akin to a folie à deux. They may feel that they are "in love with" or "hypnotized by" the father and function as the father's wife and the mother to his child(ren). These victim-mothers may fight any attempts to intervene in the family and "choose" to remain with the father or return to him. One victim-mother reported that she married her stepfather and bore four children by him after her mother divorced him. She was 13 at the time of their marriage. This man later molested his four children/grandchildren in addition to other children in the extended family.

The therapist working with adolescent and adult survivors will occasionally learn that the incest resulted in pregnancy. Whether it went to term or not, the pregnancy constitutes another "secondary secret" of incest. As such, it stays undisclosed because of the victim's sense of stigma and her fear of being condemned if the truth were known. The therapist who senses additional guilt and shame issues should consider the possibility of an unacknowledged pregnancy. If pregnancy is admitted, the therapist can further probe about its circumstance and outcome.

Clinical issues will be determined by the circumstances of the pregnancy, its outcome, the condition and upbringing of the child, and the victim-mother's method of coping. Incest pregnancy and childbirth can be conceptualized as "trauma within the trauma" requiring the methods of traumatic stress treatment as outlined in Chapter 8. The victim-mother must recall and examine the circumstances of the pregnancy and/or childbirth, explore and experience the emotions attached to it, and attend to any unfinished business. The latter may include issues ranging from locating an adopted child to disclosing to the child or to other family members the true paternity and/or maternity. The following case describes such a situation.

Jean sought therapy specifically for help in deciding whether to tell her 18-year-old daughter Lauren that Jean's father was in fact Lauren's real father. Jean had never disclosed Lauren's true paternity to anyone, preferring instead to let people believe that the conception was the result of a "one-night stand" and that the identity of the father was unknown. Jean had raised Lauren in her parents' home, where all still resided. Her father knew of his paternity and occasionally taunted her with it. He blackmailed her with threats to disclose paternity if she refused further incestuous contact. Jean's mother never indicated any suspicion (in their community, out-of-wedlock pregnancies were common) and was helpful to Jean in raising Lauren. Jean was in terrible turmoil and suffered guilt and shame about the circumstances of Lauren's conception and about the fact that she had always been ambivalent towards her, at times loving her and at other times abusing her. She felt that she had irreparably damaged Lauren and that only by "setting the record straight" could she begin to do right by her daughter.

The Child of Incest

The child of incest begins life with a taboo birth status and with a much greater than average potential for physical malformations and disabilities. Little is known about these children. The population has been largely uninvestigated due to researcher bias or indifference and/or difficulty in identifying and drawing a sample to study. Several researchers have emphasized the need for more information about children of incest, so that the magnitude of the risk for abnormalities from deleterious recessive genes can be identified (Baird & McGillivray, 1982) and information and assistance offered to these individuals and their families, whether biological or adoptive. Additionally, these children are psychologically at risk.

Some of these children are accepted and raised within the nuclear or extended biological family, while others are placed in foster care or given up for adoption. Adoption or upbringing in the extended family holds the best potential for a healthy emotional atmosphere within which the child can grow and develop, since the role strain and conflict are significantly less than in the family of origin. Whatever the placement, families should be informed about the child's birth circumstance and actual or probable genetic risk and malformations.

As discussed above, the child's birth status and the true identity of the child's parents are frequently kept secret when the child is raised within the nuclear family. The child may be raised as the victim-mother's sibling rather than as her child, with the true grandmother in the role of mother. Or, as in the case example given above, the true identity of the father is undisclosed but the child is raised within the grandfather/father's home.

Children of incest are children of conflicted roles and relationships. As when there are other family secrets with their associated shame, the child of incest is likely to develop a shamed identity and an associated low self-concept. These may be further reinforced by covert or overt family scapegoating, blaming, or rejection. The victim-mother, dealing with her own guilt, shame, and confusion, may be ambivalent or even hostile toward her child. Tragically, even more hostility or rejection can be expected to be directed toward the child if s/he has genetic malformations or develops disabilities. Finally, the child may be very vulnerable to being sexually and/or physically abused due to emotional neediness resulting from the impoverished psychological climate or to being perceived as stigmatized/disabled and therefore vulnerable. Sexual abuse may be forthcoming from the father/grandfather.

Reasonable guidelines for treatment when there is a child of incest could be adopted from Fossum and Mason's (1986) approach to dealing with family secrets and family shame. The family secrets must be admitted and disclosed. The consequences of family secrets and deceit and the emotions involved in confronting them make up the work of therapy.

The client who is a child of incest may present concern or suspicions about birth status directly, or the therapist may begin to suspect the presence of such a family secret during the course of the therapy. Once again, it is of utmost importance that the therapist be knowledgeable and accepting of such a possibility and indicate willingness to introduce it or explore it with the client. Where its possibility is suspected by the therapist but not by the client, the topic can be raised gently and explored gradually.

Determining the likelihood of an incestuous birth status and the associated deceit engaged in by the family is made difficult by the very nature of the issue and the potential reactions of family members. Reactions can range from immediate and full disclosure, accompanied by relief, fear, anger, or pleasure that the secret is finally out (this latter circumstance might be expected in the patriarchal family where the father is proud of his paternity), to denial and hostility towards the client for daring to suggest such a shameful possibility. In the absence of family honesty or support or in the case when knowledgeable family members are dead or unavailable, it may be necessary for the client to search out birth or other records or individuals who could offer verification. Feelings generated by confirmation on nonconfirmation need to be fully addressed in treatment.

Similar to disclosure of other significant family secrets, the discovery of an incestuous birth status and the true identity of one or both parents can be expected to evoke strong reactions. The client may initially respond with feelings of shock, anger, disbelief and denial, or just the opposite, with relief and acceptance. She may feel less stigmatized by learning the truth or more so due to what the truth signifies. The working-through process involves exploration or the client's emotions and perspectives on the situation and deciding whether to take any action. It is conceivable that some clients would decide not to disturb the family status quo but to use the information as an important aid in their therapy. Others may feel it necessary to pursue full family confrontation and disclosure and to work towards the establishment of different relationships between family members. Where active abuse continues or the potential for abuse is high, reporting the abuse to authorities is necessary for its cessation.

MILITARY AND FOREIGN SERVICE

Military and foreign service dependents constitute another subpopulation of incest victim/survivors not yet adequately recognized and studied. Although the military and foreign service are now open to women, in the past their ranks were almost exclusively male. The adult survivor therefore came from a "traditional" military or foreign service family with the incest occurring during the father's active duty, following discharge, or during his retirement.

While the incestuous family pattern is likely set long before military and foreign service, several characteristics of this life contribute to the occurrence and continuance of incest and aggravate its effects. These include family isolation, duty station rotations and resultant lack of a stable home base and support system, paternal absences while on assignment, a traditional family organization with father as the head of the family and all other members economically dependent on him and officially labeled his "dependents," and insensitive medical and social services. These are discussed by Crigler (1984) in her article on incest in the military family. Research by Dubanoski and McIntosh (1984) on factors contributing to child abuse and neglect (including sexual abuse) in military families found some differences but many similarities to civilian families.

The father's absences while on assignment can contribute to a family atmosphere of abandonment, which can be especially pronounced when the family is stationed far from home and familiar supports, possibly in an alien and hostile culture. Family members may turn to one another and sexualize their needs for support and nurturance. The father's absences may also inhibit father-child bonding and father's regular involvement in the early socialization of his children, factors identified by Parker and Parker (1986) as possible antecedents of father-daughter incest.

The entrapment of a child in a military or foreign service family can be even stronger than in a civilian family because she may have no stable resources around her other than her family. If her mother is dependent, passive, absent or hostile towards her, she then has no family resources. The entire family may have been strongly conditioned to protect the father's career and the family's economic livelihood (including the potential for a comfortable retirement) at all costs and to do nothing, including revealing incest, that would place it in jeopardy. In her review article, Crigler specifically notes that the Uniform Code of Military Justice (UCMJ) states that incest will not be sanctioned or tolerated by anyone in the military. Military personnel and their families can face a legal situation involving double jeopardy, since the perpetrator may be charged and tried in both the military and civilian legal systems. At least in the Navy, recent policy changes allow information about incest to be reported without terminating careers. A shift from punishment to family and individual treatment is gradually taking place.

Thus far our discussion has focused on incest that occurs when the father is on active duty status in either the military or foreign service. It can also occur after the father has left active duty. Crigler discussed the situation in which a retired military man who either cannot find an appropriate civilian job or suffers from war-related chronic illness turns to his daughter for solace. This is especially likely to occur if the wife enters the work world and leaves the husband at home with the children. I have recently learned of another variation in working with several survivors whose fathers served in World War II or the Korean War. The fathers clearly suffered some sort of war-related physical or emotional disability and by their families' descriptions "came back different from when they went in."

The daughters believed that their fathers' post-traumatic stress accounted, at least in part, for their incestuous behavior.

Father-daughter incest is probably the most frequently occurring type in military and foreign service families; however, other types occur as well. Sibling incest might very well occur because sons follow their father's example or because siblings turn to one another to cope with the family dysfunction or isolation. Crigler discussed the development of two types of mother-son incest in some military families. In both types, the father is either physically or psychologically absent or both. The first is likely to involve the oldest son and to be situational. It is most apt to occur when the husband is away for extended periods of time and the son is directed to be "the man of the house while Dad is gone." While trying to support each other psychologically, mother and son end up in a sexual relationship. The second type is more gradual in onset and, as described in Chapter 4, may involve only seductiveness or indirect sexual contact. The father is absent and unavailable by virtue of being "married to his career." The mother and son develop a strong bond to help them contend with the father's isolation from the family.

The survivor from a military or foreign service family who enters treatment may initially have difficulty disclosing anything about the family, much less the incest. The family's code of privacy and silence about family matters may be so strong as to border on paranoia. The therapist's first task is the development of some measure of trust and an alliance. The therapist can also begin by indicating an understanding of the family rules and then slowly pointing out how they might no longer be useful and discussing alternative strategies. I have found that repeated assurances of confidentiality and the privileged communication inherent in the counseling situation are necessary with this population.

Once the client is able to disclose and discuss events from the past, the counseling proceeds as outlined in previous chapters. The survivor has variations on the familiar issues and aftereffects of incest; for example, entrapment and isolation may have been much more pronounced for a child in a military family due to duty station rotations. The therapist must attend to these variations in assisting the client to work through the incest experience.

RELIGIOUS COMMUNITIES AND CULTS

We conlude this chapter with a brief discussion of one final special group — incest survivors in religious communities and cults. Although no research evidence is available on this group, clinical reports have documented that involvement in religious groups and cults is sometimes a means used by a survivor to cope with the abuse and its aftereffects. In discussing reasons for pursuing religious life, Jakubiak and Murphy (1987) discuss possible motivations:

> Some survivors struggled with their victimization and chose religious life because they felt authentically called. These women are fortunate because they received the help and support they needed to rebuild trust, freeing them to pursue their own lives as wounded healers. Others, not having had the benefit of self-disclosure and healing, may have chosen religious life because, consciously or unconsciously, they sought an environment of goodness and discipline in which to "atone" for their "dirty sins and secrets" of the past. Others were attracted to the life-style because community living and commitment to celibacy preclude having to deal with men and sexuality. (p. 23)

Additional motivations for involvement in both religious communities and cults include an attraction to a structured life dedicated to the needs of others, "loss of self" and obedience to the authority of a hierarchical structure or charismatic leader, atonement and self-punishment, and separation from family.

Some cults include a libertarian sexual philosophy, often for the pleasure of a male leader who functions as a father figure. Sexual interaction with the leader therefore serves as a traumatic reenactment of incest, as does sexual involvement with other members of the community when undertaken for the leader's gratification. Drugs and other "mind control" techniques might be used to lessen resistance to participation. Thus, a survivor involved in a cult might be repeatedly revictimized as part of the cult's activities while reenacting her past abuse.

The restrictions and structure imposed by these communities might initially counter aftereffects of the incest and lead to improvement in the survivor's functioning. Yet, in time aftereffects manifest in these communities just as they do in other environments. The survivor/member might not be able to control compulsions and acting-out tendencies or might exhibit marked symptoms of depression, lost vitality, and disengagement from others.

The healing process is the same for these survivors as it is for those not involved in a structured community. They require a nonjudgmental helper with whom they can explore the past and receive validation for long-suppressed affect. During the process or at its completion, they must assess their motivations in joining a community and reevaluate their commitment to the group. Again, quoting Jakubiak and Murphy:

> Sometimes after counseling for incest, adult survivors reassess their motives and conclude that religious life is not really an authentic choice for them but

a reaction to early traumatization. Others decide that they entered for the wrong reasons but can now, after therapy, commit themselves to religious life for different, more self-selected motives. (p. 24)

In conclusion, minority status and special group membership interact with and influence the aftereffects of incest. When a survivor, who is a member of the groups discussed in this chapter or any other special group, presents for treatment a therapist must take group membership into consideration. Special group status is but another variable in individualized assessment and treatment planning.

CHAPTER 14

Special Problems and Issues in Treatment

CERTAIN PROBLEMS and issues having to do with both process and content have been found to arise with regularity in incest treatment. Six categories of these problems and issues, which are not mutually exclusive, are discussed in this chapter, along with strategies for their management: dissociation and the return of the repressed; self-damaging behaviors; other-damaging behaviors; addictions and compulsive behaviors; sexuality and sexual difficulties; and medical treatment.

DISSOCIATION AND THE RETURN OF THE REPRESSED

The name of this category is adapted from the title of a recent chapter by van der Kolk and Kadish (1987). In it, they wrote:

> . . . Except when related to brain injury, dissociation always seems to be a response to traumatic life events. Memories and feelings connected with the trauma are forgotten and return as intrusive recollections, feeling states (such as overwhelming anxiety and panic unwarranted by current experience), fugues, delusions, states of depersonalization, and finally in behavioral reenactments. . . .
> Dissociation is adaptive: it allows relatively normal functioning for the duration of the traumatic event and leaves a large part of the personality unaffected by the trauma. (pp. 185–186)

As discussed in Chapter 8, dissociation constitutes a disturbance in the normal integration of thoughts, feelings and memories into the ongoing stream of consciousness, leading to the separation of emotions and memories from normal awareness. The process exists on a continuum and involves lesser to greater degrees of disruption and separation, the most complete being the multiple personality (Putnam 1985). Dissociation is a normative process that becomes pathological with the greater intensity of the stressor. It is involved in the identity disturbance and fragmentation described by many survivors (a sense of the self as unreal, dead, not fully present) and in such associated problems as low self-esteem, guilt, and self-damaging behavior. It is further involved in memory disturbance characterized by difficulties with concentration due to "spacing out," including trance states, depersonalization, derealization, and fainting, and in intrusive recall, including frightening images, perceptual distortions, flashbacks, nightmares, and body memories of the abuse.

In working with incest survivors, the therapist can expect to see a variety of dissociative reactions, some characterized by numbing and others by intrusive disturbances in memory, identity, and consciousness. Some actually occur during therapy as part of the treatment process, giving the therapist the opportunity to observe and experience them firsthand with the survivor. Others are reported as they occur outside of the treatment setting and in the course of everyday life. Although some of these are so mild as to be almost imperceptible, others are very flagrant and startling. Most dissociative reactions are not so complete as to involve a personality change or the total amnesia barrier found in true multiple personality disorder.* Rather, they involve partial splitting or fragments of memory, feeling, or identity. Putnam (1986) has indicated that abreaction of the traumatic memory and emotions and reintegration are the general treatment strategies for dissociative reactions. Specific strategies useful in working with both numbing and intrusive symptoms are discussed below (these supplement techniques discussed for these two categories in Chapter 10). These strategies are useful to the survivor alone and if needed can also be taught to partners, other family members, and close friends.

Numbing Symptoms

Numbing reactions vary in degree from the very subtle (a blink or eyeroll during which time the survivor has "blanked") to prolonged episodes (the client is conscious but "away" and in a trance-like state for long periods of time or she is amnesic for entire traumatic episodes). When numbing reactions occur during the course of therapy, they may serve the following functions: to withdraw from or numb the self against the anxiety associated with the therapy issues or the therapy relationship itself; to avoid recall; to avoid painful feelings; to avoid integrating the learning of the therapy; to maintain safety (one of my clients tells me "the wall just went

---

*The reader is referred to Braun (1986), Kluft (1985), and the growing literature on the treatment of multiple personality disorder.

up" when she feels unsafe with what we are discussing); and to defend against shame. They also occur outside of the therapy for similar reasons or in the aftermath of an experience of a therapy session where issues have been "stirred up." Once this type of reaction has been identified, it needs careful monitoring, especially when it involves prolonged periods of "spacing out." For example, the survivor may need to learn cues to when she might go into a trance and be careful about driving or using machinery at that time or to learn techniques to "come back" or ground herself during such episodes.

Since the survivor may think that her numbing dissociative reactions mean that she is crazy, a preliminary intervention strategy is to explain and depathologize them. During numbing episodes within the therapy, the therapist might ask the survivor where she is and how she feels while observing which topics, memories, or emotions precipitate the trance state and what functions the trance serves. For example, one of my clients "spaces out" whenever she feels her rage. By splitting if off, she is able to control it. Part of our work has been to allow her to consciously experience her rage in manageable doses. Several techniques are useful in accessing dissociated material: writing about it, having a dialogue with the split-off part of the self, and drawing the experience. Feedback and process confrontation about the perceived function of the dissociation fosters conscious examination.

In some cases it is useful to encourage a client to "go with" the dissociation and to accept it as a means she has devised to protect herself; however, the survivor must be gradually encouraged to "stay in the present" with what she formerly split away. Hypnosis can be used to assist in bringing material to consciousness. It can also be helpful in stressing the safety and security of the therapeutic setting as a context within which to face the memories, in separating the "here and now" from "then," and in grounding her or bringing her back to the present. The therapist may need to tell the client repeatedly that she is no longer alone as she was as a child.

At times the survivor may have difficulty returning to the present and may require extra time and strong sensory stimulation to do so. One of my clients has had a number of episodes of dissociation where she was "out" for several hours. On one such occasion a hospitalization was precipitated. We have learned to recognize when she is slipping into a heavy dissociative state—I interrupt it with instructions stated in a loud voice to come back and focus on the room, the colors of the room, the temperature, her breathing, etc. During a similar episode which occurred outside of therapy, one of her friends resorted to putting ice cubes down her blouse after nothing else worked. The ice caused an almost immediate return to the present!

Amnesia is a form of numbing seen frequently among survivors. Herman and Schatzow (1987) have made the most comprehensive comments about it. From their ratings of 53 women in short-term therapy groups on recall, age at onset, duration and degree of violence, they reported the following associations:

> The majority of patients (64%) did not have full recall of the sexual abuse but reported at least some degree of amnesia. . . . Just over one quarter of the women (28%) reported severe memory deficits. A strong association was observed between the degree of reported amnesia and the age of onset and duration of the sexual abuse. Women who reported no memory deficits were generally those whose abuse had begun or continued well into adolescence. Mild to moderate deficits were usually associated with abuse that began in latency and ended by early adolescence. Marked memory deficits were usually associated with abuse that began early in childhood, often in the preschool years, and ended before adolescence.
>
> In addition, a relationship was observed between frankly violent or sadistic abuse experiences and the resort to massive repression as a defense. (p. 5)

These authors remarked further:

> Characteristic differences were also observed in the adaptive styles and symptoms of patients with no memory deficits, those with mild to moderate deficits, and those with severe amnesia. Patients with full recall often commented that they wished they could repress their memories. Lacking this defensive option, they tended to depend heavily on dissociation and isolation of affect to protect themselves from the overwhelming feelings associated with the abuse. They often described themselves as "numb," "frozen," "in a fog," or "behind a glass wall." At times, some of the patients who could not repress their memories also lost the capacity for dissociation. When this resource failed, patients resorted to more maladaptive coping strategies, including somatization (conversion reactions, hypochondriasis), impulsive risk-taking, drug abuse, and transient psychotic episodes. In the group setting, patients will [sic] full recall of their abuse experiences often formulated goals that required them to tolerate and share the feelings associated with their memories, and thereby to emerge from their chronic feeling of numbness and isolation. (pp. 5–6)

Intrusive Symptoms

Survivors with the most severe memory deficits often describe almost complete amnesia for childhood but report experiencing jarring, recurrent, intrusive symptoms, particularly flashbacks and body sensations. And some survivors with complete amnesia develop acute symptoms of post-traumatic stress disorder when a recent experience (a family crisis, disclosure of other incest in the family, a TV show about incest, a sexual experience) triggers sudden, often overwhelming recall of the incest trauma. Again, quoting Herman and Schatzow:

> These patients described the return of repressed memories as extremely painful and disruptive to their established mode of functioning. They de-

scribed themselves as reliving their childhood abuse experiences as though they were occurring in the present. The reported experiences often included violence, sadism, or grotesque perversity. Recurrent images intruded both into sleep, in the form of nightmares, and into waking life. Patients experienced derealization and terror and often expressed the fear that they were losing their minds. (1987, p. 8)

Participation in an incest therapy group usually stimulates the memory recovery as members "chain" from each other's experiences. Group further allows the validation of memories and support in expression, since other members have had similar experiences. In fact, a group can be such a powerful catalyst to recall that it is sometimes necessary for the leaders to slow the process to avoid flooding of memories and emotions and to allow time for reintegration.

Similarly, in individual work the survivor is encouraged to have as much control as possible over the process. She does this by limiting exposure to sources of information that stimulate recall. The therapist might find it necessary to develop a repertoire of containment messages and techniques. I have used guided imagery and/or hypnotic instructions for this purpose. Examples include: "Close the door to the memories and lock it. Keep the key so you can unlock the door when you are again ready to do so." "Imagine yourself putting the thoughts and memories out of your mind. Put them in a safe place as you focus on something pleasant right now. Focus on being in the safety and security of this room." The client is usually given additional instructions to breathe deeply and to relax as much as possible during the closing-down process.

It appears that many survivors know much more than they think they know about their abuse experience. Given conditions that stimulate and allow recall, memories surface. Keeping a journal, writing an autobiography, and seeking corroboration of the incest from other family members or other childhood sources are effective in keeping the abuse experience concrete and in consciousness. However, it is also obvious that some survivors will never have full, lucid recall, especially for abuse which occurred when the child was preverbal. Such a situation makes it necessary for survivor and therapist to rely on whatever is available (e.g. memory fragments and/or kinesthetic memory) rather than complete recall.

Flashbacks, nightmares, and frightening images are fairly common intrusive mechanisms by which the repressed returns. They vary in intensity, duration, the degree of anxiety they stimulate, and the degree to which they interfere with daily activities or lead to avoidance of situations which function as triggers. Rieth (n.d.) provided the following definition and description of flashbacks:

Flashbacks are non-psychotic episodes in which a person actually relives the abuse as it happened. . . . She has no sense that she is here now, that she is safe, or that she has a therapist or other solid object who is for her and with

whom she can talk about what is happening to her. She is temporarily
disabled by this PTSD symptom.

Flashbacks do not occur capriciously, although it seems to be so to the
client. Rather than a flashback happening "from out of the blue," it usually
occurs in response to some stimulus in the present environment. The feelings she presents in the flashback be it the feeling of powerlessness, terror,
frustration, rage, or having been abused, or of not having been heard, is
present in some live way at the time of the flashback. . . . She is likely to be
unaware of the connection between what she is feeling in the flashback and
what is precipitating that feeling in the environment. (pp. 16–17)

The treatment of flashbacks includes teaching the survivor that they are
normal reactions to trauma and that she is not losing her mind. They may
be particularly intense during treatment and will likely be reduced in frequency and intensity over time; however, they may be present periodically
throughout the survivor's life. Flashbacks can be conceptualized and
treated in a manner similar to the treatment of phobias. The client is
assisted to control the panic rather than to avoid the object or activity that
cues the fear (DuPont, 1982). Although she will not have control over *when*
they occur, she can have some control over *what happens* when they do.
She learns to change her goal from the elimination of all flashbacks (a goal
over which she has little control and at which she is bound to fail) to one of
reducing her anxiety and improving her manner of coping with their occurrence (Sprei & Goodwin, 1983). The issue of control is paramount. As in
the treament of phobias, the survivor needs to know she has a way out of
the situation at all times. She should be encouraged to take whatever
action is necessary to feel safe. In a sexual situation, this might mean
shifting position, getting out of bed, leaving the room or creating physical
distance between herself and her partner. She is encouraged over time to
experience increased doses of anxiety as she can manage them and to re-
engage in anxiety-provoking behavior (Sprei & Courtois, 1988; Sprei and
Goodwin, 1983).

Several techniques have been developed for working with flashbacks
experienced either within or outside of the therapy. The survivor can use
these techniques whenever the flashback occurs, whether she is alone or
with others. The first step is to teach the survivor to identify and verbalize
when she is having a flashback. She is asked to describe what she is experiencing in the present as she is told that she is safe and not actually in the
situation she is experiencing. She is encouraged to reorient herself in the
present (grounding); this enables her to achieve a sense of control and to
distinguish the present from the past. She is taught to recognize that the
flashback is in her mind and that she is not having the actual experience as
she once did. Relaxation techniques are useful to assist her in controlling
and breaking the anxiety. Touching or holding the client is an additional
way to focus her in the present while assuring her of safety.

Once triggers are identified, they can be avoided or modified. For example, if a flashback occurs during sex due to a particular kind of stimulation, that stimulation can be avoided or changed until it no longer elicits the flashback reaction. Triggers which cannot be realistically eliminated, such as heavy breathing during sex, might be somewhat modified by doing something which changes them or breaks the association, such as talking during sex, avoiding strenuous sex, or changing positions. These same techniques can be applied to nightmares, with the survivor encouraged to focus herself in the "here and now" and the safety of her environment. If a partner is available, s/he should have an understanding of flashback phenomena and be encouraged to hold the survivor and to offer soothing reassurances that she is safe and in the present.

SELF-DAMAGING BEHAVIORS

This category includes many different types of behavior, all directed towards damaging or even destroying the self. These "revictimization" events are concrete manifestations of the damage of the victimization process. The individual has been so conditioned to the victim role and her self-concept so eroded that she continues the process even after the original victimization has ceased.

Sex and diagnostic differences have been found among sexual assault survivors in terms of revictimization: Females are more likely to be recipients of the aggression and abuse of others (usually of males) and to direct aggressive and hostile feelings towards themselves ("acting in") rather than towards others ('acting out"). Thus, female victims are more likely than males to engage in self-damaging behaviors. Females more often have diagnoses of major depression or borderline personality disorder, are actively or passively suicidal, and self-mutilate. In contrast, males are more prone to act out their hostilities, to direct them towards others, and to engage in other-damaging behaviors. They often engage in criminal and violent behavior and frequently carry diagnoses of antisocial personality, psychopath, or sociopath (Carmen, Rieker, & Mills, 1984). Additionally, more women than men are diagnosed as multiple personalities, not necessarily because there are fewer male multiples but because they instead are diagnosed as antisocial, psychopathic, or sociopathic. Because they act out their aggression, they are more likely to have been involved in the criminal justice rather than the mental health system.

The goals and motivations of different types of self-damaging behaviors vary quite markedly and differ by degree of seriousness; however, all involve some measure of self-directed hatred and rage often operating at an unconscious level. These behaviors can be conceptualized along a continuum from less to more severe with overlap between them. They may be solitary or may involve getting others to be hurtful or destructive. Self-damaging behaviors include the following:

- *Self-sabotage, self-defeat and self-neglect*: The survivor follows a pattern of not allowing herself to reach her goals, to succeed, or to be treated well. This category may include a disregard of health and other basic needs.
- *Unnecessary risks and "accidents"*: This type of behavior is usually impulsive and recurrent. It may involve repeated injury due to "accidents," unnecessary risk-taking, and rebelliousness and argumentativeness which provoke others.
- *Addictive and compulsive behaviors*: These include workaholism, chemical dependency, eating disorders, and compulsive shopping, gambling, relationships, and sex.
- *Self-abusive relationships and sexual practices*: The individual may be constantly involved in relationships which are psychologically, physically and/or sexually damaging to her. Dangerous sexual practices include unprotected sex, promiscuity, pornography, bondage, voyeurism, exhibitionism, etc.
- *Self-mutilation*: Self-mutilation involves inflicting some sort of injury to the body, most often through cutting, burning, gouging, pinching, hitting or breaking bones.
- *Suicidality*: Suicidal ideation and behavior may be a rather constant preoccupation or may occur sporadically when the survivor is depressed or under particular stress. Attempts range from those which are somewhat mild to those which are highly lethal.
- *Death*: Death may be self-induced or provoked. Self-induced death may be the result of a successful suicide attempt or the accidental result of a suicidal gesture or dangerous practice. Provoked death may be the result of keeping company with dangerous individuals who are murderous if sufficiently challenged or antagonized.

Most of these behaviors are discussed in other sections of this chapter, with the exception of self-mutilation, suicidality, and death, which will be discussed below.

Self-Mutilation

The severity of self-mutilation depends upon the level of the individual's pathology, according to a review article by Conn (1986). The client with an anxiety (neurotic) disorder is not conscious of an intent to harm herself and most often engages in repetitive, somewhat mild behaviors such as scratching, pinching, fingernail- and lip-biting. The client with a borderline diagnosis most frequently self-mutilates by cutting, hitting, or burning or otherwise hurting herself repeatedly and ritualistically. She may also have a serious eating disorder or may ingest substances she knows will make her ill. She is conscious of the behavior as providing some measure of relief from turmoil, pain or anxiety. Favazza (1987) noted that chronic self-mutilation is almost invariably limited to borderline personality. Multiple personalities and psychotic clients mutilate more profoundly and more dangerously than the others, in reaction to more serious perceptual or thought disorders. Self-mutilation for the multiple or psychotic is generally not stereotyped or chronic and is highly individualized and much more dramatic. For instance, it may be so serious as to involve self-stabbing, broken bones, genital mutilation, organ damage and organ removal. It often results from command hallucinations, religious preoccupations and dictates in psychotics or the vengeful rage of the persecutor personality in multiple personalities.

Physical and sexual abuse have only recently been recognized as childhood antecedents of self-injurious behavior, which may begin as a means of coping with the abuse (de Young, 1982). The goal of self-mutilation is usually the act itself and not death; however, on occasion it may accidentally result in death. Additionally, its usual purpose is not to control others (including the therapist), although sometimes it is. Most often it is a hidden, solitary practice of which the survivor is afraid and ashamed. Incest victims studied by de Young reported being evasive and deceptive when asked about their injuries. Rather than admitting that the injuries were self-inflicted, they attributed them to clumsiness or accidents. Self-mutilators quite frequently hide their injuries and their behaviors. For example, they may dress in a way that camouflages their bodies and their injuries (much like battered women) or may be very secretive regarding eating disorders. On the other hand, they may exhibit them as a physical manifestation of their psychological pain.

Self-mutilation has a variety of different motivations. Psychodynamics can be roughly organized into three groupings, as suggested by de Young: (1) entrapment and control, (2) punishment, and (3) ego reintegration.

Entrapment and Control: Self mutilation may provide the victim with a way of preventing further abuse or of demonstrating control and ownership of her body. Additionally, impotent rage about the abuse may become self-directed and expressed in self-injury. Some victims lash out at themselves rather than the abuser. They try to make themselves ugly so they will no longer be abused. For others, self-injury is a way to anesthetize the part of their body that is being abused by distracting themselves with another type of pain. This is exemplified by the survivor who would painfully pinch herself to keep from feeling her father's touch. Self-mutilation may further be a silent cry for help — a way to ask for help without breaking the injunction of silence.

Punishment: Self-mutilation may be an expression of either self-punishment or atonement. As punishment, self-mutilation may signify the introjection of the perpetrator's hostility and abuse, expressed as shame, self-hatred, and low self-esteem. In this way the survivor takes over where the perpetrator left off and continues the pattern of abuse. In particular, the victim may blame herself for the abuse and feel great disgust with her body, especially if she experienced sexual response. She may be enraged with the "child within" and see her as bad, dirty, disgusting, etc.

Ego Reintegration: Acts of self-mutilation often provide psychic calm and decrease tension associated with memories of abuse. Such acts provide a mechanism to resolve internal conflicts, particularly unexpressed guilt and rage. Mutilation may also relieve feelings of emptiness, depersonalization, unreality, anger, abandonment, and rejection, and may be used to terminate episodes of dissociation. It is a way to prove and experience one's existence. The sight of blood or the act of cutting or burning may bring feelings of relief and soothing or terminate the dissociative period (Favazza, 1987). Often no pain accompanies these behaviors because they have formerly been used as anesthesia against the pain of the abuse. For some survivors self-mutilation can be considered an addictive behavior and a way they have found to regulate intense affect.

The clinician treating incest survivors most often sees self-injurious behaviors consistent with neurotic and borderline diagnoses, although occasionally the client with a diagnosis of multiple personality, post-traumatic stress disorder, or schizophrenia will engage in more serious self-damaging acts. Whatever the severity, self-mutilation can be very frightening for both client and therapist. An understanding of the goals and motivations of the self-injury, as well as an assessment of personal reactions to self-mutilating behavior, is essential to insure a therapeutic rather than a punitive, disgusted, or panicked response. Furthermore, although the therapist must be concerned about the behavior, she must avoid having the cessation of self-mutilation as the sole focus of the treatment.

Obviously the therapist must know about the self-mutilation before being able to treat it. The initial step is asking about and assessing any self-injurious practices, keeping in mind the broad range of behaviors that can be considered self-hurtful. The function of the behavior should be explored with the survivor. Identifying and discussing formerly hidden and shameful self-mutilating practices break the secrecy surrounding them while providing some measure of relief; nevertheless, the therapist must be careful to see the behavior as a means of coping with underlying distress and not further shame the client for her symptom manifestation.

Assessment of the severity and risk of the behavior is also necessary. According to Stone (1984), the borderline patient who is both depressed and hostile is at great risk. Conn (1986) wrote that the psychotic patient who is composed rather than agitated and who experiences command hallucinations or who is deeply religious and feels God is "telling" her to harm herself is in grave danger. Similarly, the persecutor personality of the multiple personality patient may attempt to hurt or destroy other personalities and thus pose a serious threat to the individual. The decision to treat self-mutilation on an outpatient basis depends on the seriousness of the behavior and the individual's degree of impulsivity and control. The therapist can sometimes contract with the survivor to limit or prevent self-injury.

Self-mutilating behavior is not the primary focus of treatment; rather, the underlying issues must be addressed. The therapist's role is to empathically connect to the survivor and to communicate concern about how her behavior is self-damaging. The therapist must avoid becoming the rescuer (and reinforcing the survivor's rescue fantasies) and must communicate to the survivor that she is responsible for her own behavior. Initially the treatment can be directed to limit-setting and finding less damaging methods to achieve her goals. As the therapy develops and the alliance deepens, the survivor can be encouraged to talk out or otherwise express her emotional turmoil. Alternative ways to relieve anxiety include imagery, acting out of the feelings, the toleration of increased levels of emotional discomfort and stress, and anger management techniques. Conn (1986) suggests that on occasion a neuroleptic antidepressant, or antianxiety medication may be useful. Drugs should be used with caution and with attention to any addictive potential. The use of any disinhibiting substances such as alcohol and illicit drugs should be discouraged, with Antabuse recommended to assist the alcoholic survivor in maintaining sobriety. Additional treatment suggestions can be found in Favazza (1987).

Suicidality

Several recent studies conducted on different populations (Bagley & Ramsey, 1985 — community; Briere, 1984, and Briere & Runtz, 1986 — clinical; Sedney & Brooks, 1984 — college) have compared the suicide histories of sexually abused versus nonabused populations. Each found a significant relationship between a history of sexual abuse and suicidal behavior in childhood and adulthood. Briere and Runtz specifically studied the relationship between child sexual abuse and subsequent suicidality and found that sexually abused clients were twice as likely as nonabused clients to have made at least one suicide attempt in the past and more frequently reported suicidal ideation at intake. Among the sexual abuse clients, they found greater suicidality to be correlated with multiple perpetrators, concurrent physical abuse, and abuse involving intercourse.

Russell (1986) has made the point that a history of child sexual abuse as a risk factor for suicidality has been unacknowledged until just recently and that the number of former victims driven to suicide will, of course, never be known. Krystal (1984) and other researchers of prolonged trauma have reported a little known cause of death—psychogenic death. It may be seen as a type of suicide but one that is not necessarily voluntary or deliberate; rather, it is due to a prolonged state of trauma. This form of death ensues after the individual has suffered "inescapable and unmodifiable peril" and has gone into a defensive stance of surrender or learned helplessness (Krystal, 1984). As numbing and depression become more pronounced over time, the individual closes down and loses both hope and the will to live. The process eventually culminates in death. Psychogenic death would most likely only occur as the result of the most prolonged, violent, and torturous incest; however, a striking number of survivors report losing the will to live or feeling hopeless and powerless.

Summit (1986) discussed how the option of suicide may provide the abused child and later the adult with some measure of control, relief, and hope. He labeled it as the "cherished out" that some survivors keep as their final option to be exercised if all else fails. He reported the case of an incest survivor who killed herself in his office building after deciding that death was preferable to the pain of working on her abuse issues. This particular woman left a legacy of her writings and artwork to Dr. Summit so he could use them in educating others about incest aftereffects.

Thus, the therapist working with incest survivors must recognize that they are more likely than other clients to present with both suicidal ideation and a history of past attempts. They may also make more current and more lethal attempts, may be more hopeless and "shut down," and may very well be intent on self-destruction. Some incest survivors will go through repeated suicidal crises during the course of therapy due to both their life circumstance and the pain associated with working through the trauma. Suicidality is especially likely when previously repressed memories and intense emotions surface. Rage reactions, in particular, may be self-directed in the early treatment stages, when the survivor is still self-blaming. Suicidal feelings may give way to homicidal ones when the rage gets directed outward during the course of treatment.

Suicide can provide a way to be in control, to ultimately wrest control from and punish the abuser. Suicidal ideation and attempts may also be related to negative self-perceptions, particularly shame, guilt, and self-hatred. The survivor may feel so badly about herself that she sees death as the punishment she deserves. A tragic recent example in my community was the 15-year-old who threw herself in front of a train as a means of stopping her stepfather's daily molestation. Finally, suicidal gestures and attempts can further constitute a "cry for help," especially when direct mention of the abuse has been forbidden.

Standard assessment and treatment strategies for suicidal clients apply.

A thorough suicide history (including a history of suicide by other members of the immediate family) is needed, along with an assessment of the survivor's motivations, intent, psychological state, and support network. The impulsive, drug-dependent, seriously depressed, and hopeless client is clearly at great risk, as is the survivor diagnosed as multiple personality and the psychotic client.

One other type of suicidal/self-destructive behavior deserves mention here since it provides a particular challenge to the clinician: the survivor who either directly provokes others to hurt her or who is caught in a violent relationship or lifestyle which she is unable to leave. Very often both therapist and client work hard to find alternatives to the dangerous lifestyle and behaviors only to have the client return to them. Many helpers have become so frustrated at what has been commonly termed "masochism" that they eventually give up in frustration or themselves act ragefully towards the client. Thus, they too become "sadistic abusers," with the client once again relating in her most accustomed way. The clinician must understand that the process is not masochism or the enjoyment of pain but rather quite the opposite: traumatic transference due to the tendency towards revictimization as learned behavior resulting from past abuse. The survivor who provokes aggressive responses or who continually returns to dangerous relationships and lifestyles tests the therapist differently but no less strenuously than the acutely suicidal client. Continual attention to the underlying pain is essential in working with these clients; their behavior must be interpreted in the context of the original and subsequent victimization. New ways of relating and of discharging emotion must be taught. In maintaining this therapeutic stance the clinician will benefit from consultation with colleagues familiar with the strength of the revictimization process.

Death

Although difficult to contemplate, death will sometimes be the result of self-mutilation, a suicide, a homicide within or outside of the context of an abusive relationship, substance abuse or an eating disorder, or provocation or risk-taking on the part of the survivor. The death of a client is highly stressful for the therapist whatever the circumstances. Therapists' reactions include feelings of grief, anger, loss, and sometimes depression. They might be further burdened by feelings associated with their professional role, namely guilt, responsibility, inadequacy, and fear of being seen as incompetent or of being investigated. It is critical that the therapist seek immediate support and consultation, and it may be beneficial to conduct or ask a colleague to conduct a psychological autopsy.

The therapist working with incest survivors, like those working with others at high risk for death and violence, must examine their own attitudes about the possibility of these outcomes. Further, the intensity of a client's self-destructive urges calls for equally intensive clinical intervention and reaction. The therapist must be prepared to offer this type of support or have ready access to professionals and facilities that can provide assistance during crises. It is also essential for the therapist (especially the solo practitioner) to have sources of support and consultation. Finally, therapists need to be aware of legal standards (involving right to treatment and to refuse treatment, confidentiality, duty to warn, involuntary hospitalization, safe houses and shelters, restraining orders, etc.) as they affect their clients.

The therapist must demonstrate caring and concern towards the survivor while simultaneously communicating that she is responsible for her behavior and its consequences. The therapist should also communicate that s/he will do all that is possible to assist the survivor and should explain the legal mandate to break confidentiality when there is a clear and present danger to the survivor or to someone else.

OTHER-DAMAGING BEHAVIOR

Abused males are much more likely than abused females to direct their anger towards others; nevertheless, some female survivors are violent and abusive towards family members and others. On a continuum of severity, types of other-damaging behaviors include:

- *Inability to sustain an intimate relationship and inadequate parenting*: This may include faulty or nonexistent bonding between partners and between parent and child, along with failure to nurture and protect children or extreme overprotection.
- *Abuse, deprivation and neglect*: Family members may be physically and emotionally neglected, deprived and abused. Emotional abuse may include unrelenting hostility and criticism as well as threats of destruction, violence and death.
- *Physical abuse*: Family members may be subjected to battering and other forms of physical abuse, sometimes resulting in permanent damage and physical maiming. Violence can also be perpetrated outside of the home.
- *Sexual abuse*: Family members may be subject to different forms of sexual abuse or nonprotection from abuse. Nonfamily members may also be sexually assaulted and abused.
- *The killing of pets*: Family members may be threatened with or forced to witness or participate in the killing of a family pet. Stone (1984) has identified the killing of pets as the strongest indicator of danger to humans in acting-out psychopathic borderline personalities. Green (1982) described a case in which a mother developed murderous impulses towards her daughter as a traumatic reenact-

ment of her own incestuous abuse at her daughter's age. This patient's killing of the family cat preceded her wish to kill her daughter and was an indication of high lethal intent to the therapist.
- *Homicide*: Family members and other individuals have been killed
due to uncontrollable rage, revenge, pathological jealousy, or self-
defense. Homicide of a family member, whether the abuser or the
abused, is not infrequently the outcome of extensive and progressive family violence. Batterers kill as their violence escalates; those
battered kill to escape the abuse or to prevent its recurrence
(Browne, 1987; Walker, 1984).

While emotional abuse, deprivation, and neglect may occur independently of other forms of abuse, frequently they occur in conjunction with
physical and sexual abuse. The therapeutic relationship may provide the
means of learning more effective and nurturing ways of relating; however,
such self-help groups as Parents Anonymous and 12-step programs, and
such psychoeducational groups as parent and the training Helfer "crash
course in childhood for adults who abuse" (described in Chapter 10) are
also necessary to break the abuse cycle.

The therapist is likely to have strong negative countertransference reactions to abuse and violence directed towards others (whether emotional or
physical). At times this abusiveness will be directed toward the therapist,
causing additional alarm and fear, as described by Walker (1979) in her work
with battered women. Of necessity, the therapist must assess his/her own
reactions to abusive behavior that may escalate to the point of homicide
and maintain sources of support, consultation, and management in the
event of an acute episode.

The therapist may be hard pressed to empathize with a client engaged
in other-damaging behavior. As with the self-abusive client, the therapist
should clearly establish the client's responsibility for his/her own actions
and offer support for the client's feelings but not for aggressive means of
expressing them. Although the past abuse of this client may not be addressed immediately, the therapist should consider the aggressive behavior
as a consequence of having been victimized. Nevertheless, the client who
is repetitively and compulsively abusive to others must be strongly confronted by the therapist. The therapist must guard against being "conned";
many of these individuals are notorious for their inability to empathize
with those they harm and for their denial of both their actions and their
damaging consequences. Many are also expert at rationalizing and minimizing their actions. Firm limitations on behavior, including strong consequences to be enacted if the behavior recurs, are necessary with this subpopulation.

The initial approach with the aggressive/abusive client is to identify the
abusive behavior and then to assess intent, ability to empathize, motiva-

tion to change, skills deficits, impulsivity, ability to control behavior, and substance abuse or other factors that serve as disinhibitors. In cases with high potential for violence, the therapist might want to establish a stringent contract with behavioral limitations and contingencies. Hospitalization or other forms of detention or containment might be needed to prevent violence. A therapy group for abusers might be a useful adjunct.

The therapist must be familiar with professional and legal mandates and local law enforcement policies regarding the violent and/or abusive client. In all states, therapists must report suspected or confirmed cases of ongoing child physical and sexual abuse. The therapist is obligated to break confidentiality and has a "duty to warn"* intended victims when s/he has reason to believe that a client's threat of violence is serious. The knowledge that the therapist will actually warn intended victims can be a strong deterrent for some clients, especially when the therapeutic alliance is a strong one. The client can be forewarned that this type of breach of confidentiality will alter the entire character of the therapeutic relationship and will prevent the therapist from functioning exclusively as an ally.

Some survivors come to view violence, particularly homicide, as the only solution available to them, in much the same way that suicidal clients see self-destruction as their only option. Furthermore, abusiveness towards others is the way that incestuous families deal with conflict and may therefore be seen as legitimate and expected behavior. For example, one of my clients described how she was contemplating killing her abusive parents and how she saw such a murder as justified. In her family, all three siblings were murderously enraged at the parents (for paternal incest and physical abuse and for maternal emotional neglect and nonprotection) and at one another. This client fully believed a court of law would find her innocent once they heard of her childhood story, which was in fact horrendous. She was unaware and surprised to learn that many of the battered women who kill out of desperation during current episodes of abuse are usually found guilty and incarcerated (Browne, 1987). She had not thought through the full consequences to herself of murdering her parents.†

The therapist must teach the violent client other ways to discharge and channel aggressive feelings and urge the breaking of violent patterns while supporting the legitimacy of the feelings. In addition, some clients experience all of their feelings as anger. The therapist can help them disentangle rage from other emotions as part of the emotional retraining of the therapy.

---

*Laws regarding "duty to warn" are still being debated and vary by state. Therapists must keep apprised of "duty to warn" obligations in their states.

†In a recent highly publicized case, Cheryl Pierson, an 18-year-old incest survivor, was sentenced to six months in jail for her role in planning her father's murder. She had pleaded guilty to manslaughter (Kleiman, 1987).

ADDICTIONS AND COMPULSIVE BEHAVIORS

In recent years clinicians treating dysfunctional (including alcoholic and incestuous) families have found that they often have multiple problems associated with regulation and control and that overlap exists between different types of family problems. Fossum and Mason (1986) have identified this pattern and determined that many of these families are shame-bound. In describing this type of family, they write:

> . . . a shame-bound family is a family with a self-sustaining, multigenerational system of interaction with a cast of characters who are (or were in their lifetime) loyal to a set of rules and injunctions demanding control, perfectionism, blame and denial. The pattern inhibits or defeats the development of authentic intimate relationships, promotes secrets and vague personal boundaries, unconsciously instills shame in the family members, as well as chaos in their lives, and binds them to perpetuate the shame in themselves and their kin. (Authors' italics, p. 8)

They further note that addictions and different types of compulsive behaviors are mechanisms used by these families to defend against their shame issues:

> We find themes of the shame-bound family when people are *compulsively abusing themselves* in all the countless ways they can do so: abusing drugs and alcohol, physically inflicting pain or injury, overworking, overexercising, or starving themselves. We recognize the same theme when people are *compulsively abusing others*, whether it be child abuse of spouse abuse and whether the abuse be physical, sexual, or emotional.
> The pattern is recognizable in many different behaviors which we have come to identify as compulsive. They include *compulsions related to money and material goods*, such as compulsive shopping, overspending, hoarding, saving, and shoplifting. They include many compulsions *related to sexuality*, such as compulsive voyeurism, exhibitionism, masturbation, affairs and casual encounters, use of pornography, obscene phone calls, incest and rape. This host of compulsive behaviors includes *compulsions related to food*, as in anorexia nervosa, bulimia, obsessive dieting and overeating. We are also coming to see the shame-bound system as a recognizable pattern in *agoraphobia* and some *psychosomatic* problems. (pp. 9–10)

Since incest survivors often come from shame-bound families, they and their relatives suffer from many of these addictions and compulsions either directly or in association with one another. For example, a survivor from an alcoholic family may herself not be alcoholic but she may have a history of being involved with alcoholic partners (codependency). Or she may not directly abuse her children but may be involved in a relationship where both she and her children are abused. Two of the most common addictive/compulsive problems seen among survivors, chemical dependency and eating disorders, are discussed here with suggested therapeutic strategies. Other compulsions are discussed elsewhere in this chapter.

Chemical Dependency

The correlation between chemical dependency and abuse has been noted repeatedly. That incest often occurs in the context of an alcoholic family or when the abuser has used alcohol or drugs is now well documented. A history of incest in the background of a sizable percentage of alcoholic women has also been identified. Myers (n.d.) has provided a graphic description of the role drug and alcohol abuse can play for the incest victim:

> I was 11 years old when I first discovered that drugs could make the terrible world around me disappear. I began sniffing glue to get out of my pain, and it worked. Drugs became my great escape; there was nothing I wouldn't try in order to get high. I never knew how I'd feel dealing with different people, but, on drugs, I could be anything I wanted to be. . . . I could be pretty, have a good family, a nice father, a strong mother, and be happy. When I was on drugs, I felt high, happy, and in control of my life. . . .
>
> People said that taking too many drugs would burn out your brains. I used to think that I could become a vegetable if only I could succeed in burning out my brains. I *wanted* to become a vegetable. . . .
>
> I developed a kind of love/trust relationship with drugs that I had never had with people. I knew they would never fail me the way people had. I could be sure about what the drugs would do to me; I had found a way to feel good and happy — even if it was with drugs instead of people.

Concerning alcohol:

> For me, drinking had the opposite effect of drugs, . . . Drinking got me back into my pain; it allowed me to express my anger (which, of course, I couldn't do on drugs because I couldn't feel any pain). I used to get off on feeling depressed, on examining how rotten my childhood had been, and how lonely it was to be a kid. I played sad records when I was drunk and let the tears come pouring out.
>
> When I started drinking, I was much too young to buy alcohol so I got older people to buy it for me. They were usually men, and since they were always interested in sex, I always had something with which to pay. . . .
>
> I also got more physically self-destructive when I was drinking. I could tolerate more physical pain when I was drunk: I had been drinking when I burned my arms and during several suicide attempts. I could express my anger under the influence of alcohol, and I purposely started fights so my boyfriends would beat me up. I felt I deserved it. I also remember longing for human closeness, for physical contact of any kind that would prove others were paying attention to me.
>
> Drinking and drugs put me in touch with different feelings and different people. Drugs made me feel mellow and accepting and gave me passive people from whom it was easy to detach myself both physically and emotion-

ally. Drugs allowed me to be alone in my own world and made me numb to my other painful reality. By embracing the violence with my own self-destructiveness, I tried to prove that I could withstand any amount of pain and hurt. Neither of them gave me what I needed, but, in a negative way, they gave me ways of coping with what I had. (pp. 11–12)

Chemical dependency carries more stigma for women than for men and continues to be more hidden; consequently, it is a less recognized and less treated problem among women. The incest survivor who is drug-dependent often feels doubly stigmatized and may be careful to hide her addiction. During assessment and treatment, the therapist must ask about alcohol and drug use, as well as about the family history of chemical dependency.

Two main patterns are in evidence (similar to the two veteran patterns described by Jelinek and Williams, 1987). The first involves the survivor who had a family history of alcohol abuse and/or who was chemically dependent before as well as after the abuse. The second involves the survivor who began to abuse alcohol and drugs after the trauma to relieve stress and to self-medicate. Different treatment is necessary for each. In the first case, where there is a lifelong history of substance abuse and the survivor is clearly chemically dependent, she should be encouraged to enter a drug/alcohol detoxification program. The incest therapy is secondary and only becomes primary when the survivor achieves sobriety (sometimes with the help of Antabuse). Survivors in such treatment programs can be forewarned that as they progress in their detoxification they may begin to experience more intense symptoms of PTSD, since alcohol/drugs have been found to suppress these symptoms.

A study by Kovach (1983) offered research support for this position. She found that incest survivors in recovery differ from their nonabused counterparts. They were significantly more depressed and exhibited a greater degree of covert and overt anxiety. They developed a drinking problem at a younger age, perceived themselves to have experienced a greater number of traumatic life events, and reported a greater incidence of sexual dysfunction prior to abusive drinking. They also experienced a higher level of psychological stress during recovery.

In the second group, PTSD is the primary problem with chemical use secondary, a means the survivor has used to cope with the discomfort of intrusive symptoms. The incest can be treated directly with this group. As abuse issues are resolved and PTSD symptoms decrease in intensity and frequency, it is likely that alcohol and drug use will similarly decrease. With this group, the therapist wants to carefully monitor drug use and determine whether it is in fact controllable and decreasing with the PTSD symptoms. If not, involvement in a treatment program of some sort is called for.

Many survivors who themselves are not chemically dependent have developed patterns of codependency. When such a pattern is identified, involvement in Al-Anon, Adult Children of Alcoholics, or a similarly oriented self-help or therapy group is to be recommended.

Eating Disorders

In recent years an interface between eating disorders and child sexual abuse has become apparent to clinicians specializing in the treatment of each population. The following issues have been found to overlap between the two groups: concerns having to do with intimacy, shame, low self-esteem, mistrust of others, guilt, conflict and anxiety about sexuality, a negative body image, the need to succeed, and powerlessness and depression. Both groups also have problems with substance abuse and self-destructive behavior. Smolak, Levine and Sullins (1987) further comment: "In this same vein child sexual experiences and contributing conditions could also promote other prominent components of the psychopathology of eating disorders, such as mistrust of internal experiences (e.g., anger and sexual feelings), distorted body image, and even a relentless drive to perfect and purify one's body" (p. 2). In addition, eating disorders develop as a means to achieve control, as self-abuse, as a means of self-nourishment or, just the opposite, as a means of physically representing the non-nourishing atmosphere of the family.

A history of sexual abuse has been most frequently associated with bulimia, but it seems to have a relationship with compulsive overeating and anorexia as well. Sexual abuse alone does not cause an eating disorder nor is an eating disorder always the outcome of abuse. However, Kearney-Cooke (in press) has suggested that "abusive sexual experiences, as well as the feelings of powerlessness which result from them, can be important contributing factors in the development of an eating disorder and require specific treatment."

Like substance abuse problems, shame-based eating disorders are often hidden problems brought to treatment. The survivor should be asked during assessment or early in treatment about any eating disturbances and whether other family members have such a history. Treatment approaches resemble those just discussed for chemical dependency. An eating disorder of life-threatening proportions should receive primary treatment focus with incest treatment scheduled subsequently. Otherwise treatment should focus on the incest issues which underlie the eating problem, particularly body image distortions and negative feelings about sexuality. Kearney-Cooke (in press) has reported a 90% reduction in binge-purge frequency and substantial improvement in psychological functioning among bulimic women whose treatment included a focus on the aftereffects of child sexual abuse.

I have noted an intensification of eating difficulties among my clients during the course of treatment as their PTSD symptoms intensified. Usually, compulsive overeating is used as a means of dissociating from abuse issues that are being consciously addressed. Survivors from families characterized by alcoholism or compulsive overeating revert to this behavior as feelings intensify. Referral to Overeaters Anonymous or another support group is often necessary. As incest issues are addressed and symptoms become less intense and as the survivor addresses the function of eating disorders and comes to better accept herself, these disorders can be expected to abate.

SEXUALITY AND SEXUAL DIFFICULTIES

In their book *Incest and Sexuality*, Maltz and Holman (1987) stated:

Sexuality is a very sensitive and emotionally charged subject for incest survivors. (p. 1)

Incest lacks all the essential conditions for positive, healthy sexuality. (p. 11)

Incest profoundly influences what female survivors learn about sex and what they come to believe is expected sex-role behavior. (p. 52)

For many survivors, sexuality has become confused with sexual abuse, even though intellectually they understand there is a difference. (p. 7)

These statements should not be taken to mean that every incest survivor will have sexual concerns or specific sexual problems, but rather that incest can have a profound, sometimes very subtle, and often very serious, impact on sexuality. It distorts the victim's self-worth, violates her body integrity, and distorts the meaning of love and intimacy.

According to the available research evidence, concerns about sexuality, as well as problems with sexual functioning and developing satisfying sexual relationships, are very likely in a clinical population of incest survivors. Negative self-concept, including body alienation, and sexual, interpersonal, and sex-role distortions and misperceptions are usually at the root of sexual difficulties. Relationship problems and specific sexual dysfunctions were discussed in Chapter 6 (see p. 107). To briefly recapitulate, the sexual effects of incest are most pronounced in three areas: (1) sexual emergence in adulthood, (2) sexual orientation or preference, and (3) sexual arousal, response, and satisfaction (Maltz & Holman, 1987).

A sexual concern or relationship difficulty may be the reason a survivor initiates therapy. Nadelson (1982) has noted that a request for sex therapy may be a way for a client to avoid painful discussion or confrontation about sexual abuse. More commonly, concerns about sexual functioning arise during treatment and are only discussed with great difficulty due to the degree of shame involved or because the survivor feels hopeless about ever overcoming the sexual aftereffects of the abuse. Whenever sexual concerns are expressed, the therapist needs to make a preliminary determination about their cause and severity. If the sexual problem is due to a medical problem, lack of awareness, or sexual ignorance, a minor intervention may be all that is needed. However, in the majority of cases, the sexual difficulty is more complicated, is a direct result of the incest, and requires extensive treatment of the effects of the abuse itself.

Annon (1976) has developed a useful treatment model which has been recommended specifically for sexual problems arising from sexual victimization by Becker and Skinner (1984) and Sprei and Courtois (1988). His P-LI-SS-IT treatment model is organized in hierarchical treatment stages;

(1) *Permission* to do or not do something. In the case of the survivor, this may be permission to refuse certain forms of sexual activity or to try others.

(2) *Limited Information* about sexual physiology, sexual functioning, sexuality and sex roles. Because many survivors were misinformed about sex, sex education, including specific information about incest/sexual abuse, may be reassuring and provide relief.

(3) *Specific Suggestions* involves the assignment of behavioral exercises and strategies. With permission, information, and participation in suggested exercises, sexual concerns and difficulties may abate rapidly.

(4) *Intensive Therapy* involves the exploration of abuse issues as causative of the sexual difficulty.

Maltz and Holman (1987) have noted that sexual concerns are usually best addressed after the survivor has addressed incest concerns, including self-worth, responsibility for the abuse, and negative sexual conditioning. She may only then be ready to reclaim her sexuality as something positive and in her control. Thus, many survivors will need all five stages of the P.L1.SS-IT model.

Before working directly on sexual issues, the survivor can do many things for herself to feel better about her body and to increase her sense of sexual and interpersonal competence. Specifically, she can engage in self-nurturing practices and exercises designed to help her learn about and value her body. Learning to behave assertively in general and especially in intimate relationships is also useful. Through reading and discussion she can be sure she has accurate information about sexuality and sexual functioning. In particular, she must learn to distinguish loving from exploitive sex and begin the process of differentiating past abuse from present sexual functioning. She can then focus on learning about her own sexual responsiveness through self-stimulation exercises. Once she has more information, more comfort, and more control, she is in a better position to be sexual with a partner and to develop an intimate relationship.

Maltz and Holman (1987) point out the difficulties faced by a survivor's partner in working through sexual concerns. They view the partner as a secondary victim of the incest and underscore the necessity for communication and openness on the part of both the survivor and her partner. The therapist can find specific treatment recommendations for various sexual difficulties (e.g., specific aversions, flashbacks and dissociation during sex, and involvement of the partner) in Maltz and Holman and in Sprei and Courtois (1988). Both sets of authors emphasize that some survivors may not be able to fully reverse the effects of the abuse or to achieve full resolution of sexual concerns; nonetheless, improvement in sexual self-esteem and reclamation of personal sexuality are achievable.

MEDICAL TREATMENT

Many survivors had negative medical experiences in childhood. These most often were the result of the indirect behavioral and somatic cues to sexual abuse and the medical profession's ignorance about and denial of sexual abuse. Four types of negative medical experiences are most commonly described by survivors:

(1) *Missed diagnosis of sexual and/or physical abuse* due to professional ignorance or denial of the problem despite obvious signs of such abuse (no less an eminent pediatrician than C. Everett Koop, Surgeon General of the United States, has recently admitted that he overlooked obvious signs of abuse in many of the children he treated due to lack of available information about child abuse and a disbelief that parents could so injure their own children) (Rovner, 1987). Many survivors describe having had serious somatic difficulties for which no medical diagnosis could be found. Even obvious signs of abuse aroused little or no suspicion or were denied (Sgroi, 1977). In contrast some survivors were fearful that medical personnel *would* detect signs of abuse, which they sought to hide.

(2) *Unnecessary or ineffective treatment* based on lack of awareness and misdiagnosis. Some survivors underwent surgeries, hospitalizations, drug regimens, shock treatments, and years of psychotherapy to treat the somatic manifestations of their abuse experiences.

(3) *Insensitive treatment by medical personnel.* This was especially true if they were seen as malingering, diagnosed as suffering from psychosomatic illness, or were phobic, adversarial, or uncooperative about medical procedures and towards medical personnel.

(4) *Abuse by medical personnel.* Abuse of patients by medical and mental health personnel has been recognized only of late. Evidence is accumulating that incest survivors are more vulnerable to

revictimization, in general and at the hands of professionals (de Young, 1981a; Russell, 1986).

The critical role of medical personnel in the diagnosis and treatment of sexual and physical abuse of children has been recognized only since the mid-1970s. When today's survivors were children, abuse was not acknowledged unless it was too flagrant to be ignored. Four areas of concern to survivors in receiving medical treatment are discussed here together with strategies for their management: medical personnel; medical examinations and procedures; drugs; and hospitalization.

Medical Personnel

Medical personnel may be especially frightening for survivors by virtue of their being authority figures who have been imbued with a great deal of power and control. This is especially true of doctors because formerly, almost all were male. Additionally, medical personnel are feared because they treat the body and because their procedures and techniques involve touch and a full spectrum of invasive practices and techniques. Medical training has over the years been so technically focused as to almost ignore the treatment of the whole person. Established medical and clinical protocols not infrequently leave little room for the human dimension and result in the perception of a "white coat wall" by the population at large as well as by incest survivors.

Several problematic ways that survivors deal with medical personnel, particularly doctors, have been identified. The survivor might cope by complete avoidance of health maintenance, even in the face of obvious problems. This is a strategy most evident with the client who is highly anxious, phobic, dissociated and/or engaged in self-neglect and passive self-damage. One of my clients told me that she would rather die than seek medical treatment.

Another coping mechanism involves overcompliance or superficial compliance, even when not in the survivor's best interest. Survivors may feel that they have to listen to the doctor no matter what and that they have no right to ask for information, challenge the doctor, or even seek out a more compatible or human physician. For example, several of my clients never discussed preexisting medical conditions that could complicate their treatment with their doctor because they didn't want to bother him.

The opposite, oppositionalism, is another coping mechanism. The survivor who is hostile to other authority figures may extend this same style to medical personnel. This in turn usually forecloses any possibility of a doctor-patient alliance and can result in self-fulfilling negative treatment by medical personnel. Some survivors reenact the trauma of their abuse by finding an authority figure to abuse them or to assist in their self-mutilation.

The therapist can help by first understanding and accepting the survivor's feelings and establishing their legitimacy given her abuse experiences and any past negative experience with medical personnel. Relaxation, hypnotic and desensitization techniques, and assertiveness training may be of assistance. It may be particularly useful to discuss where the survivor can exert control and to use role play in preparation. The client should also be encouraged to "shop" for medical personnel and to see herself as a consumer. She should seek out a medical practitioner with whom she feels comfortable, who is fully accredited, and who shows personal sensitivity and a willingness to work with the survivor's individual concerns. She should be able to see her doctor as her ally rather than her enemy.

The medical practitioner can also be forewarned about and prepared for the client's concerns and reactions. In many instances I have found it useful for the survivor to disclose (or give me permission to disclose) that psychological trauma is at the root of her difficulties. In some cases and at the survivor's discretion the incest has been revealed; in others the physician has been told only that a traumatic episode occurred.

Physicians usually appreciate knowing about a patient's incest experience and its aftermath so they can vary their protocols and procedures to accommodate and not exacerbate the difficulties.

Maryann was extremely anxious during any medical procedure but never disclosed this to her doctor or his staff for fear that they would think she was being childish. She underwent a rather routine surgical procedure in a teaching hospital where a number of residents observed and participated. One was assigned to begin an IV tube but had difficulty and made several attempts before his supervisor took over. As a result, Maryann became so anxious she hyperventilated, resulting in cancellation of the surgery. She blamed herself for "being such a baby"; not until she discussed the situation in her therapy group did she get feedback that she needed to discuss her anxiety reactions with her doctor to avoid a repeat experience. She subsequently had additional surgery which went more smoothly because her doctor, forewarned, organized her treatment differently, with no observers and a senior staff member beginning her anesthesia.

Medical Examinations and Procedures

The survivor may experience any type of medical treatment as negative because it involves touching or is otherwise invasive. In particular, pelvic, breast, and rectal examinations may be directly reminiscent of the abuse and nearly intolerable for some survivors. Procedures like catherization, intravenous treatment, or surgery are also fear and panic-provoking, as are such additional aspects of treatment as being confined and in the control of one or more authority figures. Such procedures may stimulate direct kinesthetic memory of the abuse or precipitate flashbacks or dissociative episodes.

The survivor may fear having her body exposed and may hold the belief that anyone looking at her will somehow know of her abuse. Of course, the fears of some survivors are realistic, since some have been scarred or otherwise injured by their abuse or through self-inflicted punishment. Medical garb, instruments, and environments further contribute to fear and insecurity. Finally, bureaucratic procedures and delays can be close to intolerable for some survivors. This is due to the fact that waiting and the accompanying fear were part of their abuse experience. The bureaucratization of medicine and the seeming disregard for punctuality by some medical practitioners can have a very negative impact on some survivors.

The same strategies discussed above for medical personnel pertain to medical procedures as well. Additionally, the survivor can be coached to ask questions about medical examinations and procedures—their purpose, how they are done, their duration, whether they will involve pain and discomfort, etc. The survivor can also be encouraged to fully discuss any previous problems with medical procedures with the physician or staff and any special concerns about safety, modesty, pain, etc. In the case of a terrified or intensely phobic client, protocols may need to be substantially altered and the client desensitized as much as possible. Typically, it is necessary for the physician to take more time than usual and to fully explain what s/he is doing and for what reason. At times it may be necessary for drugs or even anesthesia to be administered, although some survivors may react negatively to the lack of control involved with their use.

I have also found that on occasion it is therapeutic for the therapist to accompany the survivor to the doctor's and even to go through the medical procedure with her. This seems to be especially beneficial when issues of safety are paramount. The implications of doing so, including possible changes in the therapeutic relationship, should be discussed fully with the survivor.

Adele had been molested by her brother and subsequently in adolescence by a male gynecologist. It took several years in therapy, innumerable discussions, and intensive relaxation training and desensitization before she agreed to schedule a routine gynecological examination, which was necessitated by severe menstrual problems. It took months of trying before this client found a female physician and office staff she felt comfortable with. I decided to accompany her to establish her safety and to coach her through the experience.

This client had very high needs for control in this situation. We began by planning that the initial visit would involve only a verbal consultation with the doctor and preparing a list of questions for her to ask. Once she felt comfortable with the doctor and received assurances that no procedure would be done against her will, she was able to be examined. The examination proceeded with the physician and I using humor to relieve her tension, the physician explaining every step of the procedure in advance, with my holding her hand, urging her to breathe and relax, and reassuring and grounding her when she unexpectedly experienced a flashback during the examination.

This experience was very beneficial because Adele felt some measure of control and, more importantly, felt safe and unviolated. Our therapeutic relationship was strengthened as a result of this intervention.

Drug Treatment

Drug treatment (whether for psychological or physical distress) may have negative connotations for some survivors, principally those whose abuse involved being drugged and those who fear that drugs will cause them to totally lose control or will signify that they are crazy. Drugs may also be perceived negatively by survivors who have had addictive problems themselves or who grew up in addicted families. The survivor may refuse recommended drug treatment or resist or sabotage its effectiveness. On the other hand, some survivors self-medicate with drugs to relieve anxiety and to lessen symptoms of physiological arousal.

Yost (1987), in discussing the psychopharmacologic management of post-traumatic stress disorder, recommended a conservative approach on the part of the clinician. He stated:

> As a general principle, I feel psychotropic medications [for] . . . stress syndromes should not be prescribed as a matter of routine. They should be used to treat those symptoms of anxiety, depression and sleep disturbance that seriously interfere with other modalities of treatment and so impair the individual that he or she cannot function adequately in the work place or in daily social activities.
>
> If a substance abuse problem exists, the primary focus of treatment should be to correct this difficulty first before proceeding to deal with anxiety and/or depression. Unfortunately, all too many victims of trauma turn to alcohol . . . to relieve anxiety or promote sleep. Even if the individual did not abuse alcohol before the traumatic event, he or she may find it provides some symptom relief in the denial phase of the disorder. Do not neglect to carefully elicit a history of substance use and other medications the individual might be taking before proceeding with the anti-anxiety or antidepressant medication. (pp. 94–95)

When the clinician has decided that symptoms are severe enough to warrant evaluation for psychotropic medications, the topic must be approached carefully. Reasons for the recommendation need to be clearly articulated, and the therapist must indicate a willingness to fully discuss both the rationale and the survivor's questions and reservations.

Some survivors are eager to try a medication to achieve some symptom relief. Others are suspicious and take the recommendation as a concrete sign that the therapist secretly thinks that they are hopeless or, worse, insane. The decision ultimately rests with the survivor, although the therapist must be clear about the consequences of her choice. For example, therapy is likely to proceed very slowly or even to be ineffective for the survivor suffering from a major depressive disorder who refuses an antidepressant.

The process can be achieved in stages, particularly with a very reluctant survivor. The first stage is to have an evaluation. Optimally, this with is a psychiatrist with whom the therapist has a good working relationship, who will completely explain recommended drugs and rationale for their use, who maintains follow-up contact with patients, and who is sensitive to issues of sexual abuse. The second stage, when a medication trial is recommended, is for the client to learn about the medication, its benefits and side effects, and the duration of treatment. Next the survivor begins the medication and monitors both physical and psychological reactions as the dosage is adjusted. Symptom relief is often positive reinforcement for reluctant and anxious clients. Difficulties arise when the survivor gets no symptom relief, suffers uncomfortable side effects, or maintains control by not following directions. The therapist must firmly yet gently interpret reasons for noncompliance and monitor reactions to the medication. When a particular drug fails, others are usually tried. As noted by Yost (1987, p. 99), "successfully encouraging the patient to persist usually requires a strong therapeutic alliance between the patient and physician (p. 99)." On occasion, the drug trial needs to be abandoned due to lack of effectiveness, noncompliance or paradoxical reactions where, instead of promoting symptom relief, the drug increases symptoms or triggers decompensation. Another possibility is that the diagnosis is wrong and may need to be reconsidered. This has been noted with multiple personality disorder in particular.

Drugs prescribed for physical illness may cause similar concerns. Fears concerning drugs should be taken seriously, especially as they relate to a survivor's history. The therapist can support and monitor the survivor's reactions and teach assertive and consumer skills (as described earlier) to assist the survivor in becoming as knowledgeable and therefore in control as possible. Occasionally, it may be necessary to use desensitization and hypnosis to decrease anxiety.

Hospitalization

Hospitalization, whether for psychological or physical concerns, most often involves all three of the problem areas described above as well as more lengthy confinement and the administration of additional procedures by anonymous medical specialists. As such, it can be terrifying for survivors. Should a client need to be hospitalized for any reason during the course of therapy, the experience should be carefully monitored due to its potential for distress, including regression and decompensation. The therapist can begin by inquiring about any specific concerns or fears the survivor might have and how she has fared in the past with other medical procedures. The therapist can then offer assistance according to what the survivor might need to insure as successful a hospitalization experience as possible. Usually, information alleviates some distress. It might also be helpful for the survivor to do some reading on patient rights and how to assertively deal with medical personnel.

Psychiatric hospitalization may be especially stressful. It may be necessitated by severe depression, acute suicidal, homicidal or mutilating episodes, debilitating bouts of depression, rage and anxiety, life-threatening eating disorders or addictions, decompensation and psychosis. If at all possible the therapist should encourage that hospitalization be voluntary rather than involuntary so that the survivor has some sense of control. In such a circumstance, the reasons favoring hospitalization should be discussed in detail, along with the ramifications of opting for hospitalization. For example, one of my clients was relieved when we discussed that her employer should be told she was hospitalized but did not need to know where or for what reason. The stigma associated with psychiatric hospitalization is another reason it should be fully discussed. Hospitalization might have a negative impact on the survivor's self-perception by reinforcing her belief that she is crazy or unable to cope. Whenever possible, family members and/or friends can be enlisted to assist with the decision and to offer support. The therapist can expect that the decision to be hospitalized will always involve some measure of ambivalence and at times active resistance.

Of course, such preparation is virtually impossible in an emergency situation involving imminent danger. At those times it is often necessary to involve the police and to use an ambulance for transportation to the hospital. Even so, if at all possible at the time or after the crisis has passed, the reasons for hospitalization should be explained and the issue of stigma discussed.

Continuity of contact between therapist and survivor should be maintained throughout the hospital stay. Whenever feasible, the therapist should continue to be active in treatment planning and implementation, as the client's primary therapist and as a member of the treatment team. Because of the prominence of trust, betrayal, separation, abandonment and rejection issues, the extent of and reasons for the therapist's involvement or non-involvement should be discussed fully with the survivor.

The length of stay will be determined by the type of admission (whether voluntary or involuntary) and the laws governing required length of stay, as well as the severity of the client's admission status, her progress during hospitalization, and her economic circumstances and insurance coverage.

Discharge can be quite stressful, particularly when hospitalization was required during an acute episode and/or was lengthy. Family members and friends should be enlisted to give intensive support in the period immediately following discharge. The therapist might also arrange to have frequent phone contact and to meet on a more frequent basis postdischarge. Further, the client should be prepared for the transition to her normal daily activities. Client and therapist can discuss how she will handle the return to her normal schedule and inquiries into her whereabouts and the reasons for her hospitalization. Feelings of stigma and shame should continue to be explored postdischarge.

This chapter has highlighted special problems and issues which might arise during the course of incest therapy. Incest survivors often exhibit numbing and intrusive symptoms in treatment and have difficulties with self- and other-damaging behaviors, addictions, and compulsions, sexual functioning and medical treatment. Suggestions for management of these problems were reviewed.

CHAPTER 15

Special Family Issues

INEVITABLY, MANY SPECIAL issues involving the family surface during therapy. The most prominent are disclosure of the incest to family and friends, confrontation of the abuser and other family members, and reporting of any current abuse of minor children within the family. A less common issue, but one holding great interest for some survivors, is legal action in the form of a civil suit seeking redress for incest injuries.

Survivors must also decide how to interact with their families of origin—whether to maintain full or limited contact or to "divorce" themselves from the family. Limited contact or total estrangement often leads a survivor to "refamily" with her partner and children or to find a surrogate family, people with whom she can develop family bonds and traditions and with whom she can celebrate special occasions and holidays. Whether family interaction is chosen or not, the issue of forgiveness typically arises at some point during treatment. The survivor wrestles with self-forgiveness as well as forgiveness of the abuser and other family members. Finally, incest and its aftermath often cause secondary victimization of a survivor's partner or other loved ones. These secondary victims often benefit from education, reassurance, a support and self-help group or therapy to cope with their own reactions and to support the survivor.

DISCLOSURE TO FAMILY MEMBERS AND OTHERS

As we have seen, societal and familial denial of incest and incest dynamics locks victims into patterns of secrecy and silence. Forced silence is traumatic; it constitutes a secondary trauma whose importance is often overlooked (Lister, 1982). Nowhere is the blackmail of incest more obvious than in this forced silence. Herman (1981) succinctly summarized the issue of disclosure for incest survivors when she wrote that disclosure is both longed for and feared. Victims long for someone to notice and to assist them but fear disbelief, blame, and disavowal instead. As we have noted, these fears are well-founded. Even when a victim dares to make a disclosure or when the incest is obvious to family members or others, assistance and intervention are not guaranteed. An inadequate response makes further attempts at disclosure more difficult, if not impossible.

We now know from available research that approximately half of all incest victims made an attempt at disclosure at the time of the incest and that most responses were unfavorable. Herman provided a description of the typical disclosure scenario of father-daughter incest undertaken at the time of the incest which illustrates the problems faced by the victim:

> Disclosure disrupts whatever fragile equilibrium has been maintained, jeopardizes the functioning of all family members, increases the likelihood of violent and desperate behavior and places everyone, but particularly the daughter, at risk for retaliation.
>
> The precipitant for disclosure is often a change in the terms of the incestuous relationship which makes it impossible for the daughter to endure it any longer.
>
> Once the decision to break secrecy has been made, the daughter must find a person to confide in. Often the daughter is too alienated from her mother to trust her with this secret. In an effort to ensure a protective response, she frequently bypasses her mother and seeks help from someone outside the family.
>
> For the mother, whether or not she suspected the incestuous relationship, disclosure of the secret is utterly shattering. First of all, she feels betrayed by her husband and daughter. But in addition to her personal feelings of hurt and outrage, she must cope with the knowledge that her marriage and livelihood are in jeopardy. . . .
>
> For the father, the disclosure is likewise a threat to his entire way of life. He stands to lose not only the sexual contact he craves, but also his wife, his family, his job, and even his liberty. Faced with this overwhelming threat, most commonly the father adopts a stance of outraged denial. He does whatever he can to discredit his daughter and to rally his wife to his side. All too often, this strategy succeeds. . . .
>
> Without active outside intervention, then, the daughter is greatly at risk within her family once the incest secret has been revealed. By defying her father's orders to maintain secrecy, she has in effect made him her enemy. Her mother was never a strong ally, and in a crisis she cannot be depended upon. If nothing is done to protect the daughter, the chances are great that the parental couple will unite against her and virtually drive her out of the family.
>
> For this reason, the person to whom the incest secret is revealed bears a heavy burden of responsibility. (1981, pp. 131–133)

Although this scenario is, unhappily, the most typical, some victims were fortunate to have received responses that were comforting and empathic and interventions which stopped the abuse. Such responses do not negate the experience of having been abused but they certainly help to ameliorate some of the effects. At the very least, the victim learns that someone believed her and that she was seen as important enough for them to intervene.

Disclosures made in adulthood offer a somewhat greater likelihood of positive response than those made in childhood or adolescence; yet, responses all too often remain inadequate. The survivor of incest in the nuclear family has a greater likelihood of receiving a supportive and empathic response from friends and distant relatives than from closer relatives. Although years may have elapsed since the incest occurred, making the family situation less conflicted and volatile than it was then, if the family received no outside assistance the dysfunctional patterns of interaction tend to persist. Responses to adult disclosure reflect these dysfunctional patterns. For many survivors, therapy may be the first time anyone ever asked about the possibility of childhood sexual abuse and the first time they ever disclosed its occurrence. Even then, some get no further than making a disclosure and either leave therapy or later recant their story.

Herman (1981) recommended that at some point during treatment, if it has not been done before, the incest secret be shared with at least one person besides the therapist. This recommendation is well-founded. The privacy and confidentiality of the therapist's office, so instrumental in fostering trust, inadvertently provide for the maintenance of secrecy. Some survivors find it easiest and safest to disclose to others who have also had incest experience and so seek out a therapy or support group. They may choose not to divulge the incest to anyone other than group members. Others find that they want to disclose to other family members, to partners, or to close friends. Preparation for these disclosures can be done in individual or group treatment but group is by far the better choice. It provides a place for sharing disclosure experiences, for brainstorming strategies and exploring options, for rehearsing, and for supporting disclosure attempts whatever their outcome. In a group, the survivor has what she did not have as a child: a support system which validates her experience as well as her right to disclose it and to expect a response.

Whether in group or individual therapy, survivors should be cautioned against making impulsive or unprepared disclosures. These hold greater potential for disappointment than do disclosures that are planned. It should be stressed that careful preparation does not, in and of itself, insure a positive outcome or an appropriate response. Rather, its goal is to assist the survivor in examining her motivations and expectations and in determining strategy and timing. She is also encouraged to anticipate and prepare for a range of possible responses.

Therapist and survivor can begin by reviewing any child abuse disclosures she or other members of her family have made in the past. The therapist will want to know when attempts at disclosure were made in the family, by whom, to whom, how they were made, how they were received, and how they affected the survivor at the time or later. Their impact on current or future disclosures should also be determined. It is not unusual to find that disclosure made outside the family had a more positive outcome than disclosure within, a fact that is infuriating and disheartening to many abuse survivors. Disclosure within the family most often results not in acknowledgement but in continued patterns of denial, minimization and scapegoating, even when more than one victim discloses. Multiple disclosures, as described in the following case example, are not unusual. Quite often, siblings are unaware that anyone else in the family has been abused until such a disclosure.

Judy joined an incest therapy group because no one in her family would take disclosures made by her and her older sister seriously. Several years before, her sister had written a letter to every member of their family except her father, the abuser, informing them of his long-term molestation of her. The letter was virtually ignored by all family members except Judy, who tried to support her sister but did not reveal her own abuse. While in therapy, Judy decided to divulge her experience to her sister, who by that time had broken off ties with the family due to her anger and disillusionment. She was unreceptive to Judy, saying she no longer wanted to even discuss things that had happened in their crazy family. Judy was crushed and felt guilty for her previous inability to disclose at a time that might have strengthened her sister's effort. She turned to the group for support.

In planning for current or future disclosures, it is advisable to explore the survivor's motivations and expectations, as well as her level of functioning, including resolution of incest issues and personality dynamics. It is equally important to discern the possible responses of those to whom she will make her revelation. Survivor motivations and expectations vary. The most common reasons for disclosure, whether to family members, partners or friends, include: making the incest real to oneself and one's family; sharing it as an important life event and important influence on the survivor's life; seeking validation and personal support for its occurrence and effects; seeking relief from guilt; ventilating anger and seeking revenge; preventing the abuse of other children in the family; and attempting to reconstitute the family. Each of these motivations should be explored in depth. The survivor needs to approach disclosure with realistic, achievable expectations. At minimum, she must not look to disclosure to validate *for her* that the incest occurred, because she might be met with a wall of denial. Nor should she expect that disclosure will result in a supportive and harmonious family. Survivors who are in crisis unrelated to abuse should be encouraged to wait for a less stressful time since disclosure can precipitate a crisis. She is better able to handle the effects of disclosure, whatever they might be, if other aspects of her life are relatively stable.

Dynamics from the incest experience can be recapitulated in the disclosure process, just as they can in the therapy process and relationship. The therapist must assess the survivor's transference issues to assist her in not repeating them when she confides the incest. For example, some survivors disclose in such a hostile or indirect way that they insure a hostile or offhand response. Some revert to their predominant family role. If they were the caretaker, they disclose but then work to minimize the conflict and make everyone feel better; if the family scapegoat, they again allow the blame and anger to be dumped on them.

The survivor should, if possible, make her initial revelations to those individuals who have the best potential for offering a supportive response. A positive experience can provide the base from which to make any additional disclosure. Confiding to one or two close friends is sufficient for some survivors, while others decide to disclose their childhood experiences to all close friends, their partner, and/or other family members. Some survivors are so invested in breaking their silence that they choose to "go public" and discuss their experience in the media, professional training programs, and in other public contexts.

Disclosure to family members, whether members of the family of origin, partners, or in-laws, holds special challenges and calls for special preparation. Survivors should have resolved issues of responsibility, guilt, and physiological arousal before attempting disclosure. Disclosure of incest within the nuclear family is clearly the most threatening—the survivor should anticipate that family members will likely resort to familiar defenses and dysfunctional patterns as they attempt to cope with the exposure of the family secret. The survivor must be far enough along in her recovery to handle these without falling back on her old patterns. She must have a level of self-esteem adequate to withstand any responses that are less than positive or supportive. She must be able to keep in focus that she was the child and the victim and that she was not to blame for either the incest itself or the pain caused by its revelation.

The family dynamics, the role of the incest in the family, and the way the family handles stress should be determined. For example, divulgence in a highly emotional or violent family may precipitate emotional outbursts, perhaps including violence or suicide threats. Other families respond by not responding, apparently denying not only the incest but also the disclosure. Between these two extremes lies a range of other possibilities. Some families are able to acknowledge the incest, to work on it together, and to reconstitute. Most often, the secret is heard and may be even addressed but is then reburied. The family strives to maintain its homeostasis without working on the dysfunctional dynamics which gave rise to the incest.

Eventually, the survivor is blamed, scapegoated, or rejected for challenging the family secrecy and causing distress in the process. This pattern directly parallels the dynamics of childhood.

The survivor must also be prepared for the possibility that other incestuous abuse occurred in the family about which she had no previous knowledge. Quite often, one family member's revelation or reporting of incest (whether past or present) precipitates and facilitates disclosure on the part of others. The survivor can be encouraged to approach other family members she suspects of having been molested before making her disclosure; however, she must be prepared for denial and even dismissal on their part if they feel overly threatened or are in the numbing/denial phase of the traumatic stress response. These defenses are likely to be disturbed by the disclosure of past abuse by another member of the family.

Partners can have a variety of responses to the news of a loved one's incestuous past. A rather common response involves minimization or avoidance. The partner hears about the abuse, offers some generally supportive comments and gestures, and then proceeds to "forget" hearing about it. Other typical responses include: rescue and protection, which may limit the survivor's self-determination and leave her feeling powerless and inadequate; anger and retribution, which may cause the survivor to feel out of control and highly anxious and fearful; rejection, which overtly or covertly blames her for the incest; and support and empathy, including sadness and anguish, which help the survivor in her recovery process (Walsh, 1986b). At some point, in-laws may learn about the incest either directly from the survivor or from her spouse, with her permission or not. In-law responses span a continuum from support and sympathy to rejection and blaming. In-laws will be concerned not only for the survivor but for her spouse, their child, and for any grandchildren.

Survivors might also choose to disclose their abuse experience to their children in order to halt the maintenance of family secrets and shame through another generation. Obviously, the extent of the disclosure should be determined by the child's age and capacity to understand. With younger children, it might suffice to talk about "bad touch" and to warn the child about the offending family member(s) if family contact is maintained. In such a circumstance, the parent must be vigilant and can explain to the child that unsupervised contact is not allowed with that relative. With older children, a revelation can serve the same purpose but might also explain past family estrangement or discomfort and/or the survivor's symptoms and difficulties. Older children might have similar reactions to those described above for partners. They too might need support and should be encouraged to talk about their reactions. Tragically, when a survivor/mother discloses to her children, she might hear that they too have been abused by the same or another family member. She must be prepared beforehand for that possibility and to take the steps necessary to protect any current children in the family. Reporting is discussed later in this chapter.

Despite all of the attention incest has recently received, survivors must still be cautious in telling about their abuse. Incest remains an uncomfortable topic for most people and one they do not know how to respond to. Although some responses are supportive, survivors complain of a general lack of understanding and comfort from family and friends. Instead of hearing something like, "I'm sorry to hear that you were abused and that you're still suffering," or "I'm sorry that the abuse has been so painful and its effects so longlasting. I will help you in any way that I can," most survivors are faced with responses along the lines of, "That happened 25 years ago. I can't understand why you're still worrying about it. Just put it behind you and get on with your life," or "I don't see what that has to do with you today," or "Pretend it didn't happen—just ignore it and it will go away," or perhaps the most insulting of all, when the incest did not involve intercourse, "If you weren't raped, I don't understand what all the fuss is about. If it were a clear case of rape, I could understand." (Of course, this last response totally ignores the fact that most rape victims are not supported and understood but instead are often blamed and told not to make a big thing out of nothing.)

As is the case with victims of other types of crimes, few guidelines exist as to how to respond to reports or disclosures of victimization. Guidelines in the form of pamphlets and brochures are now available to family members when current child sexual abuse is discovered (see, for example, the brochure reproduced in McFarlane, Waterman, et al., 1986). No such resource has been available for family members, partners, or friends concerning how to respond to the disclosure of past abuse. I have developed a set of guidelines for this purpose, which are included in Table 8.

CONFRONTATION OF THE PERPETRATOR
AND OTHER FAMILY MEMBERS

Confrontation goes beyond disclosure and builds upon it. While disclosure involves exposing the occurrence of incest, confrontation involves challenging the perpetrator and other family members to face the truth about it. It can involve a diversity of actions, including: expressing of anger, hurt, and other emotions; questioning reasons and motives for the family circumstances, the abuse, and any lack of assistance; determining why the survivor was selected for victimization; exposing the toll the incest took on her life; demanding recognition of aftereffects, accountability, apology, and sometimes restitution and family treatment; and preventing future abuse in the family.

Confrontation, like disclosure, is often a potent therapeutic strategy. It

TABLE 8
How to Respond to a Disclosure of Past Child Sexual Abuse

- Be open to the disclosure. Let the survivor know you are open to discussing what she feels comfortable telling you about her past.
- Appreciate how difficult it is to make a disclosure and to confide long-held secrets.
- Offer her support and understanding. Empathize with her without pitying her. Let her know that you hurt to hear that she had such difficult events to contend with.
- Strive to be sensitive but matter-of-fact in your initial response rather than highly emotional. Know that she needs a calm, accepting, encouraging response.
- Encourage her to tell you details as she chooses to and as she is able. Don't press for details and don't focus on the sexual details. It may suffice for her to tell you only the most minimal of details or she might want you to know more. It is her decision, to do as she is able.
- Don't blame her. Emphasize that, no matter what the circumstance, she was not to blame. Be careful of questions that sound blaming, such as "Didn't you try to stop it?" "Did you tell him that you didn't like it?" "How did you know your mother wouldn't believe you if you didn't try to tell her?" "Maybe you really did enjoy it."
- Don't try to deny that it happened and don't tell her to forget it and get on with her life or otherwise "talk the abuse into going away." It's not "all in her head" and she needs to know that she is believed and supported. Don't tell her she made it up to get attention or "things like that just don't happen in good families," etc. It is especially tempting to deny incest when the perpetrator is a respected and loved member of the family and/or "a pillar of the community."
- Allow her her emotions and expect that she will have positive as well as negative feelings or that her predominant ones might be confusion and ambivalence. Not uncommonly, survivors have feelings of warmth and love towards the perpetrator for the non-exploitive parts of their relationship especially if he was the only family member to offer her nurturance.
- Don't respond with panic. Allow yourself some time to sort out your feelings.
- Don't pressure her and don't try to rush her. She needs to make choices and take action at her discretion. She will also heal at her own pace. Unfortunately, the recovery process is often lengthy—she needs support over its duration.
- Encourage her to seek therapy if she has not yet done so. Let her know that there are professionals who specialize in treating the aftereffects of abuse and who can help her. Offer her hope that she can recover from the effects of the past.
- Encourage her to make choices that are in her best interest. Don't try to stop her from making choices and don't make them for her.
- Don't attempt to be overprotective or rescue her and don't confront the perpetrator or other family members without her knowledge and permission. Be aware that angry and retaliatory behavior can hurt her by making her feel anxious, out of control, and powerless.
- Talk to her about taking action to safeguard children in the family if the perpetrator still poses a risk. Other disclosures and reporting might be necessary. Indicate your support and willingness to explore possible avenues of action.
- Don't treat her like "damaged or spoiled goods" following disclosure. If you are her sexual partner, she needs assurances that she is still lovable and attractive. Try to maintain your normal level of sexual interaction and don't try to "make everything better with sex." Seek out professional assistance or a support group if your

TABLE 8
(*Continued*)

---

feelings are strongly negative or you find yourself obsessing about the details of abuse rather than focusing on the welfare of your partner. It is appropriate to share your feelings of anger, hurt, etc., but be sure they are directed towards the perpetrator and the abuse and are not blaming of the survivor.
- Follow up with her after her initial disclosure to you. Don't let the disclosure "go down a black hole," never to be mentioned again. And don't tell her that you forgot that she had ever made a disclosure to you.
- Maintain your normal expression of affection with the survivor. Touching, holding and hugging can be especially comforting. If you do not have a relationship with the survivor which normally includes physical contact, ask her permission before making any and respect her wishes.
- Support her in future disclosures, confrontations or reporting. Be aware that this may be especially difficult for other family members, who are bound to feel split loyalty and to get caught up in other family roles and interaction patterns.
- Respect her privacy. Do not break her confidence and don't discuss her disclosure without her permission.

---

can benefit the survivor whether she confronts the offender and other family members directly or indirectly. Through it, the survivor regains her sense of control and personal power, choosing to use them to her own advantage. She refuses to continue to bury the incest or accept responsibility for the perpetrator's behavior, instead bringing it and its effects to the fore.

The prevalence and success of confrontation are difficult to discern from available research because confrontation has not been investigated apart from disclosure. It is likely that confrontation has been undertaken less frequently because it involves more assertiveness and is more difficult in the face of strong family denial. Clinical reports suggest that retrospective confrontation differs significantly from disclosure for these very reasons. Confrontation involves a questioning of and opposition to the incest status quo. As such, it has greater potential for negative outcome, including violence, than does disclosure. It is probably accurate to assume that most confrontations are unsuccessful and meet with resistance and negative response. It is unfortunate but true that indirect confrontation, either in group or individual therapy through role play or psychodrama, a letter, an audio or videotape, offers a better chance of a positive response than does direct confrontation.

Direct confrontation of the perpetrator or family is not the final outcome of incest treatment (as some clinicians and treatment programs have somewhat forcefully suggested); rather, it should be considered as an option the survivor can exercise in resolving her incest issues. It should only be undertaken following careful preparation, including an assessment of its potential for destruction and retraumatization, the survivor's ego strength, and her stage in her treatment process. When considering confrontation, the initial question is not how, when, or where to confront, but *whether* to confront at all.

MacFarlane and Korbin (1983) recommend that the motivations of all involved, including the therapist, be examined in deciding whether to pursue personal confrontation. Therapists may find that the tenets of their treatment orientation or more personal reactions argue for or against confrontation. For example, a psychoanalytic therapist might avoid involvement with anyone beside the identified patient and avoid a confrontation, whereas the family therapist might encourage a confrontation involving all members of the family. Or the therapist might be so enraged about what happened to the client that confrontation is encouraged as a way to "get back" at the perpetrator and family.

Obviously, the therapist's orientation and personal beliefs should not determine whether confrontation is pursued. Rather, the survivor's motivations and goals are the critical factors. Many of the goals and motivations resemble those for disclosure (discussed in the previous section), but they are typically more forceful, involve more protest, and call for explanation and accountability. Confrontation involves challenge and inquiry not usually involved in disclosure. Furthermore, it typically involves the expectation of acknowledgment, accountability, concern, and apology from the perpetrator and other family members. Herman (1981) described the role of preparation and the possible benefits of confrontation:

> Patients should not be encouraged to proceed with a confrontation until they have thoroughly explored their own motives and goals, and until they have anticipated and prepared themselves emotionally for the reactions they may provoke. Once adequate preparation has been done, the confrontation can be an important milestone in the patient's mastery of the incest trauma. It becomes a kind of rite, in which the patient sheds her identity as witch, bitch, or whore and casts off her role as the guardian of the family secret. She does not expect her family to absolve her of her guilt; rather, she absolves herself in their presence. If family members respond with denial, panic, hostility, or threats, she is encouraged to observe these reactions and to judge from them how powerful the family pressures upon her must have been when she was a child. (pp. 193–194)

There are many circumstances where direct confrontation is contraindicated because of its potential for physical harm, a potential the therapist must not underestimate. According to MacFarlane and Korbin (1983):

> The primary situation that demands caution is one in which there is potential for violence or retaliation on the part of a former abuser. In cases in which acute psychosis is evident or suspected or in which the abuser has a history of assaultive and violent outbursts, any direct confrontation about

the past incest could result in physical danger to the adult client and/or the intervening clinician. Clinicians must be aware that in some cases the advantages of confronting, and thus hopefully resolving, this type of family secret, however sensitively, may be outweighed by the potential harm that could ensue. For example, there is little solace for the young woman who is afraid to pursue the criminal case against her father because her personal confrontation with him over her childhood sexual abuse resulted in a brutal beating and rape, with persistent threats on her life if she continues her allegations. Although this case is extreme, clients must be aware of the potential for such violence. (p. 232)

MacFarlane and Korbin go on to describe self-destructive behavior as another potential outcome of confrontation. Suicides of victim, perpetrator, or partner occur more frequently in response to the disclosure or confrontation of incest that has yet been publicized. Two particularly shocking circumstances of this sort were reported in the Washington, D.C. area in recent years: One involved a young woman who drank a bottle of vodka and threw herself in front of a train after having disclosed to a friend that her stepfather regularly molested her. The second involved a stepfather who shot (but did not kill) his stepdaughter and then killed himself following her disclosure to police and their subsequent confrontation of him concerning his incestuous assaults.

MacFarlane and Korbin offered these comments about suicide potential:

A related consideration is the potential for self-destructive behavior on the part of former abusers or their spouses when finally faced with the exposure and long-term consequences of the prior incest. Since the threat of incest is often one of the weapons used to obtain a child's compliance and silence, the renewed threat or persistent fear of such an outcome should not continue to serve as a form or psychological blackmail or necessarily preclude intervention with a client's extended family. Nonetheless, suicide must be considered a possibility during the disclosure phase of past as well as current child sexual abuse. Precautions in the form of backup resources and individual crisis intervention should be taken, when indicated, to insure that this possibility has been carefully guarded against before undertaking the confrontation of past abuse. (p. 232)

Even when violence is ruled out or its likelihood assessed to be low, the potential for other types of harm must receive consideration. Of foremost concern: Will the survivor suffer additional emotional damage if she receives a neutral or negative response or will she be able to step back from such a response and use it to increase her self-understanding? In other words, can it be growth-producing and have a positive outcome even if the response is poor? As part of the preliminaries, therapist and client must also assess her status in the treatment process, particularly the degree to which incest issues have been resolved, and her capacity to handle the stress entailed by a confrontation. Confrontation should be postponed if the survivor continues to blame herself or hold herself responsible for the incest. She must have adequate ego strength since direct confrontation has great potential to damage the client who is fragile or fragmented.

Another consideration: What is the potential for physical or emotional harm of other family members and does the survivor want to take this into account? For example, if the abuser or another family member is in poor health, could a confrontation precipitate a medical crisis, even a death? Or could it precipitate a dissolution of the family, a divorce, or a serious psychiatric emergency? The survivor who chooses to proceed given these possibilities must be sure that she can handle whatever ensues.

Some survivors discuss their confrontation plans with other family members before making a final decision. Their intent is usually to inform them ahead of time, to "test the waters," and to enlist their support or to encourage them to become involved in a joint confrontation if they too were also molested. Confrontation is not always greeted with enthusiasm or support even by other members of the family who were abused, something the survivor should anticipate.

As with disclosure, a full range of responses from family members can be expected. Joint confrontation by two victims does take place in some families and has the benefit of decreasing isolation, providing support, and strengthening the case for the abused. Some unmolested relatives are able to offer strong support to the abused and are more interested in her well-being than in the family conflict and discomfort likely to be generated by the confrontation. Others relatives are nonsupportive and admonish the survivor to "not rock the boat," "let sleeping dogs lie," "not bring up all that old stuff and hurt Mom and Dad," "not tell Mom about what Dad did after all this time—it would kill her," or "not make Mom and Dad choose between their children" (in the case of sibling incest). Thus, some survivors must advance without internal family approval or encouragement. In such circumstances, an outside source of support is essential.

Once all of these factors are taken into consideration, the survivor can decide whether to directly confront the abuser and/or other family members. The choice is not always to confront. Some survivors choose, in effect, to rebury the secret and to never disclose it to the family. If the nonconfrontation option is selected, other therapeutic strategies are available for exposure and integration of feelings through indirect means. These will be discussed later in this section.

When the choice is made to confront, further preparation is in order. The survivor should have a solid therapeutic alliance as a strong support base. An outside source of support from other relatives, friends, or a therapy group gives her further sustenance. She also should have achieved a fairly good understanding of the incest and its impact on her life and must have resolved guilt and self-blame issues. Overly global, naive, optimistic or enabling expectations must be reformulated to be both realistic and achievable.

MacFarlane and Korbin provide particularly useful guidelines for confrontation preparation. They note that the overall goals of incest therapy are likely to be compatible with the goals of family confrontation, but they may not be achievable by means of the confrontation. The survivor must understand this crucial distinction before proceeding. She must be prepared for the contingency that, rather than breaking through family denial, confrontation (however mild) might reinforce it. She might be treated as she was in her childhood, with blame projected onto her for causing trouble. Family members might persist in their defenses to protect themselves from the knowledge of their own behavior, whether it was the abuse or the lack of assistance. The survivor herself might be strongly pressured and tempted to return to her former role in the family. To do so could sabotage her attempt at confrontation.

Even when a confrontation is carefully mapped out, its success is not assured. The outcome can nevertheless be positive if the survivor is prepared for a variety of responses on the part of family members and has thought through her own responses. Adequate preparation helps the client cope with whatever a confrontation brings, whether old family patterns and defenses, family pain and crisis generated by acknowledgment, or the discovery of previously unknown levels of abuse or other disturbance within the family. The following are some basic guidelines, drawn from Mac-Farlane and Korbin's article, that are helpful to clients in their preparation:

- *Carefully consider timing.* Confrontation should be deferred if the family is in the midst of serious stress or crisis unrelated to the incest. Such crisis would make it impossible for the survivor to receive adequate attention or response. Likewise, the survivor should wait if she has other ongoing life crises.
- *Assess survivor readiness.* As mentioned earlier, the survivor must be at a point in treatment where she has adequate ego strength and defenses to cope positively with a confrontation. She must also be at a point where her rage has been sufficiently discharged. If she is experiencing intense, out-of-control rage, confrontation should be postponed. A rageful approach to the family can throw it into a defensive posture precluding any positive response.
- *Expect family denial and do not overreact to it.* A lifelong pattern of denial may only give way some time after the confrontation. It is unrealistic to expect that the family will react with openness when that has not been its pattern. It will likely take some time and possibly repeat confrontations to penetrate the family's denial.
- *Try to be patient with the process.* Again, reactions may occur some time after the confrontation takes place.

- *Do not look to the confrontation for validation of either the abuse or the survivor.* The survivor must not expect to receive validation or absolution from the abuser, but rather should find them elsewhere, hopefully from within herself and through the therapeutic process.
- *Expect a variety of outcomes and varying degrees of success and resolution.* I have had some clients go back to family members and be well-received (in fact, in one case of abuse by a cousin, the client's mother shared that she, too, had been sexually assaulted in childhood and could readily understand and identify with her daughter's pain. The mother was particularly upset that her daughter had not been able to seek her assistance when the abuse was ongoing). On the other hand, I have also had clients face denial and scapegoating when they dared to openly challenge the family's incest ethic.

MacFarlane and Korbin recommend that strategies and structural components of the confrontation be decided next. These include such factors as whether to confront the abuser/family alone or with other victimized family members, whether to meet only with the abuser or to include other family members, whether to hold a surprise or preannounced meeting, whether to include the therapist(s), where to hold the meeting, and whether to set time limits on it. In general, unless an element of surprise is seen as necessary for the involvement of the abuser or other family members (as is the case in alcohol intervention), the first step in the confrontation is a request for a meeting, made face-to-face, by phone or letter. The abuser can be told directly but without elaboration about the meeting's topic or, less directly, that the survivor has something important that she wishes to discuss. If the topic is disclosed, participation is more likely if privacy is assured for the meeting. The survivor needs to determine ahead of time whether others will be involved in the meeting and whether to disclose that fact ahead of time to the abuser. The unexpected involvement of other family members and/or "outsiders" such as a therapist may surprise him enough to break through his denial (again drawing from the alcohol intervention model) or may strengthen his resistance, possibly enrage him, and compromise any cooperation.

In some cases, the survivor may choose to confront within the therapy and so invite the abuser and other family members to attend one or more therapy sessions with her. Although it is not always possible or desirable for a therapist to be involved, such involvement can assist the communication process, offer support, and minimize the potential for harm and re-traumatization. If logistical considerations preclude the involvement of the survivor's primary therapist, another clinician can be recruited and prepared to participate. The involved therapist (especially when the survivor's primary therapist) is in a delicate position: She or he must be explicit about being the survivor's ally but must also maintain an assertive but nonaggressive stance towards the perpetrator and other participants. The intent is to facilitate the communication process so that the goals of the confrontation are met. Hopefully, increased understanding and possibly reconciliation of some sort also result.

Confrontation is undertaken in some cases to stop any ongoing abuse in the family or to prevent future exploitation. Strategies which have been devised to achieve these ends or to force an abuser into treatment include threats of disclosure to the extended family or to the community at large and the threat of legal action or police reporting. Very often, these threats are enough to command an abuser's attention and to obtain his cooperation. The survivor must be prepared to make good on her threats in the event that the abuse continues.

When direct confrontation is not possible because it is too risky or the abuser or others are unavailable or dead, other means may be employed which enable the survivor to express her feelings. The most widely used strategy in indirect confrontation seems to be letter-writing; other exercises such as role play or psychodrama, the empty chair technique, audiotape and videotape, drawings, and visiting a grave site can be used to achieve the same end. Models of letters and other writing are available in the books *I Never Told Anyone* and *Voices in the Night.*

A variant of direct confrontation is possible in those communities which have ongoing treatment groups for abusers, victims, and other family members. A survivor can engage in confrontation and discussion with an abuser and/or other family member(s) who act as substitutes for her own family. This confrontation becomes part of the surrogates' treatment as well, since they must own responsibility for the abuse they perpetrated and its aftereffects.

REPORTING PAST AND CURRENT ABUSE

The survivor may go beyond confrontation and the threat of reporting by making a report of her past abuse to the police or child protective services. She may be especially disposed to do so when she believes that the abuser continues to pose a risk to children. She is also faced with the decision of whether to report when current abuse of a child (either within or outside the family) is strongly suspected or known. Determining whether to report past or current abuse raises all of the issues and inhibitions that typically accompany disclosure and/or confrontation. Additional issues and pressures arise because reporting usually entails an investigation involving several social service and law enforcement agencies. The abuser is subject to arrest and prosecution and the family to public scrutiny and possible forced disruption.

The survivor who has disclosed her abuse or who has confronted the abuser or other family members may have an easier time with reporting than the survivor who still maintains the incest secret, although this is not always the case. Frequently, survivors are willing and able to take action to protect other children in the family, action that they were previously unable to take for themselves. They may also feel that the changed social milieu, including the increased emphasis on reporting and intervening in child sexual abuse, makes reporting much easier than it was in the past.

The therapist who learns of ongoing abuse of a minor child does not have the same option of choosing whether to report it or not. By state law, appropriate legal and protective services must be informed when current abuse is disclosed or strongly suspected. According to Davidson (1986), who reviewed legal issues in the failure to report child abuse:

> Since the first state mandatory child abuse and neglect reporting laws were enacted in the early 1960's, there has been a steady increase in the number of "mandated" professionals who are obligated to report known or suspected child maltreatment. Since 1967, all states have had such laws, and in most of these states physicians, dentists, interns, nurses, psychologists, teachers and other school personnel, social workers, law enforcement officers, and personnel in child care programs are now specifically identified as being required to report.
>
> To address the major legal impediments which have inhibited reporting: (1) every state has provided statutory immunity to the reporter, thus providing an absolute defense to the professional who is sued as a consequence of his fulfilling in good faith the reporting obligation; (b) most states have abolished the doctor-patient and therapist-client privilege in all child abuse related situations; (c) many states have laws which shield the reporter from having his or her identity revealed; and (d) a few states provide protection to reporters from any job-related sanctions based on their decision to report, as well as preventing any supervisor from interfering with their asking of the report. (pp. 73–74)

The duty to report past abuse is less clear. Kelly (in press) has noted that no statute of limitations currently exists on the therapist's duty to report, although a statute does exist on the criminal prosecution of cases of child sexual abuse. He believes that state law should be changed to directly address this issue and suggests that laws not *require* a therapist to report the past childhood abuse of an adult, a suggestion I agree with. Instead, a formerly molested adult should have the right to choose whether to make a report in much the same way as a rape victim has that choice.

However, in the situation where a survivor has either abused children in the past or poses a serious risk to abuse them in the future, the therapist has a duty to report. Kelly notes a second major legal obligation which limits confidentiality in such cases, the "duty to protect" or "duty to warn." This duty, derived from the 1976 Tarasoff ruling and related case law decisions, holds that a therapist must exercise reasonable care in protecting potential victims when a reasonable suspicion exists that a client may endanger another person. Because no empirically based guidelines are yet available with which to assess the dangerousness of pedophiles and incest offenders, clinical judgment must be used in deciding whether to make a report.

In order to safeguard the therapeutic alliance, the therapist should be knowledgeable about the legalities of priviledged communication and child abuse reporting laws and able to clearly articulate them. At the outset of treatment, the survivor should be advised of the limits of confidentiality and the necessity for mandatory reporting by the therapist in the event of a direct disclosure, the strong suspicion of ongoing abuse or high potential for future abuse. She should be further advised that although reporting involves breaking the confidentiality of the therapeutic relationship, reports can be made anonymously for her and disclosure of actual statements made during the course of therapy are not required in most states. Of course, if the survivor is the individual judged to be a risk to children, the report will name him/her.

The mandate to report current abuse in the family can be problematic, since it involves compromising the priviledged communication of the therapy relationship and may go against the client's wishes. She may fear that the child caught in current abuse will be harmed instead of helped by a protective services/law enforcement investigation or that the perpetrator or other members of the family will retaliate. The therapist certainly faces a dilemma in such circumstances, particularly if s/he knows that the community's protective services are not always responsive or helpful due to overwork, understaffing, or undertraining.

Some professionals who have questions about the effectiveness of child protective services (CPS), particularly when a law enforcement response is involved, and who fear reprisal against the child choose not to report abuse. Conte (1986) commented that:

> While there are numerous legitimate concerns which in part support a reluctance to report, non-reporting also presents its own problems to clients who are left in abusive situations or who fail to receive the social and mental health services which would help correct the abusive situation and the effects of such abuse in the life of the abused children and her/his family. Experience also suggests that there are personal reasons for some professionals' reluctance to report which are largely self-centered and in no way directed toward the interests of clients (e.g., fear of being sued by angry former clients). However, . . . there are a number of legitimate professional concerns which are client centered and which should not be confused with these personal, less admirable reasons. (p. 55)

An individual therapist is not in a position to put a stop to ongoing sexual abuse; instead, strong cooperation between child protective services and law enforcement (the police and the criminal justice system) with mental health services is usually needed to effectively intervene in the family and to prevent the continuation of the incestuous abuse. According to Herman (1981, p. 134), "any approach which fails to report incest to the legally designated authority, creates more problems than it solves." I concur with the recommendation that ongoing abuse be reported, even though the effectiveness of child welfare services cannot be assured. At the very least, reporting communicates to the client and to the family that the therapist will not collude in ongoing abuse and the corresponding maintenance of the incest secret. The therapist can present the necessity to make a report as policy and as an attempt to counter the abuse and to insure the child's safety. A balanced perspective on the type of response that can be expected from reporting should be presented. Child protective workers should be presented as competent fellow professionals whose job requires investigating and acting on reports of child maltreatment (Herman, 1981).

Once the therapist determines the necessity for reporting, the implications of doing so must be discussed with the client. Her feelings about both the breaking of confidentiality and the actual reporting should be explored, along with their impact on the therapeutic relationship. Although reporting is sometimes resisted, at other times it is supported with enthusiasm and relief. In the latter circumstance, therapist and survivor need to decide who will initiate the report and whether to report openly or anonymously. Reporting can prove beneficial and empowering when undertaken by a survivor, since it is further proof that she has broken out of her powerless position in the family and broken with the family's abuse ethic. If the decision is for the therapist to make the report, he or she can make it in the presence of the survivor.

The therapist should support the rationale for reporting but should also provide a realistic appraisal of the probable consequences of doing so. Adequate response on the part of reporting agencies is often less associated with the circumstances of a particular case than with the resources of the community where a report is made. It is safe to say that, in recent years, the massive increase in the number of reports of child abuse and neglect, including child sexual abuse, has overburdened many community and state child protective services, whose staffing has not kept pace with the increased volume. Unfortunately, at the current time most communities have not developed comprehensive treatment programs that insure support and effective treatment to all members of the family. The reporting of current abuse, like disclosure and confrontation, does not guarantee a positive outcome. Intervention may cause increased distress and great frustration, and may make the family situation worse instead of better. The therapist must accurately present these eventualities to insure that the survivor is forewarned, whatever the outcome of the intervention.

The therapist should be familiar enough with the procedures set in motion by a report that these can be outlined for the survivor. A description of the steps involved in the investigation of allegations of child sexual abuse can be obtained from the procedural guidelines for local or state child protection agencies or the outlines of case management contained in Sgroi's *Handbook of Clinical Intervention in Child Sexual Abuse* or Herman's *Father-Daughter Incest*.

Survivors are likely to be very frustrated and angry if the response to a report is ineffective or worse. The therapist can strongly empathize with these emotions but can also point out that, even if nothing else was achieved, the silence surrounding the incest was broken. The increased volume of reports underscores the magnitude of the problem and hopefully will lead to continued procedural changes geared towards stopping and preventing future incest. The advances of the past ten years surely give a measure of the progress that can be made on a social problem in a relatively short time span.

LEGAL REMEDIES FOR INCEST SURVIVORS

The traditional legal approach to incest is through criminal law. Criminal prosecution of incest has been pursued when the incest is discovered while the victim is still a minor. Yet, as forcefully presented by Herman (1981, p. 167), the criminal approach presents problems for the incest victim. Prosecution to the full extent of the law is the exception rather than the rule: "Even if a complaint is made, which is unlikely, the chances are slight that the case will ever go to trial, still slighter that the father [abuser] will be found guilty, and even slighter that, if convicted, he will be sentenced to prison."

Civil remedies offer a different means of redressing incest injury. According to Moore (1986):

> Tort remedies are an appropriate form of action for incest victims and survivors. For those women who have reached adulthood without any legal response to the sexual abuse . . . tort remedies provide them with the opportunity to have their day in court, to place the blame for the incest . . . and to let the world know, through a public court proceeding, that the women themselves were not to blame.
>
> Our legal system provides a person who has been wronged by another the opportunity to require that person to compensate damage caused by the wrongful action. . . .
>
> Additionally, it is within the discretion of judges and juries in many states to award punitive damages, although in some states the plaintiff may first have to establish malice. Such exemplary damage awards are generally meant to punish the wrongful actor and to serve as a warning to others. (p. 12)

As can be seen from this quote, a civil action may have many potential benefits for a survivor: compensatory and punitive damages as well as public exposure, both of which are deterrents to those who would molest their children.

At least one legal commentator (Salten, 1984) has argued for the establishment of a tort of "incest." Until such time as such a tort is available, there are only four possible causes of action under which an incest survivor can proceed (Moore, 1986): (1) assault, (2) battery (each requiring proof of intent on the part of the abuser), (3) intentional infliction of emotional distress, and (4) negligent infliction of emotional distress. In all four, the survivor would need to offer convincing proof that requirements for the tort were met by the incestuous abuse.

DeRose (1985, p. 195), in her review article on incest survivors and the statute of limitations, has noted that "incest victims have utilized various tort theories with moderate success in seeking remedies; however, the statute of limitations remains the primary stumbling block for adult survivors of incest." Currently, in all states, a one-to-three-year statute of limitations exists in tort cases. The statute usually runs from the date of injury; however, in the case of a minor, it runs from the day she reaches the age of majority. In other words, an incest survivor has from one to three years from the time she reaches the age of 18 in which to file a suit. Statutes of limitation have been provided in the law to provide a reasonable timeframe within which a plaintiff can seek compensation, while limiting the defendant's liability from continuing indefinitely. In an incest tort suit, the abuser/defendant would most likely rely on the statute of limitations as grounds for dismissal, although he has other defenses at his disposal as well.

At present incest lawsuits are being brought which challenge the statute of limitations and seek exceptions to it. Exceptions to the date of injury accrual have been granted in a variety of other types of suits on a variety of grounds, such as fraud or undue influence or duress in the relationship between plaintiff and defendant. Many of these are applicable to incest cases (see review articles by Allen, 1983; DeRose, 1985; Moore, 1986, and Salten, 1984). According to Moore: "The preferred rule for the statute of limitations in incest suits would be that the statute began running at the date of discovery of the injury rather than at the date of actual injury" (p. 14). DeRose succinctly summarized the argument: "If the date-of-injury commencement bars the relief of blameless victims who are as yet unaware of the deleterious effects of past incest, their guarantee of justice is violated" (p. 220).

As this book and the incest studies cited have demonstrated, many incest survivors do not know the full extent of their injuries at the age of majority or do not even know that they have been abused, much less injured. The severity of their injuries often does not become evident until they are in their twenties and thirties and is not understood as related to and developing from the incest. Many survivors do not even remember the incest or realize its association to their problems until they enter therapy.

Further, it is unrealistic to expect that a young woman just exiting from an incestuous family situation would have the emotional (and financial) resources to pursue such a suit during the proscribed time period.

It remains to be seen whether courts will agree with these arguments and delay the discovery rule. But even a delayed discovery rule of one to three years' time after the discovery of the incest injury is not sufficient in a great many incest cases when the survivor continues to experience severe symptomatology which makes her psychologically unable to bring a suit. Such was the case with one of my clients:

Sue sought therapy for the aftereffects of years of incestuous abuse by her father. As abuse experiences and their warded-off emotions were explored during the course of therapy, Sue became severely depressed, suicidal, and dissociative. She was hospitalized twice for these symptoms.

Sue has decided that she would like to sue her father, a retired military man, to publicly humiliate him and her mother for the abuse which she likens to concentration camp internment. She has not yet fully resolved issues of responsibility, revenge towards her mother, and physiological arousal, feels acutely rageful and homicidal towards her parents, and has strong dissociative reactions when under extreme stress. It is obvious that she is not yet psychologically ready to initiate a suit.

In exploring the possibility of a suit with an attorney, Sue learned that although she has good grounds on which to sue her father, the suit is impeded by the statute of limitations. Further, even if a delayed discovery rule were allowed, she would have a difficult time making her case because she did not initiate the suit during the first year of her treatment.

In my opinion, once delayed discovery is accepted as an exception to the statute of limitations, a new argument will need to be made that the severity of injury, at times, prevents survivors from filing civil suits during the proscribed time period. Following Salten's (1984) suggestions, state legislatures might develop a new tort of incest or might extend the statute of limitations for survivors, thus allowing them to bring suit for the incest at any time after the discovery of its injurious aftermath.

Many of the clinical issues discussed above for deciding whether to disclose, confront, and/or report incest pertain to litigation as well. In considering a suit, the survivor's motives and goals should be thoroughly explored. The most common goals for suing include: to receive financial compensation and punitive damages, to humiliate the abuser, to regain control, to gain public acknowledgment and apology, and to deter further incest by the abuser or by others. Goals and expectations should be assessed as to their feasibility. For example, a goal of achieving a large financial settlement is unrealistic and unachievable if the abuser has limited financial resources. Or the expectation that the abuser will immediately cave in and offer a financial settlement to avoid going to trial might also be unrealistic, as it was in one case I recently heard about. The survivor had not considered the possibility that her father would not settle. She was emotionally devastated and dropped her suit because she did not feel she could handle going to trial. If, however, her expectations had been to publicly call her father to task and to humiliate him, her actions might have sufficed.

As with disclosure and confrontation, an assessment of the survivor's personal resources is warranted. To broaden support and financial resources, it may be useful to enlist the assistance of national women's organizations, civil liberties organizations, and national and local victim's rights organizations. The survivor must have adequate financial resources to pursue a suit, unless such a suit is taken on a contingency or pro bono basis. In my experience, lawyers resist such a financial arrangement when there is reason to believe that the abuser does not have the means to make a large settlement if the case is won or because the survivor's suit must first successfully challenge the statute of limitations before going any further, thus making if an "iffy" case at best. When the survivor decides to pay legal expenses out of pocket, she must guard against becoming financially insolvent as a result. Becoming destitute would be self-defeating.

The survivor must be prepared for the fact that suit might actually result in a trial. She must also be prepared for intense public scrutiny when such a suit is filed. Some survivors have ended up hospitalized because they either did not expect or could not handle the pressure associated with the publicity generated by their case. In one recently publicized case, the survivor committed suicide before her case reached the trial stage (*The Boston Globe*, May 10, 1987).

It appears that so far, in most of the suits in which the statute of limitations restriction has been overcome, abusers have avoided a trial by making a financial settlement. But some cases have gone on to full jury trials. The survivor needs a clear understanding ahead of time of what such a trial will entail. She, similar to the rape victim in a criminal trial, will be the star witness, subject to intensive examination and cross-examination. Her life will be minutely scrutinized and possibly widely publicized if the case comes to the attention of the media. Although publicity might very well help her case and humiliate the abuser, she too might be humiliated as the details of the abuse and other personal issues are disclosed. Moreover, other family members are affected by a suit and may pressure her to drop it. The family's potential for violence must be evaluated when making the decision to sue.

Both survivor and therapist need to prepare for the change in their roles and relationship brought on by the legal effort. The therapist would be called on to provide intensified emotional support in the treatment setting. Additionally, if called as a witness, the therapist would publicly offer an assessment of the survivor's diagnosis, symptoms, and functioning and recount details of the treatment. The therapist herself might arrange for backup support, especially if the case goes public and is accompanied by high pressure media attention and if courtroom testimony is required.

FAMILY OUTCOMES

The degree of contact that adult incest survivors maintain with their families of origin varies considerably and ranges from reconciliation and reconstitution to estrangement and dissolution. Reconciliation of family members seems most easily achieved when the incest had little effect on family functioning and/or when members were able to intervene immediately and effectively to stop the abuse. Reconciliation between individual members of the family sometimes occurs in the absence of or instead of total family reconciliation.

The term "family reconstitution" is usually applied in the case of nuclear family incest, most often when referring to father-daughter incest. As the name implies, family reconstitution means the reconstruction of the family in such a way that incest does not recur. This is sometimes possible without the formal individual or family treatment regimen described below. According to Swink and Leveille (1986, p. 136): "Occasionally, with a new attitude and if there have been some major changes in the family (such as the abuser and spouse divorced, or an alcoholic became sober), then a new relationship can be formed."

Reconstitution is otherwise usually possible only after the incest secret is broken and with intensive treatment of the perpetrator and other family members. The perpetrator's treatment regimen resembles treatment for the alcoholic. He begins by admitting that he is powerless over his behavior and is encouraged to confront his denial and rationalizations about the incest. As treatment progresses, he must take responsibility for his abusive behavior and apologize to the victim in the presence of other family members. Similar to the alcoholic, he learns that he will always be in the process of recovery and that he will always be at risk to repeat the incest. Treatment of other family members involves strengthening them individually and strengthening the bonds between them so that they will act to prevent or halt any additional incest in the family.

Group treatment models with adjunctive self-help components seem to be most effective in achieving a reconstituted family. These programs have been criticized for their efforts to keep the family together by those who feel that once the incest taboo has been breached the family is never again safe for the child. The programs are supported by those who feel that it is in everyone's best interest for the family to be reunited once the father has been rehabilitated (Giarretto, 1982).

At the other end of the spectrum are those families which were so nonnurturing, nonprotective and/or violent that family members were estranged from one another from childhood on, estrangement which continues into adulthood. Most outcomes are not so black or white. Instead, they might involve maintaining contact with selected relatives and limiting contact with others or maintaining emotionally detached contact with all relatives or continuing full interaction with the entire family.

In incest therapy, the goal is not to reconstitute the family but to help the survivor realistically perceive her family and its functioning (i.e., its roles, messages and dynamics) and decide *what is best for her.* The therapist must respect the importance and intensity of relational bonds even in the most abusive of families. She has the sometimes difficult task of helping the survivor make a realistic family assessment while not scapegoating the family and its members. The therapist must understand when the survivor chooses to maintain family contact even when the abuse has been horrendous. In such cases the therapist's task is to assist the survivor in understanding her dynamics and needs along with the reasons she chooses to maintain contact. Such a client might be able to achieve more distance from the family only after she develops strong supports on the outside. Therapy (whether individual, group or both) can certainly provide such a support source.

THE ISSUE OF FORGIVENESS

Incest survivors are routinely urged to "forgive and forget" or to heed their religious training by forgiving the perpetrator his transgressions. Although a survivor might very well resolve her incest issues with forgiveness of the offender and other family members, *forgiveness is her choice* and is not something that every survivor will decide to do. The therapist does the survivor a disservice if forgiveness is foisted on her as something she *must do* or even if it is suggested prematurely to her as an option.

Fitzgibbons (1986) offered some useful guidelines on cognitive and emotive uses of forgiveness in the treatment of anger. He began by citing the *Webster's Dictionary* definition of forgiveness as "a process of ceasing to feel resentment against someone or to pardon someone." He continued: "The process usually begins, after the therapist has analyzed the origins of the patient's pain, as an intellectual exercise in which the patient makes a decision to forgive. At the same time the patient attempts to understand those who have inflicted the hurt. Emotional forgiveness, that is, when one truly feels like forgiving another, is normally preceded by a significant amount of time and energy spent in intellectual forgiving" (pp. 629–630).

This description of the forgiveness process can be seen to dovetail with the therapeutic process we have discussed for incest resolution. Once the survivor has surfaced the incest situation and explored cognitions and emotions, she can then decide on a course of action. Though forgiveness can have many benefits such as disengagement from painful experiences of the past and the reconciliation of relationships, it is particularly arduous when the situation involves disappointment with or exploitation by a family member. Fitzgibbons addressed this issue: "When there have been severe traumas early in life . . . the therapist must proceed gently and cautiously, and limit the time spent forgiving because of the profound pain which may enter consciousness" (p. 632). Thus, we can see that forgiveness should not be rushed, nor is it the end result for all survivors.

Full forgiveness is the decision arrived at by some survivors while others feel that they cannot forgive because they have been hurt so deeply, an apology has not been tendered, and to forgive suggests that those who caused the injury remain unaccountable for their misdeeds. If a survivor cannot forgive, she must have enough resolution or disengagement from the past to be able to claim her present and future for herself. She must not remain stuck in futile anger but rather must use it as a spur to her development.

Swink and Leveille (1986) discussed another aspect of forgiveness—that it does not mean that the abuser is trusted from that point on. They wrote:

> In those cases in which the perpetrator admits the abuse and asks for forgiveness, the survivor must determine if she is ready, willing or able to accept an apology. Sometimes they think that in order to forgive, they must now trust this person as if nothing wrong ever happened and even let him babysit his grandchildren. Unless the perpetrator has gone through many years of intensive therapy for sexual offenders with continuing support, he is no safer alone with children than an alcoholic is safe alone with a drink. Thus, the former victim may be ready to accept an apology and retribution, but she would be wrong to expect that she can now trust her abuser. (p. 139)

PARTNERS AND OTHER LOVED ONES: SECONDARY VICTIMS

A victimization experience most often has a ripple effect; the primary victim is directly affected and her intimates secondarily. Not infrequently, partners and other loved ones suffer "contact traumatization."

Partners and Other Loved Ones

As described earlier, aftereffects and symptoms may be acute and chronic from the survivor's childhood on. Or they may be delayed only becoming evident in early to mid adulthood, when the survivor goes through the separation-individuation process from her family of origin and takes on the tasks of this life stage—marriage or other intimate relationships, parent-hood, and/or a career. Whether aftereffects are acute, chronic, and/or de-layed, all have a significant (and sometimes dramatic) impact on partners and other loved ones, as shown by the following examples:

Arlene had been abused by her father from age two to 19. She had shown a variety of behavioral, interpersonal, medical, and familial symp-toms throughout her childhood and adolescence; these were sometimes noticed but never addressed. Arlene was a parentified child who excelled at school; thus, she was able to camouflage symptoms.

She met and married Phil when she was 19 to escape her family. To her, he was her "knight in shining armor" who rescued her from the horrors of her family. She clung to him desperately. Early in the marriage she dis-closed the incest and manifested acute symptoms, such as crouching in the closet when she got scared, but Phil never really noticed. He was immature, rigid, and controlling and expected that Arlene would be his "perfect wom-an" and take care of all his needs. Their marriage began to deteriorate when Arlene advanced in her career and became less dependent on and caretaking of Phil. Yet, separating from him terrified her and set off a major depression and severe dissociative episodes. Phil was concerned but unable to offer much support. He was confused and angry about how "his Arlene" had changed and blamed therapy for causing the reactions and for ulti-mately costing him his marriage.

Arlene has no contact with members of her family, so friends have become her surrogate family. They have been protective, frightened, con-cerned, and angered by the intensity of her reactions. Most have been in contact with her therapist at one time or another as they have sought to assist her. They have also at various times confronted members of her family for her and said things that, as yet, Arlene is unable to say for herself.

Diana reached adulthood in total amnesia about the abuse she had suffered as a young child at the hands of an uncle who often babysat her. The abuse included oral, anal, and vaginal sex and penetration with ob-jects. It stopped suddenly when he joined the military and she was success-ful in forgetting it and blocking it from consciousness.

She met her future husband when she was 21 and they made a con-scious choice to wait until they were married to have sex. On their wedding night, when they attempted intercourse, she experienced sudden flash-backs and physiological arousal of such intensity that she threw her hus-band out of the bed. This happened whenever they attempted to be sexual so that the couple had no choice but to be celibate. Diana subsequently became so symptomatic that she could barely function. Also, she could not tolerate being around her husband. He was patient and supportive of

Diana's therapy, but after several years and little improvement in their marriage, both decided to have the marriage annulled.

Diana's mother was appalled to learn of the abuse and at the changes she has seen in her daughter. She liked Diana's husband and had high hopes for their marriage. She herself has become depressed and anxious over the years as Diana has struggled to overcome the effects of the abuse.

Lila was abused by her grandfather, father, and brother from ages four to 14. Both her father and grandfather were alcoholic and she suspects her brother is as well. She also believes that her father and brother (her grandfather is now dead) have the potential to abuse her nieces.

Lila ran away from home when she was 16 and was heavily involved in drugs and street crime to support her habit. She suffered stranger rape on two different occasions.

Lila now lives with her lesbian lover, with whom she has an impulsive, unstable relationship. Both Lila and her lover are alcoholic and are given to bouts of depression and occasional violence. Lila works in a low-paying, deadend job that she hates. Several times a year, she becomes acutely suicidal and has been hospitalized during several of these episodes. Lila's lover is the more stable of the two and feels that she can't take much more although she loves Lila. Lila's last suicide attempt was the most serious and she's been in an acute depression for months. She was also the victim of a recent street mugging and has been having terrifying nightmares and flashbacks since that time.

Maureen recently found out that her live-in lover had been molesting her 11-year-old daughter when a report from her daughter's school triggered an investigation. She steadfastly supported her lover and blamed her daughter for being a tease. She was court-referred into treatment with her daughter, where she continued to deny the abuse. At the last session, she told the therapist she couldn't understand what all the fuss was about—her father had done some "funny things" with her when she was young and they hadn't affected her. Why would they affect her daughter?

These cases are clear examples of how partners and other loved ones can pay dearly for past incest experience and how the destructive effects of incest extend beyond the victim. These cases also show the different reactions of significant others. Many reactions parallel those described earlier: rescue, revenge, rejection, blame, ambivalence, avoidance, denial, hurt and empathy. Additionally, some of these significant others develop their own set of symptoms. They may become fearful, anxious, abusive, angry, resentful, and depressed, along with a whole host of other reactions. Some loved ones totally miss the mark in being able to support the survivor, as they are caught up in their own reactions and concerns. But another group offer empathy and appropriate support and seek out information so they can assist as much as possible.

At times I have found it very useful to have a consultation with a partner or loved one, sometimes with the survivor, sometimes not. A consultation may involve a face-to-face meeting or a telephone call. Its purpose is the exchange of information—the partner can offer his/her perceptions and observations about the survivor and size up the therapist while the therapist can do likewise. The partner/loved one can give the therapist valuable information about the survivor's everyday functioning and can share fears and concerns. Such a meeting communicates to the survivor that loved ones care enough to attempt to learn more about what she is going through and how best to extend support and understanding.

A consultation can further serve to somewhat demystify the therapy process and the therapist. Therapy may be very threatening for the partner whose life is directly affected by the changes (good or bad) brought on as a result of it. For example, he or she is affected when a survivor moves away from a pattern of caretaking or has flashbacks, self-mutilates or suffers debilitating anxiety reactions in response to treatment. The partner may also become jealous of the therapist-client relationship, especially when a strong dependency, idealization, or other transference reaction has developed. A consultation can then be used to include the partner in the process, to offer an opportunity for reality-testing (e.g., the partner would likely see the transference distortion, especially when the therapist maintains a professional stance, explains the reaction, and offers reassurance that it will change during treatment).

A consultation also provides the opportunity to explain the course of therapy, particularly how things might get worse before they get better and how the survivor might become increasingly symptomatic before recovering. I have heard of a number of cases where the difficulties inherent in the therapy put such a strain on a marriage or relationship that the partners separated. Such an occurrence almost always causes an additional and overwhelming level of stress for the survivor. As part of a consultation, the therapist can enlist the aid and support of the partner or loved one, can devise specific strategies for assistance, can offer the partner support, and can formulate plans if the survivor enters an acute state. It can be very reassuring for significant others to know that a mental health professional is involved and responsible. It often relieves them of the feeling that they are shouldering the burden alone. A final and related point: I have found consultation time to be well spent. It quite often results in one or more "therapeutic allies" outside of the therapy, individuals who support the goals of the treatment and encourage the survivor in her quest for healing.

Partners or loved ones might themselves profit from outside support. Although the purpose of the consultation is not to formally assess their psychological functioning, the therapist might discern the need for treatment during a consultation and make such a recommendation. Otherwise, a group for the partners or significant others of sexual abuse survivors might be recommended. These groups, in educational, self-help or therapy format, are increasingly available. Whatever the format, groups usually begin by educating members about the aftereffects of child sexual abuse/incest and about the reactions they might have to learning about past or ongoing abuse of a loved one by someone in her family. They also offer education about helpful and nonhelpful responses to the survivor. (See Table 8 for suggested responses.) Members then have the opportunity to explore and ventilate reactions to the abuse itself, to the perpetrator, to the survivor, and to her reactions and symptoms. In the event that a survivor is in the process of confronting or suing the perpetrator or other family members and needing extensive support herself, the group offers the partner backup support for his/her own needs.

Self-help and therapy groups are also geared to assisting members in their own personal growth and in making changes alone or in conjunction with the changes that survivors undertake. Survivors and their partners and friends may have unconsciously selected one another because their personal and interpersonal dynamics were complementary. For example, the overresponsible incest survivor often chooses a partner who is highly dependent and childlike and further surrounds herself with family and friends who require her nurturing and caretaking but give her little in return. Through her therapy, she learns about family dynamics and roles and is encouraged to make changes, changes that affect these relationships. Treatment of partners and other loved ones assists them to learn about family roles and how they interact with the survivor. As a result, they better understand, respond to, and even initiate role changes with the survivor.

Finally, during the course of group participation, a partner/loved one might acknowledge or disclose that he or she too was abused as a child. This pattern is being seen more frequently and should be anticipated by professionals working with these significant others. As is increasingly recognized with the children of other dysfunctional families (the most obvious being adult children of alcoholics), a substantial number of them marry or develop friendships with individuals who themselves come from dysfunctional families. Thus, it is to be expected that incest survivors are quite frequently involved with others who were sexually abused or who come from incestuous families. It may be very difficult for a survivor to learn that her partner/loved one also suffered past sexual abuse and that it had been previously undisclosed. The group can provide support during the time of disclosure and can assist the individual in beginning the process of exploring his/her own abuse history.

Children of Survivors

One final group must be mentioned: children of survivors. Many survivors function quite adequately as mothers but some are unable to do so because they lack parenting skills, their interactions with their own mothers were so deficient that they lack an adequate model, they lack support, and mothering is impeded by the effects of incest and traumatic stress reactions. The case of Maureen on page 351 illustrates a mother's incapacity to safeguard her daughter because of her denial responses to her own abuse. A woman's capacity to mother her children also varies dramatically depending upon the degree of stress she is experiencing and how she fares during the treatment process. If the mother is so debilitated that she cannot function in her role as a parent or if she is unable to provide her children with protection from sexual molestation (either inside or outside of the home), others need to function in her place and, on occasion, the children removed from her supervision.

A temporary inability to parent was described by survivor Sheila Sisk and therapist Charlotte Foster Hoffman in their book *Inside Scars: Incest Recovery as Told by a Survivor and Her Therapist*, (1987). At one point during treatment, Sheila, a single parent of two young daughters, was so overwhelmed by her symptoms and the initial effects of disclosing the incest in therapy that her ability to parent was compromised. Her children were removed from her custody until she was better able to care for them, when her symptoms lessened somewhat. For her, the restitution of her parenting rights became an early goal and focus of her therapy.

As mentioned earlier in this chapter, children should be informed of their mother's past trauma and any present difficulties according to the child's age and maturity, level of comprehension, and the degree of support available. Optimally, the other parent or another adult is available in addition to the survivor/mother to provide support and explanation. Disclosure to children should be made only after careful consideration of motivations and possible consequences. Another reason has to do with the perceived potential for abuse of the children by the original abuser or other family members. Disclosure of previous abuse can be used to safeguard the children and to warn off the perpetrator from further abuse.

Direct disclosure to children is not always necessary as illustrated by one survivor's actions following the birth of her daughter. She revised her will to stipulate that, in the event of she and her husband's deaths, her parents not receive custody of her child or be allowed unsupervised visitation rights. Her alcoholic father had a multigenerational history of abuse. The mother consistently denied his past abuse and abuse potential; she had inadequately supervised another granddaughter on a family visit despite warnings and her assurances of safety, with the result that the child was molested. The grandparents are both high-status professionals of good standing in their community. The survivor, herself a professional, decided on this strong course of action because her parents' social and professional status made it likely that a court would rule in their favor in a custody dispute. The will also stipulates that, in the event of parental death, the child would be informed of the reasons for the custody arrangements once she is old enough to understand them.

When children are directly informed (whatever their age but especially with younger, dependent children), every effort must be made to provide for their security and to keep communication open. The disclosed past abuse of a parent by other family members is likely to generate strong reactions, including anger, disbelief, hurt, sadness, anxiety, depression, mistrust, and fear, and a secondary victimization or "contact traumatization." Concern for the abused mother's well-being and fears of abandonment or family dissolution also might well be stimulated, especially when the mother is debilitated by her symptoms and by the rigors of the therapy. When severe, these will warrant therapeutic attention and strong reassurance by other family members and friends. Peer support groups are of particular utility with children as they are with partners. Additionally, children can be provided with age-appropriate reading material and encouraged to watch audiovisual programs on child sexual abuse. These materials enable them to develop a cognitive understanding of incest/child sexual abuse, to put it in a broader context and to learn prevention and safety techniques.

The special family problems faced by incest survivors were discussed in this chapter. Survivors often struggle with issues of disclosure, confrontation, and reporting, as well as whether to maintain contact with their family of origin and whether to forgive the perpetrator or other family members. Although legal redress for past incest is limited by the statute of limitations in all states, a number of survivors and their advocates are pursuing legal action to extend the statute of limitations and the delayed discovery rule and to establish a tort of "incest." As secondary victims of incest, partners and other loved ones have special needs which sometimes require education, consultation, and treatment.

APPENDICES

Incest History
Questionnaire

INSTRUCTIONS

This 52-question Incest History Questionnaire is designed to assist you in describing your incest experience. It consists of five sections: (1) Family Description; (2) Pre-Incest Self-Description; (3) Description of the Incest; (4) Initial Aftereffects Rating Scale; and, (5) Long-Term Aftereffects Rating Scale. The questionnaire can be completed in several ways: as a whole or in sections inside or outside of therapy. Discussions or responses with your therapist might be tape-recorded for later use.

The Incest History Questionnaire asks detailed questions. Respond according to your ability to answer and your degree of comfort. Do not rush yourself or put yourself under intense pressure. Respond in as much detail as you can remember and you are comfortable with. Another version of this questionnaire has been used in research. The survivors who completed it were unanimous in a indicating that it asks direct questions pertinent to the family and the incest. They found it a helpful tool in disclosure and discussion. This revised version is designed to assist with information-gathering for the therapy process. It will help you to analyze your family and its functioning, the incest and its aftermath, including direct and indirect aftereffects.

I. YOUR FAMILY DESCRIPTION

1. Briefly describe what you know of your grandparents on both your mother's and your father's side. What were they like? How were your parents raised? Can you remember anything about what their relationship was like? Did they have any outstanding personal or family problems that you know about or have heard about? What was their socioeconomic level?

   a. mother's parents:

   b. father's parents:

This questionnaire is a version of the Incest History Questionnaire, © Courtois, 1979, modified for use in a clinical setting.

c. their relationship, parenting, family deficits or assets, etc.:

2. How many children were there in your parents' respective families?

   a. mother:
      number of siblings _____
      mother's birth order _____

   b. father:
      number of siblings _____
      father's birth order _____

3. Are you aware of any physical or sexual abuse in either of your parents' families? How about serious emotional problems or illness, alcoholism or drug abuse?

   a. mother:

   b. father:

4. Describe your parents as individuals. Note any particular personal strengths, weaknesses, and/or problems or assets they have.

   a. mother:

   b. father:

5. Describe your parents' relationship/marital history.

   a. How old were they when they met? When they married?

   b. Did they get together or marry under any special circumstances or strains (e.g., extreme economic hardship, "had to get married")?

   c. Have they ever separated, or divorced and/or remarried? Please describe the circumstances.

   d. Describe your parents' relationship as best you can.

   e. Do you recall any major changes (good or bad) occurring in their relationship? When and of what type?

   f. Describe how your parents interacted with the extended family.

   g. Briefly describe as best you can the educational, occupational and work history of each of your parents.

      mother:

      father:

   h. Briefly describe how your parents and your family functioned in the community at large (e.g., Were they isolated? Did they have friends?).

   i. What was/is your parents' religion? How did religious traditions, beliefs influence family functioning?

    j. What was your family's ethnic or cultural background? How did traditions, beliefs influence family functioning?

6. How many children are in your family (include self and any half-brothers/sisters and stepbrothers/sisters). List all according to birth and note their order, sex, and the number of years between them. Also note children who died and their birth order.

	Sex	Age Difference
_____	_____	_____
_____	_____	_____
_____	_____	_____
_____	_____	_____
_____	_____	_____
_____	_____	_____

7. Now describe as best you can the roles in your family, including any roles you think you held (e.g., older sister acted like a mother, brother was the family clown or scapegoat, mother was the "softy," father was the authoritarian).

father:

mother:

siblings:

self:

8. Describe as best you can what your household was like, how it functioned internally (e.g., mother was boss, father was quiet; father was domineering but mother was the power behind the throne; parents always did what the children wanted/always gave in).

    a. Do you recall any major changes in functioning in your family? Describe them and when they occurred.

9. Describe any family problems, trauma or upheavals you can think of that occurred before, during or after the incest (please note when). (E.g., death in the family, divorce, alcoholism, severe illness or injury, desertion, child running away.)

10. Describe your relationship with your family and its members as you were growing up (e.g., warm, distant, conflicted).

mother:

father:

siblings:

11. Describe your current relationship with family members and current interaction patterns (e.g., warm, distant, conflicted).

    mother:

    father:

    siblings:

II. PRE-INCEST SELF-DESCRIPTION

12. If you can, describe what you can remember about yourself before the incest occurred.

13. Answer the next 4 questions on a scale of 1 to 5.

    a. How did you feel about yourself?

1	2	3	4	5
___/ _____/ _____/ _____/ _____/ ___

good   neutral/   bad
                                      don't know/
                                      don't remember

    b. How did you feel you compared to your friends?

1	2	3	4	5
___/ _____/ _____/ _____/ _____/ ___

felt better   about the   felt worse
about myself   same   about myself

    c. What was your degree of comfort with others?

1	2	3	4	5
___/ _____/ _____/ _____/ _____/ ___

comfortable   neutral/   uncomfortable
                                      don't know/
                                      don't remember

    d. How well did you relate to others?

1	2	3	4	5
___/ _____/ _____/ _____/ _____/ ___

good   neutral/   bad
                                      don't know/
                                      don't remember

14. Indicate your general level of awareness of the following before the incest situation began. Using the following scale, please place the appropriate number next to the subject.

	1		2		3		4		5

___/ _____/ _____/ _____/ _____/ ___

very aware   somewhat aware   unaware

_____ a. sexuality, e.g., sexual behavior and functioning

_____ b. rape

_____ c. incest

_____ d. that strangers could be dangerous and that you should be cautious around them

_____ e. that family members could be dangerous and that you should be cautious around them

15. Did you experience any type of major disruption, crisis or trauma when you were young prior to the incest situation? Please describe (e.g., a family death, a separation from family).

III. DESCRIPTION OF THE INCEST

A. *The Incest*

16. Describe the incest situation which you were involved in as a child/adolescent.

a. Please describe the type of sexual activity that took place. Describe if there was a progression of activity over time.

17. Onset of the incest.

a. When did it begin?

b. How did it begin?

c. Do you have any idea why it began or took place?

18. Termination of the incest.

a. When did it stop? How old were you at the time?

b. How did it stop?

c. Do you have any idea why it stopped?

d. Did you or anyone else do anything to stop it?

19. Duration. How long did the incest go on?

20. Frequency.

a. How often did the incest occur?

b. Were there any patterns or particular circumstances surrounding the occurrence (e.g., drunkenness, violence, loneliness)?

21. Location. Where did the incest take place?

22. The Perpetrator.

    a. Who was the perpetrator?

    b. What was his/her age when the incest began? When it ended?

    c. Can you remember anything about this person that would have caused him/her to engage in incest (e.g., loneliness, temper, drinking)?

    d. Please describe this individual as best you can.

23. Describe your relationship with the perpetrator.

    a. prior to the incest:

    b. during the incest:

    c. after the incest:

24. Involvement.

    a. Were you ever offered any favors or enticements for your participation?

    b. Did you ever refuse to participate? What happened when you did?

    c. Did you ever choose to participate? Please describe.

    d. Were you ever threatened if you didn't comply?

    e. Did you ever struggle? What happened when you did?

    f. Did you ever engage in any other type of behavior to get out of the situation (e.g., running away, getting married)?

25. Reactions at the time of the incest.

    a. What were your reactions to the incest?

    b. How do you think you coped with the incest? What did you do?

    c. What were your reactions to the perpetrator?

    d. What were your reactions to yourself/within yourself?

    e. What were your reactions to other family members?

26. Describe what you were like while the incest was ongoing.

27. How did you function at the time of the incest? Do you believe any aspects of your life suffered or improved at the time due to the incest (e.g., school, relations with others)?

28. Are you aware of any other incest in your family (nuclear or extended) (e.g., sister with father, brother and sister).

29. Were you ever sexually approached by or involved with any other family member?

   _____ Yes   _____ No

   If yes, return to the beginning of this section and answer the questions for that incest. (Repeat this as necessary.)

   a. If yes, was there any connection between this situation and the first incest?

B. *The Issue of Disclosure*

30. In your opinion, did anyone else besides you and the perpetrator know of the incest without a direct disclosure?

   _____ No   _____ Yes

   If yes, describe why you believe so.

31. Do you know if you had observable symptoms that would have cued someone to the incest?

32. Did the incest result in a pregnancy? If yes, what was the outcome?

33. If the situation was overt or became known, did the people who knew ever intervene?

   _____ Yes   _____ No

   a. What action did they take?

   b. What reaction did you have?

34. Did you ever disclose the incest to anyone and/or seek help in any way?

   _____ Yes   _____ No

   If no, skip the rest of this section and continue at section IV.

   a. To whom did you disclose?

   b. When did you disclose the incest? How old were you then?

   c. Describe your reasons for disclosure and any expectations and fears that you had.

   d. What was your reaction after disclosure to this individual and to any action that was taken?

   e. Did the perpetrator know of your disclosing to this person? What was his/her reaction?

C. *Involvement of Social Agencies and Personnel*

35. Was the incest ever reported outside the family to a social agency?

_____ Yes _____ No

If no, go on to section IV.

Which of the following agencies or personnel became involved?

a. _____ police

b. medical services and personnel

_____ hospital

_____ clinic

_____ physician

_____ nurse

_____ other:

c. social service/mental health agency and personnel

_____ child protective agency

_____ community mental health center/family services

_____ psychiatrist

_____ psychologist

_____ counselor

_____ social worker

_____ other:

d. minister, priest or church member

e. legal agency and personnel

_____ the courts

_____ State Attorney's office

_____ private attorney

_____ other:

36. Go back and describe your involvement with and response from the agencies and personnel that you checked above.

37. Describe your reaction to these same involved agencies and personnel.

38. Describe your reaction to the perpetrator at this time.

39. Were you or the perpetrator ever removed from your home after reporting?

_____ Yes _____ No

If no, go on to section IV.

a. For what reason were you or the perpetrator removed?

b. By whom?

c. Where were you removed to?

d. What were your reactions?

e. What was the experience like for you?

40. Have you ever received psychological counseling?

_____ Yes   _____ No

If no, go on to section IV.

a. If yes, reasons for seeking treatment.

b. Did you disclose the incest experience in the counseling?

_____ Yes   _____ No

c. If yes, how and why did you make the disclosure? How did the counselor deal with your disclosure?

d. If no, why did you choose not to disclose it in counseling?

IV. THE INITIAL AFTEREFFECTS

41. Describe any aftereffects you experienced in the following eight areas. These aftereffects are what you perceive were the immediate (rather than long-term) effects of the incest. After describing each one, rate its effect on you using the following scale and explain your rating.
A scale of from 1 to 7: 1 = strongly positive; 2 = moderately positive; 3 = somewhat positive; 4 = neutral; 5 = somewhat negative; 6 = moderately negative; 7 = strongly negative

a. social (e.g., feeling isolated, different from others, unable to interact, mistrustful of others).

_/ _____/ _____/ _____/ _____/ _____/ _____/ __
1   2   3   4   5   6   7

b. psychological/emotional (e.g., not being able to feel anything or having too many emotions). Please discuss specific emotions.

_/ _____/ _____/ _____/ _____/ _____/ _____/ __
1   2   3   4   5   6   7

c. physical (e.g., feeling sick at the mention of certain activities, pain, soreness, headaches).

_/ _____/ _____/ _____/ _____/ _____/ _____/ __
1   2   3   4   5   6   7

d. sexual (e.g., sexual confusion, sexual fears, wanting sex all the time or avoiding it, sexual preference).

_/ _____/ _____/ _____/ _____/ _____/ _____/ __
1   2   3   4   5   6   7

e. familial (within or with your family) (e.g., family members were estranged, got closer, parents got divorced).

_/ _____/ _____/ _____/ _____/ _____/ _____/ __
1   2   3   4   5   6   7

f. sense of self (e.g., powerful, ashamed, improved, or lowered self-concept)

_/ _____/ _____/ _____/ _____/ _____/ _____/ __
1   2   3   4   5   6   7

g. relation to men (e.g., close, trusting, mistrusting, hostile)

_/ _____/ _____/ _____/ _____/ _____/ _____/ __
1   2   3   4   5   6   7

h. relation to women (e.g., close, trusting, mistrusting, hostile)

_/ _____/ _____/ _____/ _____/ _____/ _____/ __
1   2   3   4   5   6   7

42. Please describe any other aftereffects and symptoms.

V. THE LONG-TERM AFTEREFFECTS

43. Describe any aftereffects in the following eight areas that you experienced in the long-term aftermath of the incest. After describing each one, indicate how severe you believe the effect was on you from a scale of from 1 to 7. 1=strongly positive; 2=moderately positive; 3=somewhat positive; 4=neutral; 5=somewhat negative; 6=moderately negative; 7=strongly negative

a. social (e.g., feeling isolated, different from others, unable to interact, mistrustful of others).

_/ _____/ _____/ _____/ _____/ _____/ _____/ __
1   2   3   4   5   6   7

b. psychological/emotional (e.g., not being able to feel anything or having too many emotions). Please discuss specific emotions.

_/ _____/ _____/ _____/ _____/ _____/ _____/ __
1   2   3   4   5   6   7

c. physical (e.g., feeling sick at the mention of certain activities, pain, soreness, headaches).

_/ _____/ _____/ _____/ _____/ _____/ _____/ __
1   2   3   4   5   6   7

d. sexual (e.g., sexual confusion, sexual fears, wanting sex all the time or avoiding it, sexual preference).

_/ _____/ _____/ _____/ _____/ _____/ _____/ __
 1   2   3   4   5   6   7

e. familial (within or with your family) (e.g., family members were estranged, got closer, parents got divorced).

_/ _____/ _____/ _____/ _____/ _____/ _____/ __
 1   2   3   4   5   6   7

f. sense of self (e.g., powerful, ashamed, improved or lowered self-concept)

_/ _____/ _____/ _____/ _____/ _____/ _____/ __
 1   2   3   4   5   6   7

g. relation to men (e.g., close, trusting, mistrusting, hostile)

_/ _____/ _____/ _____/ _____/ _____/ _____/ __
 1   2   3   4   5   6   7

h. relation to women (e.g., close, trusting, mistrusting, hostile)

_/ _____/ _____/ _____/ _____/ _____/ _____/ __
 1   2   3   4   5   6   7

44. Please describe any other aftereffects and symptoms.

45. Using the scale provided, indicate what type of effect the incest had on your life.

       1   2   3   4   5   6   7
/ _____/ _____/ _____/ _____/ _____/ _____/ __
 very   positive somewhat neutral   somewhat negative   very
 positive   positive no effect negative   negative

a. Please discuss why you think this.

46. Describe your current feelings about the perpetrator.

47. Describe your current feelings about any other significant person(s) in your life.

48. Describe your current feelings about the incest. How do you understand your incest experience? Does it have any meaning to you?

49. Describe your current feelings about yourself.

50. Describe any difficulties or complaints you have concerning your present functioning or lifestyle (e.g., headaches, inability to concentrate, poor social skills).

51. Is there any other information you would like to add?

52. Do you have any immediate reactions to having discussed your incest experience in this way?

Recommended Books and Audiovisual Material

BOOKS

Allen, V. (1982). *Daddy's girl*. New York: Berkely Books.

Armstrong, L. (1978). *Kiss daddy good-night: A speak-out on incest*. New York: Hawthorne Books.

Bass, E. & Davis, L. (1988). *The courage to heal: Women healing from child sexual abuse*. New York: Harper & Row.

Bass, E. & Thornton, L. (Eds.). (1983). *I never told anyone: Writing by women survivors of child sexual abuse*. New York: Harper & Row.

Brady, K. (1979). *Father's days*. New York: Dell.

Brownmiller, S. (1975). *Against our will: Men, women and rape*. New York: Simon and Schuster.

Butler, S. (1978). *Conspiracy of silence: The trauma of incest*. New York: Bantam Books.

Carnes, P. (1983). *Out of the shadows: Understanding sexual addiction*. Minneapolis, MN: CompCare Publications.

Cleveland, D. (1986). *Incest: The story of three women*. Lexington, MA: D C Heath.

Donaldson, M. A. (1983). *Incest years after: Putting the pain to rest*. Fargo, ND: The Village Family Service Center.

Donaldson, M. A. & Green, S. C. (1987). *Incest, years after: Learning to cope successfully*. Fargo, ND: The Village Family Service Center.

Forward, S. & Buck, C. (1978). *Betrayal of innocence: Incest and its devastation*. Los Angeles: J. P. Tarcher.

Fossum, M. A. & Mason, M. J. (1986). *Facing shame*. New York: W. W. Norton.

Gil, E. (1983). *Outgrowing the pain: A book for and about adults abused as children*. San Francisco: Launch Press.

Helfer, R. E. (1978). *Childhood comes first: A crash course in childhood for adults*. East Lansing, MI: Ray E. Helfer.

Herman, J. (1981). *Father-daughter incest*. Cambridge, MA: Harvard University Press.

Lerner, H. G. (1985). *The dance of anger*. New York: Harper & Row.

Maltz, W. & Holman, B. (1987). *Incest and sexuality*. Lexington, MA: D.C. Heath.

McNaron, T. A. H. & Morgan, Y. (Eds.) (1982). *Voices in the night: Women speaking about incest.* Minneapolis, MN: Cleis Press.

Meiselman, K. C. (1978). *Incest: A psychological study of cause and effect with treatment recommendations.* San Francisco: Jossey-Bass.

Morris, J. M. (1982). *If I should die before I wake.* Los Angeles: J. P. Tarcher, Inc.

Rush, F. (1980). *The best kept secret: Sexual abuse of children.* Englewood Cliff, NJ: Prentice Hall, Inc.

Russell, D. E. H. (1986). *The secret trauma: Incest in the lives of girls and women.* New York: Basic Books.

Sisk, S. & Hoffman, C. F. (1987). *Inside scars: Incest recovery as told by a survivor and her therapist.* Gainesville, FL: Pandora Press.

Ward, E. (1985). *Father-daughter rape.* New York: Grove Press.

AUDIOVISUALS

Breaking silence. Future Educational Films, Inc. 1628 Union Street, San Francisco, California 94123.

Incest: The victim nobody believes.

Incest, years after: A lecture on theory and treatment. Mary Ann Donaldson. The Village Family Service Center, P.O. Box 7398, Fargo, ND.

The last taboo. Produced by Dale McCulley.

Bibliography

Adams, M. S. & Neel, J. S. (1967). Children of incest. *Pediatrics, 40,* 55–62.

Allen, J. (1983). Tort remedies for incestuous abuse. *Golden Gate University Law Review, 7,* 609–619.

Allen, V. (1982). *Daddy's girl.* New York: Berkely Books.

Allison, R. B. (1974). A new treatment approach for multiple personalities. *American Journal of Clinical Hypnosis, 17,* 15–32.

American Humane Association. (1981). *National study on child neglect and reporting.* Denver: Author.

American Psychiatric Association. (1987). *Diagnostic and statistical manual of mental disorders.* (3rd ed., rev.). Washington, D.C.: Author.

American Psychiatric Association. (1980). *Diagnostic and statistical manual of mental disorders.* (3rd ed.). Washington, D.C.: Author.

Andreason, N. C. (1985). Posttraumatic stress disorder. In H. I. Kaplan & B. J. Sadock (Eds.), *Comprehensive textbook of psychiatry.* (4th ed.) (pp. 918–924). Baltimore: Williams & Wilkins.

Annon, J. S. (1976). *Behavioral treatment of sexual problems: Brief therapy.* New York: Harper & Row.

Armstrong, L. (1982). The cradle of sexual politics. In Kirkpatrick, M. (Ed.), *Women's sexual experience: Explorations of the dark continent.* (pp. 109–125). New York: Plenum.

Armstrong, L. (1978). *Kiss daddy good-night: A speak-out on incest.* New York: Hawthorne Books.

Armsworth, M. W. (1984). *Posttraumatic stress responses in women who experienced incest as children or adolescents.* Unpublished doctoral dissertation, University of Cincinnati, Cincinnati, OH.

Armsworth, M. W. (1987, August). *Abuse and support of adult incest survivors by helping professionals.* Paper presented at the annual meeting of the American Psychological Association, New York City.

Arroyo, W., Eth, S., & Pynoos, R. (1984). Sexual assault of a mother by her preadolescent son. *American Journal of Psychiatry, 141,* 1107–1108.

Bagley, C. & Ramsey, R. (1985, February). *Disrupted childhood and vulnerability to sexual assault: Long-term sequels with implications for counselling.* Paper presented at the conference on Counselling the Sexual Abuse Survivor, Klinic Community Health Centre, Winnipeg, Manitoba.

Baird, P. A. & McGillivray, B. (1982). Children of incest. *Journal of Pediatrics, 101,* 854–857.

Bard, M. & Sangrey, D. (1986). *The crime victim's book.* New York: Brunner/Mazel.

Barnhouse, R. T. (1978). Sex between patient and therapist. *Journal of the American Academy of Psychoanalysis, 61,* 533–546.

Bass, E. & Thornton, L. (Eds.). (1983). *I never told anyone: Writing by women survivors of child sexual abuse.* New York: Harper & Row.

Beahrs, J. O. (1982). *Unity and multiplicity: Multilevel consciousness of self in hypnosis, psychiatric disorder and mental health.* New York: Brunner/Mazel.

Beck, J. & van der Kolk. *Women with a history of incest in the mental hospital.* Manuscript submitted for publication.

Becker, J. V. & Skinner, L. J. (1984). Behavioral treatment of sexual dysfunctions in sexual assault survivors. In I. R. Stuart & J. G. Greer (Eds.). *Victims of sexual aggression: Treatment of children, women, and men.* New York: Van Nostrand Reinhold.

Becker, J. V., Skinner, L. J., Abel, G. G., & Treacy, E. C. (1982). Incidence and types of sexual dysfunctions in rape and incest victims. *Journal of Sex and Marital Therapy, 8,* 65–74.

Benedek, E. P. (1985). Children and psychic trauma: A brief review of contemporary thinking. In S. Eth & R. S. Pynoos (Eds.). *Post-traumatic stress disorder in children.* Washington, D.C.: American Psychiatric Press, Inc.

Benward, J. & Densen-Gerber, J. (1975). Incest as a causative factor in anti-social behavior: An exploratory study. *Contemporary Drug Problems, 4*(3), 323–340.

Bergart, A. M. (1986). Isolation to intimacy: Incest survivors in group therapy. *Social Casework, 67,* 266–275.

Berry, G. W. (1975). Incest: Some clinical variations on a classical theme. *Journal of the American Academy of Psychoanalysis, 3,* 151–161.

Blank, A. (March, 1985). *Lessons learned from the treatment of combat veterans relevant for crime victims.* Paper presented at the colloquium, The Aftermath of Crime: A Mental Health Crisis. National Institute of Mental Health and National Organization of Victim Assistance, Washington, D.C.

Brady, K. (1979). *Father's days.* New York: Dell.

Braun, B. G. (1986a). Issues in the treatment of multiple personality disorder. In B. G. Braun (Ed.). *Treatment of multiple personality disorder.* Washington, DC: American Psychiatric Press, Inc.

Braun, B. G. (Ed.). (1986b). *Treatment of multiple personality disorder.* Washington, D.C.: American Psychiatric Press, Inc.

Braun, B. G. (1980). Hypnosis for multiple personalities. In H. J. Wain (Ed.). *Clinical hypnosis in medicine.* Chicago: Year Book Medical Publishers.

Brickman, J. (1984). Feminist, nonsexist, and traditional models of therapy: Implications for working with incest. *Women and Therapy, 3*(1) 49–67.

Brickman, J. (1985, February). *Counselling issues and techniques for working with sexual abuse survivors.* Workshop presented at the conference on Counselling the Sexual Abuse Survivor, Klinic Community Health Centre, Winnipeg, Manitoba.

Briere, J. (April, 1984). *The effects of childhood sexual abuse on later psychological functioning: Defining a post-sexual abuse syndrome.* Paper presented at the Third National Conference on the Sexual Victimization of Children, Children's Hospital National Medical Center, Washington, D.C.

Briere, J. & Runtz, M. (1985). *Symptomatology associated with prior sexual abuse in a non-clinical sample.* Paper presented at the annual meeting of the American Psychological Association, Los Angeles, CA.

Briere, J. & Runtz, M. (1986). Suicidal thoughts and behaviours in former sexual abuse victims. *Canadian Journal of Behavioral Science, 18,* 413–423.

Brooks, B. (1983). Preoedipal issues in a postincest daughter. *American Journal of Psychotherapy, 37,* 129–136.

Browne, A. (1987). *When battered women kill.* New York: The Free Press.

Browne, A. & Finkelhor, D. (1986). Impact of child sexual abuse: A review of the literature. *Psychological Bulletin, 99,* 66–77.

Browning, D. & Boatman, B. (1977). Incest: Children at risk. *American Journal of Psychiatry, 134,* 69–72.

Brownmiller, S. (1975). *Against our will: Men, women and rape.* New York: Simon and Schuster.

Bryer, J. B., Miller, J. B., Nelson, B., & Krol, P. (n.d.). *Adult psychiatric symptoms, diagnoses, and medications as indicators of childhood abuse.* Unpublished manuscript. Charles River Hospital, Wellesley, MA.

Burgess, A. W., Groth, A. N., Holmstrom, L. L., & Sgroi, S. M. (1978). *Sexual assault of children and adolescents.* Lexington, MA: D. C. Heath.

Burgess, A. W. & Holmstrom, L. L. (1974). Sexual trauma of children and adolescents: Pressure, sex and secrecy. *Nursing Clinics of North America, 10,* 554–563.

Burgess, A. W. & Holmstrom, L. L. (1979). *Rape: Crisis and Recovery.* New York: Prentice-Hall.

Butler, S. (1978). *Conspiracy of silence: The trauma of incest.* New York: Bantam Books.

Butler, S. (February, 1985). *Treatment perspectives: A feminist view.* Presentation made at the Conference on Counselling the Sexual Abuse Survivor, Klinic Community Health Centre, Winnipeg, Manitoba.

Calof, D. (1987). *Treating adult survivors of incest and child abuse.* Workshop presented at The Family Network Symposium, Washington, D.C.

Carmen, E. H., Rieker, P. R., & Mills, T. (1984). Victims of violence and psychiatric illness. *American Journal of Psychiatry, 143,* 378–383.

Carnes, P. (1983). *Out of the shadows: Understanding sexual addiction.* Minneapolis, MN: Compcare Publications.

Caul, D. & Wilbur, C. B. (n.d.). *General Amnesia Profile.*

Chasnoff, I., Burns, W., Schnoll, S., Burns, K., Chisum, G., & Kyle-Spore, L. (1986). Maternal neonatal incest. *American Journal of Orthopsychiatry, 56,* 577–580.

Clary, W. F., Burstin, K. J., & Carpenter, J. S. (1984). Multiple personality and borderline personality disorder. *Psychiatric Clinics of North America, 7,* 89–100.

Cohen, J. A. (1981). Theories of narcissism and trauma. *American Journal of Psychotherapy, 35,* 93–100.

Cohen, P. (1984). Violence in the family — An act of loyalty? *Psychotherapy, 21,* 249–253.

Cohen, T. (1983). The incestuous family revisited. *Social Casework, 64,* 154–161.

Cole, C. L. (1985). A group design for adult female survivors of childhood incest. *Women & Therapy, 4,* 71–82.

Cole, E. (1982). Sibling incest: The myth of benign sibling incest. *Women and Therapy, 5,* 79–89.

Conn, L. N. (1986). Self-mutilation: The symptom and its management. *Treatment Trends,* Ellicott City, MD: Taylor Manor Hospital, 1–5.

Conte, J. (1986). Failure to report sexual victimization of children: The context of professional behavior. In *Proceedings of Symposium on Professional Ethics and Child Abuse.* Jointly sponsored by the American Bar Association and the National Institute of Mental Health. (Contract No. 85-MO-420617-01D). Rockville, MD: National Institute of Mental Health.

Coons, P. M. (1980). Multiple personality: Diagnostic considerations. *Journal of Clinical Psychiatry*, 41, 330–336.

Cooper, I. & Cormier, M. (1982). Inter-generational transmission of incest. *Canadian Journal of Psychiatry*, 278, 231–235.

Corwin, D. (May, 1986). *The sexually abused child disorder: Fact or fantasy?* Panel presented at the Fourth National Conference on the Sexual Victimization of Children, Children's Hospital National Medical Center, New Orleans, LA.

Courtois, C. A. (1979). Characteristics of a volunteer sample of adult women who experienced incest in childhood and adolescence. *Dissertation Abstracts International*, 40A, Nov.–Dec. 1979, 3194-A.

Courtois, C. A. (1982, April). *The conditions and aftereffects of childhood incest experience.* Paper presented at the Second National Conference on Sexual Victimization of Children, Children's Hospital National Medical Center, Washington, D.C.

Courtois, C. A. (1986, May). *Treatment for serious mental health sequelae of child sexual abuse: Post-Traumatic Stress Disorder in children and adults.* Paper presented at the Fourth National Conference on the Sexual Victimization of Children, Children's Hospital National Medical Center, New Orleans, LA.

Courtois, C. A. & Hinckley, J. A. (1981). Grandfather-granddaughter incest. *Journal of Sex Education and Therapy*, 7, 37–42.

Courtois, C. A. & Leehan, J. (1982). Group treatment for grown-up abused children. *The Personnel and Guidance Journal*, 60, 564–566.

Courtois, C. A. & Sprei, J. E. (1988). Retrospective incest therapy for women. In L. E. Walker (Ed.). *Handbook on sexual abuse of children.* New York: Springer.

Courtois, C. A. & Watts, D. (1982). Counseling adult women who experienced incest in childhood or adolescence. *Personnel and Guidance Journal*, 275–279.

Crigler, P. (1984). Incest in the military family. In Kaslow, F. and Ridenour, R. (Eds.). *The military family.* New York: Guilford.

Cupchik, W. (1984). Reintrojection therapy: A procedure for altering parental introjects. *Psychotherapy*, 21, 213–217.

Danieli, Y. (1984). Psychotherapists' participation in the conspiracy of silence about the Holocaust. *Psychoanalytic Psychology*, 1, 23–42.

Davidson, H. (1986). Failure to report child abuse: Legal penalties and emerging issues. In *Proceedings of Symposium on Professional Ethics and Child Abuse.* Jointly sponsored by the American Bar Association and the National Institute of Mental Health. (Contract No. 85-MO-420617-01D). Rockville, MD: National Institute of Mental Health.

DeRose, D. M. (1985). Adult incest survivors and the statute of limitations: The delayed discovery rule and long-term damages. *The Santa Clara Law Review*, 25, 191–225.

DeYoung, M. (1981a). Case reports: The sexual exploitation of incest victims by helping professionals. *Victimology: An International Journal*, 1-4, 91–101.

De Young, M. (1981b). Siblings of Oedipus: Brothers and sisters of incest victims. *Child Welfare*, 60, 561–568.

De Young, M. (1982). Self-injurious behavior in incest victims: A research note. *Child Welfare*, 61, 577–584.

Dixon, K. N., Arnold, L. E., & Calestro, K. (1978). Father-son incest: Underreported psychiatric problem? *American Journal of Psychiatry*, 135, 835–838.

Donaldson, M. A. (1983). *Responses to childhood incest: A tool for self-assessment.* Fargo, ND: The Village Family Service Center.

Donaldson, M. A. & Green, S. C. (1987). *Incest, years after: Learning to cope sucessfully (An educational guide for self-assessment).* Fargo, ND: The Village Family Service Center.

Donaldson, M. A. & Gardner, R. (1985). Diagnosis and treatment of traumatic stress among women after childhood incest. In C. R. Figley (Ed.). *Trauma and its wake: The study and treatment of post-traumatic stress disorder.* New York: Brunner/Mazel.

Dubanoski, R. A. & McIntosh, S. R. (1984). Child abuse and neglect in military and civilian families. *Child Abuse and Neglect, 8,* 55–67.

DuPont, R. L. (Ed.). (1982). *Phobia: A comprehensive summary of modern treatments.* New York: Brunner/Mazel.

Ellenson, G. S. (1986). Disturbances of perception in adult female incest survivors. *Social Casework, 67,* 149–159.

Emslie, G. J. & Rosenfeld, A. A. (1983). Incest reported by children and adolescents hospitalized for severe psychiatric problems. *American Journal of Psychiatry, 140,* 708–711.

Erikson, E. H. (1980). *Identity and the life cycle.* New York: W. W. Norton.

Eth, S., & Pynoos, R. S. (Eds.). (1985). *Post-traumatic stress disorder in children.* Washington, D.C.: American Psychiatric Press, Inc.

Faria, G. & Belohlavek, N. (1984). Treating female adult survivors of childhood incest. *Social Casework, 465–471.*

Favazza, A. R. (1987). *Bodies under siege: Self-mutilation in culture and psychiatry.* Baltimore: The Johns Hopkins University Press.

Figley, C. R. (Ed.). (1985). *Trauma and its wake: The study and treatment of post-traumatic stress disorder.* New York: Brunner/Mazel.

Finkelhor, D. (1978). Psychological, cultural and family factors in incest and family sexual abuse. *Journal of Marriage and Family Counseling, 4,* 41–49.

Finkelhor, D. (1979). *Sexually victimized children.* New York: Free Press.

Finkelhor, D. (1984). *Child sexual abuse: New theory and research.* New York: The Free Press.

Finkelhor, D. (1986). *A sourcebook on child sexual abuse.* Beverly Hills: Sage Publications.

Finkelhor, D. & Baron, L. (1986). High risk children. In D. Finkelhor and associates (Eds.). *A sourcebook on child sexual abuse.* Beverly Hills, CA: Sage Publications.

Finkelhor, D. & Browne, A. (1985). The traumatic impact of child sexual abuse: A conceptualization. *American Journal of Orthopsychiatry, 55,* 530–541.

Fitzgibbons, T. P. (1986). The cognitive and emotive uses of forgiveness in the treatment of anger. *Psychotherapy, 23,* 629–633.

Flannery, R. B., Jr. (1987). From victim to survivor: A stress management approach to the treatment of learned helplessness. In B. van der Kolk (Ed.). *Psychological trauma.* Washington, D.C.: American Psychiatric Press, Inc.

Forward, S., & Buck, C. (1978). *Betrayal of innocence: Incest and its devastation.* Los Angeles: J. P. Tarcher.

Fossum, M. A. & Mason, M. J. (1986). *Facing shame.* New York: W. W. Norton & Company.

Frederick, C. (1985). Children traumatized by catastrophic situations. In S. Eth & R. S. Pynoos (Eds.). *Post-traumatic stress disorder in children.* Washington, D.C.: American Psychiatric Press, Inc.

Freud, A. (1981). A psychoanalyst's view of sexual abuse by parents. In P. B. Mrazek & C. H. Kempe (Eds.). *Sexually abused children and their families.* New York: Pergamon Press.

Fromouth, M. E. (1986). The relationship of childhood sexual abuse with later psychological adjustment in a sample of college women. *Child Abuse and Neglect, 10,* 5–15.

Gelinas, D. J. (1983). The persisting negative effects of incest. *Psychiatry, 46,* 313–332.

Giarretto, H. (1976). The treatment of father-daughter incest: A psych-social approach. *Children Today, 34,* 2-5.

Giarretto, H. (1982). A comprehensive child sexual abuse treatment program. *Child Abuse & Neglect, 6,* 263–278.

Glueck, B. C., Jr. (1965). Pedophilia. In R. Slovenko (Ed.). *Sexual behavior and the law.* Springfield, IL: Charles C. Thomas.

Gold, E. R. (1986). Long-term effects of sexual victimization in childhood: An attributional approach. *Journal of Consulting and Clinical Psychology, 54,* 471–475.

Goodwin, J. (1982). *Sexual abuse: Incest victims and their families.* Littleton, MA: PGS Publishing.

Goodwin, J. (1985). Post-traumatic symptoms in incest victims. In S. Eth & R. S. Pynoos (Eds.). *Post-traumatic stress disorder in children.* Washington, D.C.: American Psychiatric Press, Inc.

Goodwin, J., Attias, R., McCarty, T., Chandler, S., & Romanik, R. (in press). Effects on psychiatric inpatients of routine questioning about childhood sexual abuse. *Victimology: An International Journal.*

Goodwin, J., Cormier, L., & Owen, J. (1983). Grandfather-granddaughter incest: A trigenerational view. *Child Abuse & Neglect, 7,* 163–170.

Goodwin, J. & DiVasto, P. (1979). Mother-daughter incest. *Child Abuse & Neglect, 3,* 953–957.

Goodwin, J., McCarthy, T., & DiVasto, P. (1981). Prior incest in mothers of abused children. *Child Abuse & Neglect, 5,* 87–95.

Gordy, P. L. (1983). Group work that supports adult victims of childhood incest. *Social Casework, 64,* 300–307.

Green, A. H. (1978). Psychopathology of abused children. *Journal of the American Academy of Child Psychiatry, 17,* 92–103.

Green, A. H. (1983). Dimensions of psychological trauma in abused children. *Journal of the American Academy of Child Psychiatry, 22,* 231–237.

Green, C. M. (1982). Filicidal impulses as an anniversary reaction to childhood incest. *American Journal of Psychotherapy, 36,* 264–271.

Greer, J. G. (1986). *Psychoanalytic treatment of adult incest survivors.* Paper presented at the Fourth National Conference on the Sexual Victimization of Children. Children's Hospital National Medical Center. New Orleans, L.A.

Greenberg, M. S. & van der Kolk, B. (1987). Retrieval and integration of traumatic memories with the "painting cure." In B. van der Kolk (Ed.). *Psychological trauma.* Washington, D.C.: American Psychiatric Press, Inc.

Groth, A. N. (1982). The incest offender. In S. M. Sgroi (Ed.). *Handbook of Clinical Intervention in Child Sexual Abuse.* Lexington, MA: D. C. Heath.

Groves, D. (1987). *Resolving traumatic memories: Competency based training for mental health professionals.* Munster, IN: David Groves Seminars.

Harris, J. M. (1986, May). *A model training seminar for adult incest survivors.* Paper presented at the Fourth National Conference on the Sexual Victimization of Children, Children's Hospital National Medical Center, New Orleans, LA.

Helfer, R. E. (1978). *Childhood comes first: A crash course in childhood for adults.* East Lansing, MI: Ray E. Helfer.

Herman, J. (1981). *Father-daughter incest.* Cambridge: Harvard University Press.

Herman, J. (1987, April). *Incest Therapy.* Workshop sponsored by The Therapy Center, Alexandria, VA.

Herman, J. & Hirschman, L. (1977). Father-daughter incest. *Signs: Journal of Women in Culture and Society, 2,* 735–756.

Herman, J. & Hirschman, L. (1981). Families at risk for father-daughter incest. *American Journal of Psychiatry, 138,* 967–970.

Herman, J. & Schatzow, E. (1984). Time-limted group therapy for women with a history of incest. *International Journal of Group Psychotherapy, 34*(4), 605–616.

Herman, J. & Schatzow, E. (1987). Recovery and verification of memories of childhood sexual trauma. *Psychoanalytic Psychology, 4,* 1–14.

Herman, J. & van der Kolk, B. (1987). Traumatic antecedents of borderline personality disorder. In B. van der Kolk (Ed.). *Psychological trauma.* Washington, D.C.: American Psychiatric Press, Inc.

Horevitz, P. P. & Braun, B. G. (1984). Are multiple personalities borderline? In B. G. Braun (Ed.). *Symposium on multiple personality. Psychiatric Clinics of North America, 7,* 69–87.

Horowitz, M. J. (1976). *Stress response syndromes.* New York: Jason Aronson.

Horowitz, M. J. (1986). *Stress response syndromes* (2nd ed.). Northvale, NJ: Jason Aronson.

Jakubiak, M. & Murphy, S. (1987). Incest survivors in women's communities. *Human Development, 8,* 19–25.

James, K. (1977). Incest: The teenager's perspective. *Psychotherapy: Theory, Research, and Practice, 14,* 146–155.

Janoff-Bulman, R. (1979). Characterological versus behavioral self-blame: Inquiries into depression and rape. *Journal of Personality and Social Psychology, 37,* 1798–1809.

Janoff-Bulman, R. & Frieze, I. (1983). A theoretical perspective for understanding reactions to victimization. *Journal of Social Issues, 39,* 1–18.

Jehu, D., Klassen, C., & Gazan, M. (1985). Cognitive restructuring of distorted beliefs associated with childhood sexual abuse. *Journal of Social Work and Human Sexuality, 4,* 49–69.

Jehu, D., Gazan, M., & Klassen, C. (1985). Common therapeutic targets among women who were sexually abused in childhood. In *Feminist Perspectives on Social Work and Human Sexuality,* New York: Haworth Press.

Jelinek, J. M. & Williams, T. (1987). Post-traumatic stress disorder and substance abuse: Treatment problems, strategies and recommendations. In T. Williams (Ed.). *Post-traumatic stress disorders: A handbook for clinicians.* Cincinnati, OH: Disabled American Veterans.

Johns, M. B. (1987). Therapists, incest and countertransference: The effects of experience and theoretical orientation on therapists beliefs and practices. Unpublished manuscript. The Woodburn Community Mental Health Center, Annandale, VA.

Josephson, G. S. & Fong-Beyette, M. L. (1987). Factors assisting female clients' disclosure of incest during counseling. *Journal of Counseling and Development, 65,* 475–478.

Joy, S. (1987). Retrospective presentations of incest: Treatment strategies for use with adult women. *Journal of Counseling and Development, 65,* 317–319.

Justice, B. & Justice, R. (1979). *The broken taboo: Sex in the family.* New York: Human Sciences Press.

Kaplan, H. S. & Sadock, B. J. (Eds.). (1985). *Comprehensive textbook of psychiatry.* (4th ed.). Baltimore: Williams & Wilkins.

Kaslow, F., Haupt, D., Arce, A. A., & Werblowsky, J. (1981). Homosexual incest. *Psychiatric Quarterly, 53,* 184–193.

Keane, T. M., Fairbank, J. A., Caddell, J. M., Zimering, R. T., & Bender, M. E. (1985). A behavioral approach to assessing and treating post-traumatic stress disorder in Vietnam veterans. In C. R. Figley (Ed.). *Trauma and its wake: The study and treatment of post-traumatic stress disorder.* New York: Brunner/Mazel.

Kearney-Cooke, A. (in press). Group treatment of sexual abuse among women with eating disorders. *Women and Therapy.*

Keating, K. (1983). *The hug therapy book.* Minneapolis, MN: Compcare Publications.

Kelly, R. J. (in press). Limited confidentiality and the pedophile. *Hospital and Community Psychiatry.*

Kelly, R. J., MacDonald, V. M., & Waterman, J. M. (1987, January). *Psychological symptomatology in adult male victims of child sexual abuse: A preliminary study.* Paper presented at the joint conference of the American Psychological Association Division 12 and the Hawaii Psychological Association. Honolulu, HI.

Kelly, R. J. & Scott, M. M. (1986). Sociocultural considerations in child sexual abuse. In K. MacFarlane, J. Waterman et al. (Eds.). *Sexually abused young children: Evaluation and treatment.* New York: Guilford.

Kempe, R. & Kempe, H. (1984). *The common secret.* New York: W. H. Freeman.

Kersher, G. & McShane, M. (1984). The prevalence of child sexual abuse victimization in an adult sample of Texas residents. *Child Abuse & Neglect, 8,* 495–501.

Kinsey, A. C., Pomeroy, W. B., Martin, C. E., & Gebhard, P. (1953). *Sexual behavior in the human female.* Philadelphia: Saunders.

Kleiman, D. (1987, October 6). 6-month term for teen-ager in L. I. murder. *The New York Times,* Section B 1–2.

Kluft, R. P. (1984). Treatment of multiple personality disorder. *Psychiatric Clinics of North America, 7,* 9–30.

Kluft, R. P. (Ed.). (1985). *Childhood antecedents of multiple personality.* Washington, DC: American Psychiatric Press.

Korbin, J. (1981). *Child abuse and neglect: Cross-cultural perspectives.* Berkeley: University of California Press.

Kovach, J. A. (1983). The relationship between treatment failures of alcoholic women and incestuous histories with possible implications for post-traumatic stress disorder symptomatology. *Dissertation Abstracts International, 44*(3-A), 710.

Krugman, S. (1987). Trauma in the family: Perspectives on the intergenerational transmission of violence. In B. van der Kolk (Ed.). *Psychological trauma.* Washington, DC: American Psychiatric Press.

Krystal, H. (1984). Psychoanalytic views on human emotional damage. In B. A. van der Kolk (Ed.). *Post-traumatic stress disorder: Psychological and biological sequelae.* Washington, DC: American Psychiatric Press.

Lamb, S. (1986). Treating sexually abused children: Issues of blame and responsibility. *American Journal of Orthopsychiatry, 56,* 303–307.

Leehan, J. & Wilson, L. (1985). *Grown-up abused children.* Springfield, IL: Charles C. Thomas.

Lees, S. W. (1981). *Guidelines for helping female victims and survivors of incest.* Cambridge, MA: Incest Resources, Inc.

Lerner, M. J. (1980). *The belief in a just world.* New York: Plenum.

Lewis, M. & Sarrel, P. (1969). Some psychological aspects of seduction, incest, and rape in childhood. *Journal of the American Academy of Child Psychiatry, 8* 609–619.

Lindberg, F. H. & Distad, L. J. (1985a). Post-traumatic stress disorders in women who experienced childhood incest. *Child Abuse and Neglect, 9,* 329–334.

Lindberg, F. H. & Distad, L. J. (1985b). Survival responses to incest: Adolescents in crisis. *Child Abuse and Neglect, 9,* 521–526.

Lister, E. D. (1982). Forced silence: A neglected dimension of trauma. *American Journal of Psychiatry, 139,* 872–876.

Loredo, C. (1982). Sibling incest. In S. M. Sgroi (Ed.). *Handbook of clinical intervention in child sexual abuse*. Lexington, MA: D. C. Heath.

MacFarlane, K. & Korbin, J. (1983). Confronting the incest secret long after the fact: A family study of multiple victimization with strategies for intervention. *Child Abuse & Neglect, 7*, 225–240.

MacFarlane, K. & Waterman, J. with Conerly, S., Dramon, L., Durfee, M., & Long, S. (1986). *Sexual abuse of young children*. New York: Guilford.

Maltz, W. & Holman, B. (1987). *Incest and Sexuality*. Lexington, MA: Lexington Books.

Mann, J. (1973). *Time limited psychotherapy*. Cambridge, MA: Harvard University Press.

Margolis, M. (1984). A case of mother-adolescent son incest: A follow-up study. *Psychoanalytic Quarterly, 53*, 355–385.

Mayer, A. (1983). *Incest: A treatment manual for therapy with victims, spouses and offenders*. Holmes Beach, FL: Learning Publications, Inc.

McCarty, L. M. (1986). Mother-child incest: Characteristics of the offender. *Child Welfare, 65*, 447–458.

McNaron, T. A. H. & Morgan, Y. (Eds.). (1982). *Voices in the night: Women speaking about incest*. Minneapolis, MN: Cleis Press.

Meichenbaum, D. & Jaremko, M. E. (Eds.). (1983). *Stress reduction and prevention*. New York: Plenum.

Meiselman, K. C. (1978). *Incest: A psychological study of cause and effects with treatment recommendations*. San Francisco: Josey-Bass.

Messer, A. A. (1969). The "Phaedra complex". *Archives of General Psychiatry, 21*, 213–218.

Miller, A. (1981). *Prisoners of childhood: The drama of the gifted child and the search for the true self*. New York: Basic Books.

Miller, A. (1984). *Thou shalt not be aware: Society's betrayal of the child*. New York: Farrar, Straus, Giroux.

Moore, J. M. (1986). Civil remedies for incest survivors. *Response, 9*, 11–16.

Morris, M. (1982). *If I should die before I wake*. Los Angeles: J. P. Tarcher, Inc.

Morrissey, K. (1982). Self-help for women with a history of incest. In *Therapeutic interventions in father-daughter incest*. Symposium conducted at the annual meeting of the American Psychological Association, Toronto, Ontario.

Mrazek, P. B. (1981). The nature of incest: A review of contributing factors. In P. B. Mrazek & C. H. Kempe (Eds.). *Sexually abused children and their families*. New York: Pergamon.

Mrazek, P. B. & Kempe, C. H. (Eds.). (1981). *Sexually abused children and their families*. New York: Pergamon.

Myers, B. (n.d.). *Developmental disruptions of victims of incest and childhood abuse*. Minneapolis, MN: Christopher Street.

Nadelson, C. C. (1982). Incest and rape: Repercussions in sexual behavior. In L. Greenspoon (Ed.). *The Annual Review of Psychiatry*. Washington, DC: American Psychiatric Association Press, Inc.

Nasjleti, M. (1980). Suffering in silence: The male incest victim. *Child Welfare, LIX*, 269–275.

O'Connor, D. (1986, March). Later-life consequences of childhood sexual abuse. *Development, trauma, treatment: Sexual issues of young adulthood*. The Metropolitan College Mental Health Association, New York City.

Parker, H. & Parker, S. (1986). Father-daughter sexual abuse: An emerging perspective. *American Journal of Orthopsychiatry, 56*, 531–549.

Parson, E. R. (1985). Ethnicity and traumatic stress: The intersecting point in psychotherapy. In C. R. Figley (Ed.). *Trauma and its wake: The study and treatment of post-traumatic stress disorder.* New York: Brunner/Mazel.

Pasternak, S. (1987, December). *The effects of childhood sexual abuse on later adult functioning and the complexities of its treatment.* Paper presented at the conference, Adult Child Therapy—Treating the Adult Survivor of Child Abuse. The Psychiatric Institute Foundation. Washington, DC.

Pelto, V. L. (1981). Male incest offenders and non-offenders: A comparison of early sexual history. *Dissertation Abstracts International, 42*(3-B), 1154.

Peters, J. J. (1976). Children who are victims of sexual assault and the psychology of offenders. *American Journal of Psychotherapy, 30,* 398-421.

Peters, S. D. (1984). *The relationship between childhood sexual victimization and adult depression among Afro-American and white women.* Unpublished doctoral dissertation, University of California, Los Angeles.

Price, R. (1987). Dissociative disorders of the self: A continuum extending into multiple personality. *Psychotherapy, 24,* 387-391.

Putnam, F. W. (1984). Multiple personality. *Psychiatric Annals, 14,* 58-61.

Putnam, F. W. (1986, May). *Treatment for serious mental health sequelae.* Panel presented at the Fourth National Conference on the Sexual Victimization of Children. Children's Hospital National Medical Center. New Orleans, LA.

Putnam, F. W. (1985). Pieces of the mind: Recognizing the psychological effects of abuse. *Justice for Children, 1,* 6-7.

Putnam, F. W., Post, R. M., & Guroff, J. J. (1983). *One hundred cases of multiple personality disorder.* Presented at the annual meeting of the American Psychiatric Association.

Raybin, J. (1969). Homosexual incest. *The Journal of Nervous and Mental Disease, 148,* 105-110.

Renshaw, D. (1982). *Incest: Understanding and treatment.* Boston: Little, Brown.

Rieker, P. & Carmen, E. (1986). The victim-to-patient process: The disconfirmation and transformation of abuse. *American Journal of Orthopsychiatry, 56,* 360-370.

Rieth, S. M. (n.d.). *A new model for the treatment of adult survivors of sexual abuse.* Buffalo, NY: The Samaritan Counseling Center of the Niagara Frontier, Inc.

Rist, K. (1979). Incest: Theoretical and clinical views. *American Journal of Orthopsychiatry, 49,* 680-691.

Rogers, C. M. & Tremaine, T. (1984). Clinical intervention with boy victims of sexual abuse. In I. R. Stuart & J. G. Greer (Eds.). *Victims of sexual aggression: Treatment of children, women, and men.* New York: Van Nostrand Reinhold.

Rose, D. S. (1986). "Worse than death": Psychodynamics of rape victims and the need for psychotherapy. *American Journal of Psychiatry, 143,* 817-824.

Rosenfeld, A. A. (1977). Sexual misuse and the family. *Victimology: An International Journal, 2,* 226-235.

Rosenfeld, A. A. (1979). Endogamic incest and the victim-perpetrator model. *American Journal of Diseases of Children, 133,* 406-410.

Rosenfeld, A. A. (1986, May). *Treatment for serious mental health sequelae.* Panel presented at the Fourth National Conference on the Sexual Victimization of Children. Children's Hospital National Medical Center. New Orleans, LA.

Rovner, S. (1987, August 11). Violence hits home: When the abused child grows up. *The Washington Post.* 12, 14-15.

Roybal, L. & Goodwin, J. (1982). The incest pregnancy. In J. Goodwin (Ed.). *Sexual abuse: Incest victims and their families.* Littleton, MA: PSG Publishing Company, Inc.

Runtz, M. G. (1987). *The sexual victimization of women: The link between child*

abuse and revictimization. Paper presented at the annual meeting of the Canadian Psychological Association, Vancouver, BC.

Rush, F. (1977). The Freudian cover-up. *Chrysalis*, 31–45.

Rush, F. (1980). *The best kept secret: Sexual abuse of children.* Englewood Cliff, NJ:
Prentice Hall.

Russell, D. E. H. (1983). The incidence and prevalence of intrafamilial and extrafamilial sexual abuse of female children. *Child Abuse & Neglect*, 7, 133–146.

Russell, D. E. H. (1985, February). *Key new findings on incest.* Presentation made at
the Conference on Counselling the Sexual Abuse Survivor, Klinic Community
Health Centre, Winnipeg, Manitoba.

Russell, D. E. H. (1986). *The secret trauma: Incest in the lives of girls and women.*
New York: Basic Books.

Salten, (1984). Statutes of limitations in civil incest suits: Preserving the victim's
remedy. *Harvard Women's Law Journal*, 7, 189–190.

Schover, L. R., Friedman, J. M., Weiler, S. J., Heiman, J. R., & LoPiccolo, J. (1980).
*A multi-axial descriptive system for the sexual dysfunctions: Categories and manu-
al.* Stoneybrook: New York: Sex Therapy Center.

Schover, L. R., Friedman, J. M., Weiler, S. J., Heiman, J. R., & LoPiccolo, J. (1980).
*A multi-axial descriptive system for the sexual dysfunctions: Categories and manu-
al.* Stoneybrook, New York: Sex Therapy Center.

Schultz, R., Braun, B. G., & Kluft, R. P. (1987). [*The most significant findings of the
interface between multiple personality disorder (MPD) and Borderline Personality
Disorder (BPD)*]. Unpublished raw data.

Scurfield, R. M. (1985). Post-trauma stress assessment and treatment: Overview
and formulations. In C. R. Figley (Ed.). *Trauma and its wake: The study and
treatment of post-traumatic stress disorder.* New York: Brunner/Mazel.

Sedney, M. A. & Brooks, B. (1984). Factors associated with history of childhood
sexual experience in a nonclinical female population. *Journal of the American of
Child Psychiatry*, 23, 215–218.

Sgroi, S. M. (1977). Kids with clap: Gonorrhea as an indicator of child sexual
assault. *Victimology: An International Journal*, 2, 251–267.

Sgroi, S. M. (1978). Comprehensive examination for child sexual assault: Diagnostic, therapeutic and child protection issues. In A. W. Burgess, A. N. Groth, L. L.
Holstrom, & S. M. Sgroi (Eds.). *Sexual assault of children and adolescents.* Lexington, MA: D. C. Heath.

Sgroi, S. M. (Ed.). (1982). *Handbook of clinical intervention in child sexual abuse.*
Lexington, MA: D.C. Heath.

Sgroi, S. M., Blick, L. C., & Porter, F. S. (1982). A conceptual framework for child
sexual abuse. In S. M. Sgroi (Ed.). *Handbook of clinical intervention in child
sexual abuse.* Lexington, MA: D. C. Heath.

Shengold, L. (1979). Child aubse and deprivation: Soul murder. *Journal of the
American Psychoanalytic Association*, 27, 533–559.

Shengold, L. (1980). Some reflections on a case of mother/adolescent son incest.
International Journal of Psychoanalysis, 60, 461–476.

Silver, R. L., Boon, C., & Stones, M. H. (1983). Searching for meaning in misfor-
tune: Making sense of incest, *Journal of Social Issues*, 39, 2, 81–102.

Simari, C. G. & Baskin, D. (1982). Incestuous experiences within homosexual
populations: A preliminary study. *Archives of Sexual Behavior*, 11, 329–344.

Sisk, S. & Hoffman, C. F. (1987). *Inside scars: Incest recovery as told by a survivor and
her therapist.* Gainesville, FL: Pandora Press.

Slaikeu, K. A. (1984). *Crisis intervention.* Boston, MA: Allyn and Bacon.

Smolak, L., Levine, M. P., & Sullins, E. (1987, August). *Child sexual experiences and eating disorders in a college population.* Paper presented at the annual convention of the American Psychological Association, New York City.

Solin, C. A. (1986). Displacement of affect in families following incest disclosure. *American Journal of Orthopsychiatry, 56,* 570–576.

Speigel, D. (1986). Dissociation, double binds, and posttraumatic stress in multiple personality disorder. In B. G. Braun (Ed.). *Treatment of multiple personality disorder.* Washington, DC: American Psychiatric Press, Inc.

Spencer, J. (1978). Father-daughter incest. *Child Welfare, 57,* 581–589.

Sprei, J. (1987). Group treatment of adult incest survivors. In C. Brody (Ed.). *Women in Groups,* New York: Springer.

Sprei, J. & Courtois, C. (1988). The treatment of women's sexual dysfunctions arising from sexual assault. In J. R. Field & R. A. Brown (Eds.). *Advances in the understanding and treatment of sexual problems: Compendium for the individual and marital therapist.* New York: Spectrum.

Sprei, J. & Goodwin, R. (1983). The group treatment of sexual assault survivors. *The Journal for Specialists in Group Work, 8,* 39–46.

Sprei, J. with Unger, P. (1986). *A training manual for the group treatment of adults molested as children.* Rockville, MD: Montgomery County Sexual Assault Service.

Staff. (1984, April). Sexual exploitation and abuse of people with disabilities. *Response.* Washington, DC: Center for Women Policy Studies.

Stampfl, T. G. & Levis, D. J. (1967). Essentials of implosive therapy: A learning-theory-based psychodynamic behavioral therapy. *Journal of Abnormal Psychology, 86,* 276–284.

Steele, B. F. (1986). Notes on the lasting effects of early child abuse throughout the life cycle. *Child Abuse & Neglect, 10,* 283–291.

Stone, M. H. (1981). Borderline syndromes: A consideration of subtypes and an overview, directions for research. *Psychiatric Clinics of North America, 4,* 3–13.

Stone, M. H. (1984). *Self-defeat, self-mutilation and suicide in the borderline patient.* Workshop presentation, The Washington Psychological Center, New Carollton, MD.

Stuart, I. R. & Greer, J. G. (Eds.). (1984). *Victims of sexual aggression: Treatment of children, women and men.* New York: Van Nostrand Reinhold.

Summit, R. (1982). Beyond belief: The reluctant discovery of incest. In M. Kirkpatrick (Ed.). *Women's sexual experience: Explorations of the dark continent.* New York: Plenum.

Summit, R. (1983). The child sexual abuse accommodation syndrome. *Child Abuse and Neglect, 7,* 177–193.

Summit, R. (1986, May). *Treatment for serious mental health sequelae.* Panel presented at the Fourth National Conference on the Sexual Victimization of Children. Children's Hospital National Medical Center. New Orleans, LA.

Summit, R. & Kryso, J. (1978). Sexual abuse of children: A clinical spectrum. *American Journal of Orthopsychiatry, 48,* 237–251.

Swink, K. K. & Leveille, A. E. (1986). From victim to survivor: A new look at the issues and recovery process for adult incest survivors. Special issue of *Women & Therapy, The Dynamics of Feminist Therapy, 5,* 119–141.

Symonds, M. (1980). The "second injury" to victims [Special issue]. *Evaluation and Change.* 36–38.

Terr, L. (1983). Chowchilla revisited: The effects of psychic trauma four years after a school-bus kidnapping. *American Journal of Psychiatry, 140,* 1543–1550.

Tomarchio, D. (n.d.). *Adults sexually abused as children: Impact on career development and implications for career counseling.* Unpublished manuscript, Seton Hall University, South Orange.

Tsai, M., Feldman-Summers, S., & Edgar, M. (1979). Childhood molestation: Variables related to differential impacts on psychosexual functioning in adult women. *Journal of Abnormal Psychology, 88,* 407–417.

Tsai, M. & Wagner, N. (1978). Therapy groups for women sexually molested as children. *Archives of Sexual Behavior, 7,* 417–427.

Tufts New England Medical Center, Division of Child Psychiatry. (1984). *Sexually exploited children: Service and research project.* Final report for the Office of Juvenile Justice and Delinquency Prevention, Washington, D.C.: U.S. Department of Justice.

Urquiza, A. J. & Crowley, C. (1986, May). *Sex differences in the survivors of child sexual abuse.* Paper presented at the Fourth National Conference on the Sexual Victimization of Children, Children's Hospital National Medical Center, New Orleans, LA.

Van Buskirk, S. & Cole, C. (1983). Characteristics of eight women seeking therapy for the effects of incest. *Psychotherapy: Theory, Research and Practice, 20,* 503–514.

van der Kolk, B. (1984). *Post-traumatic stress disorder: Psychological and biological sequelae.* Washington, DC: American Psychiatric Press, Inc.

van der Kolk, B. (1987a). *Psychological trauma.* Washington, DC: American Psychiatric Association Press, Inc.

van der Kolk, B. (1987b). The role of the group in the origin and resolution of the trauma response. In B. van der Kolk (Ed.). *Psychological trauma.* Washington, DC: American Psychiatric Press, Inc.

van der Kolk, B. & Kadish, W. (1987). Amnesia, dissociation, and the return of the repressed. In B. van der Kolk (Ed.). *Psychological trauma.* Washington, DC: American Psychiatric Press, Inc.

Veronen, L. J. & Kilpatrick, D. G. (1983). Stress management for rape victims. In D. Meichenbaum & M. E. Jaremko (Eds.). *Stress reduction and prevention.* New York: Plenum.

Walker, L. E. (1979). *The battered woman.* New York: Harper & Row.

Walker, L. E. (1984). *The battered woman syndrome.* New York: Springer.

Walsh, C. P. (1986a). *The self-concept and sex-role orientation of adult females in therapy with and without incest history.* Unpublished doctoral dissertation, University of Florida, Gainesville.

Walsh, C. P. (1986b). Special issues in retrospective therapy for child sexual abuse. Panel presented at the Fourth National Conference on the Sexual Vicitimization of Children. Children's Hospital National Medical Center, New Orleans, LA.

Ward, E. (1985). *Father-daughter rape.* New York: Grove Press.

Waterman, J. (1986). Family dynamics of incest with young children. In K. MacFarlane & J. Waterman (Eds.). *Sexual abuse of young children.* New York: The Guilford Press.

Weeks, R. B. (1976). The sexually exploited child. *Southern Medical Journal, 69,* 848–850.

Weinberg, K. (1955). *Incest behavior.* New York: Citadel Press.

Weiner, I. B. (1964). On incest: A survey. *Excerpta Criminologica, 4,* 137–155.

Wells, L. A. (1981). Family pathology and father-daughter incest: Restricted psychopathology. *Journal of Clinical Psychiatry, 42,* 197–202.

Westerlund, E. (1983). Counseling women with histories of incest. *Women & Therapy, 2,* 17–30.

Westermeyer, J. (1978). Incest in psychiatric practice: A description of patients and incestuous relationships. *Journal of Clinical Psychiatry, 39,* 643–648.

Wheeler, B. R. & Walton, E. (1987, December). Personality disturbances of adult incest victims. *Social Casework*, 597–602.

Wilhelm, D. (1987, May 10). Suicide closes an incest suit. *The Boston Globe*. pp. 41, 43.

Williams, T. (Ed.). (1987). *Post-traumatic stress disorders: A handbook for clinicians*. Cincinnati, OH: Disabled American Veterans.

Wise, M. L. (1985, April). *Incest victim survivor paradox: Therapeutic strategies and issues*. Presented at the annual convention of the American Association of Counseling and Development, New York City.

Wood, B. L. (1987). *Children of alcoholism: The struggle for self and intimacy in adult life*. New York: New York University Press.

Wooley, M. J. & Vigilanti, M. A. (1984). Psychological separation and the sexual abuse victim. *Psychotherapy: Theory, Research and Practice, 21*, 347–352.

Wyatt, G. (1985). The sexual abuse of Afro-American and white women in childhood. *Child Abuse & Neglect, 9*, 507–519.

Yates, A. (1982). Children eroticized by incest. *American Journal of Psychiatry, 139*, 482–485.

Yates, M. & Pawley, K. (1987). Utilizing imagery and the unconscious to explore and resolve the trauma of sexual abuse. *Art Therapy, 3*, 36–41.

Yost, J. F. (1987).The psychopharmacologic management of post-traumatic stress disorder (PTSD) in Vietnam veterans and in civilian situations. In T. Williams (Ed.). *Post-traumatic stress disorders: A handbook for clinicians*. Cincinnati, OH: Disabled American Veterans.

Index